POPOL

The Mayan Book
of the Dawn of Life

Translated by

DENNIS TEDLOCK

with commentary based on the
ancient knowledge of the modern Quiché Maya

VUH

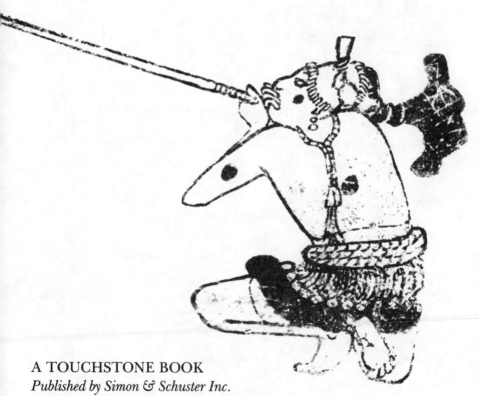

A TOUCHSTONE BOOK
Published by Simon & Schuster Inc.
New York London Toronto Sydney Tokyo Singapore

Copyright © 1985 by Dennis Tedlock
All rights reserved
including the right of reproduction
in whole or in part in any form
First Touchstone Edition, 1986

Published by Simon & Schuster, Inc.
Simon & Schuster Building
Rockefeller Center
1230 Avenue of the Americas
New York, New York 10020

TOUCHSTONE and colophon are registered trademarks
of Simon & Schuster, Inc.

Designed by Edith Fowler

Manufactured in the United States of America

10 9 8 7 6 5 4 3 2
10 9 8   Pbk.

Library of Congress Cataloging in Publication Data

Popol vuh. English.
  Popol vuh.

  Translated from the Quiché.
  Bibliography: p.
  1. Quichés—Religion and mythology. 2. Indians of Central
America—Guatemala—Religion and mythology.
I. Tedlock, Dennis. II. Title.
F1465.P813   1985   299'.79281   84-23644
ISBN: 0-671-45241-X
ISBN: 0-671-61771-0 Pbk.

Are 4u ua nuta4alibal, nupresenta
chiquiuach ri nantat, comon chuchkajauib
mu4hulic uleu, mu4hulic poklaj, mu4hulic bak.

CONTENTS

ILLUSTRATIONS

PREFACE

You cannot erase time.
—ANDRÉS XILOJ

THE TRANSLATOR of the Popol Vuh, as if possessed by the story the Popol Vuh tells, must wander in darkness and search long for the clear light. The task is not a matter of deciphering Maya hieroglyphs, since the only surviving version of the Popol Vuh is a transcription into alphabetic writing, but the manuscript nevertheless abounds with ambiguities and obscurities. My work took me not only into dark corners of libraries but into the forests and tall cornfields and smoky houses of highland Guatemala, where the people who speak and walk and work in the pages of the Popol Vuh, the Quiché Maya, have hundreds of thousands of descendants. Among them are diviners called "daykeepers," who know how to interpret illnesses, omens, dreams, messages given by sensations internal to their own bodies, and the multiple rhythms of time. It is their business to bring what is dark into "white clarity," just as the gods of the Popol Vuh first brought the world itself to light.

The Quiché people speak a Mayan language, say prayers to Mayan mountains and Mayan ancestors, and keep time according to the Mayan calendar. They are also interested citizens of the larger contemporary world, but they find themselves surrounded and attacked by those who have yet to realize they have something to teach the rest of us. For them it is not that the time of Mayan civilization has passed, to be followed by the time of European civilization, but that the two have begun to run alongside one another. A complete return to conditions that existed before Europeans first arrived is unthinkable, and so is a complete abandonment of indigenous traditions in favor of European ones. What most worries daykeepers about people from Europe, and specifically about missionaries, is that they confuse the Earth, whose divinity is equal to that of the celestial God, with the devil. As daykeepers put it, "He who makes an enemy of the Earth makes an enemy of his own body."

In the western part of what was once the Quiché kingdom is a town called Chuua 4,ak or "Before the Building." It is listed in the Popol Vuh as one of the citadels that were added to the kingdom during the reign of two great lords named Quicab and Cauizimah. When they sent "guardians of the land" to occupy newly conquered towns, Before the Building was assigned to nobles whose descendants still possess documents that date from the period of the Popol Vuh manuscript. Among contemporary Guatemalan towns it is without rival in the degree to which its ceremonial life is timed according to the Mayan calendar and mapped according to the relative elevations and directional positions of outdoor shrines. Once each 260 days, on the day named Eight Monkey, daykeepers converge from all over the Guatemalan highlands for the largest of all present-day Mesoamerican ceremonies that follow the ancient calendar. That Before the Building was already a religious center before the fall of the Quiché kingdom is indicated by the Nahua name that Pedro de Alvarado's Mexican-Indian allies gave it: Momostenango, meaning "Citadel of Shrines." It was in this town that I began my search for someone who might be able to light my way through some of the darker passages of the Popol Vuh. At the same time I began making sound recordings of contemporary narratives, speeches, and prayers, looking for passages that might resemble the Popol Vuh.

For fieldworkers in a Citadel of Shrines, visiting sacred places, listening to prayers and chants, and learning how to reckon time according to the continuing rhythms of the Mayan calendar can be a dangerous business. Barbara Tedlock and I almost came to the point of giving up our various research projects and leaving town when a daykeeper named Andrés Xiloj divined that we had not only annoyed people at shrines but had entered the presence of these shrines without even realizing that we must be ritually clean in order to do so. But it was this same daykeeper, a man who is also the head of his patrilineage, who took on the task of answering all our inquiries about the shrines, the people who went there, the calendar, and the process by which he had divined the nature of our offense. One day, when we had come to the point of asking for a detailed description of the training and initiation of daykeepers, he dropped what seemed to be a broad hint that the best way to find out the answer to such questions would be to undertake an actual apprenticeship. After debating the meaning of his remarks all night, we asked him the next day whether he had meant that he would in fact be willing to take us on as apprentices, and he said, "Of course." There followed four and a half months of formal training, timed according to the Mayan calendar, that left us much more knowledgeable than we had ever intended to be.

Diviners are, by profession, interpreters of difficult texts. They can even start from a nonverbal sign, such as an ominous invasion of a house by a wild animal, and arrive at a "reading," as we would say, or *ubixic*, "its saying" or "its announcement," as is said in Quiché. When they start from a verbal sign such as the name of a day on the Mayan calendar, they may treat it as if it were a sign from a writing system rather than a word in itself, arriving at "its saying" by finding a different word with similar sounds. It should therefore come as no surprise that a diviner might be willing to take on the task of reading the Popol Vuh, whose text presents its own intriguing difficulties of interpretation.

When Andrés Xiloj was given a chance to look at the text of the Popol Vuh, he produced a pair of spectacles and began reading aloud, word by word. His previous knowledge of alphabetic reading and writing was limited to Spanish, but he was able to grasp the orthography of the Popol Vuh text with very little help. When he was puzzled by archaic words, I offered definitions drawn from Quiché dictionaries compiled during the colonial period; in time, of course, he readily recognized the more frequent archaic forms. He was never content with merely settling on a Quiché reading of a particular passage and then offering a simple Spanish translation; instead, he was given to frequent interpretive asides, some of which took the form of entire stories. In the present volume the effects of the three-way dialogue among Andrés Xiloj, the Popol Vuh text, and myself are most obvious in the Glossary and the Notes and Comments, but they are also present in the Introduction and throughout the translation of the Popol Vuh itself.

My work in Guatemala took me not only to the town called Before the Building (Momostenango), but to the ruins of Rotten Cane (Utatlán), to the mountain called Patohil, to the pile of broken stones at Petatayub, and to towns such as Santa Cruz Quiché, Spilt Water (Zacualpa), Above the Nettles (Chichicastenango), Above the Hot Springs (Totonicapán), Willow Tree (Santa María Chiquimula), and Under Ten Deer (Quezaltenango). To the patron saints and earthly spirits of all these places I pay my respects, especially to Santiago and his scribe, San Felipe, at Momostenango; to San Juan and to the divine Uhaal and Roz Utz stones at Agua Tibia; and above all to Uhaal Zabal, 4huti Zabal, and Nima Zabal.

Library pilgrimages have taken me to nearby Cambridge, Massachusetts, to the Tozzer Library at Harvard; to the National Anthropological Archives at the Smithsonian Institution in Washington, D.C.; to the Latin American libraries at Tulane in New Orleans and the University of Texas in Austin; to the special-collections library at Brigham Young University in Provo, Utah; to the Museo Nacional de Antropología in Mexico City; to the Archivo General de Centroamérica in Guatemala City; and to the Newberry Library in Chicago, where I saw, felt, smelled, and heard the rustle of the manuscript of the Popol Vuh.

Such is the magnitude of the present project that it stretched over nine years; except for one of these years and part of another, it necessarily took a backseat to the countless complexities of university life. Most of the Guatemalan fieldwork was carried out during the summer of 1975 and throughout 1976. Much of my effort to transform masses of research and multiple trial runs at translation into a book was made during evenings and weekends at home, and it was also carried on during all-too-brief retreats to such places as Tepoztlán, south of Mexico City; Panajachel, on the shore of Lake Atitlán in Guatemala; and in the woodlands and rocks near Cerrillos, New Mexico, south of Santa Fe. But even when one is confined to Massachusetts, there are ways in which the world of the Popol Vuh makes itself felt. During the months in which I completed the manuscript for the book you now hold in your hands, I could see Venus as the morning star if I looked out the window of my study early enough.

Thinking back over my work on the Popol Vuh brings a great many people to mind; I apologize in advance to those who should have been remembered here but were not. Having learned my lessons about ancestors from my Quiché master, I will begin with persons who are now deceased. Robert Wauchope, when I first began my graduate work at Tulane in 1961, soon became convinced that I should eventually go to Guatemala to do archaeological fieldwork; he lived long enough to know that fourteen years later I finally did get to Guatemala, but as an ethnologist, linguist, and translator rather than an archaeologist. My first lessons in how to read and interpret manuscript sources from Spanish America were given to me by France V. Scholes in the Coronado Library at the University of New Mexico, during the summer of 1964. He and Wauchope enjoyed full careers, but the career of Thelma Sullivan, the finest of all scholars working with texts in the Nahuatl language, was cut short; she stood out among Americanists in general as one of those rare individuals who realize and demonstrate that precision in translation is not to be confused with mechanical literalness. Also cut short was the career of Fernando Horcasitas, who gave a splendid lecture on Nahuatl theater one fine warm evening in Cuernavaca when Barbara Tedlock and I were waiting for the Guatemalan border to reopen after the great earthquake of 1976.

And then there is Abelino Zapeta y Zapeta, who in 1979 became the first Quiché to serve as mayor of Santa Cruz Quiché in centuries. He offered gracious words of greeting to an international conference on the Popol Vuh that took place in his town. For the time being it must also be said that he was the last Quiché to serve as mayor. A year after the conference, while he was riding home from work on his bicycle, he was assassinated by gunmen who were seen driving away in an army jeep. The day may come when the Popol Vuh will be entirely at home in Santa Cruz Quiché, the town where it was written, but that day may not be soon.

Turning to those who are still living, and beginning with graduate school, I first think of Munro S. Edmonson. I have come to disagree with him about a great many matters affecting the Popol Vuh, as he well knows, but I have not forgotten his seminar on the Maya at Tulane, which I took more than twenty years ago. When he offered a list of possible research topics to the students in that seminar, I was the one who chose to do a class presentation and term paper on the Popol Vuh. But my first fieldwork in anthropology took me closer to my home in New Mexico: I went to the Zuni, who live on the northern frontier of Mesoamerica. When it came, at long last, to doing field research among the people whose ancestors wrote the Popol Vuh, it was Robert M. Carmack, of the State University of New York at Albany, who introduced Barbara Tedlock and myself to the western highlands of Guatemala. He did this with a generosity that is rare among ethnographers—and with a wisdom, still rarer, that led him to abandon us to our fate once he had gotten us into the field.

Among the people of Guatemala, I give special thanks to Andrés Xiloj Peruch, who not only traveled with me through the Quiché text of the Popol Vuh but taught me how to read dreams, omens, and the rhythms of the Mayan calendar. Thanks also go to his daughter María, who has boundless patience and kindness; to Santiago Guix, who showed the way down many a path; to Gustavo Lang, who offers a steady hand in any emergency; to Lucas Pacheco Benítez, who combines a warm heart with an intimate knowledge of the spiritual properties of stones; to Celso Akabal, who offers genial toasts at his home near the shrine called the Great Place of Declaration; to Vicente de León Abac, who knows how the ancient customs originated; to Esteban Ajxub, who eloquently prays and sings for others; and to Flavio Rojas Lima, who knows how to make foreigners feel welcome at the Seminario de Integración Social Guatemalteca.

In matters of Native American linguistics and poetics, I am especially thankful for more than fifteen years of unceasing dialogue with Dell Hymes. Others who come to mind here are Allan Burns, the first to reveal that conversation is the root of all Mayan discourse; Lyle Campbell, who went beyond his normal duties in providing myself and others with an introductory course in Quiché at the State University of New York at Albany in the fall of 1975 and who taught me the value of Cakchiquel sources; Ives Goddard, who convinced me that even the most intractable manuscript materials on Native American languages may conceal moments of great accuracy; T. J. Knab, who helped me with Nahuatl loanwords in the Popol Vuh and with Nahuatl metaphors; and James L. Mondloch, who answered some of my questions about Quiché syntax.

In matters of ethnography, ethnohistory, and archaeology I think of Duncan Earle, who revealed that the "mushroom head" of the Popol Vuh is in fact an herb; Gary Gossen, who knows that in trying to comprehend the contemporary highland Maya we are dealing with nothing less than a civilization; Doris Heyden, the first to reveal the full meaning of the secret cave at Teotihuacan; Alain Ichon, who excavated the site called Thorny Place in the Popol Vuh; David H. Kelley, who personally convinced me in far-off Calgary that classic Maya vase paintings do indeed illustrate scenes from the Popol Vuh; J. Jorge Klor de Alva, who knows that the "spiritual conquest" of Mesoamerica has in fact never taken place; Linda Schele, who brought the hieroglyphic texts of Palenque closer than ever to the Popol Vuh at the eighth Workshop on Maya Hieroglyphic Writing in Austin; and Nathaniel Tarn, who in earlier times played the role of anthropologist among neighbors of the Quiché and later returned as a poet.

Anthony Aveni, John B. Carlson, and Floyd G. Lounsbury have heard out my ideas concerning the calendrical and astronomical interpretation of the Popol Vuh. Michael D. Coe, who well knows what a calabash tree is, not only provided welcome praise for the translation but generously permitted the use of the vase drawings reproduced here. Peter T. Furst and Jill Leslie Furst are steady friends who can be counted upon to do unexpected things, like raising toads, cooking sharks, and praising the fertility of skeletons. But above all I am grateful to my wife-colleague Barbara Tedlock, scholar and artist, who has meanwhile been telling her own story about places and times in Guatemala.

At various times over the years I have discussed portions of this work with four past and present colleagues in the University Professors Program at Boston University, all of whom have views on the subject of translation: William Arrowsmith, Rodolfo Cardona, D. S. Carne-Ross, and Herbert Mason. Others who have lent patient ears include the poets Robert Kelly, George Quasha, Jerome Rothenberg, and Charles Stein, along with the book-rancher Gus Blaisdell and the apple-farmer Jeff Titon. Thanks also go to Richard Lewis, of the Touchstone Center in New York, who provided me with the opportunity to do a public performance of parts of the translation at the American Museum of Natural History.

My fieldwork in Guatemala in 1976 was done with the aid of a Fellowship for Independent Study and Research from the National Endowment for the Humanities. Released time for the continuation of the translation of the Popol Vuh was provided, during the academic years 1979–80 and 1980–81, by a grant from the Translations Program at the National Endowment for the Humanities, which is ably and thoughtfully administered by Susan Mango. During 1980–81 I received additional aid in the form of a sabbatical leave from Boston University.

From the beginning of our work on the Popol Vuh, Andrés Xiloj felt certain that if one only knew how to read it perfectly, borrowing the knowledge of the day lords, the moist breezes, and the distant lightning, it should reveal everything under the sky and on the earth, all the way out to the four corners. As a help to my own reading and pondering of the book, he suggested an addition to the prayer that daykeepers recite when they go to public shrines. It goes like this:

Make my guilt vanish,
Heart of Sky, Heart of Earth;
do me a favor,
give me strength, give me courage
in my heart, in my head,
since you are my mountain and my plain;
may there be no falsehood and no stain,
and may this reading of the Popol Vuh
come out clear as dawn,
and may the sifting of ancient times
be complete in my heart, in my head;
and make my guilt vanish,
my grandmothers, grandfathers,
and however many souls of the dead there may be,
you who speak with the Heart of Sky and Earth,
may all of you together give strength
to the reading I have undertaken.

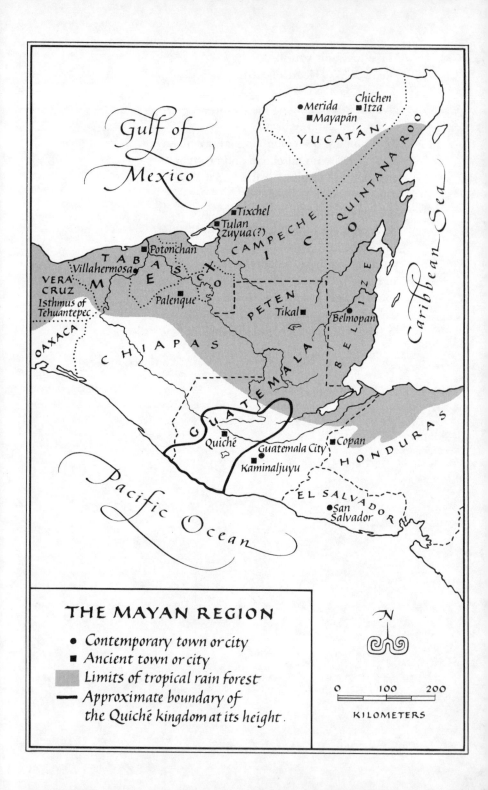

THE MAYAN REGION

- Contemporary town or city
- Ancient town or city
- Limits of tropical rain forest
- Approximate boundary of the Quiché kingdom at its height.

0   100   200

KILOMETERS

INTRODUCTION

THE FIRST FOUR HUMANS, the first four earthly beings who were truly articulate when they moved their feet and hands, their faces and mouths, and who could speak the very language of the gods, could also see everything under the sky and on the earth. All they had to do was look around from the spot where they were, all the way to the limits of space and the limits of time. But then the gods, who had not intended to make and model beings with the potential of becoming their own equals, limited human sight to what was obvious and nearby. Nevertheless, the lords who once ruled a kingdom from a place called Quiché, in the highlands of Guatemala, once had in their possession the means for overcoming this nearsightedness, an *ilbal*, a "seeing instrument" or a "place to see"; with this they could know distant or future events. The instrument was not a telescope, not a crystal for gazing, but a book.

The lords of Quiché consulted their book when they sat in council, and their name for it was Popol Vuh or "Council Book." Because this book contained an account of how the forefathers of their own lordly lineages had exiled themselves from a far-away city called Tulan, they sometimes described it as "the writings about Tulan." Because a later generation of lords had obtained the book by going on a pilgrimage that took them across water on a causeway, they titled it "The Light That Came from Across the Sea." And because the book told of events that happened before the first sunrise and of a time when the forefathers hid themselves and the stones that contained the spirit familiars of their gods in forests, they also titled it "Our Place in the Shadows." And finally, because it told of the first rising of the morning star and the sun and moon, and of the rise and radiant splendor of the Quiché lords, they titled it "The Dawn of Life."

Those who wrote the version of the Popol Vuh that comes down to us do not give us their personal names but rather call themselves "we" in its opening pages and "we who are the Quiché people" later on. In contemporary usage "the Quiché people" are an ethnic group in Guatemala, consisting of all those who speak the particular Mayan language that itself has come to be called Quiché; they presently number over half a million and occupy most of the former territory of the kingdom whose development is described in the Popol Vuh. To the west and northwest of them are other Mayan peoples, speaking other Mayan languages, who extend across the Mexican border into the highlands of Chiapas and down into the Gulf coastal plain of Tabasco. To the east and northeast still other Mayans extend just across the borders of El Salvador and Honduras, down into the lowlands of Belize, and across the peninsula of Yucatán. These are the peoples, with a total population of about four million today, whose ancestors developed what has become known to the outside world as Maya civilization.

The roots of Maya civilization may lie in the prior civilization of the Olmecs, which reached its peak on the Gulf coastal plain about three thousand years ago. Maya hieroglyphic writing and calendrical reckoning probably have antecedents that go back at least that far, but they did not find expression in the lasting form of inscriptions on stone monuments until the first century B.C., in a deep river valley that cuts through the highlands of Chiapas. From there, the erection of inscribed monuments spread south to the Pacific and eastward along the Guatemalan coastal plain, then reached back into the highlands at the site of Kaminaljuyu, on the western edge of what is now Guatemala City. During the so-called classic period, beginning about A.D. 300, the center of literate civilization in the Mayan region shifted northward into the lowland rain forest that separates the mountain pine forest of Chiapas and Guatemala from the low and thorny scrub forest of northern Yucatán. Swamps were drained and trees were cleared to make way for intensive cultivation. Hieroglyphic texts in great quantity were sculpted in stone and stucco, painted on pottery and plaster, and inked on long strips of paper that were folded like screens to make books. This is the period that accounts for the glories of such sites as Palenque, Tikal, and Copan, leaving a legacy that has made Maya civilization famous in the fields of art and architecture. The Mayan languages spoken at most of these sites probably corresponded to the ones now known as Cholan, which are still spoken by the Mayan peoples who live at the extreme eastern and western ends of the old classical heartland.

Near the end of the classic period, the communities that had carved out a place for themselves in the rain forest were caught in a deepening vortex of overpopulation, environmental degradation, and malnutrition. The organizational and technological capacities of Maya society were strained past the breaking point, and by A.D. 900 much of the region had been abandoned. That left Maya civilization divided between two areas that had been peripheral during classic times, one in northern Yucatán and the other in the Guatemalan highlands. The subsequent history of both these areas was shaped by invaders from the western end of the old classical heartland, from Tabasco and neighboring portions of the Gulf coastal plain, who set up militaristic states among the peoples they conquered. The culture they carried with them has come to be called Toltec; it is thought to have originated among speakers of Nahua languages, who are presently concentrated in central Mexico (where they include the descendants of the Aztecs) and who once extended eastward to Tabasco. In the Mayan area, Toltec culture was notable for giving mythic prominence to the god-king named Plumed Serpent, technical prominence to the use of spear-throwers in warfare, and sacrificial prominence to the human heart. Those who carried this culture to highland Guatemala brought many Nahua words with them, but they themselves were probably Gulf-coast Maya of Cholan descent. Among them were the founders of the kingdom whose people have come to be known as the Quiché Maya.

DRAWING BY CARLOS A. VILLACORTA

26

Mayan monuments and buildings no longer featured inscriptions after the end of the classic period, but scribes went right on making books for another six centuries, sometimes combining Mayan texts with Toltecan pictures. Then, in the sixteenth century, Europeans arrived in Mesoamerica. They forcibly imposed a monopoly on all major forms of visible expression, whether in drama, architecture, sculpture, painting, or writing. Hundreds of hieroglyphic books were tossed into bonfires by ardent missionaries; between this disaster and the slower perils of decay, only four books made it through to the present day. Three of them, all thought to come from the lowlands, found their way to Europe in early colonial times and eventually turned up in libraries in Madrid, Paris, and Dresden; a fragment from a fourth book was recovered more recently from looters who had found it in a dry cave in Chiapas. But the survival of Mayan literature was not dependent on the survival of its outward forms. Just as Mayan peoples learned to use the symbolism of Christian saints as a mask for ancient gods, so they learned to use the Roman alphabet as a mask for ancient texts.

There was no little justice in the fact that it was the missionaries themselves, the burners of the ancient books, who worked out the problems of adapting the alphabet to the sounds of

---

SCRIBES WENT RIGHT ON MAKING BOOKS: This is a page from the Maya hieroglyphic book known as the Dresden Codex, which dates to the thirteenth century. The left-hand column describes the movements of Venus during one of five different types of cycles reckoned for that planet. The right-hand column describes the auguries for the cycle and gives both pictures and names for the attendant deities. The top picture, in which the figure at right is seated on two glyphs that name constellations, may have to do with the position of Venus relative to the fixed stars during the cycle. In the middle picture is the god who currently accounts for Venus itself, holding a dart-thrower in his left hand and darts in his right; in the bottom picture is his victim, with a dart piercing his shield. The Venus gods of the Popol Vuh are more conservatively Mayan than those of the Dresden Codex; they are armed with old-fashioned blowguns rather than Toltecan dart-throwers.

Mayan languages, and while they were at it they charted grammars and compiled dictionaries. Their official purpose in doing this linguistic work was to facilitate the writing and publishing of Christian prayers, sermons, and catechisms in the native languages. But very little time passed before some of their native pupils found political and religious applications for alphabetic writing that were quite independent of those of Rome. These independent writers have left a literary legacy that is both more extensive than the surviving hieroglyphic corpus and more open to understanding. Their most notable works, created as alphabetic substitutes for hieroglyphic books, are the Chilam Balam or "Jaguar Priest" books of Yucatán and the Popol Vuh of Guatemala.

The authors of the alphabetic Popol Vuh were members of the three lordly lineages that had once ruled the Quiché kingdom: the Cauecs, the Greathouses, and the Lord Quichés. They worked in the middle of the sixteenth century, shortly before the end of one of the fifty-two-year cycles measured out by their own calendar. The scene of their writing was the town of Quiché, northwest of what is now Guatemala City. The east side of this town, on flat land, was new in their day, with buildings in files on a grid of streets and the bell towers of a church at the center. The west side, already in ruins, was on fortified promontories above deep canyons, with pyramids and palaces clustered around multiple plazas and courtyards. The buildings of the east side displayed broad expanses of blank stone and plaster, but the ruined walls of the west side bore tantalizing traces of multicolored murals. What concerned the authors of the new version of the Popol Vuh was to preserve the story that lay behind the ruins.

During the early colonial period the town of Quiché was eclipsed, in both size and prosperity, by the neighboring town of Chuui La or "Above the Nettles," better known today as Chichicastenango. The residents of the latter town included members of the Cauec and Lord Quiché lineages, and at some point a copy of the alphabetic Popol Vuh found its way there. Between 1701 and 1703, a friar named Francisco Ximénez happened to get a look at this manuscript while he was serving as the parish

ARE V XE OHER ESTE ES EL PRINCÍPIO DE LAS

THE ONLY SURVIVING COPY OF THE QUICHÉ TEXT OF THE POPOL
VUH: The first page of the copy of the alphabetic Popol Vuh
made by Francisco Ximénez in Chichicastenango; the
Quiché text is on the left and his own Spanish translation is
on the right.

priest for Chichicastenango. He made the only surviving copy of the Quiché text of the Popol Vuh and added a Spanish translation (see the illustration on p. 29). His work remained in the possession of the Dominican order until after Guatemalan independence, but when liberal reforms forced the closing of all monasteries in 1830, it was acquired by the library of the University of San Carlos in Guatemala City. Carl Scherzer, an Austrian physician, happened to see it there in 1854, and Charles Etienne Brasseur de Bourbourg, a French priest, had the same good fortune a few months later. In 1857 Scherzer published Ximénez' Spanish translation under the patronage of the Hapsburgs in Vienna, members of the same royal lineage that had ruled Spain at the time of the conquest of the Quiché kingdom, and in 1861 Brasseur published the Quiché text and a French translation in Paris. The manuscript itself, which Brasseur spirited out of Guatemala, eventually found its way back across the Atlantic from Paris, coming to rest in the Newberry Library in 1911. The town graced by this library, with its magnificent collection of Native American texts, is not in Mesoamerica, but it does have an Indian name: Chicago, meaning "Place of Wild Onions."

The manuscript Ximénez copied in the place called "Above the Nettles" may have included a few illustrations and even an occasional hieroglyph, but his version contains nothing but solid columns of alphabetic prose. Mayan authors in general made only sparing use of graphic elements in their alphabetic works, but nearly every page of the ancient books combined writing (including signs meant to be read phonetically) and pictures. In the Mayan languages, as well as in Nahua, the terms for writing and painting were and are the same, the same artisans practiced both skills, and the patron deities of both skills were twin monkey gods born on the day bearing a name translatable (whether from Mayan or Nahua) as One Monkey. In the books made under the patronage of these twin gods there is a dialectical relationship between the writing and the pictures: the writing not only records words but sometimes has elements that picture or point to their meaning without the necessity of a detour through words. As for the pictures, they not only depict what they mean but have elements that can be read as words. When we say that Mesoamerican writing is strongly ideographic relative to our own, this observation should be balanced with the realization that Mesoamerican painting is more conceptual than our own.

At times the writers of the alphabetic Popol Vuh seem to be describing pictures, especially when they begin new episodes in narratives. In passages like the following, the use of sentences beginning with phrases like "this is" and the use of verbs in the Quiché equivalent of the present tense cause the reader to linger, for a moment, over a lasting image:

> This is the great tree of Seven Macaw, a nance, and this is the food of Seven Macaw. In order to eat the fruit of the nance he goes up the tree every day. Since Hunahpu and Xbalanque have seen where he feeds, they are now hiding beneath the tree of Seven Macaw, they are keeping quiet here, the two boys are in the leaves of the tree.

It must be cautioned, of course, that "word pictures" painted by storytellers, in Quiché or in any other language, need not have physical counterparts in the world outside the mind's eye. But the present example has an abruptness that suggests a sudden still picture from a story already well under way rather than a moving picture unfolded in the course of the events of that story. The narrators do not describe how the boys arrived "in the leaves of the tree"; the opening scene is already complete, waiting for the blowgun shot that comes in the next sentence, where the main verb is in the Quiché equivalent of the past tense and the still picture gives way to a moving one.

More than any other Mayan book, whether hieroglyphic or alphabetic, the Popol Vuh tells us something about the conceptual place of books in the pre-Columbian world. The writers of the alphabetic version explain why the hieroglyphic version was among the most precious possessions of Quiché rulers:

> They knew whether war would occur; everything they saw was clear to them. Whether there would be death, or whether there would be famine, or whether quarrels would occur, they knew it for certain, since there was

a place to see it, there was a book. "Council Book" was their name for it.

When "everything they saw was clear to them" the Quiché lords were recovering the vision of the first four humans, who at first "saw everything under the sky perfectly." That would mean that the Popol Vuh made it possible, once again, to sight "the four sides, the four corners in the sky, on the earth," the corners and sides that mark not only the earth but are the reference points for the movements of celestial lights.

If the ancient Popol Vuh was like the surviving hieroglyphic books, it contained systematic accounts of cycles in astronomical and earthly events that served as a complex navigation system for those who wished to see and move beyond the present. In the case of a section dealing with the planet Venus, for example, there would have been tables of rising and setting dates, pictures of the attendant gods, and brief texts outlining what these gods did when they established the pattern for the movements of Venus. When the ancient reader of the Popol Vuh took the role of a diviner and astronomer, seeking the proper date for a ceremony or a momentous political act, we may guess that he looked up a specific passage, pondered its meaning, and rendered an opinion. But the authors of the alphabetic Popol Vuh tell us that there were also occasions on which the reader offered "a long performance and account" whose subject was the emergence of the whole *cahuleu* or "sky-earth," which is the Quiché way of saying "world." If a divinatory reading or pondering was a way of recovering the depth of vision enjoyed by the first four humans, a "long performance," in which the reader may well have covered every major subject in the entire book, was a way of recovering the full cosmic sweep of that vision.

If the authors of the alphabetic Popol Vuh had transposed the ancient Popol Vuh directly, on a glyph-by-glyph basis, they might have produced a text that would have made little sense to anyone but a fully trained diviner and performer. What they did instead was to quote what a reader of the ancient book would say when he gave a "long performance," telling the full story that lay behind the charts, pictures, and plot outlines of the ancient book. Lest we miss the fact that they are quoting, they periodically insert such phrases as "This is the account, here it is," or "as it is said." At one point they themselves take the role of a performer, *speaking directly to us* as if we were members of a live audience rather than mere readers. As they introduce the first episode of a long cycle of stories about the gods who prepared the sky-earth for human life, they propose that we all drink a toast to the hero.

At the beginning of their book, the authors delicately describe the difficult circumstances under which they work. When they tell us that they are writing "amid the preaching of God, in Christendom now," we can catch a plaintive tone only by noticing that they make this statement immediately after asserting that their own gods "accounted for everything—and did it, too—as enlightened beings, in enlightened words." What the authors propose to write down is what Quichés call the Oher Tzih, the "Ancient Word" or "Prior Word," which has precedence over "the preaching of God." They have chosen to do so because "there is no longer" a Popol Vuh, which makes it sound as though they intend to re-create the original book solely on the basis of their memory of what they have seen in its pages or heard in the "long performance." But when we remember their complaint about being "in Christendom," there remains the possibility that they still have the original book but are protecting it from possible destruction by missionaries. Indeed, their next words make us wonder whether the book might still exist, but they no sooner raise our hopes on this front than they remove the book's reader from our grasp: "There is the original book and ancient writing, but he who reads and ponders it hides his face." Here we must remember that the authors of the alphabetic Popol Vuh have chosen to remain anonymous; in other words, they are hiding their own faces. If they are protecting anyone with their enigmatic statements about an inaccessible book or a hidden reader, it could well be themselves.

The authors begin their narrative in a world that has nothing but an empty sky above and a calm sea below. The action gets under way when the gods who reside in the primordial sea, named Maker, Modeler, Bearer, Begetter, Heart of the Lake,

Heart of the Sea, and Sovereign Plumed Serpent, are joined by gods who come down from the primordial sky, named Heart of Sky, Heart of Earth, Newborn Thunderbolt, Raw Thunderbolt, and Hurricane. These two parties engage in a dialogue, and in the course of it they conceive the emergence of the earth from the sea and the growth of plants and people on its surface. They wish to set in motion a process they call the "sowing" and "dawning," by which they mean several different things at once. There is the sowing of seeds in the earth, whose sprouting will be their dawning, and there is the sowing of the sun, moon, and stars, whose difficult passage beneath the earth will be followed by their own dawning. Then there is the matter of human beings, whose sowing in the womb will be followed by their emergence into the light at birth, and whose sowing in the earth at death will be followed by dawning when their souls become sparks of light in the darkness.

For the gods, the idea of human beings is as old as that of the earth itself, but they fail in their first three attempts (all in Part One) to transform this idea into a living reality. What they want is beings who will walk, work, and talk in an articulate and measured way, visiting shrines, giving offerings, and calling upon their makers by name, all according to the rhythms of a calendar. What they get instead, on the first try, is beings who have no arms to work with and can only squawk, chatter, and howl, and whose descendants are the animals of today. On the second try they make a being of mud, but this one is unable to walk or turn its head or even keep its shape; being solitary, it cannot reproduce itself, and in the end it dissolves into nothing.

Before making a third try the gods decide, in the course of a further dialogue, to seek the counsel of an elderly husband and wife named Xpiyacoc and Xmucane. Xpiyacoc is a divine matchmaker and therefore prior to all marriage, and Xmucane is a divine midwife and therefore prior to all birth. Like contemporary Quiché matchmakers and midwives, both of them are *ah3ih* or "daykeepers," diviners who know how to interpret the auguries given by thirteen day numbers and twenty day names that combine to form a calendrical cycle lasting 260 days. They are older than all the other gods, who address them as grandparents, and the cycle they divine by is older than the longer cycles that govern Venus and the sun, which have not yet been established at this point in the story. The question the younger gods put to them here is whether human beings should be made out of wood. Following divinatory methods that are still in use among Quiché daykeepers, they give their approval. The wooden beings turn out to look and talk and multiply themselves something like humans, but they fail to time their actions in an orderly way and forget to call upon the gods in prayer. Hurricane brings a catastrophe down on their heads, not only flooding them with a gigantic rainstorm but sending monstrous animals to attack them. Even their own dogs, turkeys, and household utensils rise against them, taking vengeance for past mistreatment. Their only descendants are the monkeys who inhabit the forests today.

At this point the gods who have been working on the problem of making human beings will need only one more try before they solve it, but the authors of the Popol Vuh postpone the telling of this episode, turning their attention to stories about heroic gods whose adventures make the sky-earth a safer place for human habitation. The gods in question are the twin sons of Xpiyacoc and Xmucane, named One Hunahpu and Seven Hunahpu, and the twin sons of One Hunahpu, named Hunahpu and Xbalanque. Both sets of twins are players of the Mesoamerican ball game, in which the rubber ball (an indigenous American invention) is hit with a yoke that rides on the hips rather than with the hands. In addition to being ballplayers, One and Seven Hunahpu occupy themselves by gambling with dice, whereas Hunahpu and Xbalanque go out hunting with blowguns.

The adventures of the sons and grandsons of Xpiyacoc and Xmucane are presented in two different cycles, with the episodes divided between the cycles more on the basis of where they take place in space than when they take place in time. The first cycle deals entirely with adventures on the face of the earth, while the second, though it has two separate above-ground passages, deals mainly with adventures in the Mayan underworld, named Xibalba. If the events of these two cycles were combined in a single chronological sequence, the above-ground episodes would probably alternate with those below, with the heroes descending into the underworld, emerging on the earth again, and so forth. These sowing and dawning movements of the heroes, along with those of their supporting cast, prefigure the present-day movements of the sun, moon, planets, and stars.

Hunahpu and Xbalanque are the protagonists of the first of the two hero cycles (corresponding to Part Two in the present translation), and their enemies are a father and his two sons, all of them pretenders to lordly power over the affairs of the earth. Hurricane, or Heart of Sky, is offended by this threesome, and it is he who sends Hunahpu and Xbalanque against them. The first to get his due is the father, named Seven Macaw, who claims to be both the sun and moon. In chronological terms this episode overlaps with the story of the wooden people (at the end of Part One), since Seven Macaw serves as their source of celestial light and has his downfall at the same time they do. The twins shoot him while he is at his meal, high up in a fruit tree, breaking his jaw and bringing him down to earth. Later they pose as curers and give him the reverse of a face-lift, pulling out all his teeth and removing the metal disks from around his eyes; this puts an end to his career as a lordly being. His earthly descendants are scarlet macaws, with broken and toothless jaws and mottled white patches beneath their eyes. He himself remains as the seven stars of the Big Dipper, and his wife, named Chimalmat, corresponds to the Little Dipper. The rising of Seven Macaw (in mid-October) now marks the coming of the dry season, and his fall to earth and his disappearance (beginning in mid-July) signal the beginning of the hurricane season. It was his first fall, brought on by the blowgun shot of Hunahpu and Xbalanque, that opened the way for the great flood that brought down the wooden people. Just as Seven Macaw only pretended to be the sun and moon, so the wooden people only pretended to be human.

Hunahpu and Xbalanque next take on Zipacna, the elder of Seven Macaw's two sons, a crocodilian monster who claims to be the maker of mountains. But first comes an episode in which Zipacna has an encounter with the gods of alcoholic drinks, the Four Hundred Boys. Alarmed by Zipacna's great strength, these boys trick him into digging a deep hole and try to crush him by dropping a great log down behind him. He survives, but he waits in the hole until they are in the middle of a drunken victory celebration and then brings their own house down on top of them. At the celestial level they become the stars called Motz, the Quiché name for the Pleiades, and their downfall corresponds to early-evening settings of these stars. At the earthly level, among contemporary Quichés, the Pleiades symbolize a handful of seeds, and their disappearance in the west marks the proper time for the sowing of crops.

Zipacna meets his own downfall when Hunahpu and Xbalanque set out to avenge the Four Hundred Boys. At a time when Zipacna has gone without food for several days, they set a trap for him by making a device that appears to be a living, moving crab. Having placed this artificial crab in a tight space beneath an overhang at the bottom of a great mountain, they show him the way there. Zipacna goes after the crab with great passion, and his struggles to wrestle himself into the right position to consummate his hunger become a symbolic parody of sexual intercourse. When the great moment comes the whole mountain falls on his chest (which is to say he ends up on the bottom), and when he heaves a sigh he turns to stone.

Finally there comes the demise of the younger son of Seven Macaw, named Earthquake, who bills himself as a destroyer of mountains. In his case the lure devised by Hunahpu and Xbalanque is the irresistibly delicious aroma given off by the roasting of birds. They cast a spell on the bird they give him to eat: just as it was cooked inside a coating of earth, so he will end up covered by earth. They leave him buried in the east, opposite his elder brother, whose killing of the Four Hundred Boys associates him with the west (where the Pleiades may be seen to fall beneath the earth). Seven Macaw, as the Big Dipper, is of course in the north. He is near the pivot of the movement of the night sky, whereas his two sons make the earth move—though they cannot raise or level whole mountains in a single day as they once did.

Having accounted for three of the above-ground episodes in the lives of Hunahpu and Xbalanque, the Popol Vuh next moves back in time to tell the story of their father, One Hunahpu, and his twin brother, Seven Hunahpu (at the beginning of Part

Three). This is the point at which the authors treat us as if we were in their very presence, introducing One Hunahpu with these words: "Let's drink to him, and let's just drink to the telling and accounting of the begetting of Hunahpu and Xbalanque." The story begins long before One Hunahpu meets the woman who will bear Hunahpu and Xbalanque; in the opening episode, he marries a woman named Xbaquiyalo and they have twin sons named One Monkey and One Artisan. One Hunahpu and his brother sometimes play ball with these two boys, and a messenger from Hurricane, a falcon, sometimes comes to watch them. The boys become practitioners of all sorts of arts and crafts, including flute playing, singing, writing, carving, jewelry making, and metalworking. At some point Xbaquiyalo dies, but we are not told how; that leaves Xmucane, the mother of One and Seven Hunahpu, as the only woman in the household.

The ball court of One and Seven Hunahpu lies on the eastern edge of the earth's surface at a place called Great Abyss at Carchah. Their ballplaying offends the lords of Xibalba, who dislike hearing noises above their subterranean domain. The head lords are named One Death and Seven Death, and under them are other lords who specialize in causing such maladies as lesions, jaundice, emaciation, edema, stabbing pains, and sudden death from vomiting blood. One and Seven Death decide to challenge One and Seven Hunahpu to come play ball in the court of Xibalba, which lies at the western edge of the underworld. They therefore send their messengers, who are monstrous owls, to the Great Abyss. One and Seven Hunahpu leave One Monkey and One Artisan behind to keep Xmucane entertained and follow the owls over the eastern edge of the world. The way is full of traps, but they do well until they come to the Crossroads, where each of four roads has a different color corresponding to a different direction. They choose the Black Road, which means, at the terrestrial level, that their journey through the underworld will take them from east to west. At the celestial level, it means that they were last seen in the black cleft of the Milky Way when they descended below the eastern horizon; to this day the cleft is called the Road of Xibalba.

Entering the council place of the lords of Xibalba is a tricky business, beginning with the fact that the first two figures seated there are mere manikins, put there as a joke. The next gag that awaits visitors is a variation on the hot seat, but after that comes a deadly serious test. One and Seven Hunahpu must face a night in Dark House, which is totally black inside. They are given a torch and two cigars, but they are warned to keep these burning all night without consuming them. They fail this test, so their hosts sacrifice them the next day instead of playing ball with them. Both of them are buried at the Place of Ball Game Sacrifice, except that the severed head of One Hunahpu is placed in the fork of a tree that stands by the road there. Now, for the first time, the tree bears fruit, and it becomes difficult to tell the head from the fruit. This is the origin of the calabash tree, whose fruit is the size and shape of a human head.

Blood Woman, the maiden daughter of a Xibalban lord named Blood Gatherer, goes to marvel at the calabash tree. The head of One Hunahpu, which is a skull by now, spits in her hand and makes her pregnant with Hunahpu and Xbalanque. The skull explains to her that henceforth, a father's face will survive in his son, even after his own face has rotted away and left nothing but bone. After six months, when Blood Woman's father notices that she is pregnant, he demands to know who is responsible. She answers that "there is no man whose face I've known," which is literally true. He orders the owl messengers of Xibalba to cut her heart out and bring it back in a bowl; armed with the White Dagger, the instrument of sacrifice, they take her away. But she persuades them to spare her, devising a substitute for her heart in the form of a congealed nodule of sap from a croton tree. The lords heat the nodule over a fire and are entranced by the aroma; meanwhile the owls show Blood Woman to the surface of the earth. As a result of this episode it is destined that the lords of Xibalba will receive offerings of incense made from croton sap rather than human blood and hearts. At the astronomical level Blood Woman corresponds to the moon, which appears in the west at nightfall when it begins to wax, just as she appeared before the skull of One Hunahpu at the Place of Ball Game Sacrifice when she became pregnant.

Once she is out of the underworld, Blood Woman goes to

Xmucane and claims to be her daughter-in-law, but Xmucane resists the idea that her own son, One Hunahpu, could be responsible for Blood Woman's pregnancy. She puts Blood Woman to a test, sending her to get a netful of corn from the garden that One Monkey and One Artisan have been cultivating. Blood Woman finds only a single clump of corn plants there, but she produces a whole netful of ears by pulling out the silk from just one ear. When Xmucane sees the load of corn she goes to the garden herself, wondering whether Blood Woman has stripped it. On the ground at the foot of the clump of plants she notices the imprint of the carrying net, which she reads as a sign that Blood Woman is indeed pregnant with her own grandchildren.

To understand how Xmucane is able to interpret the sign of the net we must remember that she knows how to read the auguries of the Mayan calendar, and that one of the twenty day names that go into the making of that calendar is "Net." Retold from a calendrical point of view, the story so far is that Venus rose as the morning star on a day named Hunahpu, corresponding to the ballplaying of Xmucane's sons, One and Seven Hunahpu, in the east; then, after being out of sight in Xibalba, Venus reappeared as the evening star on a day named Death, corresponding to the defeat of her sons by One and Seven Death and the placement of One Hunahpu's head in a tree in the west. The event that is due to come next in the story is the rebirth of Venus as the morning star, which should fall, as she already knows, on a day named Net. When she sees the imprint of the net in the field, she takes it as a sign that this event is coming near, and that the faces of the sons born to Blood Woman will be reincarnations of the face of One Hunahpu.

When Hunahpu and Xbalanque are born they are treated cruelly by their jealous half-brothers, One Monkey and One Artisan, and even by their grandmother. They never utter a complaint, but keep themselves happy by going out every day to hunt birds with their blowguns. Eventually they get the better of their brothers by sending them up a tree to get birds that failed to fall down when they were shot. They cause the tree to grow tall enough to maroon their brothers, whom they transform into monkeys. When Xmucane objects they give her four chances to see the faces of One Monkey and One Artisan again, calling them home with music. They warn her not to laugh, but the monkeys are so ridiculous she cannot contain herself; finally they swing up and away through the treetops for good. One Monkey and One Artisan, both of whose names refer to a single day on the divinatory calendar, correspond to the planet Mars, which thereafter begins its period of visibility on a day bearing these names, and their temporary return to the house of Xmucane corresponds to the retrograde motion of Mars. They are also the gods of arts and crafts, and they probably made their first journey through the sky during the era of the wooden people, who were the first earthly beings to make and use artifacts and who themselves ended up as monkeys.

With their half-brothers out of the way, Hunahpu and Xbalanque decide to clear a garden plot of their own, but when they return to the chosen spot each morning they find that the forest has reclaimed it. By hiding themselves at the edge of the plot one night, they discover that the animals of the forest are restoring the cleared plants by means of a chant. They try to grab each of these animals in turn, but they miss the puma and jaguar completely, break the tails off the rabbit and deer, and finally get their hands on the rat. In exchange for his future share of stored crops, the rat reveals to them that their father and uncle, One and Seven Hunahpu, left a set of ball game equipment tied up under the rafters of their house, and he agrees to help them get it down. At home the next day, Hunahpu and Xbalanque get Xmucane out of the house by claiming her chili stew has made them thirsty; she goes after water but is delayed when her water jar springs a leak. Then, when Blood Woman goes off to see why Xmucane has failed to return, the rat cuts the ball game equipment loose and the twins take possession of it.

When Hunahpu and Xbalanque begin playing ball at the Great Abyss they disturb the lords of Xibalba, just like their father and uncle before them. Once again the lords send a summons, but this time the messengers go to Xmucane, telling her that the twins must present themselves in seven days. She sends a louse to relay the message to her grandsons, but the louse is swallowed by a toad, the toad by a snake, and the snake by a falcon. The falcon arrives over the ball court and the twins shoot him in the eye. They cure his eye with gum from their ball, which is why the laughing falcon now has a black patch around the eye. The falcon vomits the snake, who vomits the toad, who still has the louse in his mouth, and the louse recites the message, quoting what Xmucane told him when she quoted what the owls told her when they quoted what the lords of Xibalba told them to say.

Having been summoned to the underworld, Hunahpu and Xbalanque go to take leave of their grandmother, and in the process they demonstrate a harvest ritual that Quichés follow to this day. They "plant" ears of corn in the center of her house, in the attic; these ears are neither to be eaten nor used as seed corn but are to be kept as a sign that corn remains alive throughout the year, even between the drying out of the plants at harvest time and the sprouting of new ones after planting. They tell their grandmother that when a crop dries out it will be a sign of their death, but that the sprouting of a new crop will be a sign that they live again.

The twins play a game with language when they instruct their grandmother; only now, instead of a quotation swallowed up inside other quotations we get a word hidden within other words. The secret word is "Ah," one of the twenty day names; the twins point to it by playing on its sounds rather than simply mentioning it. When they tell their grandmother that they are planting corn ears (*ah*) in the house (*ha*), they are making a pun on Ah in the one case and reversing its sound in the other. The play between Ah and *ha* is familiar to contemporary Quiché daykeepers, who use it when they explain to clients that the day Ah is portentous in matters affecting households. If the twins planted their corn ears in the house on the day Ah, then their expected arrival in Xibalba, seven days later, would fall on the day named Hunahpu. This fits the Mayan Venus calendar perfectly: whenever Venus rises as the morning star on a day named Net, corresponding to the appearance of Hunahpu and Xbalanque on the earth, its next descent into the underworld will always fall on a day named Hunahpu.

Following in the footsteps of their father and uncle, Hunahpu and Xbalanque descend the road to Xibalba, but when they come to the Crossroads they do things differently. They send a spy ahead of them, a mosquito, to learn the names of the lords. He bites each one of them in turn; the first two lords reveal themselves as mere manikins by their lack of response, but the others, in the process of complaining about being bitten, address each other by name, all the way down the line. When the twins themselves arrive before the lords, they ignore the manikins (unlike their father and uncle) and address each of the twelve real lords correctly. Not only that, but they refuse to fall for the hot seat, and when they are given a torch and two cigars to keep lit all night, they trick the lords by passing off a macaw's tail as the glow of the torch and putting fireflies at the tips of their cigars.

The next day Hunahpu and Xbalanque play ball with the Xibalbans, something their father and uncle did not survive long enough to do. The Xibalbans insist on putting their own ball into play first, though the twins protest that this ball, which is covered with crushed bone, is nothing but a skull. When Hunahpu hits it back to the Xibalbans with the yoke that rides on his hips, it falls to the court and reveals the weapon that was hidden inside it. This is nothing less than the White Dagger, the same instrument of sacrifice that the owls were supposed to use on Blood Woman; it twists its way all over the court, but it fails to kill the twins.

The Xibalbans consent to use the rubber ball belonging to the twins in a further game; this time four bowls of flowers are bet on the outcome. After playing well for awhile the twins allow themselves to lose, and they are given until the next day to come up with the flowers. This time they must spend the night in Razor House, which is full of voracious stone blades that are constantly looking for something to cut. In exchange for a promise that they will one day have the flesh of animals as their food, the blades stop moving. This leaves the boys free to attend to the matter of the flowers; they send leaf-cutting ants to steal them from the very gardens of the lords of Xibalba. The birds who guard this garden, poorwills and whippoorwills, are so oblivious that they fail to notice that their own tails and wings are being trimmed along with the flowers. The lords, who are aghast when they receive bowls filled with their own flowers, split the birds' mouths open, giving them the wide gape that birds of the nightjar family have today.

Next, the hero twins survive stays in Cold House, which is full of drafts and falling hail; Jaguar House, which is full of hungry, brawling jaguars; and a house with fire inside. After these horrors comes Bat House, full of moving, shrieking bats, where they spend the night squeezed up inside their blowgun. When the house grows quiet and Hunahpu peeks out from the muzzle, one of the bats swoops down and takes his head off. The head ends up rolling on the ball court of Xibalba, but Xbalanque replaces it with a carved squash. While he is busy with this head transplant the eastern sky reddens with the dawn, and a possum, addressed in the story as "old man," makes four dark streaks along the horizon. Not only the red dawn but the possum and his streaks are signs that the time of the sun (which has never before been seen) is coming nearer. In the future a new solar year will be brought in by the old man each 365 days; the four streaks signify that only four of the twenty day names—Deer, Tooth, Thought, and Wind—will ever correspond to the first day of a solar year. Contemporary Quiché daykeepers continue to reckon the solar dimension of the Mayan calendar; in 1986, for example, they will expect the old man to arrive on February 28, which will be the day Thirteen Deer.

Once Hunahpu has been fitted out with a squash for a head, he and Xbalanque are ready to play ball with the Xibalbans again. When the lords send off Hunahpu's original head as the ball, Xbalanque knocks it out of the court and into a stand of oak trees. A rabbit decoys the lords, who mistake his hopping for the bouncing of the ball, while Xbalanque retrieves the head, puts it back on Hunahpu's shoulders, and then pretends to find the squash among the oaks. Now the squash is put into play, but it wears out and eventually splatters its seeds on the court, revealing to the lords of Xibalba that they have been played for fools. The game played with the squash, like the games played with the bone-covered ball and with Hunahpu's severed head, corresponds to an appearance of Venus in the west, the direction of evening and death. If these events were combined in chronological order with those that take place entirely above ground, they would probably alternate with the episodes in which the twins defeat One Monkey and One Artisan, Seven Macaw, Zipacna, and Earthquake, with each of these latter episodes corresponding to an appearance of Venus in the east, the direction of morning and life.

At this point we are ready for the last of the episodes that prefigure the cycles of Venus and prepare the way for the first rising of the sun. Knowing that the lords of Xibalba plan to burn them, Hunahpu and Xbalanque instruct two seers named Xulu and Pacam as to what they should say when the lords seek advice as to how to dispose of their remains. This done, the twins cheerfully accept an invitation to come see the great stone pit where the Xibalbans are cooking the ingredients for an alcoholic beverage. The lords challenge them to a contest in which the object is to leap clear across the pit, but the boys cut the deadly game short and jump right in. Thinking they have triumphed, the Xibalbans follow the advice of Xulu and Pacam, grinding the bones of the boys and spilling the powder into a river.

After five days Hunahpu and Xbalanque reappear as catfish; the day after that they take human form again, only now they are disguised as vagabond dancers and actors. They gain great fame as illusionists, their most popular acts being the ones in which they set fire to a house without burning it and perform a sacrifice without killing the victim. The lords of Xibalba get news of all this and invite them to show their skills at court; they accept with pretended reluctance. The climax of their performance comes when Xbalanque sacrifices Hunahpu, rolling his head out the door, removing his heart, and then bringing him back to life. One and Seven Death go wild at the sight of this and demand that they themselves be sacrificed. The twins oblige— and, as might already be imagined, these final sacrifices are real ones. Hunahpu and Xbalanque now reveal their true identities before all the inhabitants of the underworld. They declare that henceforth, the offerings received by Xibalbans will be limited to incense made of croton sap and to animals, and that Xibalbans will limit their attacks on future human beings to those who have weaknesses or guilt.

At this point the narrative takes us back to the twins' grandmother, telling us what she has been doing all this time. She cries when the season comes for corn plants to dry out, signifying the death of her grandsons, and rejoices when they sprout again, signifying rebirth. She burns incense in front of ears from the new crop and thus completes the establishment of the custom whereby humans keep consecrated ears in the house, at the center of the stored harvest. Then the scene shifts back to Hunahpu and Xbalanque, who are about to establish another custom.

Having made their speech to the defeated Xibalbans, the twins go to the Place of Ball Game Sacrifice with the intention of reviving Seven Hunahpu, whose head and body still lie buried there. The full restoration of his face depends on his own ability to pronounce the names of all the parts it once had, but he gets no further than the mouth, nose, and eyes, which remain as notable features of skulls. They leave him there, but they promise that human beings will keep his day (the one named Hunahpu), coming to pray where his remains are. To this day, Hunahpu days are set aside for the veneration of the dead, and graveyards are called by the same word (*hom*) as the ball courts of the Popol Vuh.

At the astronomical level the visit of Hunahpu and Xbalanque to their uncle's grave signals the return of a whole new round of Venus cycles, starting with a morning star that first appears on a day named Hunahpu. As for the twins themselves, they rise as the sun and moon. Contemporary Quichés regard the full moon as a nocturnal equivalent of the sun, pointing out that it has a full disk, is bright enough to travel by, and goes clear across the sky in the same time it takes the sun to do the same thing. Most likely the twin who became the moon is to be understood specifically as the full moon, whereas Blood Woman, the mother of the twins, would account for the other phases of the moon.

With the ascent of Hunahpu and Xbalanque the Popol Vuh returns to the problem the gods confronted at the beginning: the making of beings who will walk, work, talk, and pray in an articulate manner. The account of their fourth and final attempt at a solution is a flashback, since it takes us to a time when the sun had not yet appeared. As we have already seen, the gods failed when they tried using mud and then wood as the materials for the human body, but now they get news of a mountain filled with yellow corn and white corn, discovered by the fox, coyote, parrot, and crow (at the beginning of Part Four). Xmucane grinds the corn from this mountain very finely, and the flour, mixed with the water she rinses her hands with, provides the substance for human flesh, just as the ground bone thrown in the river by the Xibalbans becomes the substance for the rebirth of her grandsons. The first people to be modeled from the corn dough are four men named Jaguar Quitze, Jaguar Night, Mahucutah, and True Jaguar. They are the first four heads of Quiché patrilineages; as in the case of the men who occupy such positions today, they are called "mother-fathers," since in ritual matters they serve as symbolic androgynous parents to everyone in their respective lineages.

This time the beings shaped by the gods are everything they hoped for and more: not only do the first four men pray to their makers, but they have perfect vision and therefore perfect knowledge. The gods are alarmed that beings who were merely manufactured by them should have divine powers, so they decide, after their usual dialogue, to put a fog on human eyes. Next they make four wives for the four men, and from these couples come the leading Quiché lineages. Celebrated Seahouse becomes the wife of Jaguar Quitze, who founds the Cauec lineage; Prawn House becomes the wife of Jaguar Night, who founds the Greathouse lineage; and Hummingbird House becomes the wife of Mahucutah, who founds the Lord Quiché lineage. True Jaguar is also given a wife, Macaw House, but they have no male children. Other lineages and peoples also come into being, and they all begin to multiply.

All these early events in human history take place in darkness, somewhere in the "east," and all the different peoples wander about and grow weary as they go on watching and waiting for the rising of the morning star and the sun. Jaguar Quitze, Jaguar Night, Mahucutah, and True Jaguar decide to change their situ-

47

PHOTO BY THE AUTHOR

THEY ARE CALLED "MOTHER-FATHERS": Andrés Xiloj (at left), who read through the Popol Vuh text with the present translator and provided numerous comments, is himself a mother-father, or patrilineage head. He is shown here at his house in Momostenango, with his son Anselmo and his daughter-in-law Manuela.

ation by acquiring patron deities they can burn offerings in front of, and it is with this purpose in mind that they go to a great eastern city bearing the names Tulan Zuyua, Seven Caves, Seven Canyons. These are grand names that call up broad reaches of the Mesoamerican past. Tulan (or Tollan) means "Place of Reeds" or more broadly "metropolis" in Nahua, and it was prefixed to the names of many different towns during Toltecan times. The particular Tulan called Zuyua was probably near the Gulf coast in Tabasco or Campeche, "eastern" because it was east of the principal Tulan of the Toltecs, near Mexico City at the site now known as Tula. But in giving Tulan Zuyua the further name Seven Caves, the Popol Vuh preserves the memory of a metropolis much older and far grander than any Toltec town.

48

This ultimate Tulan was at the site now known as Teotihuacan, northeast of Mexico City. It was the greatest city in Mesoamerican history, dating from the same period as the classic Maya. Only recently it has been discovered that beneath the Pyramid of the Sun at Teotihuacan lies a natural cave whose main shaft and side chambers add up to seven.

Countless lineages and tribes converge on the Tulan Zuyua of the Popol Vuh, and each of them, starting with the Quichés, is given a god. The Cauecs receive the god named Tohil, the Greathouses receive Auilix, and the Lord Quichés receive Hacauitz. Ultimately the patronage of the first-ranking god, Tohil, extended to all three of these lineages, and to two other Quiché lineages of lesser rank, the Tams and Ilocs. The worship of Tohil has recently been traced back to the classic period; in the inscriptions at Palenque, he bears the name Tahil, a Cholan word meaning "Obsidian Mirror," and he is shown with a smoking mirror in his forehead.

The Popol Vuh tells us that although "all the tribes were sown and came to light in unity," their languages differentiated while they were at Tulan. The cause of this was that some peoples were given patron deities whose names differed from that of the god of the Quichés. The language of the Rabinals became only slightly different, since they were given a god named One Toh rather than Tohil, but others, who received gods with completely distinctive names, ended up speaking distinctive languages, including the Cakchiquels, the Bird House people, and the Yaqui people. Today, indeed, the Rabinals, who live to the northeast of the Quiché proper, speak a dialect of Quiché, whereas the Cakchiquels (still known by this name) and the Bird House people (better known as the Tzutuhils) speak related but separate languages. What the Popol Vuh calls the Yaqui people are the speakers of Nahua languages, in Mexico. Those languages belong to a family that not only stands apart from Quiché, Cakchiquel, and Tzutuhil, but from Mayan languages in general.

Tohil is the source of the first fires kept by human beings, making it possible for them to keep warm in the cold of the predawn world. When a great hailstorm puts all these fires out,

Tohil restores fire to the Quichés by pivoting inside his sandal, which is to say that he originates the technology whereby fire is started by rotating a drill in the socket of a wooden platform. The other tribes, shivering with cold, come to the Quichés to beg for fire, but Tohil refuses to let them have it unless they promise to embrace him someday, allowing themselves to be suckled. They agree, not realizing that when the time comes for the Quiché lords to subjugate them, being "suckled" by Tohil will mean having their hearts cut out in sacrifice. Only the Cakchiquels, who get their fire by sneaking past everyone else in the smoke, escape this fate.

At the suggestion of Tohil the Quichés leave Tulan. They sacrifice their own blood to him, passing cords through their ears and elbows, and they sing a song called "The Blame Is Ours," lamenting the fact that they will not be in Tulan when the time comes for the first dawn. Packing their gods on their backs and watching continuously for the appearance of the morning star, they begin a long migration. At a place called Rock Rows, Furrowed Sands they cross a "sea" on a causeway; this would be somewhere in Tabasco or Campeche, perhaps at Potonchan or Tixchel, both lowland Maya sites where causeways pass through flooded areas. They also pass the Great Abyss, the location of the eastern ball court used by the sons and grandsons of Xmucane, a long way east and a little south of any likely location for Rock Rows, Furrowed Sands. Next they enter the highlands, turning west and continuing at a slight southward angle until they reach a mountain called Place of Advice, not very far short of the site where they will one day reach their greatest glory. With them at Place of Advice, having accompanied them ever since they left Tulan, are the Rabinals, Cakchiquels, and Bird House people.

Jaguar Quitze, Jaguar Night, Mahucutah, and True Jaguar, together with their wives, observe a great fast at Place of Advice. Tohil, Auilix, and Hacauitz speak to them, asking to be given hiding places so that they will not be captured by enemies of the Quichés. After a search through the forest, each of these gods is hidden at the place that bears his name today. They are not yet placed in temples atop pyramids, but merely in arbors decorated with bromelias and hanging mosses. At the place of Hacauitz, on a mountaintop, the Cauecs, Greathouses, and Lord Quichés weep while they wait for the dawn; the Tams and Ilocs wait on nearby mountains, while peoples other than the Quichés wait at more distant places. When, at last, they all see the daybringer, the morning star, they give thanks by burning the incense they have kept for this occasion, ever since they left Tulan.

At this point we reach the moment in the account of human affairs that corresponds to the final event in the account of the lives of the gods: the Sun himself rises. On just this one occasion he appears as an entire person, so hot that he dries out the face of the earth. His heat turns Tohil, Auilix, and Hacauitz to stone, along with such pumas, jaguars, and snakes as had existed until now. A diminutive god called White Sparkstriker escapes petrifaction by going into the shade of the trees, becoming the keeper of the stone animals. He remains to this day as a gamekeeper, with stone fetishes (volcanic concretions and meteorites) that resemble animals, together with flesh-and-blood game animals, in his care. He may be encountered in forests and caves, or on dark nights and in dreams; he appears in contemporary masked dramas dressed entirely in red, the color of the dawn.

At first the Quichés rejoice when they see the first sunrise, but then they remember their "brothers," the tribes who were with them at Tulan, and they sing the song called "The Blame Is Ours" once again. In the words of this song they wonder where their brothers might be at this very moment. In effect, the coming of the first sunrise reunites the tribes, despite the fact that they remain widely separated in space; as the Popol Vuh has it, "there were countless peoples, but there was just one dawn for all tribes." The orderly movements of the lights of the sky, signs of the deeds of the gods, enable human beings to coordinate their actions even when they cannot see one another. In point of fact Mesoamerican peoples in general shared a common calendar, consisting of the 260-day cycle, whose auguries were first read by Xpiyacoc and Xmucane, and the cycles of Mars, Venus, and the sun and moon, as measured off by the movements of their sons and grandsons and by Blood Woman.

Having seen the first sunrise from the mountain of Hacauitz, the Quichés eventually build a citadel there. But at first, even while the people of other tribes are becoming thickly settled and are seen traveling the roads in great numbers, the Quichés remain rustic and rural, gathering the larvae of yellow jackets, wasps, and bees for food and staying largely out of sight. When they go before the petrified forms of Tohil, Auilix, and Hacauitz, they burn bits of pitchy bark and wildflowers as substitutes for refined incense and offer blood drawn from their own bodies. The three gods are still able to speak to them, but only by appearing in spirit form. Tohil tells them to augment their offerings with the blood of deer and birds taken in the hunt, but they grow dissatisfied with this arrangement and begin to cast eyes on the people they see walking by in the roads. From hiding places on mountain peaks, they begin imitating the cries of the coyote, fox, puma, and jaguar.

Finally Tohil tells the Quichés to go ahead and take human beings for sacrifice, reminding them that when they were at Tulan the other tribes promised to allow him to "suckle" them. They begin to seize people they find out walking alone or in pairs, taking them away to cut them open before Tohil, Auilix, and Hacauitz and then rolling their heads out onto the roads. At first the lords who rule the victimized tribes think these deaths are the work of wild animals, but then they suspect the worshipers of Tohil, Auilix, and Hacauitz and attempt to track them down. Again and again they are foiled by rain, mist, and mud, but they do discover that the three gods, whose spirit familiars take the form of adolescent boys, have a favorite bathing place. They send two beautiful maidens, Xtah and Xpuch, to wash clothes there, instructing them to tempt the boys and then yield to any advances. They warn the maidens to return with proof of the success of their mission, which must take the form of presents from the boys.

Contrary to plan, the three Quiché gods fail to lust after Xtah and Xpuch, but they do agree to provide them with presents. They give them three cloaks with figures on the inside, one painted with a jaguar by Jaguar Quitze, another painted with an eagle by Jaguar Night, and the third painted with swarms of yellow jackets and wasps by Mahucutah. When the maidens return the enemy lords are so pleased with the cloaks that they cannot resist trying them on. All is well until the wasps painted on the inside of the third cloak turn into real ones. Xtah and Xpuch are spurned; despite their failure to tempt Tohil, Auilix, and Hacauitz they become the first prostitutes, or what Quichés call "barkers of shins." As for the enemy lords, they resolve to make war and launch a massive attack on the Quiché citadel at Hacauitz.

The enemy warriors come at night in order to get as far as possible without resistance, but they fall into a deep sleep on the road. The Quichés not only strip them of all the metal ornaments on their weapons and clothes, but pluck out their eyebrows and beards as well. Even so the enemy warriors press on the next day, determined to recover their losses, but the Quichés are well prepared. What the enemy lookouts see all around the citadel of Hacauitz is a wooden palisade; visible on the parapet are rows of warriors, decked out with the very metal objects that were stolen during the night. What the lookouts do not see is that these warriors are mere wooden puppets, and that behind the palisade, on each of its four sides, is a large gourd filled with yellow jackets and wasps, put there at the suggestion of Tohil. As for the Quichés on the inside, what they see, once the attack begins, is more than twenty-four thousand warriors converging on them, bristling with weapons and shouting continuously. But Tohil has made them so confident that they treat the attack as a great spectacle, bringing their women and children up on the parapet to see it. When they release the yellow jackets and wasps their enemies drop their weapons and attempt to flee, so badly stung they hardly even notice the blows they receive from conventional Quiché weapons. The survivors become permanent payers of tribute to the Quiché lords.

After their great victory, Jaguar Quitze, Jaguar Night, Mahucutah, and True Jaguar begin preparing, with complete contentment, for what they know to be their approaching death. First they sing "The Blame Is Ours," and then they explain to their wives and successors that "the time of our Lord Deer" has come around again. This is a reference to the day named Deer, one of the four days on which a new solar year can begin, and specifically to the first day of a longer period, lasting fifty-two years, which falls on One Deer. Such a major temporal transition is an occasion for rites of renewal; the Quiché forefathers declare that their time as lords among the living has been completed and that they intend to return to the place where they came from, far in the east. Jaguar Quitze leaves a sacred object called the "Bundle of Flames," a sort of cloth-wrapped ark with mysterious contents, as a "sign of his being." He and the others "die" by simply departing; they are never seen again, but their descendants burn incense before the Bundle of Flames in remembrance of them, just as Xmucane burned incense before the ears of corn in remembrance of Hunahpu and Xbalanque.

The Quiché lords of the second generation, following the instructions of their departed fathers, go on a pilgrimage to the east (at the beginning of Part Five). Unlike their fathers, they do this with the intention of returning in the flesh. Cocaib, the firstborn son of Jaguar Quitze, goes on behalf of the Cauec lineage; Coacutec, the second son of Jaguar Night, represents the Greathouses; and Coahau, the only son of Mahucutah, represents the Lord Quichés. They go all the way back down into the lowlands, to the other side of the same "sea" their fathers once crossed on the way up to the highlands. If they were retracing their fathers' route in detail, they must have descended into the lowlands by way of the Great Abyss. They do not go to Tulan Zuyua, which may have been in ruins by this time, but they do come before the ruler of a great kingdom. His name is Nacxit, one of the epithets Nahua speakers give to the god-king Plumed Serpent. He gives them the emblems that go with the two highest titles of Mayan nobility, Keeper of the Mat and Keeper of the Reception House Mat. Both these titles, the one belonging to a head of state and the other to an overseer of tribute collection, go to the Cauecs. From other sources we know that the Greathouse and Lord Quiché lineages also receive emblems at this time, with the title of Lord Minister (ranking third) going to one and that of Crier to the People (ranking fourth) to the other.

Cocaib, Coacutec, and Coahau return "from across the sea" with the regalia given them by Nacxit, including canopies, thrones, musical instruments, cosmetics, jewelry, the feet and feathers of various animals and birds, and "the writings about Tulan." Since one of the titles of the Popol Vuh is "The Light That Came from Across the Sea," we may guess that it was the Popol Vuh they brought back, and that the hieroglyphic version of the book contained not only writings about the gods whose movements prefigured those of celestial lights, but about such human affairs as those of Tulan. The sovereign lordship of the returned pilgrims is recognized not only by the Quichés themselves, but by the Rabinals, Cakchiquels, and Bird House people as well. Only now do the Quiché lords begin to have what the Popol Vuh calls "fiery splendor." It seems likely that their pilgrimage was conceived as a reenactment of the adventures of Hunahpu and Xbalanque in Xibalba, who had only the planet Venus to their credit when they first descended in the east at the Great Abyss, but who eventually returned with the greater splendor of the sun and full moon.

Later, after the death of the widows of Jaguar Quitze, Jaguar Night, and Mahucutah, the Quichés leave Hacauitz and settle at a succession of other sites. The Popol Vuh mentions only one of these by name, Thorny Place, settled at some point after the deaths of Cocaib, Coacutec, and Coahau. The ruins of Thorny Place, which are divided into four parts just as the Popol Vuh indicates they should be, are some distance east and a little north of Hacauitz, in the direction of the Great Abyss. This location may have been chosen because it was a step backward on the Quiché migration route, placing the ruling lords closer to their forefathers than they were before. But when the Quichés move again, two generations later, they go west and a little south again, ending up even farther in that direction than Hacauitz. This time, with Cotuha as Keeper of the Mat and Iztayul as Keeper of the Reception House Mat, they found the citadel of Bearded Place, directly across a canyon to the south from the site of what will one day be their greatest citadel.

At Bearded Place there is great harmony among the Cauecs, Greathouses, and Lord Quichés; these three lineages, each with its own palace, are tied together through intermarriage. At Thorny Place women were married off in exchange for modest favors and gifts, but now, at Bearded Place, wedding arrangements are accompanied by elaborate feasting and drinking. The only disturbance during this period comes when the Ilocs not only try to get Iztayul involved in a plot to assassinate Cotuha, but come to the point of making a military attack on Bearded Place. They are defeated, and some of their own number are sacrificed before the gods of their intended victims. The Cauec, Greathouse, and Lord Quiché lineages now rise to greater and greater power, defeating some tribes in direct attacks and terrorizing still others by having them witness the sacrifice of prisoners of war.

In the next generation the Keeper of the Mat bears the divine name Plumed Serpent, while the Keeper of the Reception House Mat is Cotuha, named after the previous Keeper of the Mat. They build a new and larger citadel across the canyon from Bearded Place, at Rotten Cane. The three leading lineages, faced with increased numbers and torn by quarrels over inflation in bride prices, break apart into smaller groups. The Cauecs divide into nine segments, the Greathouses into nine, and the Lord Quichés into four, with each of these segments headed by a titled lord and occupying its own palace. In addition, the inhabitants of Rotten Cane include the Zaquics, a lineage not previously mentioned in the Popol Vuh, divided into two segments but occupying only a single palace, making twenty-three palaces in all. Along with all these palaces, Rotten Cane is provided with three pyramids that bear the temples of Tohil, Auilix, and Hacauitz, ranged around a central plaza; elsewhere is a fourth pyramid for Corntassel, the god of the Zaquics.

The Popol Vuh identifies Plumed Serpent, who holds the titles of both Keeper of the Mat and Keeper of the Reception House Mat during at least part of his reign at Rotten Cane, as "a true lord of genius." He has the power to manifest his personal spirit familiars, putting on performances in which he transforms himself into a snake, an eagle, a jaguar, or a puddle of blood, climbing to the sky or descending to Xibalba. As the Popol Vuh explains it, his displays are "just his way of revealing himself," but they have the effect of terrorizing the lords of other tribes. The next Quiché lords to manifest genius, coming two generations later, are Quicab, who serves as Keeper of the Mat, and

Cauizimah, who serves as Keeper of the Reception House Mat. Under their rule the dominion of the Quichés reaches its greatest extent. Where Plumed Serpent gained power through spectacular displays of shamanic skill, Quicab now gains it by military force. Not content with merely overpowering the citadels of surrounding peoples, he sends out loyal vassals, called "guardians of the land" or "lookout lineages," to serve as forces of occupation. The stationing of these guardians is conceived as analogous to the construction of a palisade; they turn the entire Quiché kingdom into one great fortress.

During this period the settlement at the center of the Quiché kingdom embraced a cluster of four citadels, with Rotten Cane at the focal point. Together with the ordinary houses that occupied the lower ground around them, these four sites made up a larger town that took the name Quiché. It was perhaps the most densely built-up area that had existed in highland Guatemala since early in the classic period, and it took on the stature of the place where Cocaib, Coacutec, and Coahau had gone to receive the titles and emblems of truly glorious lordship. Five generations after their pilgrimage a new conferring of titles took place, only now it was not Quichés but the heads of the leading "lookout" lineages who were ennobled, and it happened not under the authority of Nacxit, lord of a domain in the mythic "east," but under Quicab, who ruled from Quiché.

The town of Quiché not only took on the status of the place visited by the pilgrims who saw Nacxit, but of the Tulan visited by their forefathers as well. When the founders of the ruling Quiché lineages and their closest allies left Tulan Zuyua before the first sunrise, they had come away with tribal gods whose names were "meant to be in agreement," and they were "in unity" when they passed the Great Abyss and convened at Place of Advice. Now, in this latter day, "the word came from just one place" again, and the allies convened in a town and "came away in unity" again, but this time they came away "having heard, there at *Quiché*, what all of them should do." It was probably during this period that the Quiché lords went so far as to have a branching tunnel constructed directly beneath Rotten Cane, a tunnel that brought the Seven Caves of Tulan Zuyua, or of the ultimate Tulan that was Teotihuacan, to the time and place of their own greatest glory.

It is in the course of explaining the greatness of lords like Plumed Serpent and Quicab that the writers of the alphabetic Popol Vuh tell us how its hieroglyphic predecessor was put to use, serving as a way of seeing into distant places and times. Greatness also came to the lords through their participation in religious retreats. For long periods they would stay in the temples, praying, burning incense, bleeding themselves, sleeping apart from their wives, and abstaining not only from meat but from corn products, eating nothing but the fruits of various trees. The shortest fast lasted 180 days, corresponding to half the 360-day cycle (separate from the solar year) that was used in keeping chronologies of historical events, and another lasted 260 days, or one complete run of the cycle whose days were counted by Xpiyacoc and Xmucane when they divined for the gods. The longest fast, 340 days, corresponded to a segment of the Mayan Venus calendar, beginning with the departure of Venus as the morning star and continuing through its stay in the underworld and its period of reappearance as the evening star, leaving just eight days to go before its rebirth as the morning star. This fast probably commemorated the heroic adventures of Hunahpu and Xbalanque in Xibalba, the long darkness endured by the first generation of lords as they watched for the appearance of the morning star, and the lowland pilgrimage undertaken by Cocaib, Coacutec, and Coahau.

The Quiché lords sought identification with the very gods, not only in their pilgrimages, shamanic feats, limitless vision, and long fasts, but in the requirements they set for their subjects. Just as the gods needed human beings to nurture them with offerings, so human lords required subjects to bring them tribute. As the Popol Vuh points out, the "nurture" required by the Quiché lords consisted not only of the food and drink that were prepared for them, but of turquoise, jade, and the iridescent blue-green feathers of the quetzal bird. Apparently such precious objects as these were considered the ultimate fruits of the earth and sky, which were themselves described as the "blue-green plate" and "blue-green bowl."

Near the end, the Popol Vuh lists all the noble titles held by the various segments of the Cauec, Greathouse, and Lord Quiché lineages (in rank order), and it gives the names of those who held the highest titles (in the order of their succession). In the case of the two leading segments of the Cauec lineage, those whose heads held the titles of Keeper of the Mat and Keeper of the Reception House Mat, the text lists four generations after Quicab and Cauizimah, who were in the seventh generation, without comment. Then, in the twelfth generation, the names Three Deer and Nine Dog are followed by two sentences whose combination of gravity and brevity gives the reader a chill. The first is, "And they were ruling when Tonatiuh arrived," Tonatiuh or "Sun" being the name given by the Aztecs to Pedro de Alvarado, the man whose forces destroyed Rotten Cane in 1524. And the second sentence about Three Deer and Nine Dog is simply, "They were hanged by the Castilian people."

In the thirteenth generation of Cauecs the Popol Vuh lists Tecum and Tepepul, who were "tributary to the Castilian people." Then, at the end of the list of Cauec generations, come the first lords who adopted Spanish names, Juan de Rojas and Juan Cortés, the living holders of the titles of Keeper of the Mat and Keeper of the Reception House Mat when the alphabetic Popol Vuh was written. Today Quichés ideally list either nine or thirteen generations when they invoke their ancestors in prayer; from this we can see that the thirteen generations of lords named as preceding Juan de Rojas and Juan Cortés need not be taken as constituting an exhaustive genealogy but may simply be a list of the names these two men used in their own prayers.

By giving us the names of Quiché lords who were alive while they were writing, the authors of the alphabetic Popol Vuh also give us the means for dating their work. They could not have finished it any later than 1558, since by that year the name of Juan de Rojas is missing from documents he would have signed had he still been among the living. And since they mention Pedro de Robles of the Greathouse lineage as the current Lord Minister, they could not have finished any earlier than 1554, at which time his predecessor was still in office. This places the writing of the Popol Vuh during the very same decade as the writing of the majority of the native *títulos* that exist for colonial Guatemala, documents that were composed by indigenous authors for the express purpose of reasserting the rights formerly enjoyed by specific lordly lineages living in specific places. The version of the Popol Vuh that comes down to us does not include a copy of the original title page or of whatever explicitly legal statements might have been appended to the original alphabetic manuscript, but it makes the lineage and place names plain enough, and it contains two different lists of towns that had once been tributary to Quiché.

It may be that the indigenous lords of highland Guatemala chose the 1550s to make their claims because they thought they saw an opening in Spanish policy, but they may also have been preparing for the major temporal transition that Jaguar Quitze, Jaguar Night, Mahucutah, and True Jaguar had once called "the time of our Lord Deer." A new fifty-two-year cycle, with the first day of its first year falling on One Deer, was due to begin on June 2, 1558 (on the Julian calendar). Juan Cortés, whose duties as Keeper of the Reception House Mat would have included tribute collection had he served before the coming of Alvarado, worked constantly to restore tribute rights to the lordly lineages of the town of Quiché. In 1557 he went all the way to Spain to press his case, and it may well be that he took a copy of the alphabetic Popol Vuh with him. He continued to make claims when he returned to Guatemala in 1558, prompting a missionary to warn Philip II that "this land is new and not confirmed in the faith," and that Cortés, "son of idolatrous parents, would need to do very little to restore their ceremonies and attract their former subjects to himself." Quiché rights to collect tribute never were restored, but over the next thirty years Juan Cortés did take a considerable role in appointing and installing the leaders of various towns that had once been under Quiché rule.

By the time the authors of the Popol Vuh have finished giving the rank order of noble titles and the names of the individuals who held the highest titles, they are only a few sentences away from finishing their work. At this point they single out one of the lesser titles for further discussion, a move that seems anticlimactic until we realize that they are giving us a clue to their own identity. Without naming any individuals, they point out that each of the three leading lineages included one lord bearing the title of Great Toastmaster, also translatable as Great Convener of Banquets. Here we may recall that when the authors introduced the story of One Hunahpu, they themselves proposed a toast to the reader. If we look for a convener of banquets and maker of toasts among the contemporary Quiché, we find the professional matchmaker, who serves as an eloquent master of ceremonies at the feasts where marriage arrangements are completed. If our mysterious authors were themselves the three Great Toastmasters, and if their duties included the convening of wedding banquets, that would help explain why they took a special interest in marriage customs when they recounted the life and times of successive Quiché citadels. Indeed, they specifically noted the point at which feasting and drinking first became a part of the negotiations for a bride.

The authors give us one final clue to their identity when they tell us that the three Great Toastmasters are "Mothers of the Word" and "Fathers of the Word." The combination of "Mother" and "Father" suggests the contemporary daykeepers called mother-fathers, who serve as the ritual heads of patrilineages; it is from their ranks that matchmakers are drawn. The focus on "the Word," coming as it does near the very end of a work whose opening line promised to give us the "Ancient Word," suggests that the Word parented by the Great Toastmasters and the Word written down in the alphabetic Popol Vuh are one and the same. If so, we know the name of at least one of the writers: when Juan de Rojas and Juan Cortés signed a document known as the "Title of the Lords of Totonicapán" in 1554, a man named Cristobal Velasco signed himself as Great Toastmaster of the Cauecs.

At the end of their work the authors repeat the enigma they presented near the beginning, allowing us to wonder whether the hieroglyphic Popol Vuh might still exist somewhere, only now they say it has been "lost" instead of telling us that the reader is hiding his face. They close on a note of reassurance, asking us, in effect, to accept what they have written without demanding a closer look at their sources, since "everything has been completed here concerning Quiché," meaning the place named Quiché. Then, lest we forget their difficult circumstances, they add the phrase, "which is now named Santa Cruz," or "Holy Cross." Here again they take us back to the beginning, where they told us, "We shall write about this now amid the preaching of God, in Christendom now."

Today, even when Quiché daykeepers go to a remote mountaintop shrine, sending up great clouds of incense for multitudes of deities and ancestors, they sometimes begin and end by running through an "Our Father" and a "Hail Mary" and crossing themselves. It is as if the alien eye and ear of the conqueror were present even under conditions of solitude and required the recitation of two spells, one to ward them off for awhile and the other to readmit their existence. Between these protective spells daykeepers are left to enter, in peace, a world whose obligations they know to be older than those of Christianity, obligations to the mountains and plains where they continue to live and to all those who have ever lived there before them. So it is with the authors of the Popol Vuh, who mention Christendom on the first page, Holy Cross on the last page, and open up the whole sky-earth, vast and deep, within.

Perhaps the most remarkable thing about the Popol Vuh, considered in its entirety, is the vast temporal sweep of its narrative. It begins in darkness, with a world inhabited only by gods, and continues all the way past the dawn into the time of the humans who wrote it. The surviving Maya hieroglyphic books abound with gods, but they seem to stop short of dealing directly with the acts of mortals. The Dresden book does have one page that shifts the action to the human sphere, but the following pages were torn off at some time in the past. If we wish to find hieroglyphic texts that have the same proportion between divine and human affairs as the alphabetic Popol Vuh, we must leave the time and place in which it was written and go a thousand years back and hundreds of miles away to the classic Maya site of Palenque, in the Gulf-coast lowlands.

At Palenque, in the sanctuary of each temple in what is now known as the Cross Group, is a stone tablet bearing a hieroglyphic narrative. In each case the text is divided into two panels, one of which begins with the deeds of gods who include the classic equivalents of Hunahpu and Xbalanque, and the other of which ends with the deeds of human lords whose own scribes were the authors of the inscriptions. In the middle of this narrative, where the reader passes from one panel to the other, are characters who are neither fully divine nor quite human. So also with the Popol Vuh: about halfway through, the reader comes to a transition between what might be called "myth" and "history" (at the end of Part Three). The characters in the narrative are still divine at this point, but they are described as performing rituals for the veneration of ripened corn and deceased relatives, rituals that are meant to be followed by future humans rather than by ancient gods. After this episode, in which the gods act like people, comes another in which people act like gods (at the beginning of Part Four). The people in question are the first four humans, the ones who saw and understood everything in the sky-earth. Once their perfect vision has been taken away the narrative begins to sound more like history as it moves along, though human characters continue to aspire to deeds of divine proportions.

We tend to think of myth and history as being in conflict with one another, but the authors of the inscriptions at Palenque and the alphabetic text of the Popol Vuh treated the mythic and historical parts of their narratives as belonging to a single, balanced whole. By their sense of proportion, the Egyptian Book of the Dead would need a second half devoted to human deeds in the land of the living, and the Hebrew Testament would need a first half devoted to events that took place before the fall of Adam and Eve. In the case of ancient Chinese literature the Book of Changes, which is like the Popol Vuh in being subject to divinatory interpretation, would have to be combined with the Book of History in a single volume.

To this day the Quiché Maya think of dualities in general as complementary rather than opposed, interpenetrating rather than mutually exclusive. Instead of being in logical opposition to one another, the realms of divine and human actions are joined by a mutual attraction. If we had an English word that fully expressed the Mayan sense of narrative time, it would have to embrace the duality of the divine and the human in the same way the Quiché term *cahuleu* or "sky-earth" preserves the duality of what we call the "world." In fact we already have a word that comes close to doing the job: *mythistory*, taken into English from Greek by way of Latin. For the ancient Greeks, who set about driving a wedge between the divine and the human, this term became a negative one, designating narratives that should have been properly historical but contained mythic impurities. For Mayans, the presence of a divine dimension in narratives of human affairs is not an imperfection but a necessity, and it is balanced by a necessary human dimension in narratives of divine affairs. At one end of the Popol Vuh the gods are preoccupied with the difficult task of making humans, and at the other humans are preoccupied with the equally difficult task of finding the traces of divine movements in their own deeds.

The difference between a fully mythistorical sense of narrative time and the European quest for pure history is not reducible to a simple contrast between cyclical and linear time. Mayans are always alert to the reassertion of the patterns of the past in present events, but they do not expect the past to repeat itself exactly. Each time the gods of the Popol Vuh attempt to make human beings they get a different result, and except for the solitary person made of mud, each attempt has a lasting result rather than completely disappearing into the folds of cyclical time. Later, when members of the second generation of Quiché lords go on a pilgrimage that takes them into the lowlands, their journey is not described as a literal repetition of the journey of Hunahpu and Xbalanque to Xibalba, nor even as a retracing of the journey of the human founders of the ruling Quiché lineages, but is allowed its own character as a unique event, an event that nevertheless carries echoes of the past. The effect of these events, like others, is cumulative, and it is a specifically human capacity to take each of them into account separately while at the same time recognizing that they double back on one another.

In theory, if we who presently claim to be human were to forget our efforts to find the traces of divine movements in our own actions, our fate should be something like that of the wooden people in the Popol Vuh. For them, the forgotten force of divinity reasserted itself by inhabiting their own tools and utensils, which rose up against them and drove them from their homes. Today they are swinging through the trees.

> On the holy day Eight Monkey
> in the year Eleven Thought,
> June 22, 1984,
> Menotomy, Massachusetts

PRONOUNCING QUICHÉ WORDS

VOWELS

a	Like *a* in English "father," or Spanish *a*.
e	Like *ai* in English "wait," or Spanish *e*.
i	Like *ee* in English "seed," or Spanish *i*.
o	Like *o* in English "bone," or Spanish *o*.
u	Like *oo* in English "hoot," or Spanish *u*.
aa, ee, ii, oo, uu	The doubling of a vowel normally indicates that it is followed by a glottal stop, which is like *tt* in the Scottish pronunciation of "bottle"; when *uu* begins a word or follows another vowel it is pronounced like English "woo."

CONSONANTS

b	Like English *b*, but pronounced together with a glottal stop.
c, qu	Pronounced without the puff of air that follows *c* in English "cat."
ch	Like English *ch*.
h	Pronounced deeper in the throat than English *h*, like Spanish *j* or German *ch*.
k	Pronounced with the tongue farther back in the mouth than for *c* or *qu*, like the Hebrew letter qoph.
l	Pronounced with the tongue moved forward from the position of English *l* so as to touch the teeth, as in the *ll* of Welsh "Lloyd."
m	Like English *m*.
n	Like English *n*.

p	Pronounced without the puff of air that follows *p* in English "pit."
r	Pronounced with a flap if between two vowels, like Spanish *r;* otherwise trilled like Spanish *rr*.
t	Pronounced without the puff of air that follows *t* in English "ten."
tt	Like *t*, but pronounced together with a glottal stop.
tz	Like *ts* in English "mats."
x	Like English *sh*.
y	Like English *y*.
z	Like English *s*.
3	Like *k*, but pronounced together with a glottal stop.
4	Like *c* or *qu*, but pronounced together with a glottal stop.
4h	Like *ch*, but pronounced together with a glottal stop.
4,	Like *tz*, but pronounced together with a glottal stop.

Stress is always on the final syllable of a word.

PART
ONE

MAKER OF THE BLUE-GREEN PLATE, MAKER OF THE BLUE-GREEN BOWL: One of the hundreds of altars used for burning offerings at the shrine called 4huti Zabal, or "Little Place of Declaration," at Momostenango. The potsherds, deliberately made by breaking new vessels into quarters, are used to burn copal incense in the houses of novice daykeepers and are brought here during initiation ceremonies. Pine boughs (along the top) and flowers (lower left) are brought to adorn the altar during the burning of offerings and the saying of prayers. On the flat surface of the altar itself are the coals and ashes of copal; some incompletely burned pieces, about the size and shape of a quarter, may be seen at front center. It is forbidden to touch an altar's surface with the hands; the stick at right is used to stir the burning copal or to move stray pieces of it into the fire.

THIS IS THE BEGINNING OF THE ANCIENT WORD, here in this place called Quiché. Here we shall inscribe, we shall implant the Ancient Word, the potential and source for everything done in the citadel of Quiché, in the nation of Quiché people. And here we shall take up the demonstration, revelation, and account of how things were put in shadow and brought to light

by the Maker, Modeler, named Bearer, Begetter,
Hunahpu Possum, Hunahpu Coyote,
Great White Peccary, Tapir,
Sovereign Plumed Serpent,
Heart of the Lake, Heart of the Sea,
Maker of the Blue-Green Plate,
Maker of the Blue-Green Bowl,

as they are called, also named, also described as

the midwife, matchmaker
named Xpiyacoc, Xmucane,
defender, protector,
twice a midwife, twice a matchmaker,

as is said in the words of Quiché. They accounted for everything—and did it, too—as enlightened beings, in enlightened words. We shall write about this now amid the preaching of God, in Christendom now. We shall bring it out because there is no longer a place to see it, a Council Book,

a place to see "The Light That Came from
Across the Sea,"
the account of "Our Place in the Shadows,"
a place to see "The Dawn of Life,"

as it is called. There is the original book and ancient writing, but he who reads and ponders it hides his face. It takes a long perfor-

mance and account to complete the emergence of all the sky-
earth:

> the fourfold siding, fourfold cornering,
> measuring, fourfold staking,
> halving the cord, stretching the cord
> in the sky, on the earth,
> the four sides, the four corners,

as it is said,

> by the Maker, Modeler,
> mother-father of life, of humankind,
> giver of breath, giver of heart,
> bearer, upbringer in the light that lasts
> of those born in the light, begotten in the light;
> worrier, knower of everything, whatever there is:
> sky-earth, lake-sea.

THIS IS THE ACCOUNT, here it is:
Now it still ripples, now it still murmurs, ripples, it still
sighs, still hums, and it is empty under the sky.

Here follow the first words, the first eloquence:

There is not yet one person, one animal, bird, fish, crab, tree,
rock, hollow, canyon, meadow, forest. Only the sky alone is
there; the face of the earth is not clear. Only the sea alone is
pooled under all the sky; there is nothing whatever gathered together. It is at rest; not a single thing stirs. It is held back, kept at
rest under the sky.

Whatever there is that might be is simply not there: only the
pooled water, only the calm sea, only it alone is pooled.

Whatever might be is simply not there: only murmurs, ripples, in the dark, in the night. Only the Maker, Modeler alone,

Sovereign Plumed Serpent, the Bearers, Begetters are in the water, a glittering light. They are there, they are enclosed in quetzal feathers, in blue-green.

Thus the name, "Plumed Serpent." They are great knowers, great thinkers in their very being.

And of course there is the sky, and there is also the Heart of Sky. This is the name of the god, as it is spoken.

And then came his word, he came here to the Sovereign Plumed Serpent, here in the blackness, in the early dawn. He spoke with the Sovereign Plumed Serpent, and they talked, then they thought, then they worried. They agreed with each other, they joined their words, their thoughts. Then it was clear, then they reached accord in the light, and then humanity was clear, when they conceived the growth, the generation of trees, of bushes, and the growth of life, of humankind, in the blackness, in the early dawn, all because of the Heart of Sky, named Hurricane. Thunderbolt Hurricane comes first, the second is Newborn Thunderbolt, and the third is Raw Thunderbolt.

So there were three of them, as Heart of Sky, who came to the Sovereign Plumed Serpent, when the dawn of life was conceived:

"How should it be sown, how should it dawn? Who is to be the provider, nurturer?"

"Let it be this way, think about it: this water should be removed, emptied out for the formation of the earth's own plate and platform, then comes the sowing, the dawning of the sky-earth. But there will be no high days and no bright praise for our work, our design, until the rise of the human work, the human design," they said.

And then the earth arose because of them, it was simply their word that brought it forth. For the forming of the earth they said "Earth." It arose suddenly, just like a cloud, like a mist, now forming, unfolding. Then the mountains were separated from the water, all at once the great mountains came forth. By their genius alone, by their cutting edge alone they carried out the conception of the mountain-plain, whose face grew instant groves of cypress and pine.

"How should it be sown, how should it dawn?": Corn-fields amid pine forests near Momostenango. In this passage sowing and dawning have three meanings: the begetting and bearing of human beings, the sowing and sprouting of plants, and the setting and dawning (or rising) of heavenly bodies.

And the Plumed Serpent was pleased with this:

"It was good that you came, Heart of Sky, Hurricane, and Newborn Thunderbolt, Raw Thunderbolt. Our work, our design will turn out well," they said.

And the earth was formed first, the mountain-plain. The channels of water were separated; their branches wound their ways among the mountains. The waters were divided when the

74

great mountains appeared.

Such was the formation of the earth when it was brought forth by the Heart of Sky, Heart of Earth, as they are called, since they were the first to think of it. The sky was set apart, and the earth was set apart in the midst of the waters.

Such was their plan when they thought, when they worried about the completion of their work.

THEN THE MOUNTAINS WERE SEPARATED FROM THE WATER:
Lake Atitlán, called Nahachel in Quiché, with the volcanoes
of Cerro de Oro (in the middle distance) and San Pedro (beyond). The contemporary Quichés of Momostenango reckon
Nahachel as the lake of the south; it is one of four sacred
lakes that mark the four sides of their world.

N OW THEY PLANNED THE ANIMALS OF THE MOUNTAINS, all the
guardians of the forests, creatures of the mountains: the
deer, birds, pumas, jaguars, serpents, rattlesnakes, yellowbites,
guardians of the bushes.

A Bearer, Begetter speaks:

"Why this pointless humming? Why should there merely be
rustling beneath the trees and bushes?"

"Indeed—they had better have guardians," the others replied.
As soon as they thought it and said it, deer and birds came forth.

And then they gave out homes to the deer and birds:

"You, the deer: sleep along the rivers, in the canyons. Be here
in the meadows, in the thickets, in the forests, multiply yourselves. You will stand and walk on all fours," they were told.

So then they established the nests of the birds, small and great:

"You, precious birds: your nests, your houses are in the trees, in the bushes. Multiply there, scatter there, in the branches of trees, the branches of bushes," the deer and birds were told.

When this deed had been done, all of them had received a place to sleep and a place to stay. So it is that the nests of the animals are on the earth, given by the Bearer, Begetter. Now the arrangement of the deer and birds was complete.

A ND THEN THE DEER AND BIRDS WERE TOLD by the Maker, Modeler, Bearer, Begetter:

"Talk, speak out. Don't moan, don't cry out. Please talk, each to each, within each kind, within each group," they were told—the deer, birds, puma, jaguar, serpent.

"Name now our names, praise us. We are your mother, we are your father. Speak now:

> 'Hurricane,
> Newborn Thunderbolt, Raw Thunderbolt,
> Heart of Sky, Heart of Earth,
> Maker, Modeler,
> Bearer, Begetter,'

speak, pray to us, keep our days," they were told. But it didn't turn out that they spoke like people: they just squawked, they just chattered, they just howled. It wasn't apparent what language they spoke; each one gave a different cry. When the Maker, Modeler heard this:

"It hasn't turned out well, they haven't spoken," they said among themselves. "It hasn't turned out that our names have been named. Since we are their mason and sculptor, this will not do," the Bearers and Begetters said among themselves. So they told them:

"You will simply have to be transformed. Since it hasn't turned out well and you haven't spoken, we have changed our word:

"What you feed on, what you eat, the places where you sleep, the places where you stay, whatever is yours will remain in the canyons, the forests. Although it turned out that our days were not kept, nor did you pray to us, there may yet be strength in the keeper of days, the giver of praise whom we have yet to make. Just accept your service, just let your flesh be eaten.

"So be it, this must be your service," they were told when they were instructed—the animals, small and great, on the face of the earth.

And then they wanted to test their timing again, they wanted to experiment again, and they wanted to prepare for the keeping of days again. They had not heard their speech among the animals; it did not come to fruition and it was not complete.

And so their flesh was brought low: they served, they were eaten, they were killed—the animals on the face of the earth.

A GAIN THERE COMES AN EXPERIMENT WITH THE HUMAN WORK, the human design, by the Maker, Modeler, Bearer, Begetter:

"It must simply be tried again. The time for the planting and dawning is nearing. For this we must make a provider and nurturer. How else can we be invoked and remembered on the face of the earth? We have already made our first try at our work and design, but it turned out that they didn't keep our days, nor did they glorify us.

"So now let's try to make a giver of praise, giver of respect, provider, nurturer," they said.

So then comes the building and working with earth and mud. They made a body, but it didn't look good to them. It was just separating, just crumbling, just loosening, just softening, just disintegrating, and just dissolving. Its head wouldn't turn, either. Its face was just lopsided, its face was just twisted. It couldn't look around. It talked at first, but senselessly. It was quickly dissolving in the water.

"It won't last," the mason and sculptor said then. "It seems to be dwindling away, so let it just dwindle. It can't walk and it can't multiply, so let it be merely a thought," they said.

So then they dismantled, again they brought down their work and design. Again they talked:

"What is there for us to make that would turn out well, that would succeed in keeping our days and praying to us?" they said. Then they planned again:

"We'll just tell Xpiyacoc, Xmucane, Hunahpu Possum, Hunahpu Coyote, to try a counting of days, a counting of lots," the mason and sculptor said to themselves. Then they invoked Xpiyacoc, Xmucane.

THEN COMES THE NAMING OF THOSE WHO ARE THE MIDMOST SEERS: the "Grandmother of Day, Grandmother of Light," as the Maker, Modeler called them. These are names of Xpiyacoc and Xmucane.

When Hurricane had spoken with the Sovereign Plumed Serpent, they invoked the daykeepers, diviners, the midmost seers:

"There is yet to find, yet to discover how we are to model a person, construct a person again, a provider, nurturer, so that we are called upon and we are recognized: our recompense is in words.

> Midwife, matchmaker,
> our grandmother, our grandfather,
> Xpiyacoc, Xmucane,
> let there be planting, let there be the dawning
> of our invocation, our sustenance, our recognition
> by the human work, the human design,
> the human figure, the human mass.

So be it, fulfill your names:

> Hunahpu Possum, Hunahpu Coyote,
> Bearer twice over, Begetter twice over,
> Great Peccary, Great Tapir,
> lapidary, jeweler,
> sawyer, carpenter,

THEY INVOKED THE DAYKEEPERS, DIVINERS, THE MIDMOST
SEERS: All the adults in this picture are daykeepers; in addition, the woman is a midwife and the man wearing a hat is a
matchmaker. The two men between them (the one bending
down being Andrés Xiloj) serve as mother-fathers, or patrilineage heads, and the man at right is a singer.

Maker of the Blue-Green Plate,
Maker of the Blue-Green Bowl,
incense maker, master craftsman,
Grandmother of Day, Grandmother of Light.

You have been called upon because of our work, our design. Run
your hands over the kernels of corn, over the seeds of the coral
tree, just get it done, just let it come out whether we should
carve and gouge a mouth, a face in wood," they told the daykeepers.

And then comes the borrowing, the counting of days; the hand
is moved over the corn kernels, over the coral seeds, the days,
the lots.

81

THE HAND IS MOVED OVER THE CORN KERNELS, OVER THE CORAL SEEDS, THE DAYS, THE LOTS: A divination in progress in front of burning offerings on top of Patohil, a mountain mentioned in the Popol Vuh. Coral seeds and crystals from a random handful are being set out in lots of four each; once the arrangement is complete the daykeeper will count the days of the 260-day calendar (one day for each lot), starting from the current day or from the day the client's problem began. The seeds and crystals left over from the handful are in the pile at extreme right. At left is the bundle in which the daykeeper carries his paraphernalia; the coin on top of it is the fee paid by the client. The hands are those of the author, who is a trained and initiated daykeeper.

Then they spoke to them, one of them a grandmother, the other a grandfather.

This is the grandfather, this is the master of the coral seeds: Xpiyacoc is his name.

And this is the grandmother, the daykeeper, diviner who stands behind others: Xmucane is her name.

And they said, as they set out the days:

"Just let it be found, just let it be discovered,
say it, our ear is listening,
may you talk, may you speak,
just find the wood for the carving and sculpting
by the builder, sculptor.
Is this to be the provider, the nurturer
when it comes to the planting, the dawning?
You corn kernels, you coral seeds,
you days, you lots:
may you succeed, may you be accurate,"

they said to the corn kernels, coral seeds, days, lots. "Have shame, you up there, Heart of Sky: attempt no deception before the mouth and face of Sovereign Plumed Serpent," they said. Then they spoke straight to the point:

"It is well that there be your manikins, woodcarvings, talking, speaking, there on the face of the earth."

"So be it," they replied. The moment they spoke it was done: the manikins, woodcarvings, human in looks and human in speech.

This was the peopling of the face of the earth:

They came into being, they multiplied, they had daughters, they had sons, these manikins, woodcarvings. But there was nothing in their hearts and nothing in their minds, no memory of their mason and builder. They just went and walked wherever they wanted. Now they did not remember the Heart of Sky.

And so they fell, just an experiment and just a cutout for humankind. They were talking at first but their faces were dry. They were not yet developed in the legs and arms. They had no blood, no lymph. They had no sweat, no fat. Their complexions

83

were dry, their faces were crusty. They flailed their legs and arms, their bodies were deformed.

And so they accomplished nothing before the Maker, Modeler who gave them birth, gave them heart. They became the first numerous people here on the face of the earth.

A GAIN THERE COMES A HUMILIATION, destruction, and demolition. The manikins, woodcarvings were killed when the Heart of Sky devised a flood for them. A great flood was made; it came down on the heads of the manikins, woodcarvings.

The man's body was carved from the wood of the coral tree by the Maker, Modeler. And as for the woman, the Maker, Modeler needed the pith of reeds for the woman's body. They were not competent, nor did they speak before the builder and sculptor who made them and brought them forth, and so they were killed, done in by a flood:

There came a rain of resin from the sky.

There came the one named Gouger of Faces: he gouged out their eyeballs.

There came Sudden Bloodletter: he snapped off their heads.

There came Crunching Jaguar: he ate their flesh.

There came Tearing Jaguar: he tore them open.

They were pounded down to the bones and tendons, smashed and pulverized even to the bones. Their faces were smashed because they were incompetent before their mother and their father, the Heart of Sky, named Hurricane. The earth was blackened because of this; the black rainstorm began, rain all day and rain all night. Into their houses came the animals, small and great. Their faces were crushed by things of wood and stone. Everything spoke: their water jars, their tortilla griddles, their plates, their cooking pots, their dogs, their grinding stones, each and every thing crushed their faces. Their dogs and turkeys told them:

"You caused us pain, you ate us, but now it is *you* whom *we* shall eat." And this is the grinding stone:

"We were undone because of you.

> Every day, every day,
> in the dark, in the dawn, forever,
> r-r-rip, r-r-rip,
> r-r-rub, r-r-rub,
> right in our faces, because of you.

This was the service we gave you at first, when you were still people, but today you will learn of our power. We shall pound and we shall grind your flesh," their grinding stones told them.

And this is what their dogs said, when they spoke in their turn:

"Why is it you can't seem to give us our food? We just watch and you just keep us down, and you throw us around. You keep a stick ready when you eat, just so you can hit us. We don't talk, so we've received nothing from you. How could you not have known? You *did* know that we were wasting away there, behind you.

"So, this very day you will taste the teeth in our mouths. We shall eat you," their dogs told them, and their faces were crushed.

And then their tortilla griddles and cooking pots spoke to them in turn:

"Pain! That's all you've done for us. Our mouths are sooty, our faces are sooty. By setting us on the fire all the time, you burn us. Since *we* felt no pain, *you* try it. We shall burn you," all their cooking pots said, crushing their faces.

The stones, their hearthstones were shooting out, coming right out of the fire, going for their heads, causing them pain. Now they run for it, helter-skelter.

They want to climb up on the houses, but they fall as the houses collapse.

They want to climb the trees; they're thrown off by the trees.

They want to get inside caves, but the caves slam shut in their faces.

Such was the scattering of the human work, the human design. The people were ground down, overthrown. The mouths and faces of all of them were destroyed and crushed. And it used to be said that the monkeys in the forests today are a sign of this.

They were left as a sign because wood alone was used for their flesh by the builder and sculptor.

So this is why monkeys look like people: they are a sign of a previous human work, human design—mere manikins, mere woodcarvings.

T HIS WAS WHEN THERE WAS JUST A TRACE OF EARLY DAWN on the face of the earth, there was no sun. But there was one who magnified himself; Seven Macaw is his name. The sky-earth was already there, but the face of the sun-moon was clouded over. Even so, it is said that his light provided a sign for the people who were flooded. He was like a person of genius in his being.

"I am great. My place is now higher than that of the human work, the human design. I am their sun and I am their light, and I am also their months.

"So be it: my light is great. I am the walkway and I am the foothold of the people, because my eyes are of metal. My teeth just glitter with jewels, and turquoise as well; they stand out blue with stones like the face of the sky.

"And this nose of mine shines white into the distance like the moon. Since my nest is metal, it lights up the face of the earth. When I come forth before my nest, I am like the sun and moon for those who are born in the light, begotten in the light. It must be so, because my face reaches into the distance," says Seven Macaw.

It is not true that he is the sun, this Seven Macaw, yet he magnifies himself, his wings, his metal. But the scope of his face lies right around his own perch; his face does not reach everywhere beneath the sky. The faces of the sun, moon, and stars are not yet visible, it has not yet dawned.

And so Seven Macaw puffs himself up as the days and the months, though the light of the sun and moon has not yet clarified. He only wished for surpassing greatness. This was when the flood was worked upon the manikins, woodcarvings.

And now we shall explain how Seven Macaw died, when the people were vanquished, done in by the mason and sculptor.

PART
TWO

THE FIRST NAMED HUNAHPU AND THE SECOND NAMED XBA-
LANQUE: These are the portrait glyphs for the classic Maya
equivalents of Hunahpu (left) and Xbalanque (right) at
Palenque.

HERE IS THE BEGINNING OF THE DEFEAT AND DESTRUCTION OF THE DAY OF SEVEN MACAW by the two boys, the first named Hunahpu and the second named Xbalanque. Being gods, the two of them saw evil in his attempt at self-magnification before the Heart of Sky. So the boys talked:

"It's no good without life, without people here on the face of the earth."

"Well then, let's try a shot. We could shoot him while he's at his meal. We could make him ill, then put an end to his riches, his jade, his metal, his jewels, his gems, the source of his brilliance. Everyone might do as he does, but it should not come to be that fiery splendor is merely a matter of metal. So be it," said the boys, each one with a blowgun on his shoulder, the two of them together.

And this Seven Macaw has two sons: the first of these is Zipacna, and the second is the Earthquake. And Chimalmat is the name of their mother, the wife of Seven Macaw.

And this is Zipacna, this is the one to build up the great mountains: Fire Mouth, Hunahpu, Cave by the Water, Xcanul, Macamob, Huliznab, as the names of the mountains that were there at the dawn are spoken. They were brought forth by Zipacna in a single night.

And now this is the Earthquake. The mountains are moved by him; the mountains, small and great, are softened by him. The sons of Seven Macaw did this just as a means of self-magnification.

"Here am I: I am the sun," said Seven Macaw.

"Here am I: I am the maker of the earth," said Zipacna.

"As for me, I bring down the sky, I make an avalanche of all the earth," said Earthquake. The sons of Seven Macaw are alike, and like him: they got their greatness from their father.

And the two boys saw evil in this, since our first mother and

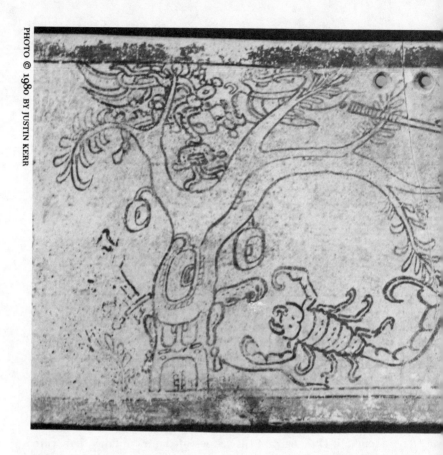

father could not yet be made. Therefore deaths and disappearances were planned by the two boys.

ND HERE IS THE SHOOTING OF SEVEN MACAW BY THE TWO BOYS. We shall explain the defeat of each one of those who engaged in self-magnification.

This is the great tree of Seven Macaw, a nance, and this is the food of Seven Macaw. In order to eat the fruit of the nance he goes up the tree every day. Since Hunahpu and Xbalanque have seen where he feeds, they are now hiding beneath the tree of

THEY ARE NOW HIDING BENEATH THE TREE OF SEVEN MACAW:
In this classic Maya vase painting from the lowlands, Seven
Macaw is shown perched in the top of a fruit tree. The tree
itself is portrayed as animate, with a face and ears at its base.
Hidden behind the tree is Xbalanque, whose pawlike hand
protrudes above the tree's left ear. Crouching at the right is
Hunahpu, in the act of shooting Seven Macaw with his
blowgun. The presence of a scorpion beneath the tree remains unexplained.

Seven Macaw, they are keeping quiet here, the two boys are in
the leaves of the tree.

And when Seven Macaw arrived, perching over his meal, the
nance, it was then that he was shot by Hunahpu. The blowgun

shot went right to his jaw, breaking his mouth. Then he went up over the tree and fell flat on the ground. Suddenly Hunahpu appeared, running. He set out to grab him, but actually it was the arm of Hunahpu that was seized by Seven Macaw. He yanked it straight back, he bent it back at the shoulder. Then Seven Macaw tore it right out of Hunahpu. Even so, the boys did well: the first round was not their defeat by Seven Macaw.

And when Seven Macaw had taken the arm of Hunahpu, he went home. Holding his jaw very carefully, he arrived:

"What have you got there?" said Chimalmat, the wife of Seven Macaw.

"What is it but those two tricksters! They've shot me, they've dislocated my jaw. All my teeth are just loose, now they ache. But once what I've got is over the fire—hanging there, dangling over the fire—then they can just come and get it. They're real tricksters!" said Seven Macaw, then he hung up the arm of Hunahpu.

Meanwhile Hunahpu and Xbalanque were thinking. And then they invoked a grandfather, a truly white-haired grandfather, and a grandmother, a truly humble grandmother—just bent-over, elderly people. Great White Peccary is the name of the grandfather, and Great White Tapir is the name of the grandmother. The boys said to the grandmother and grandfather:

"Please travel with us when we go to get our arm from Seven Macaw; we'll just follow right behind you. You'll tell him:

'Do forgive us our grandchildren, who travel with us. Their mother and father are dead, and so they follow along there, behind us. Perhaps we should give them away, since all we do is pull worms out of teeth.' So we'll seem like children to Seven Macaw, even though *we're* giving *you* the instructions," the two boys told them.

"Very well," they replied.

After that they approached the place where Seven Macaw was in front of his home. When the grandmother and grandfather passed by, the two boys were romping along behind them. When they passed below the lord's house, Seven Macaw was yelling his mouth off because of his teeth. And when Seven

Macaw saw the grandfather and grandmother traveling with them:

"Where are you headed, our grandfather?" said the lord.

"We're just making our living, your lordship," they replied.

"Why are you working for a living? Aren't those your children traveling with you?"

"No, they're not, your lordship. They're our grandchildren, our descendants, but it is nevertheless *we* who take pity on *them*. The bit of food they get is the portion we give them, your lordship," replied the grandmother and grandfather. Since the lord is getting done in by the pain in his teeth, it is only with great effort that he speaks again:

"I implore you, please take pity on me! What sweets can you make, what poisons can you cure?" said the lord.

"We just pull the worms out of teeth, and we just cure eyes. We just set bones, your lordship," they replied.

"Very well, please cure my teeth. They really ache, every day. It's insufferable! I get no sleep because of them—and my eyes. They just shot me, those two tricksters! Ever since it started I haven't eaten because of it. Therefore take pity on me! Perhaps it's because my teeth are loose now."

"Very well, your lordship. It's a worm, gnawing at the bone. It's merely a matter of putting in a replacement and taking the teeth out, sir."

"But perhaps it's not good for my teeth to come out—since I am, after all, a lord. My finery is in my teeth—and my eyes."

"But then we'll put in a replacement. Ground bone will be put back in." And this is the "ground bone": it's only white corn.

"Very well. Yank them out! Give me some help here!" he replied.

And when the teeth of Seven Macaw came out, it was only white corn that went in as a replacement for his teeth—just a coating shining white, that corn in his mouth. His face fell at once, he no longer looked like a lord. The last of his teeth came out, the jewels that had stood out blue from his mouth.

And then the eyes of Seven Macaw were cured. When his eyes were trimmed back the last of his metal came out. Still he felt no pain; he just looked on while the last of his greatness left him. It was just as Hunahpu and Xbalanque had intended.

And when Seven Macaw died, Hunahpu got back his arm. And Chimalmat, the wife of Seven Macaw, also died.

Such was the loss of the riches of Seven Macaw: only the doctors got the jewels and gems that had made him arrogant, here on the face of the earth. The genius of the grandmother, the genius of the grandfather did its work when they took back their arm: it was implanted and the break got well again. Just as they had wished the death of Seven Macaw, so they brought it about. They had seen evil in his self-magnification.

After this the two boys went on again. What they did was simply the word of the Heart of Sky.

A ND HERE ARE THE DEEDS OF ZIPACNA, the first son of Seven Macaw.

"I am the maker of mountains," says Zipacna.

And this is Zipacna, bathing on the shore. Then the Four Hundred Boys passed by dragging a log, a post for their hut. The Four Hundred Boys were walking along, having cut a great tree for the lintel of their hut.

And then Zipacna went there, he arrived where the Four Hundred Boys were:

"What are you doing, boys?"

"It's just this log. We can't lift it up to carry it."

"I'll carry it. Where does it go? What do you intend to use it for?"

"It's just a lintel for our hut."

"Very well," he replied.

And then he pulled it, or rather carried it, right on up to the entrance of the hut of the Four Hundred Boys.

"You could just stay with us, boy. Do you have a mother and father?"

"Not so," he replied.

"We'd like some help tomorrow in cutting another one of our logs, a post for our hut."

"Good," he replied.

After that the Four Hundred Boys shared their thoughts:

"About this boy: what should we do with him?"

"We should kill him, because what he does is no good. He lifted that log all by himself. Let's dig a big hole for him, and then we'll throw him down in the hole. We'll say to him:

'Why are you spilling dirt in the hole?' And when he's wedged down in the hole we'll wham a big log down behind him. Then he should die in the hole," said the Four Hundred Boys.

And when they had dug a hole, one that went deep, they called for Zipacna:

"We're asking you to please go on digging out the dirt. We can't go on," he was told.

"Very well," he replied.

After that he went down in the hole.

"Call out when enough dirt has been dug, when you're getting down deep," he was told.

"Yes," he replied, then he began digging the hole. But the only hole he dug was for his own salvation. He realized that he was to be killed, so he dug a separate hole to one side, he dug a second hole for safety.

"How far is it?" the Four Hundred Boys called down to him.

"I'm digging fast. When I call up to you, the digging will be finished," said Zipacna, from down in the hole. But he's not digging at the bottom of the hole, in his own grave; rather, the hole he's digging is for his own salvation.

After that, when Zipacna called out, he had gone to safety in his own hole. Then he called out:

"Come here, take the dirt, the fill from the hole. It's been dug. I've really gone down deep! Can't you hear my call? As for your call, it just echoes down here, it sounds to me as if you were on another level, or two levels away," said Zipacna from his hole. He's hidden in there, he calls out from down in the hole.

Meanwhile, a big log is being dragged along by the boys.

And then they threw the log down in the hole.

"Isn't he there? He doesn't speak."

"Let's keep on listening. He should cry out when he dies,"

they said among themselves. They're just whispering, and they've hidden themselves, each one of them, after throwing down the log.

And then he did speak, now he gave a single cry. He called out when the log fell to the bottom.

"Right on! He's been finished!"

"Very good! We've done him in, he's dead."

"What if he had gone on with his deeds, his works? He would've made himself first among us and taken our place—we, the Four Hundred Boys!" they said. Now they enjoyed themselves:

"On to the making of our sweet drink! Three days will pass, and after three days let's drink to dedicate our hut—we, the Four Hundred Boys!" they said. "And tomorrow we'll see, and on the day after tomorrow we'll see whether or not ants come from the ground when he's stinking and rotting. After that our hearts will be content when we drink our sweet drink," they said. But Zipacna was listening from the hole when the boys specified "the day after tomorrow."

And on the second day, when the ants collected, they were running, swarming. Having taken their pickings under the log, they were everywhere, carrying hair in their mouths and carrying the nails of Zipacna. When the boys saw this:

"He's finished, that trickster! Look here how the ants have stripped him, how they've swarmed. Everywhere they carry hair in their mouths. It's his nails you can see. We've done it!" they said among themselves.

But this Zipacna is still alive. He just cuts the hair off his head and chews off his nails to give them to the ants.

And so the Four Hundred Boys thought he had died.

After that, their sweet drink was ready on the third day, and then all the boys got drunk, and once they were drunk, all four hundred of those boys, they weren't feeling a thing.

After that the hut was brought down on top of them by Zipacna. All of them were completely flattened. Not even one or two were saved from among all the Four Hundred Boys. They were killed by Zipacna, the son of Seven Macaw.

Such was the death of those Four Hundred Boys. And it used

to be said that they entered a constellation, named Hundrath after them, though perhaps this is just a play on words.

And this is where we shall explain the defeat of Zipacna by the two boys, Hunahpu and Xbalanque.

N OW THIS IS THE DEFEAT AND DEATH OF ZIPACNA, when he was beaten by the two boys, Hunahpu and Xbalanque. What now weighed heavily on the hearts of the two boys was that the Four Hundred Boys had been killed by Zipacna.

It's mere fish and crabs that Zipacna looks for in the waters, but he's eating every day, going around looking for his food by day and lifting up mountains by night.

Next comes the counterfeiting of a great crab by Hunahpu and Xbalanque.

And they used bromelia flowers, picked from the bromelias of the forests. These became the forearms of the crab, and where they opened were the claws. They used a flagstone for the back of the crab, which clattered.

After that they put the shell beneath an overhang, at the foot of a great mountain. Meauan is the name of the mountain where the defeat took place.

After that, when the boys came along, they found Zipacna by the water:

"Where are you going, boy?" Zipacna was asked.

"I'm not going anywhere. I'm just looking for my food, boys," Zipacna replied.

"What's your food?"

"Just fish and crabs, but there aren't any that I can find. It's been two days since I stopped getting meals. By now I can't stand the hunger," Zipacna told Hunahpu and Xbalanque.

"There *is* that crab that's down in the canyon. A really big crab! Perhaps you might manage to eat her. We were just getting bitten. We wanted to catch her, but we got scared by her. If she hasn't gone away you could catch her," said Hunahpu and Xbalanque.

97

"Take pity on me, please come point her out, boys," said Zipacna.

"We don't want to, but you go ahead. You can't miss her. Just follow the river, and you go straight on over there below a great mountain. She's clattering there at the bottom of the canyon. Just head on over there," said Hunahpu and Xbalanque.

"But won't you please take pity on me? What if she can't be found, boys? If you come along I'll show you a place where there are plenty of birds. Please come shoot them, I know where they are," Zipacna replied. They consented. He went ahead of the boys.

"What if you can't catch the crab? Just as we had to turn back, so will you. Not only didn't we eat her, but all at once *she* was biting *us*. We were entering face down, but when she got scared we were entering on our back. We just barely missed reaching her then, so you'd better enter on your back," he was told.

"Very well," Zipacna replied, and then they went on. Now Zipacna had company as he went. They arrived at the bottom of the canyon.

The crab is on her side, her shell is gleaming red there. In under the canyon wall is their contrivance.

"Very good!" Zipacna is happy now. He wishes she were already in his mouth, so she could really cure his hunger. He wanted to eat her, he just wanted it face down, he wanted to enter, but since the crab got on top of him with her back down, he came back out.

"You didn't reach her?" he was asked.

"No indeed—she was just getting on top with her back down. I just barely missed her on the first try, so perhaps I'd better enter on my back," he replied.

After that he entered again, on his back. He entered all the way—only his kneecaps were showing now! He gave a last sigh and was calm. The great mountain rested on his chest. He couldn't turn over now, and so Zipacna turned to stone.

Such, in its turn, was the defeat of Zipacna by the two boys, Hunahpu and Xbalanque. He was "the maker of mountains," as his previous pronouncements had it, the first son of Seven

Macaw. He was defeated beneath the great mountain called Meauan, defeated by genius alone. He was the second to magnify himself, and now we shall speak what is spoken of another.

A ND THE THIRD TO MAGNIFY HIMSELF IS THE SECOND SON OF SEVEN MACAW, NAMED EARTHQUAKE.

"I am the breaker of mountains," he said. But even so, Hunahpu and Xbalanque defeated the Earthquake. Then Hurricane spoke, Newborn Thunderbolt, Raw Thunderbolt; he spoke to Hunahpu and Xbalanque:

"The second son of Seven Macaw is another one, another who should be defeated. This is my word, because what they do on the face of the earth is no good. They are surpassing the sun in size, in weight, and it should not be that way. Lure this Earthquake into settling down over there in the east," Hurricane told the two boys.

"Very well, your lordship. There is more to be done. What we see is no good. Isn't it a question of your position and your eminence, sir, Heart of Sky?" the two boys said when they responded to the word of Hurricane.

Meanwhile he presses on, this Earthquake, breaker of mountains. Just by lightly tapping his foot on the ground he instantly demolishes the mountains, great and small. When he met up with the two boys:

"Where are you going, boy?" they asked Earthquake.

"I'm not going anywhere. I just scatter the mountains, and I'm the one who breaks them, in the course of the days, in the course of the light," he said when he answered. Then the Earthquake asked Hunahpu and Xbalanque:

"Where did you come from? I don't know your faces. What are your names?" said Earthquake.

"We have no names. We just hunt and trap in the mountains. We're just orphans, we have nothing to call our own, boy. We're just making our way among the mountains, small and great, boy. And there's one great mountain we saw that's just growing right

AND THEN THE BOYS MADE FIRE WITH A DRILL: In this illustration from the lowland Maya hieroglyphic book now known as the Madrid Codex, two figures turn a fire drill while sparks fly up from the wooden platform where the point of the drill is inserted. They are seated on or beside a road, marked by footprints.

---

along. It's rising really high! It's just swelling up, rising above all the other mountains. And there weren't even one or two birds to be found, boy. So how could it be that you destroy all mountains, boy?" Hunahpu and Xbalanque said to Earthquake.

"It can't be true you saw the mountain you're talking about. Where is it? You'll see me knock it down yet. Where did you see it?"

"Well, it's over there in the east," said Hunahpu and Xbalanque.

"Good. Lead the way," the two boys were told.

"Not so. You take the middle. Stay here between us—one of us at your left, the other at your right hand—because of our blowguns. If there are birds, we'll shoot," they said. They enjoy practicing their shooting.

And this is the way they shoot: the shot of their blowguns isn't made of earth—they just blow at the birds when they shoot, to the amazement of the Earthquake.

And then the boys made fire with a drill and roasted the birds over the fire. And they coated one of the birds with plaster, they put gypsum on it.

"So this is the one we'll give him when he's hungry, and when he savors the aroma of our birds. That will be victory, since we've covered his bird with baked earth. In earth we must cook it, and in earth must be his grave—if the great knower, the one to be made and modeled, is to have a sowing and dawning," said the boys.

"Because of this, the human heart will desire a bite of meat, a meal of flesh, just as the heart of the Earthquake will desire it," Hunahpu and Xbalanque said to one another. Then they roasted the birds and cooked them until they were brown, dripping with fat that oozed from the backs of the birds, with an overwhelmingly fragrant aroma.

And this Earthquake wants to be fed, his mouth just waters, he gulps and slurps with spittle and saliva because of the fragrance of the birds. So then he asked:

"What are you eating? I smell a truly delicious aroma! Please give me a little bit," he said. And when they gave a bird to Earthquake, he was as good as defeated.

After he had finished off the bird, they went on until they arrived in the east, where the great mountain was.

Meanwhile, Earthquake had lost the strength in his legs and arms. He couldn't go on because of the earth that coated the bird he'd eaten. So now there was nothing he could do to the mountain. He never recovered; he was destroyed. So then he was bound by the two boys; his hands were bound behind him. When his hands had been secured by the boys, his ankles were bound to his wrists.

After that they threw him down, they buried him in the earth.

Such is the defeat of Earthquake. It's Hunahpu and Xbalanque yet again. Their deeds on the face of the earth are countless.

And now we shall explain the birth of Hunahpu and Xbalanque, having first explained the defeat of Seven Macaw, along with Zipacna and Earthquake, here on the face of the earth.

PART
THREE

A ND NOW WE SHALL NAME THE NAME OF THE FATHER OF HUNAHPU AND XBALANQUE. Let's drink to him, and let's just drink to the telling and accounting of the begetting of Hunahpu and Xbalanque. We shall tell just half of it, just a part of the account of their father. Here follows the account.

These are the names: One Hunahpu and Seven Hunahpu, as they are called.

And these are their parents: Xpiyacoc, Xmucane. In the blackness, in the night, One Hunahpu and Seven Hunahpu were born to Xpiyacoc and Xmucane.

And this One Hunahpu had two children, and the two were sons, the firstborn named One Monkey and the second named One Artisan.

And this is the name of their mother: she is called Xbaquiyalo, the wife of One Hunahpu. As for Seven Hunahpu, he has no wife. He's just a partner and just secondary; he just remains a boy.

They are great thinkers and great is their knowledge. They are the midmost seers, here on the face of the earth. There is only good in their being and their birthright. They taught skills to One Monkey and One Artisan, the sons of One Hunahpu. One Monkey and One Artisan became flautists, singers, and writers; carvers, jewelers, metalworkers as well.

And as for One and Seven Hunahpu, all they did was throw dice and play ball, every day. They would play each other in pairs, the four of them together. When they gathered in the ball court for entertainment a falcon would come to watch them, the messenger of Hurricane, Newborn Thunderbolt, Raw Thunderbolt. And for this falcon it wasn't far to the earth here, nor was it far to Xibalba; he could get back to the sky, to Hurricane, in an instant.

The four ballplayers remained here on the face of the earth after the mother of One Monkey and One Artisan had died.

105

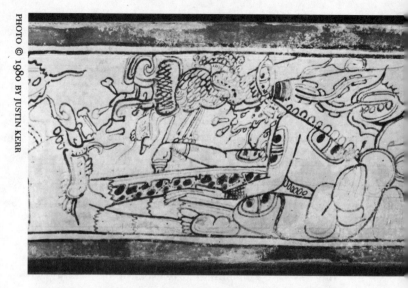

ONE MONKEY AND ONE ARTISAN BECAME FLAUTISTS, SINGERS, AND WRITERS: In this classic Maya funerary vase painting from northern Guatemala, the twin monkey gods are shown seated in a cross-legged position, pointing to screen-folded books while speaking or singing. The books they hold in their hands have jaguar-skin covers; other books are piled up at their feet. (*Vase in the New Orleans Museum of Art.*)

Since it was on the road to Xibalba that they played, they were heard by One Death and Seven Death, the lords of Xibalba:

"What's happening on the face of the earth? They're just stomping and shouting. They should be summoned to come play ball here. We'll defeat them, since we simply get no deference from them. They show no respect, nor do they have any shame. They're really determined to run right over us!" said all of Xibalba, when they all shared their thoughts, the ones named One and Seven Death. They are great lawgivers.

A ND THESE ARE THE LORDS OVER EVERYTHING, each lord with a commission and a domain assigned by One and Seven Death:

There are the lords named House Corner and Blood Gatherer. And this is their commission: to draw blood from people.

Next are the lordships of Pus Master and Jaundice Master. And this is their domain: to make people swell up, to make pus come out of their legs, to make their faces yellow, to cause jaundice, as it is called. Such is the domain of Pus Master and Jaundice Master.

Next are the lords Bone Scepter and Skull Scepter, the staff bearers of Xibalba; their staffs are just bones. And this is their staff-bearing: to reduce people to bones, right down to the bones and skulls, until they die from emaciation and edema. This is the commission of the ones named Bone Scepter and Skull Scepter.

Next are the lords named Trash Master and Stab Master. This is their commission: just to catch up with people whenever they have filth or grime in the doorway of the house, the patio of the house. Then they're struck, they're just punctured until they crawl on the ground, then die. And this is the domain of Trash Master and Stab Master, as they are called.

Next are the lords named Wing and Packstrap. This is their domain: that people should die in the road, just "sudden death," as it is called. Blood comes to the mouth, then there is death from vomiting blood. So to each of them his burden, the load on

AND THESE ARE THE LORDS OVER EVERYTHING: This late classic Maya funerary vase painting from northern Guatemala shows seven lords of Xibalba, with the head lord, corresponding to One Death of the Popol Vuh, smoking a cigar and sitting on a jaguar skin at right. The two lords immediately to his left may be Bone Scepter (in the bottom row) and Skull Scepter (in the top row), one with a staff that looks like a spinal column in front of him and the other with a rounded bundle that could contain a skull. All seven lords wear ball game yokes on their hips. The Popol Vuh mentions fourteen lords, counting two manikins that are meant to be mistaken for lords. Perhaps each pair of names mentioned in the Popol Vuh originally belonged to a single lord, or perhaps each of the lords shown here is understood to have another seated at his side.

---

his shoulders: just to strike people on the neck and chest. Then there is death in the road, and then they just go on causing suffering, whether one is coming or going. And this is the domain of Wing and Packstrap.

Such are those who shared their thoughts when they were piqued and driven by One and Seven Hunahpu. What Xibalba desired was the gaming equipment of One and Seven Hunahpu: their kilts, their yokes, their arm guards, their panaches and headbands, the costumes of One and Seven Hunahpu.

And this is where we shall continue telling of their trip to Xibalba. One Monkey and One Artisan, the sons of One Hunahpu, stayed behind. Their mother died—and, what is more, they were to be defeated by Hunahpu and Xbalanque.

A	ND NOW FOR THE MESSENGERS OF ONE AND SEVEN DEATH: "You're going, you Military Keepers of the Mat, to summon One and Seven Hunahpu. You'll tell them, when you arrive:

' "They must come," the lords say to you. "Would that they might come to play ball with us here. Then we could have some excitement with them. We are truly amazed at them. Therefore they should come," say the lords, "and they should bring their playthings, their yokes and arm guards should come, along with their rubber ball," say the lords,' you will say when you arrive," the messengers were told.

And these messengers of theirs are owls: Shooting Owl, One-legged Owl, Macaw Owl, Skull Owl, as the messengers of Xibalba are called.

There is Shooting Owl, like a point, just piercing.

And there is One-legged Owl, with just one leg; he has wings.

And there is Macaw Owl, with a red back; he has wings.

And there is also Skull Owl, with only a head alone; he has no legs, but he does have wings.

There are four messengers, Military Keepers of the Mat in rank.

And when they came out of Xibalba they arrived quickly, alighting above the ball court where One and Seven Hunahpu were playing, at the ball court called Great Abyss at Carchah. The owls, arriving in a flurry over the ball court, now repeated their words, reciting the exact words of One Death, Seven Death, Pus Master, Jaundice Master, Bone Scepter, Skull Scepter, House Corner, Blood Gatherer, Trash Master, Stab Master, Wing, Packstrap, as all the lords are named. Their words were repeated by the owls.

"Don't the lords One and Seven Death speak truly?"

"Truly indeed," the owls replied. "We'll accompany you. 'They're to bring along all their gaming equipment,' say the lords."

"Very well, but wait for us while we notify our mother," they replied.

And when they went to their house, they spoke to their mother; their father had died:

"We're going, our dear mother, even though we've just arrived. The messengers of the lord have come to get us:

' "They should come," he says,' they say, giving us orders. We'll leave our rubber ball behind here," they said, then they went to tie it up under the roof of the house. "Until we return— then we'll put it in play again."

They told One Monkey and One Artisan:

"As for you, just play and just sing, write and carve to warm our house and to warm the heart of your grandmother." When they had been given their instructions, their grandmother Xmucane sobbed, she had to weep.

"We're going, we're not dying. Don't be sad," said One and Seven Hunahpu, then they left.

A FTER THAT ONE AND SEVEN HUNAHPU LEFT, guided down the road by the messengers.

And then they descended the road to Xibalba, going down a steep cliff, and they descended until they came out where the rapids cut through, the roaring canyon narrows named Neck Canyon. They passed through there, then they passed on into the River of Churning Spikes. They passed through countless spikes but they were not stabbed.

And then they came to water again, to blood: Blood River.

They crossed but did not drink. They came to a river, but a river filled with pus. Still they were not defeated, but passed through again.

And then they came to the Crossroads, but here they were defeated, at the Crossroads:

Red Road was one and Black Road another.

White Road was one and Yellow Road another.

There were four roads, and Black Road spoke:

"I am the one you are taking. I am the lord's road," said the road. And they were defeated there: this was the Road of Xibalba.

And then they came to the council place of the lords of Xibalba, and they were defeated again there. The ones seated first there are just manikins, just woodcarvings dressed up by Xibalba. And they greeted the first ones:

"Morning, One Death," they said to the manikin. "Morning, Seven Death," they said to the woodcarving in turn.

So they did not win out, and the lords of Xibalba shouted out with laughter over this. All the lords just shouted with laughter because they had triumphed; in their hearts they had beaten One and Seven Hunahpu. They laughed on until One and Seven Death spoke:

"It's good that you've come. Tomorrow you must put your yokes and arm guards into action," they were told.

"Sit here on our bench," they were told, but the only bench they were offered was a burning-hot rock.

So now they were burned on the bench; they really jumped around on the bench now, but they got no relief. They really got up fast, having burned their butts. At this the Xibalbans laughed again, they began to shriek with laughter, the laughter rose up like a serpent in their very cores, all the lords of Xibalba laughed themselves down to their blood and bones.

"Just go in the house. Your torch and cigars will be brought to your sleeping quarters," the boys were told.

After that they came to the Dark House, a house with darkness alone inside. Meanwhile the Xibalbans shared their thoughts:

"Let's just sacrifice them tomorrow. It can only turn out to be quick; they'll die quickly because of our playing equipment, our gaming things," the Xibalbans are saying among themselves.

This ball of theirs is just a spherical knife. White Dagger is the name of the ball, the ball of Xibalba. Their ball is just ground down to make it smooth; the ball of Xibalba is just surfaced with crushed bone to make it firm.

A ND ONE AND SEVEN HUNAHPU WENT INSIDE DARK HOUSE. And then their torch was brought, only one torch, already lit, sent by One and Seven Death, along with a cigar for each of them, also already lit, sent by the lords. When these were brought to One and Seven Hunahpu they were cowering, here in the dark. When the bearer of their torch and cigars arrived, the torch was bright as it entered; their torch and both of their cigars were burning. The bearer spoke:

" 'They must be sure to return them in the morning—not finished, but just as they look now. They must return them intact,' the lords say to you," they were told, and they were defeated. They finished the torch and they finished the cigars that had been brought to them.

And Xibalba is packed with tests, heaps and piles of tests.

This is the first one: the Dark House, with darkness alone inside.

And the second is named Rattling House, heavy with cold inside, whistling with drafts, clattering with hail. A deep chill comes inside here.

And the third is named Jaguar House, with jaguars alone inside, jostling one another, crowding together, with gnashing teeth. They're scratching around; these jaguars are shut inside the house.

Bat House is the name of the fourth test, with bats alone inside the house, squeaking, shrieking, darting through the house. The bats are shut inside; they can't get out.

And the fifth is named Razor House, with blades alone inside. The blades are moving back and forth, ripping, slashing through the house.

These are the first tests of Xibalba, but One and Seven Hunahpu never entered into them, except for the one named earlier, the specified test house.

And when One and Seven Hunahpu went back before One and Seven Death, they were asked:

"Where are my cigars? What of my torch? They were brought to you last night!"

"We finished them, your lordship."

"Very well. This very day, your day is finished, you will die, you will disappear, and we shall break you off. Here you will hide your faces: you are to be sacrificed!" said One and Seven Death.

And then they were sacrificed and buried. They were buried at the Place of Ball Game Sacrifice, as it is called. The head of One Hunahpu was cut off; only his body was buried with his younger brother.

"Put his head in the fork of the tree that stands by the road," said One and Seven Death.

And when his head was put in the fork of the tree, the tree bore fruit. It would not have had any fruit, had not the head of One Hunahpu been put in the fork of the tree.

This is the calabash tree, as we call it today, or "the head of One Hunahpu," as it is said.

And then One and Seven Death were amazed at the fruit of the tree. The fruit grows out everywhere, and it isn't clear where the head of One Hunahpu is; now it looks just the way the calabashes look. All the Xibalbans see this, when they come to look.

The state of the tree loomed large in their thoughts, because it came about at the same time the head of One Hunahpu was put in the fork. The Xibalbans said among themselves:

"No one is to pick the fruit, nor is anyone to go beneath the tree," they said. They restricted themselves; all of Xibalba held back.

It isn't clear which is the head of One Hunahpu; now it's exactly the same as the fruit of the tree. Calabash tree came to be its name, and much was said about it. A maiden heard about it, and here we shall tell of her arrival.

A ND HERE IS THE ACCOUNT OF A MAIDEN, the daughter of a lord named Blood Gatherer.

And this is when a maiden heard of it, the daughter of a lord. Blood Gatherer is the name of her father, and Blood Woman is the name of the maiden.

And when he heard the account of the fruit of the tree, her father retold it. And she was amazed at the account:

"I'm not acquainted with that tree they talk about. ' "Its fruit is truly sweet!" they say,' I hear," she said.

Next, she went all alone and arrived where the tree stood. It stood at the Place of Ball Game Sacrifice:

"What? Well! What's the fruit of this tree? Shouldn't this tree bear something sweet? They shouldn't die, they shouldn't be wasted. Should I pick one?" said the maiden.

And then the bone spoke; it was here in the fork of the tree:

"Why do you want a mere bone, a round thing in the branches of a tree?" said the head of One Hunahpu when it spoke to the maiden. "You don't want it," she was told.

"I do want it," said the maiden.

"Very well. Stretch out your right hand here, so I can see it," said the bone.

"Yes," said the maiden. She stretched out her right hand, up there in front of the bone.

And then the bone spit out its saliva, which landed squarely in the hand of the maiden.

And then she looked in her hand, she inspected it right away, but the bone's saliva wasn't in her hand.

"It is just a sign I have given you, my saliva, my spittle. This, my head, has nothing on it—just bone, nothing of meat. It's just the same with the head of a great lord: it's just the flesh that makes his face look good. And when he dies, people get frightened by his bones. After that, his son is like his saliva, his spittle, in his being, whether it be the son of a lord or the son of a craftsman, an orator. The father does not disappear, but goes on being fulfilled. Neither dimmed nor destroyed is the face of a lord, a warrior, craftsman, orator. Rather, he will leave his daughters and sons. So it is that I have done likewise through you. Now go up there on the face of the earth; you will not die. Keep the word. So be it," said the head of One and Seven Hunahpu—they were of one mind when they did it.

This was the word Hurricane, Newborn Thunderbolt, Raw Thunderbolt had given them. In the same way, by the time the maiden returned to her home, she had been given many instructions. Right away something was generated in her belly, from the saliva alone, and this was the generation of Hunahpu and Xbalanque.

And when the maiden got home and six months had passed, she was found out by her father. Blood Gatherer is the name of her father.

A ND AFTER THE MAIDEN WAS NOTICED BY HER FATHER, when he saw that she was now with child, all the lords then shared their thoughts—One and Seven Death, along with Blood Gatherer:

"This daughter of mine is with child, lords. It's just a bastard," Blood Gatherer said when he joined the lords.

"Very well. Get her to open her mouth. If she doesn't tell, then sacrifice her. Go far away and sacrifice her."

"Very well, your lordships," he replied. After that, he questioned his daughter:

"Who is responsible for the child in your belly, my daughter?" he said.

"There is no child, my father, sir; there is no man whose face I've known," she replied.

"Very well. It really is a bastard you carry! Take her away for sacrifice, you Military Keepers of the Mat. Bring back her heart in a bowl, so the lords can take it in their hands this very day," the owls were told, the four of them.

Then they left, carrying the bowl. When they left they took the maiden by the hand, bringing along the White Dagger, the instrument of sacrifice.

"It would not turn out well if you sacrificed me, messengers, because it is not a bastard that's in my belly. What's in my belly generated all by itself when I went to marvel at the head of One Hunahpu, which is there at the Place of Ball Game Sacrifice. So please stop: don't do your sacrifice, messengers," said the maiden. Then they talked:

"What are we going to use in place of her heart? We were told by her father:

'Bring back her heart. The lords will take it in their hands, they will satisfy themselves, they will make themselves familiar with its composition. Hurry, bring it back in a bowl, put her heart in the bowl.' Isn't that what we've been told? What shall we deliver in the bowl? What we want above all is that you should not die," said the messengers.

"Very well. My heart must not be theirs, nor will your homes be here. Nor will you simply force people to die, but hereafter, what will be truly yours will be the true bearers of bastards. And hereafter, as for One and Seven Death, only blood, only nodules of sap, will be theirs. So be it that these things are presented before them, and not that hearts are burned before them. So be it: use the fruit of a tree," said the maiden. And it was red tree sap she went out to gather in the bowl.

After it congealed, the substitute for her heart became round. When the sap of the croton tree was tapped, tree sap like blood, it became the substitute for her blood. When she rolled the blood around inside there, the sap of the croton tree, it formed a surface like blood, glistening red now, round inside the bowl. When the tree was cut open by the maiden, the so-called cochineal croton, the sap is what she called blood, and so there is talk of "nodules of blood."

"So you have been blessed with the face of the earth. It shall be yours," she told the owls.

"Very well, maiden. We'll show you the way up there. You just walk on ahead; we have yet to deliver this apparent duplicate of your heart before the lords," said the messengers.

And when they came before the lords, they were all watching closely:

"Hasn't it turned out well?" said One Death.

"It has turned out well, your lordships, and this is her heart. It's in the bowl."

"Very well. So I'll look," said One Death, and when he lifted it up with his fingers, its surface was soaked with gore, its surface glistened red with blood.

"Good. Stir up the fire, put it over the fire," said One Death.

After that they dried it over the fire, and the Xibalbans savored the aroma. They all ended up standing here, they leaned over it intently. They found the smoke of the blood to be truly sweet!

And while they stayed at their cooking, the owls went to show the maiden the way out. They sent her up through a hole onto the earth, and then the guides returned below.

In this way the lords of Xibalba were defeated by a maiden; all of them were blinded.

And here, where the mother of One Monkey and One Artisan lived, was where the woman named Blood Woman arrived.

A ND WHEN THE BLOOD WOMAN CAME TO THE MOTHER OF ONE MONKEY AND ONE ARTISAN, her children were still in her belly, but it wasn't very long before the birth of Hunahpu and Xbalanque, as they are called.

And when the woman came to the grandmother, the woman said to the grandmother:

"I've come, mother, madam. I'm your daughter-in-law and I'm your child, mother, madam," she said when she came here to the grandmother.

"Where do you come from? As for my lastborn children, didn't they die in Xibalba? And these two remain as their sign and their word: One Monkey and One Artisan are their names. So if you've come to see my children, get out of here!" the maiden was told by the grandmother.

"Even so, I really am your daughter-in-law. I am already his, I belong to One Hunahpu. What I carry is his. One Hunahpu and Seven Hunahpu are alive, they are not dead. They have merely made a way for the light to show itself, madam mother-in-law, as you will see when you look at the faces of what I carry," the grandmother was told.

And One Monkey and One Artisan have been keeping their grandmother entertained: all they do is play and sing, all they work at is writing and carving, every day, and this cheers the heart of their grandmother.

And then the grandmother said:

"I don't want you, no thanks, my daughter-in-law. It's just a bastard in your belly, you trickster! These children of mine who are named by you are dead," said the grandmother.

"Truly, what I say to you is so!"

"Very well, my daughter-in-law, I hear you. So get going, get their food so they can eat. Go pick a big netful of corn, then come back—since you are already my daughter-in-law, as I understand it," the maiden was told.

"Very well," she replied.

After that, she went to the garden; One Monkey and One Artisan had a garden. The maiden followed the path they had cleared and arrived there in the garden, but there was only one clump, there was no other plant, no second or third. That one clump had borne its ears. So then the maiden's heart stopped:

"It looks like I'm a sinner, a debtor! Where will I get the netful of food she asked for?" she said. And then the guardians of food were called upon by her:

"Come thou, rise up, come thou, stand up:
Generous Woman, Harvest Woman,
Cacao Woman, Cornmeal Woman,
thou guardian of the food of One Monkey, One Artisan,"

said the maiden.

And then she took hold of the silk, the bunch of silk at the top of the ear. She pulled it straight out, she didn't pick the ear, and the ear reproduced itself to make food for the net. It filled the big net.

And then the maiden came back, but animals carried her net. When she got back she went to put the pack frame in the corner of the house, so it would look to the grandmother as if she had arrived with a load.

And then, when the grandmother saw the food, a big netful:

"Where did that food of yours come from? You've leveled the place! I'm going to see if you've brought back our whole garden!" said the grandmother.

And then she went off, she went to look at the garden, but the one clump was still there, and the place where the net had been put at the foot of it was still obvious.

And the grandmother came back in a hurry, and she got back home, and she said to the maiden:

"The sign is still there. You really are my daughter-in-law! I'll have to keep watching what you do. These grandchildren of mine are already showing genius," the maiden was told.

Now this is where we shall speak of the birth of Hunahpu and Xbalanque.

A ND THIS IS THEIR BIRTH; WE SHALL TELL OF IT HERE. Then it came to the day of their birth, and the maiden named Blood Woman gave birth. The grandmother was not present when they were born; they were born suddenly. Two of them were born, named Hunahpu and Xbalanque. They were born in the mountains, and then they came into the house. Since they weren't sleeping:

"Throw them out of here! They're really loudmouths!" said the grandmother.

After that, when they put them on an anthill, they slept soundly there. And when they removed them from there, they put them in brambles next.

And this is what One Monkey and One Artisan wanted: that they should die on the anthill and die in the brambles. One Monkey and One Artisan wanted this because they were rowdyish and flushed with jealousy. They didn't allow their younger brothers in the house at first, as if they didn't even know them, but even so they flourished in the mountains.

And One Monkey and One Artisan were great flautists and singers, and as they grew up they went through great suffering and pain. It had cost them suffering to become great knowers. Through it all they became flautists, singers, and writers, carvers. They did everything well. They simply knew it when they were born, they simply had genius. And they were the successors of their fathers who had gone to Xibalba, their dead fathers.

Since One Monkey and One Artisan were great knowers, in their hearts they already realized everything when their younger brothers came into being, but they didn't reveal their insight because of their jealousy. The anger in their hearts came down on their own heads; no great harm was done. They were decoyed by Hunahpu and Xbalanque, who merely went out shooting every day. These two got no love from the grandmother, or from One Monkey and One Artisan. They weren't given their meals; the meals had been prepared and One Monkey and One Artisan had already eaten them before they got there.

But Hunahpu and Xbalanque aren't turning red with anger; rather, they just let it go, even though they know their proper place, which they see as clear as day. So they bring birds when they arrive each day, and One Monkey and One Artisan eat them. Nothing whatsoever is given to Hunahpu and Xbalanque, either one of them. All One Monkey and One Artisan do is play and sing.

And then Hunahpu and Xbalanque arrived again, but now they came in here without bringing their birds, so the grandmother turned red:

"What's your reason for not bringing birds?" Hunahpu and Xbalanque were asked.

"There are some, our dear grandmother, but our birds just got hung up in a tree," they said, "and there's no way to get up the tree after them, our dear grandmother, and so we'd like our elder brothers to please go with us, to please go get the birds down," they said.

"Very well. We'll go with you at dawn," the elder brothers replied.

Now they had won, and they gathered their thoughts, the two of them, about the fall of One Monkey and One Artisan:

"We'll just turn their very being around with our words. So be it, since they have caused us great suffering. They wished that we might die and disappear—we, their younger brothers. Just as they wished us to be slaves here, so we shall defeat them there. We shall simply make a sign of it," they said to one another.

And then they went there beneath a tree, the kind named yellowwood, together with the elder brothers. When they got there they started shooting. There were countless birds up in the tree, chittering, and the elder brothers were amazed when they saw the birds. And not one of these birds fell down beneath the tree:

"Those birds of ours don't fall down; just go throw them down," they told their elder brothers.

"Very well," they replied.

And then they climbed up the tree, and the tree began to grow, its trunk got thicker.

After that, they wanted to get down, but now One Monkey and One Artisan couldn't make it down from the tree. So they said, from up in the tree:

"How can we grab hold? You, our younger brothers, take pity on us! Now this tree looks frightening to us, dear younger brothers," they said from up in the tree. Then Hunahpu and Xbalanque told them:

"Undo your pants, tie them around your hips, with the long end trailing like a tail behind you, and then you'll be better able to move," they were told by their younger brothers.

"All right," they said.

And then they left the ends of their loincloths trailing, and all at once these became tails. Now they looked like mere monkeys.

After that they went along in the trees of the mountains, small and great. They went through the forests, now howling, now keeping quiet in the branches of trees.

Such was the defeat of One Monkey and One Artisan by Hunahpu and Xbalanque. They did it by means of their genius alone.

And when they got home they said, when they came to their grandmother and mother:

"Our dear grandmother, something has happened to our elder brothers. They've become simply shameless, they're like animals now," they said.

"If you've done something to your elder brothers, you've

knocked me down and stood me on my head. Please don't do anything to your elder brothers, my dear grandchildren," the grandmother said to Hunahpu and Xbalanque. And they told their grandmother:

"Don't be sad, our dear grandmother. You will see the faces of our elder brothers again. They'll come, but this will be a test for you, our dear grandmother. Will you please not laugh while we test their destiny?" they said.

And then they began playing. They played "Hunahpu Monkey."

A ND THEN THEY SANG, THEY PLAYED, THEY DRUMMED. When they took up their flutes and drums, their grandmother sat down with them, then they played, they sounded out the tune, the song that got its name then. "Hunahpu Monkey" is the name of the tune.

And then One Monkey and One Artisan came back, dancing when they arrived.

And then, when the grandmother looked, it was their ugly faces the grandmother saw. Then she laughed, the grandmother could not hold back her laughter, so they just left right away, out of her sight again, they went up and away in the forest.

"Why are you doing that, our dear grandmother? We'll only try four times; only three times are left. We'll call them with the flute, with song. Please hold back your laughter. We'll try again," said Hunahpu and Xbalanque.

Next they played again, then they came back, dancing again, they arrived again, in the middle of the patio of the house. As before, what they did was delightful; as before, they tempted their grandmother to laugh. Their grandmother laughed at them soon enough. The monkeys looked truly ridiculous, with the skinny little things below their bellies and their tails wiggling in front of their breasts. When they came back the grandmother had to laugh at them, and they went back into the mountains.

"Please, why are you doing that, our dear grandmother? Even

DRAWING BY THE AUTHOR

SUDDENLY SCRATCHING THEMSELVES: This spider monkey was painted on a classic Maya funerary vase from northern Guatemala. Note the dangling genitals, or what the Popol Vuh calls "the skinny little things below their bellies." (*The vase is in the collection of Edwin Pearlman.*)

so, we'll try it a third time now," said Hunahpu and Xbalanque.

Again they played, again they came dancing, but their grandmother held back her laughter. Then they climbed up here, cutting right across the building, with thin red lips, with faces blank, puckering their lips, wiping their mouths and faces, suddenly scratching themselves. And when the grandmother saw them again, the grandmother burst out laughing again, and again they went out of sight because of the grandmother's laughter.

"Even so, our dear grandmother, we'll get their attention."

So for the fourth time they called on the flute, but they didn't come back again. The fourth time they went straight into the forest. So they told their grandmother:

"Well, we've tried, our dear grandmother. They came at first, and we've tried calling them again. So don't be sad. We're here—we, your grandchildren. Just love our mother, dear grandmother. Our elder brothers will be remembered. So be it: they have lived here and they have been named; they are to be called One Monkey and One Artisan," said Hunahpu and Xbalanque.

So they were prayed to by the flautists and singers among the ancient people, and the writers and carvers prayed to them. In ancient times they turned into animals, they became monkeys, because they just magnified themselves, they abused their younger brothers. Just as they wished them to be slaves, so they themselves were brought low. One Monkey and One Artisan were lost then, they became animals, and this is now their place forever.

Even so, they were flautists and singers; they did great things while they lived with their grandmother and mother.

AND NOW THEY BEGAN TO ACT OUT THEIR SELF-REVELATION before their grandmother and mother. First they made a garden:

"We'll just do some gardening, our dear grandmother and mother," they said. "Don't worry. We're here, we're your grandchildren, we're the successors of our elder brothers," said Hunahpu and Xbalanque.

And then they took up their axe, their mattock, their hoe; each of them went off with a blowgun on his shoulder. They left the house having instructed their grandmother to give them their food:

"At midday bring our food, dear grandmother," they said.

"Very well, my dear grandchildren," said their grandmother.

After that, they went to their gardening. They simply stuck their mattock in the ground, and the mattock simply cultivated the ground.

And it wasn't only the mattock that cultivated, but also the axe. In the same way, they stuck it in the trunk of a tree; in the same way, it cut into the tree by itself, felling, scattering, felling all the trees and bushes, now leveling, mowing down the trees.

Just the one axe did it, and the mattock, breaking up thick masses, countless stalks and brambles. Just one mattock was doing it, breaking up countless things, just clearing off whole mountains, small and great.

And then they gave instructions to that creature named the mourning dove. They sat up on a big stump, and Hunahpu and Xbalanque said:

"Just watch for our grandmother, bringing our food. Cry out right away when she comes, and then we'll grab the mattock and axe."

"Very well," said the mourning dove.

This is because all they're doing is shooting; they're not really doing any gardening.

And as soon as the dove cries out they come running, one of them grabbing the mattock and the other grabbing the hoe, and they're tying up their hair.

One of them deliberately rubs dirt on his hands; he dirties his face as well, so he's just like a real gardener.

And as for the other one, he deliberately dumps wood chips on his head, so he's like a real woodcutter.

Once their grandmother has seen them they eat, but they aren't really doing their gardening; she brings their food for nothing. And when they get home:

"We're really ready for bed, our dear grandmother," they say when they arrive. Deliberately they massage, they stretch their legs, their arms in front of their grandmother.

And when they went on the second day and arrived at the garden, it had all grown up high again. Every tree and bush, every stalk and bramble had put itself back together again when they arrived.

"Who's been picking us clean?" they said.

And these are the ones who are doing it, all the animals, small and great: puma, jaguar, deer, rabbit, fox, coyote, peccary, coati, small birds, great birds. They are the ones who did it; they did it in just one night.

After that, they started the garden all over again. Just as before, the ground worked itself, along with the woodcutting.

PHOTO BY THE AUTHOR

And then they shared their thoughts, there on the cleared and broken ground:

"We'll simply have to keep watch over our garden. Then, whatever may be happening here, we'll find out about it," they said when they shared their thoughts. And when they arrived at the house:

"How could we get picked clean, our dear grandmother? Our garden was tall thickets and groves all over again when we got there awhile ago, our dear grandmother," they said to their

126

Just clearing off whole mountains, small and great: Terraced cornfields just beginning to sprout in a forest clearing near the Quiché town of Nahualá.

grandmother and mother. "So we'll go keep watch, because what's happening to us is no good," they said.

After that, they wound everything up, and then they went back to the clearing.

And there they took cover, and when they were well hidden there, all the animals gathered together, each one sat on its haunches, all the animals, small and great.

And this was the middle of the night when they came. They all spoke when they came. This is what they said:

"Arise, conjoin, you trees!
Arise, conjoin, you bushes!"

they said. Then they made a great stir beneath the trees and bushes, then they came nearer, and then they showed their faces.

The first of these were the puma and jaguar. The boys tried to grab them, but they did not give themselves up. When the deer and rabbit came near they only got them by the tail, which just broke off: the deer left its tail in their hands. When they grabbed the tail of the deer, along with the tail of the rabbit, the tails were shortened. But the fox, coyote, and peccary, coati did not give themselves up. All the animals went by in front of Hunahpu and Xbalanque.

S O NOW THERE WAS FIRE IN THEIR HEARTS, because they didn't catch them. And one more came, the last one now, jumping as he came, then they cut him off. In their net they caught the rat.

And then they grabbed him and squeezed him behind the head. They tried to choke him; they burned his tail over a fire. Ever since the rat's tail got caught, there's been no hair on his tail, and his eyes have been the way they are since the boys tried to choke him, Hunahpu and Xbalanque.

"I will not die by your hand! Gardening is not your job, but there is something that is," said the rat.

"Where is what is ours? Go ahead and name it," the boys told the rat.

"Will you let me go then? My word is in my belly, and after I name it for you, you'll give me my morsel of food," said the rat.

"We'll give you your food, so name it," he was told.

"Very well. It's something that belonged to your fathers, named One Hunahpu and Seven Hunahpu, who died in Xibalba. What remains is their gaming equipment. They left it up under the roof of the house: their kilts, their arm guards, their rubber ball. But your grandmother doesn't take these down in front of you, because this is how your fathers died."

"You know the truth, don't you!" the boys told the rat.

There was great joy in their hearts when they got word of the rubber ball. When the rat had named it they gave the rat his food, and this is his food: corn kernels, squash seeds, chili, beans, pataxte, cacao. These are his.

"If anything of yours is stored or gets wasted, then gnaw away," the rat was told by Hunahpu and Xbalanque.

"Very well, boys. But what will your grandmother say if she sees me?" he said.

"Don't be fainthearted. We're here. We know what our grandmother needs to be told. We'll set you up under the corner of the roof right away. When that's taken care of you'll go straight to where the things were left, and we'll look up there under the roof, but it's our stew we'll be looking at," they told the rat when they gave him his instructions.

Hunahpu and Xbalanque made their plans overnight and arrived right at noon, and it wasn't obvious that they had a rat with them when they arrived. One of them went right inside the house when he reached it, while the other went to the corner of the house, quickly setting up the rat. And then they asked their grandmother for their meal:

"Just grind something for our stew, we want chili sauce, our dear grandmother," they said.

After that, she ground chili for their stew. A bowl of broth was set out in front of them, but they were just fooling their grandmother and mother. They had emptied the water jar:

"We're really parched! Bring us a drink," they told their grandmother.

"Yes," she said, then she went, and they kept on eating. They weren't really hungry; they just put on false appearances.

And then they saw the rat reflected in their chili sauce: here was the rat loosening the ball that had been left in the peak of the roof. When they saw him in the chili sauce they sent a mosquito, that creature the mosquito, similar to a gnat. He went to the water, then he punctured the side of the grandmother's jar. The water just gushed out from the side of her jar. She tried, but she could not stop up the side of her jar.

"What has our grandmother done? We're choking for lack of

water, our parched throats will do us in," they told their mother, then they sent her there.

After that, the rat cut the ball loose. It dropped from beneath the roof, along with the yokes, arm guards, kilts. These were taken away then; they went to hide them on the road, the road to the ball court.

After that, they went to join their grandmother at the water, and their grandmother and mother were unable to stop up the side of the jar, either one of them.

After that, the boys arrived, each with his blowgun. When they arrived at the water:

"What have you done? We got weary at heart, so we came," they said.

"Look at the side of my jar! It cannot be stopped," said their grandmother, and they quickly stopped it up.

And they came back together, the two of them ahead of their grandmother.

In this way, the matter of the rubber ball was arranged.

HAPPY NOW, THEY WENT TO PLAY BALL AT THE COURT. So they played ball at a distance, all by themselves. They swept out the court of their fathers.

And then it came into the hearing of the lords of Xibalba:

"Who's begun a game again up there, over our heads? Don't they have any shame, stomping around this way? Didn't One and Seven Hunahpu die trying to magnify themselves in front of us? So, you must deliver another summons," they said as before, One and Seven Death, all the lords.

"They are hereby summoned," they told their messengers. "You are to say, on reaching them:

' "They must come," say the lords. "We would play ball with them here. In seven days we'll have a game," say the lords,' you will say when you arrive," the messengers were told.

And then they came along a wide roadway, the road to the house of the boys, which actually ended at their house, so that the messengers came directly to their grandmother. As for the boys, they were away playing ball when the messengers of Xibalba got there.

" 'Truly, they are to come,' say the lords," said the messengers of Xibalba. So then and there the day was specified by the messengers of Xibalba:

" 'In seven days our game will take place,' " Xmucane was told there.

"Very well. They'll go when the day comes, messengers," said the grandmother, and the messengers left. They went back.

So now the grandmother's heart was broken:

"How can I send for my grandchildren? Isn't it really Xibalba, just as it was when the messengers came long ago, when their fathers went to die?" said the grandmother, sobbing, at home by herself.

After that, a louse fell on her elbow, and then she picked it up and put it in her hand, and the louse moved around with fits and starts.

"My grandchild, perhaps you might like to take my message, to go where my grandchildren are, at the ball court," the louse was told, then he went as a message bearer:

" 'A messenger has come to your grandmother,' you will say. ' "You are to come:

'In seven days they are to come,' say the messengers of Xibalba," says your grandmother,' you will say," the louse was told.

Then he went off, and he went in fits and starts, and sitting in the road was a boy named Tamazul, the toad.

"Where are you going?" said the toad to the louse.

"My word is contained in my belly. I'm going to the two boys," said the louse to Tamazul.

"Very well. But I notice you're not very fast," the louse was told by the toad. "Wouldn't you like me to swallow you? You'll see, I'll run bent over this way, we'll arrive in a hurry."

"Very well," said the louse to the toad.

After that, when he had been united with the toad, the toad hopped. He went along now, but he didn't run.

After that, the toad met a big snake named Zaquicaz:

131

"Where are you going, Tamazul boy?" the toad was asked next by Zaquicaz.

"I'm a messenger. My word is in my belly," the toad next said to the snake.

"But I notice you're not fast. Listen to me, I'll get there in a hurry," said the snake to the toad.

"Get going," he was told, so then the toad was next swallowed by Zaquicaz. When snakes get their food today they swallow toads.

So the snake was running as he went, then the snake was met from overhead by a laughing falcon, a large bird. The snake was swallowed up by the falcon, and then he arrived above the court. When hawks get their food, they eat snakes in the mountains.

And when the falcon arrived he alighted on the rim of the ball court. Hunahpu and Xbalanque were happy then, they were playing ball when the falcon arrived.

So then the falcon cried out:

"Wak-ko! Wak-ko!"

said the falcon as he cried.

"Who's crying out there? Come on! Our blowguns!" they said. And they shot the falcon, landing their blowgun shot right in his eye. Wobbling, he fell down and they went right there to grab him, then they asked him:

"What are you after?" they said to the falcon.

"My word is contained in my belly. But heal my eye first, then I'll name it," said the falcon.

"Very well," they said.

Next they took a bit of gum off the surface of the ball, then they put it on the eye of the falcon. "Sorrel gum" was their name for it. As soon as it was treated by them, the vision of the falcon became good again.

"So name it," they said to the falcon, and then he vomited a big snake.

"Speak up," they said next to the snake.

"Yes," he said next, then he vomited the toad.

"What's your errand? Tell it," the toad was told next.

"My word is contained in my belly," the toad said next, and then he tried to throw up, but there was no vomit, he just sort of drooled. He was trying, but there was no vomit.

After that, he had to be kicked by the boys.

"You trickster!" he was told, then they kicked him in the rear, and they crushed the bones of his rear end with their feet. When he tried again, he just sort of spit.

And then they pried the toad's mouth open, it was opened by the boys. They searched his mouth, and the louse had simply stuck in the toad's teeth, it was right there in his mouth. He hadn't swallowed it, but had only seemed to swallow.

And such was the defeat of the toad. It's not clear what kind of food they gave him, and because he didn't run he became mere meat for snakes.

"Tell it," the louse was told next, so then he named his word:

"Boys, your grandmother says:

'Summon them. A message came for them:

"From Xibalba comes the messenger of One and Seven Death:

' "In seven days they are to come here. We'll play ball. Their gaming equipment must come along: rubber ball, yokes, arm guards, kilts. This will make for some excitement here," say the lords,' is the word that came from them," ' says your grandmother. So your grandmother says you must come. Truly your grandmother cries, she calls out to you to come."

"Isn't it the truth!" the boys said in their thoughts. When they heard it they left at once and got to their grandmother, but they went there only to give their grandmother instructions:

"We're on our way, dear grandmother. We're just giving you instructions. So here is the sign of our word. We'll leave it with you. Each of us will plant an ear of corn. We'll plant them in the center of our house. When the corn dries up, this will be a sign of our death:

'Perhaps they died,' you'll say, when it dries up. And when the sprouting comes:

'Perhaps they live,' you'll say, our dear grandmother and mother. From now on, this is the sign of our word. We're leaving it with you," they said, then they left.

Hunahpu planted one and Xbalanque planted another. They

were planted right there in the house: neither in the mountains nor where the earth is damp, but where the earth is dry, in the middle of the inside of their house. They left them planted there, then went off, each with his own blowgun.

THEY WENT DOWN TO XIBALBA, quickly going down the face of a cliff, and they crossed over the bottom of a canyon with rapids. They passed right through the birds—the ones called throng birds—and then they crossed Pus River and Blood River, intended as traps by Xibalba. They did not step in, but simply crossed over on their blowguns, and then they went on over to the Crossroads. But they knew about the roads of Xibalba: Black Road, White Road, Red Road, Green Road.

And there they summoned that creature named the mosquito. Having heard that he's a spy, they sent him ahead:

"Bite them one by one. First bite the first one seated there, then bite every last one of them, and it will be yours alone to suck the blood of people in the roads," the mosquito was told.

"Very well," replied the mosquito, then he took Black Road and stopped at the two manikins, the woodcarvings, that were seated first. They were all dressed up, and he bit the first of them. It didn't speak, so he bit again. When he bit the one seated second, again it didn't speak, and then he bit the third one, the one seated third actually being One Death.

"Yeow!" each one said as he was bitten.

"What?" each one replied.

"Ouch!" said One Death.

"What is it, One Death?"

"Something's bitten me."

"It's—ouch! There's something that's bitten me," the one seated fourth said next.

"What is it, Seven Death?"

"Something's bitten me." The one seated fifth spoke next:

"Ow! Ow!" he said.

"What, House Corner?" Seven Death said to him.

"Something's bitten me," he said next. The one seated sixth was bitten:

"Ouch!"

"What is it, Blood Gatherer?" House Corner said to him.

"Something's bitten me," he said next. Then the one seated seventh was bitten:

"Ouch!" he said next.

"What is it, Pus Master?" Blood Gatherer said to him.

"Something's bitten me," he said next. The one seated eighth was bitten next:

"Ouch!" he said next.

"What is it, Jaundice Master?" Pus Master said to him next.

"Something's bitten me," he said next. Then the one seated ninth was bitten next:

"Ouch!" he said.

"What is it, Bone Scepter?" Jaundice Master said to him.

"Something's bitten me," he said next. Then the one seated tenth in order was bitten next:

"Ouch!"

"What is it, Skull Scepter?" said Bone Scepter.

"Something's bitten me," he said next. Then the one seated eleventh was bitten next:

"Ouch!" he said next.

"What is it, Wing?" Skull Scepter said to him next.

"Something's bitten me," he said next. Then the one seated twelfth was bitten next:

"Ouch!" he said next.

"What, Packstrap?" he was asked next.

"Something's bitten me," he said next. Then the one seated thirteenth was bitten next:

"Ouch!"

"What is it, Bloody Teeth?" Packstrap said to him.

"Something's bitten me," he said next. Then the one seated fourteenth was bitten next:

"Ouch! Something's bitten me," he said next.

"Bloody Claws?" Bloody Teeth said to him next.

And such was the naming of their names, they named them all among themselves. They showed their faces and named their names, each one named by the one ranking above him, and naming in turn the name of the one seated next to him. There wasn't a single name they missed, naming every last one of their names when they were bitten by the hair that Hunahpu had plucked from his own shin. It wasn't really a mosquito that bit them. It went to hear all their names for Hunahpu and Xbalanque.

After that Hunahpu and Xbalanque went on, and then they came to where the Xibalbans were:

"Bid the lords good day," said someone who was seated there. It was a deceiver who spoke.

"These aren't lords! These are manikins, woodcarvings!" they said as they came up.

And after that, they bid them good morning:

> "Morning, One Death.   Morning, Seven Death.
> Morning, House Corner.   Morning, Blood Gatherer.
> Morning, Pus Master.   Morning, Jaundice Master.
> Morning, Bone Scepter.   Morning, Skull Scepter.
> Morning, Wing.   Morning, Packstrap.
> Morning, Bloody Teeth.   Morning, Bloody Claws,"

they said when they arrived, and all of their identities were accounted for. They named every one of their names; there wasn't a single name they missed. When this was required of them, no name was omitted by them.

"Sit here," they were told. They were wanted on the bench, but they didn't want it:

"This bench isn't for us! It's just a stone slab for cooking," said Hunahpu and Xbalanque. They were not defeated.

"Very well. Just get in the house," they were told.

And after that, they entered Dark House. They were not defeated there. This was the first test they entered in Xibalba, and as far as the Xibalbans were concerned they were as good as defeated.

F IRST THEY ENTERED DARK HOUSE.
And after that, the messenger of One Death brought their torch, burning when it arrived, along with one cigar apiece.

" 'Here is their torch,' says the lord. 'They must return the torch in the morning, along with the cigars. They must return them intact,' say the lords," the messenger said when he arrived.

"Very well," they said, but they didn't burn the torch—instead, something that looked like fire was substituted. This was the tail of the macaw, which looked like a torch to the sentries. And as for the cigars, they just put fireflies at the tips of those cigars, which they kept lit all night.

"We've defeated them," said the sentries, but the torch was not consumed—it just looked that way. And as for the cigars, there wasn't anything burning there—it just looked that way. When these things were taken back to the lords:

"What's happening? Where did they come from? Who begot them and bore them? Our hearts are really hurting, because what they're doing to us is no good. They're different in looks and different in their very being," they said among themselves. And when they had summoned all the lords:

"Let's play ball, boys," the boys were told. And then they were asked by One and Seven Death:

"Where might you have come from? Please name it," Xibalba said to them.

"Well, wherever did we come from? We don't know," was all they said. They didn't name it.

"Very well then, we'll just go play ball, boys," Xibalba told them.

"Good," they said.

"Well, this is the one we should put in play, here's our rubber ball," said the Xibalbans.

"No thanks. This is the one to put in, here's ours," said the boys.

"No it's not. This is the one we should put in," the Xibalbans said again.

"Very well," said the boys.

DRAWING FROM ALFRED M. TOZZER,
CHICHEN ITZA AND ITS CENOTE OF SACRIFICE;
PHOTO BY HILLEL BURGER © 1984
BY THE PRESIDENT AND FELLOWS OF HARVARD COLLEGE.

"IT'S JUST A SKULL": In this section from the relief panels in the ball court at Chichen Itza, the ball (at center) bears a skull motif. Like One and Seven Hunahpu and their sons in the Popol Vuh, the players in this scene wear kilts, yokes (the belts with objects protruding upward from them at an angle), arm guards, panaches, and headbands. From the mouths of the two players at left and the one at extreme right comes speech (resembling curling smoke), probably in the form of taunts like those the lords of Xibalba hurl at Hunahpu and Xbalanque in a later Popol Vuh episode. The kneeling player to the right of the ball has been decapitated; from his neck emerge serpents and a vine with flowers and fruits. This may be a squash vine, corresponding to the squash that was substituted for Hunahpu's head when he lost his own to a snatch-bat.

"After all, it's just a decorated one," said the Xibalbans.

"Oh no it's not, it's just a skull! We've said enough," said the boys.

"No it's not," said the Xibalbans.

"Very well," said Hunahpu. When it was sent off by Xibalba, the ball was stopped by Hunahpu's yoke.

And then, while Xibalba watched, the White Dagger came

out from inside the ball. It went clattering, twisting all over the floor of the court.

"What's that!" said Hunahpu and Xbalanque. "Death is the only thing you want for us! Wasn't it *you* who sent a summons to us, and wasn't it *your* messenger who went? Truly, take pity on us, or else we'll just leave," the boys told them.

And this is what had been ordained for the boys: that they should have died right away, right there, defeated by that knife. But it wasn't like that. Instead, Xibalba was again defeated by the boys.

"Well, don't go, boys. We can still play ball, but we'll put yours into play," the boys were told.

"Very well," they said, and this was the time for their rubber ball, so the ball was dropped in.

And after that, they specified the prize:

"What should our prize be?" asked the Xibalbans.

"It's yours for the asking," was all the boys said.

"We'll just win four bowls of flowers," said the Xibalbans.

"Very well. What kinds of flowers?" the boys asked Xibalba.

"One bowl of red petals, one bowl of white petals, one bowl of yellow petals, and one bowl of whole ones," said the Xibalbans.

"Very well," said the boys, and then their ball was dropped in. The boys were their equals in strength and made many plays, since they only had very good thoughts. Then the boys gave themselves up in defeat, and the Xibalbans were glad when they were defeated:

"We've done well. We've beaten them on the first try," said the Xibalbans. "Where will they go to get the flowers?" they said in their hearts.

"Truly, before the night is over, you must hand over our flowers and our prize," the boys, Hunahpu and Xbalanque, were told by Xibalba.

"Very well. So we're also playing ball at night," they said when they accepted their charge.

A ND AFTER THAT, THE BOYS NEXT ENTERED RAZOR HOUSE, the second test of Xibalba.

And this is when it was ordained that they be cut clear through with knives. It was intended to be quick, intended that they should die, but they did not die. They spoke to the knives then, they instructed them:

"This is yours: the flesh of all the animals," they told the knives, and they no longer moved—rather, each and every knife put down its point.

And this is how they stayed there overnight, in Razor House. Now they summoned all the ants:

"Cutting ants, conquering ants, come now,
all of you fetch all of them for us:
flowers in bloom, prizes for lords."

"Very well," they replied. Then all the ants went to get the flowers, the plantings of One and Seven Death, who had already given instructions to the guardians of the flowers of Xibalba:

"Would you please watch our flowers? Don't let them get stolen. We've defeated these boys, so won't they come looking for the prize they owe us? Don't sleep tonight."

"Very well," they replied, but the guardians of the plants

never knew a thing. Their only inclination was to stretch their mouths wide open, going from one perch to another in the trees and plants, repeating the same song:

"Whip-poor-will! Whip-poor-will!"

one of them says as he cries.

"Poor-willow! Poor-willow!"

says the other as he cries, the one named poorwill.

The two of them are the guards of the garden, the garden of One and Seven Death, but they don't notice the ants stealing what's under their guard, swarming, carrying away loads of flowers, coming to cut down the flowers in the trees, gathering these together with the flowers beneath the trees, while the guards just stretch their mouths wide open, not noticing the nibbling at their own tails, the nibbling at their own wings. The severed flowers rain down into the gathering and bunching here below, so that four bowls of flowers are easily filled, an acrobatic performance that lasts till dawn.

After that the messengers, the pages, arrive:

" 'They are to come,' says the lord. 'They must bring our prizes here right away,' " the boys were told.

"Very well," they said. Having loaded up the flowers, four bowls of them, they left and came before the lord, or lords, who received the flowers with pained looks.

With this, the Xibalbans were defeated. The boys had sent mere ants; in just one night the ants had taken the flowers and put them in the bowls.

With this, all the Xibalbans looked sick, they paled at the sight of the flowers.

After that, they summoned the flower guards:

"How did you allow our flowers to get stolen? These are *our* flowers! Here! Look!" the guards were told.

"We took no notice, your lordship, though our tails are the worse for it," they said.

And then their mouths were split wide, their payment for the theft of what was under their guard.

Such was the defeat of One and Seven Death by Hunahpu and

Xbalanque, on account of which the whippoorwills got gaping mouths. Their mouths gape to this day.

Now after that, when the ball was dropped in, they just played to a tie. When they finished the game they made an arrangement with each other:

"At dawn again," said Xibalba.

"Very well," said the boys, then they were finished.

A ND NOW THEY ENTERED COLD HOUSE. There are countless drafts, thick-falling hail inside the house, the home of cold. They diminished the cold right away by shutting it out. The cold dissipated because of the boys. They did not die, but were alive when it dawned.

So, although Xibalba had wanted them to die there, they did not, but were alive when it dawned. They came out when the pages arrived and the guards left.

"Why haven't they died?" said the rulers of Xibalba. Again they were amazed at the feats of the boys, Hunahpu and Xbalanque.

S O NEXT THEY ENTERED JAGUAR HOUSE, the jaguar-packed home of jaguars:

"Don't eat *us*. There *is* something that should be yours," the jaguars were told.

With that, they scattered bones before the animals.

After that, the jaguars were wrestling around there, over the bones.

"So they've made good work of them, they've eaten their very hearts. Now that the boys have given themselves up, they've already been transformed into skeletons," said the sentries, all of them finding it sweet. But they hadn't died; they were well. They came out of Jaguar House.

"What sort of people are they? Where did they come from?" said all the Xibalbans.

S O NEXT THEY ENTERED THE MIDST OF THE FIRE, a house of fire with only fire alone inside. They weren't burned by it, just toasted, just simmered, so they were well when it dawned. Although it had been ordained that they be quickly killed in there, overcome, they weren't, and instead it was the Xibalbans who lost heart over this.

N OW THEY WERE PUT INSIDE BAT HOUSE, with bats alone inside the house, a house of snatch-bats, monstrous beasts, their snouts like knives, the instruments of death. To come before these is to be finished off at once.

When they were inside they just slept in their blowgun; they were not bitten by the members of the household. But this is where they gave one of themselves up because of a snatch-bat that came down, he came along just as one of them showed himself. They did it because it was actually what they were asking for, what they had in mind.

And all night the bats are making noise:

"Squeak! Squeak!"

they say, and they say it all night.

Then it let up a little. The bats were no longer moving around. So there, one of the boys crawled to the end of the blowgun, since Xbalanque said:

"Hunahpu? Can you see how long it is till dawn?"

"Well, perhaps I should look to see how long it is," he replied. So he kept trying to look out the muzzle of the blowgun, he tried to see the dawn.

And then his head was taken off by a snatch-bat, leaving Hunahpu's body still stuffed inside.

"What's going on? Hasn't it dawned?" said Xbalanque. No

SNATCH-BATS, MONSTROUS BEASTS: The bats of Xibalba were frequently painted on classic Maya funerary vases of the Chamá style, from sites in the same region as the Great Abyss where Hunahpu and Xbalanque descended into the underworld. The designs on the present bat's wings represent plucked-out eyes, and he wears two eyes on his collar; the scroll-like forms issuing from his mouth, with ragged upper edges, may represent his shrieks. (*The vase is in the collection of Edwin Pearlman.*)

---

longer is there any movement from Hunahpu. "What's this? Hunahpu hasn't left, has he? What have you done?" He no longer moves; now there is only heavy breathing.

After that, Xbalanque despaired:

"Alas! We've given it all up!" he said. And elsewhere, the head meanwhile went rolling onto the court, in accordance with the word of One and Seven Death, and all the Xibalbans were happy over the head of Hunahpu.

After that, Xbalanque summoned all the animals: coati, peccary, all the animals, small and great. It was at night, still nighttime when he asked them for their food:

"Whatever your foods are, each one of you: that's what I summoned you for, to bring your food here," Xbalanque told them.

"Very well," they replied, then they went to get what's theirs, then indeed they all came back.

There's the one who only brought his rotten wood.

There's the one who only brought leaves.

There's the one who only brought stones.

There's the one who only brought earth, on through the varied foods of the animals, small and great, until the very last one remained: the coati. He brought a squash, bumping it along with his snout as he came.

And this became a simulated head for Hunahpu. His eyes were carved right away, then brains came from the thinker, from the sky. This was the Heart of Sky, Hurricane, who came down, came on down into Bat House. The face wasn't finished any too quickly; it came out well. His strength was just the same, he looked handsome, he spoke just the same.

And this is when it was trying to dawn, reddening along the horizon:

"Now make the streaks, man," the possum was told.

"Yes," said the old man. When he made the streaks he made it dark again; the old man made four streaks.

"Possum is making streaks," people say today, ever since he made the early dawn red and blue, establishing its very being.

"Isn't it good?" Hunahpu was asked.

"Good indeed," he replied. His head was as if it had every bone; it had become like his real head.

After that, they had a talk, they made arrangements with each other:

"How about not playing ball yourself? You should just make lots of threats, while I should be the one to take all the action," Xbalanque told him. After that, he gave instructions to a rabbit:

"Your place is there above the court, on top. Stay there in the oaks," the rabbit was told by Xbalanque, "until the ball comes to you, then take off while I get to work," the rabbit was told. He got his instructions while it was still dark.

DRAWINGS BY CARLOS A. VILLACORTA

THE OLD MAN MADE FOUR STREAKS: In these drawings from the Dresden Codex; the possum deity is shown bringing in each of the four types of solar years. The repeated glyphs in the column to the left of each figure give the names of the four year-beginning day names; in Quiché the names are E or "Tooth" (upper left), Naoh or "Thought" (upper right), I3 or "Wind" (lower left), and Queh or "Deer." Each figure bears the patron deity of a given type of year on his back.

After that, when it dawned, both of them were just as well as ever.

And when the ball was dropped in again, it was the head of Hunahpu that rolled over the court:

"We've won! You're done!
Give up! You lost!"

they were told. But even so Hunahpu was shouting:

"Punt the head as a ball!" he told them.

"Well, we're not going to do them any more harm with threats," and with this the lords of Xibalba sent off the ball and

Xbalanque received it, the ball was stopped by his yoke, then he hit it hard and it took off, the ball passed straight out of the court, bouncing just once, just twice, and stopping among the oaks. Then the rabbit took off hopping, then they went off in pursuit, then all the Xibalbans went off, shouting, shrieking, they went after the rabbit, off went the whole of Xibalba.

After that, the boys got Hunahpu's head back. Then Xbalanque planted the squash; this is when he went to set the squash above the court.

So the head of Hunahpu was really a head again, and the two of them were happy again. And the others, those Xibalbans, were still going on in search of the ball.

After that, having recovered the ball from among the oaks, the boys cried out to them:

"Come back! Here's the ball! We've found it!" they said, so they stopped. When the Xibalbans got back:

"Have we been seeing things?" they said. Then they began their ball game again, and they made equal plays on both sides again.

After that, the squash was punted by Xbalanque. The squash was wearing out; it fell on the court, bringing to light its light-colored seeds, as plain as day right in front of them.

"How did you get ahold of that? Where did it come from?" said Xibalba.

With this, the masters of Xibalba were defeated by Hunahpu and Xbalanque. There was great danger there, but they did not die from all the things that were done to them.

A ND HERE IT IS: THE EPITAPH, THE DEATH OF HUNAHPU AND XBALANQUE.

Here it is: now we shall name their epitaph, their death. They did whatever they were instructed to do, going through all the dangers, the troubles that were made for them, but they did not die from the tests of Xibalba, nor were they defeated by all the voracious animals that inhabit Xibalba.

After that, they summoned two midmost seers, similar to readers. Here are their names: Xulu, Pacam, both knowers.

"Perhaps there will be questions from the lords of Xibalba about our death. They are thinking about how to overcome us because we haven't died, nor have we been defeated. We've exhausted all their tests. Not even the animals got us. So this is the sign, here in our hearts: their instrument for our death will be a stone oven. All the Xibalbans have gathered together. Isn't our death inevitable? So this is your plan, here we shall name it: if you come to be questioned by them about our death, once we've been burned, what will you say, Xulu and Pacam? If they ask you:

'Wouldn't it be good if we dumped their bones in the canyon?'

'Perhaps it wouldn't be good, since they would only come back to life again,' you will say.

'Perhaps this would be good: we'll just hang them up in a tree,' they'll say to you next.

'Certainly that's no good, since you would see their faces,' you will say, and then they'll speak to you for the third time:

'Well, here's the only good thing: we'll just dump their bones in the river.' If that's what they ask you next:

'This is a good death for them, and it would also be good to grind their bones on a stone, just as corn is refined into flour, and refine each of them separately, and then:

> Spill them into the river,
> sprinkle them on the water's way,
> among the mountains, small and great,'

you will say, and then you will have carried out the instructions we've named for you," said Hunahpu and Xbalanque. When they gave these instructions they already knew they would die.

THIS IS THE MAKING OF THE OVEN, the great stone oven. The Xibalbans made it like the places where the sweet drink is cooked, they opened it to a great width.

After that, messengers came to get the boys, the messengers of One and Seven Death:

" 'They must come. We'll go with the boys, to see the treat we've cooked up for them,' say the lords, you boys," they were told.

"Very well," they replied. They went running and arrived at the mouth of the oven.

And there they tried to force them into a game:

"Here, let's jump over our drink four times, clear across, one of us after the other, boys," they were told by One Death.

"You'll never put that one over on us. Don't we know what our death is, you lords? Watch!" they said, then they faced each other. They grabbed each other by the arms and went head first into the oven.

And there they died, together, and now all the Xibalbans were happy, raising their shouts, raising their cheers:

"We've really beaten them! They didn't give up easily," they said.

After that they summoned Xulu and Pacam, who kept their word: the bones went just where the boys had wanted them. Once the Xibalbans had done the divination, the bones were ground and spilled in the river, but they didn't go far—they just sank to the bottom of the water. They became handsome boys; they looked just the same as before when they reappeared.

A ND ON THE FIFTH DAY THEY REAPPEARED. They were seen in the water by the people. The two of them looked like channel catfish when their faces were seen by Xibalba. And having germinated in the waters, they appeared the day after that as two vagabonds, with rags before and rags behind, and rags all over too. They seemed unrefined when they were examined by Xibalba; they acted differently now.

It was only the Dance of the Poorwill, the Dance of the Weasel, only Armadillos they danced.

DRAWING BY THE AUTHOR

ONLY ARMADILLOS THEY DANCED: This dancer, who wears an
armadillo mask, plays a flute, and shakes a rattle, was
painted on a classic Maya funerary vase of the Chamá style,
which pertains to sites in the same general region as the
Great Abyss where Hunahpu and Xbalanque descended into
the underworld. The cross-hatching represents the scales of
an armadillo.

Only Swallowing Swords, only Walking on Stilts now they
danced.

They performed many miracles now. They would set fire to a
house, as if they were really burning it, and suddenly bring it
back again. Now Xibalba was full of admiration.

Next they would sacrifice themselves, one of them dying for
the other, stretched out as if in death. First they would kill
themselves, but then they would suddenly look alive again. The
Xibalbans could only admire what they did. Everything they did
now was already the groundwork for their defeat of Xibalba.

And after that, news of their dances came to the ears of the
lords, One and Seven Death. When they heard it they said:

"Who are these two vagabonds? Are they really such a delight? And is their dancing really that pretty? They do everything!" they said. An account of them had reached the lords. It sounded delightful, so then they entreated their messengers to notify them that they must come:

" ' "If only they'd come make a show for us, we'd wonder at them and marvel at them," say the lords,' you will say," the messengers were told. So they came to the dancers, then spoke the words of the lords to them.

"But we don't want to, because we're really ashamed. Just plain no. Wouldn't we be afraid to go inside there, into a lordly house? Because we'd really look bad. Wouldn't we just be wide-eyed? Take pity on us! Wouldn't we look like mere dancers to them? What would we say to our fellow vagabonds? There are others who also want us to dance today, to liven things up with us, so we can't do likewise for the lords, and likewise is not what we want, messengers," said Hunahpu and Xbalanque.

Even so, they were prevailed upon: through troubles, through torments, they went on their tortuous way. They didn't want to walk fast. Many times they had to be forced; the messengers went ahead of them as guides but had to keep coming back. And so they went to the lord.

A ND THEY CAME TO THE LORDS. Feigning great humility, they bowed their heads all the way to the ground when they arrived. They brought themselves low, doubled over, flattened out, down to the rags, to the tatters. They really looked like vagabonds when they arrived.

So then they were asked what their mountain and tribe were, and they were also asked about their mother and father:

"Where do you come from?" they were asked.

"We've never known, lord. We don't know the identity of our mother and father. We must've been small when they died," was all they said. They didn't give any names.

"Very well. Please entertain us, then. What do you want us to give you in payment?" they were asked.

"Well, we don't want anything. To tell the truth, we're afraid," they told the lord.

"Don't be afraid. Don't be ashamed. Just dance this way: first you'll dance to sacrifice yourselves, you'll set fire to my house after that, you'll act out all the things you know. We want to be entertained. This is our heart's desire, the reason you had to be sent for, dear vagabonds. We'll give you payment," they were told.

So then they began their songs and dances, and then all the Xibalbans arrived, the spectators crowded the floor, and they danced everything: they danced the Weasel, they danced the Poorwill, they danced the Armadillo. Then the lord said to them:

"Sacrifice my dog, then bring him back to life again," they were told.

"Yes," they said.

> When they sacrificed the dog
>   he then came back to life.
> And that dog was really happy
>   when he came back to life.
> Back and forth he wagged his tail
>   when he came back to life.

And the lord said to them:

"Well, you have yet to set my home on fire," they were told next, so then they set fire to the home of the lord. The house was packed with all the lords, but they were not burned. They quickly fixed it back again, lest the house of One Death be consumed all at once, and all the lords were amazed, and they went on dancing this way. They were overjoyed.

And then they were asked by the lord:

"You have yet to kill a person! Make a sacrifice without death!" they were told.

"Very well," they said.

And then they took hold of a human sacrifice.

And they held up a human heart on high.

And they showed its roundness to the lords.

And now One and Seven Death admired it, and now that person was brought right back to life. His heart was overjoyed when he came back to life, and the lords were amazed:

"Sacrifice yet again, even do it to yourselves! Let's see it! At heart, that's the dance we really want from you," the lords said now.

"Very well, lord," they replied, and then they sacrificed themselves.

A ND THIS IS THE SACRIFICE OF HUNAHPU BY XBALANQUE. One by one his legs, his arms were spread wide. His head came off, rolled far away outside. His heart, dug out, was smothered in a leaf, and all the Xibalbans went crazy at the sight.

So now, only one of them was dancing there: Xbalanque.

"Get up!" he said, and Hunahpu came back to life. The two of them were overjoyed at this—and likewise the lords rejoiced, as if they were doing it themselves. One and Seven Death were as glad at heart as if they themselves were actually doing the dance.

And then the hearts of the lords were filled with longing, with yearning for the dance of Hunahpu and Xbalanque, so then came these words from One and Seven Death:

"Do it to us! Sacrifice us!" they said. "Sacrifice both of us!" said One and Seven Death to Hunahpu and Xbalanque.

"Very well. You ought to come back to life. After all, aren't you Death? And aren't we making you happy, along with the vassals of your domain?" they told the lords.

And this one was the first to be sacrificed: the lord at the very top, the one whose name is One Death, the ruler of Xibalba.

And with One Death dead, the next to be taken was Seven Death. They did not come back to life.

And then the Xibalbans were getting up to leave, those who had seen the lords die. They underwent heart sacrifice there, and the heart sacrifice was performed on the two lords only for the purpose of destroying them.

AND THEN THEY TOOK HOLD OF A HUMAN SACRIFICE: In this classic Maya funerary vase painting from northern Guatemala, the head lord of Xibalba, One Death, is seated on his throne at right; perched on his hat is one of the messengers of Xibalba, Macaw Owl, who is like an owl except in having the tail of a macaw. In front of One Death are Hunahpu (left) and Xbalanque (right), acting out the roles of sacrificial priests; Xbalanque's identity is marked by the jaguar paw on the nose of his mask. The women around the platform are all of noble rank; the one at extreme left is tapping the foot of the one who faces One Death, calling her attention to the sacrificial performance. (*The vase is in the Princeton University Art Museum.*)

As soon as they had killed the one lord without bringing him back to life, the other lord had been meek and tearful before the dancers. He didn't consent, he didn't accept it:

"Take pity on me!" he said when he realized. All their vassals took the road to the great canyon, in one single mass they filled

154

up the deep abyss. So they piled up there and gathered together, countless ants, tumbling down into the canyon, as if they were being herded there. And when they arrived, they all bent low in surrender, they arrived meek and tearful.

Such was the defeat of the rulers of Xibalba. The boys accomplished it only through wonders, only through self-transformation.

AND THEN THEY NAMED THEIR NAMES, they gave themselves names before all of Xibalba:

"Listen: we shall name our names, and we shall also name the names of our fathers for you. Here we are: we are Hunahpu and Xbalanque by name. And these are our fathers, the ones you killed: One Hunahpu and Seven Hunahpu by name. And we are

155

"SACRIFICE YET AGAIN, EVEN DO IT TO YOURSELVES!": This classic Maya funerary vase painting from the lowlands shows Hunahpu (at extreme left) about to swing the stone axe in his right hand and decapitate his brother Xbalanque, while an ecstatic lord of Xibalba (in skeletal form) looks on. The dog at right is doubtless the one already sacrificed and brought back to life earlier in this same episode. The insect above the dog holds a torch and may be one of the fireflies with which Hunahpu and Xbalanque made their cigars appear to be burning while they spent the night in Dark House, in an earlier episode. In the present scene Hunahpu is identifiable, in part, by the catfish barbel that emerges just behind his nostril; he acquired this attribute in a previous episode, when he and Xbalanque appeared as channel catfish after their ground bones had been thrown in water. Xbalanque, whose name is partly derived from *balam* or "jaguar," is identifiable from his jaguar ears, paws, feet, and tail. (*This vase can be seen at the Metropolitan Museum of Art.*)

here to clear the road of the torments and troubles of our fathers. And so we have suffered all the troubles you've caused us. And so we are putting an end to all of you. We're going to kill you. No one can save you now," they were told. And then all the Xibalbans got down on the ground and cried out:

"Take pity on us, Hunahpu and Xbalanque! It is true that we wronged your fathers, the ones you name. Those two are buried at the Place of Ball Game Sacrifice," they replied.

"Very well. Now this is our word, we shall name it for you. All of you listen, you Xibalbans: because of this, your day and your descendants will not be great. Moreover, the gifts you receive will no longer be great, but reduced to scabrous nodules of sap. There will be no cleanly blotted blood for you, just griddles, just gourds, just brittle things broken to pieces. Further, you will only feed on creatures of the meadows and clearings. None of those who are born in the light, begotten in the light will be yours. Only the worthless will yield themselves up before you. These will be the guilty, the violent, the wretched, the afflicted. Wherever the blame is clear, that is where you will come in, rather than just making sudden attacks on people in general. And you will hear petitions over headed-up sap," all the Xibalbans were told.

Such was the beginning of their disappearance and the denial of their worship.

> Their ancient day was not a great one,
> these ancient people only wanted conflict,
> their ancient names are not really divine,
> but fearful is the ancient evil of their faces.
>
> They are makers of enemies, users of owls,
> they are inciters to wrongs and violence,
> they are masters of hidden intentions as well,
> they are black and white,
> masters of stupidity, masters of perplexity,

as it is said. By putting on appearances they cause dismay.

Such was the loss of their greatness and brilliance. Their domain did not return to greatness. This was accomplished by Hunahpu and Xbalanque.

A ND THIS IS THEIR GRANDMOTHER, CRYING AND CALLING OUT IN FRONT OF THE CORN EARS they left planted. Corn plants grew, then dried up.

And this was when they were burned in the oven; then the corn plants grew again.

And this was when their grandmother burned something, she burned copal before the corn as a memorial to them. There was happiness in their grandmother's heart the second time the corn plants sprouted. Then the ears were deified by their grandmother, and she gave them names: Middle of the House, Middle of the Harvest, Living Corn, Earthen Floor became their names.

And she named the ears Middle of the House, Middle of the Harvest, because they had planted them right in the middle of the inside of their home.

And she further named them Earthen Floor, Living Corn, since the corn ears had been placed up above an earthen floor.

And she also named them Living Corn, because the corn plants had grown again. So they were named by Xmucane. They had been left behind, planted by Hunahpu and Xbalanque, simply as a way for their grandmother to remember them.

And the first to die, a long time before, had been their fathers, One Hunahpu and Seven Hunahpu. And they saw the face of their father again, there in Xibalba. Their father spoke to them again when they had defeated Xibalba.

A ND HERE THEIR FATHER IS PUT BACK TOGETHER BY THEM. They put Seven Hunahpu back together; they went to the Place of Ball Game Sacrifice to put him together. He had wanted his face to become just as it was, but when he was asked to name everything, and once he had found the name of the mouth, the nose, the eyes of his face, there was very little else to be said. Although his mouth could not name the names of each of his former parts, he had at least spoken again.

And so it remained that they were respectful of their father's heart, even though they left him at the Place of Ball Game Sacrifice:

"You will be prayed to here," his sons told him, and his heart was comforted. "You will be the first resort, and you will be the first to have your day kept by those who will be born in the light, begotten in the light. Your name will not be lost. So be it," they told their father when they comforted his heart.

"We merely cleared the road of your death, your loss, the pain, the suffering that were inflicted upon you."

And such was the instruction they gave when all the Xibalbans had been finally defeated. And then the two boys ascended this way, here into the middle of the light, and they ascended straight on into the sky, and the sun belongs to one and the moon to the other. When it became light within the sky, on the face of the earth, they were there in the sky.

And this was also the ascent of the Four Hundred Boys killed by Zipacna.

And these came to accompany the two of them. They became the sky's own stars.

PART
FOUR

A ND HERE IS THE BEGINNING OF THE CONCEPTION OF HUMANS, and of the search for the ingredients of the human body. So they spoke, the Bearer, Begetter, the Makers, Modelers named Sovereign Plumed Serpent:

"The dawn has approached, preparations have been made, and morning has come for the provider, nurturer, born in the light, begotten in the light. Morning has come for humankind, for the people of the face of the earth," they said. It all came together as they went on thinking in the darkness, in the night, as they searched and they sifted, they thought and they wondered.

And here their thoughts came out in clear light. They sought and discovered what was needed for human flesh. It was only a short while before the sun, moon, and stars were to appear above the Makers and Modelers. Broken Place, Bitter Water Place is the name: the yellow corn, white corn came from there.

And these are the names of the animals who brought the food: fox, coyote, parrot, crow. There were four animals who brought the news of the ears of yellow corn and white corn. They were coming from over there at Broken Place, they showed the way to the break.

And this was when they found the staple foods.

And these were the ingredients for the flesh of the human work, the human design, and the water was for the blood. It became human blood, and corn was also used by the Bearer, Begetter.

And so they were happy over the provisions of the good mountain, filled with sweet things, thick with yellow corn, white corn, and thick with pataxte and cacao, countless zapotes, anonas, jocotes, nances, matasanos, sweets—the rich foods filling up the citadel named Broken Place, Bitter Water Place. All the edible fruits were there: small staples, great staples, small plants, great plants. The way was shown by the animals.

And then the yellow corn and white corn were ground, and Xmucane did the grinding nine times. Corn was used, along with

163

PHOTO BY THE AUTHOR

"MORNING HAS COME FOR THE PROVIDER, NURTURER": A Quiché mother-father, Lucas Pacheco, gives nourishment to the gods at his household altar. The celestial deities, who have been given paraffin candles, are represented by the wooden saints on top of the table, while the terrestrial deities, who have been given tallow candles, are represented by the stones underneath. Don Lucas is in the process of giving libations of liquor to the stones; the large one at right has already been doused.

the water she rinsed her hands with, for the creation of grease; it became human fat when it was worked by the Bearer, Begetter, Sovereign Plumed Serpent, as they are called.

After that, they put it into words:

the making, the modeling of our first mother-father,
with yellow corn, white corn alone for the flesh,
food alone for the human legs and arms,
for our first fathers, the four human works.

It was staples alone that made up their flesh.

T HESE ARE THE NAMES OF THE FIRST PEOPLE WHO WERE MADE AND MODELED.

This is the first person: Jaguar Quitze.

And now the second: Jaguar Night.

And now the third: Mahucutah.

And the fourth: True Jaguar.

And these are the names of our first mother-fathers. They were simply made and modeled, it is said; they had no mother and no father. We have named the men by themselves. No woman gave birth to them, nor were they begotten by the builder, sculptor, Bearer, Begetter. By sacrifice alone, by genius alone they were made, they were modeled by the Maker, Modeler, Bearer, Begetter, Sovereign Plumed Serpent. And when they came to fruition, they came out human:

They talked and they made words.

They looked and they listened.

They walked, they worked.

They were good people, handsome, with looks of the male kind. Thoughts came into existence and they gazed; their vision came all at once. Perfectly they saw, perfectly they knew everything under the sky, whenever they looked. The moment they turned around and looked around in the sky, on the earth, everything was seen without any obstruction. They didn't have to walk around before they could see what was under the sky; they just stayed where they were.

As they looked, their knowledge became intense. Their sight passed through trees, through rocks, through lakes, through seas, through mountains, through plains. Jaguar Quitze, Jaguar Night, Mahucutah, and True Jaguar were truly gifted people.

And then they were asked by the builder and mason:

"What do you know about your being? Don't you look, don't you listen? Isn't your speech good, and your walk? So you must look, to see out under the sky. Don't you see the mountain-plain clearly? So try it," they were told.

And then they saw everything under the sky perfectly. After that, they thanked the Maker, Modeler:

"Truly now,
double thanks, triple thanks
that we've been formed, we've been given
our mouths, our faces,
we speak, we listen,
we wonder, we move,
our knowledge is good, we've understood
what is far and near,
and we've seen what is great and small
under the sky, on the earth.
Thanks to you we've been formed,
we've come to be made and modeled,
our grandmother, our grandfather,"

they said when they gave thanks for having been made and modeled. They understood everything perfectly, they sighted the four sides, the four corners in the sky, on the earth, and this didn't sound good to the builder and sculptor:

"What our works and designs have said is no good:
'We have understood everything, great and small,' they say."
And so the Bearer, Begetter took back their knowledge:

"What should we do with them now? Their vision should at least reach nearby, they should see at least a small part of the face of the earth, but what they're saying isn't good. Aren't they merely 'works' and 'designs' in their very names? Yet they'll become as great as gods, unless they procreate, proliferate at the sowing, the dawning, unless they increase."

"Let it be this way: now we'll take them apart just a little, that's what we need. What we've found out isn't good. Their deeds would become equal to ours, just because their knowledge reaches so far. They see everything," so said

the Heart of Sky, Hurricane,
Newborn Thunderbolt, Raw Thunderbolt,
Sovereign Plumed Serpent,
Bearer, Begetter,
Xpiyacoc, Xmucane,
Maker, Modeler,

as they are called. And when they changed the nature of their works, their designs, it was enough that the eyes be marred by the Heart of Sky. They were blinded as the face of a mirror is breathed upon. Their eyes were weakened. Now it was only when they looked nearby that things were clear.

And such was the loss of the means of understanding, along with the means of knowing everything, by the four humans. The root was implanted.

And such was the making, modeling of our first grandfather, our father, by the Heart of Sky, Heart of Earth.

A ND THEN THEIR WIVES AND WOMEN CAME INTO BEING. Again, the same gods thought of it. It was as if they were asleep when they received them, truly beautiful women were there with Jaguar Quitze, Jaguar Night, Mahucutah, and True Jaguar. With their women there they became wider awake. Right away they were happy at heart again, because of their wives.

Celebrated Seahouse is the name of the wife of Jaguar Quitze.

Prawn House is the name of the wife of Jaguar Night.

Hummingbird House is the name of the wife of Mahucutah.

Macaw House is the name of the wife of True Jaguar.

So these are the names of their wives, who became ladies of rank, giving birth to the people of the tribes, small and great.

A ND THIS IS OUR ROOT, WE WHO ARE THE QUICHÉ PEOPLE. And there came to be a crowd of penitents and sacrificers. It wasn't only four who came into being then, but there were four mothers for us, the Quiché people. There were different names for each of the peoples when they multiplied, there in the east. Their names became numerous: Sovereign Oloman,

Cohah, Quenech Ahau, as the names of the people who were there in the east are spoken. They multiplied, and it is known that the Tams and Ilocs began then. They came from the same place, there in the east.

Jaguar Quitze was the grandfather and father of the nine great houses of the Cauecs.

Jaguar Night was the grandfather and father of the nine great houses of the Greathouses.

Mahucutah was the grandfather and father of the four great houses of the Lord Quichés.

There were three separate lineages. The names of the grandfathers and fathers are not forgotten. These multiplied and flowered there in the east, but the Tams and Ilocs also came forth, along with thirteen allied tribes, thirteen principalities, including:

The Rabinals, Cakchiquels, those of the Bird House.

And the White Cornmeals.

And also the Lamacs, Serpents, Sweatbath House, Talk House, those of the Star House.

And those of the Quiba House, those of the Yokes House, Acul people, Jaguar House, Guardians of the Spoils, Jaguar Ropes.

It is sufficient that we speak only of the largest tribes from among the allied tribes; we have only noted the largest. Many more came out afterward, each one a division of that citadel. We haven't written their names, but they multiplied there, from out of the east. There came to be many peoples in the blackness; they began to abound even before the birth of the sun and the light. When they began to abound they were all there together; they stood and walked in crowds, there in the east.

There was nothing they could offer for sustenance, but even so they lifted their faces to the sky. They didn't know where they were going. They did this for a long time, when they were there in the grasslands: black people, white people, people of many faces, people of many languages, uncertain, there at the edge of the sky.

And there were mountain people. They didn't show their faces, they had no homes. They just traveled the mountains, small and great. "It's as if they were crazy," they used to say.

THEY WERE GIVERS OF PRAISE, GIVERS OF RESPECT: Pilgrims praying, singing, and burning copal (note the rising smoke) at a hilltop shrine near Pologuá, an outlying hamlet of Momostenango. Scattered about are the leaf wrappings from copal packages.

They derided the mountain people, it was said. There they watched for the sunrise, and for all the mountain people there was just one language. They did not yet pray to wood and stone.

These are the words with which they remembered the Maker, Modeler, Heart of Sky, Heart of Earth. It was said that these were enough to keep them mindful of what was in shadow and what was dawning. All they did was ask; they had reverent words. They were reverent, they were givers of praise, givers of respect, lifting their faces to the sky when they made requests for their daughters and sons:

> "Wait!
> thou Maker, thou Modeler,
> look at us, listen to us,

don't let us fall, don't leave us aside,
thou god in the sky, on the earth,
Heart of Sky, Heart of Earth,
give us our sign, our word,
as long as there is day, as long as there is light.
When it comes to the sowing, the dawning,
will it be a greening road, a greening path?
Give us a steady light, a level place,
a good light, a good place,
a good life and beginning.
Give us all of this, thou Hurricane,
Newborn Thunderbolt, Raw Thunderbolt,
Newborn Nanahuac, Raw Nanahuac,
Falcon, Hunahpu,
Sovereign Plumed Serpent,
Bearer, Begetter,
Xpiyacoc, Xmucane,
Grandmother of Day, Grandmother of Light,
when it comes to the sowing, the dawning,"

they said when they made their fasts and prayers, just watching intently for the dawn. There, too, they looked toward the east, watching closely for the daybringer, the great star at the birth of the sun, of the heat for what is under the sky, on the earth, the guide for the human work, the human design.

They spoke, those who are Jaguar Quitze, Jaguar Night, Mahucutah, and True Jaguar:

"We're still waiting for the dawning," they said, these great knowers, great thinkers, penitents, praisers, as they are called. And there was nothing of wood and stone in the keeping of our first mother-fathers, and they were weary at heart there, waiting for the sun. Already there were many of them, all the tribes, including the Yaqui people, all penitents and sacrificers.

"Let's just go. We'll look and see whether there is something to keep as our sign. We'll find out what we should burn in front of it. The way we are right now, we have nothing to keep as our own," said Jaguar Quitze, Jaguar Night, Mahucutah, and True Jaguar. They got word of a citadel. They went there.

A ND THIS IS THE NAME OF THE MOUNTAIN WHERE THEY WENT, Jaguar Quitze, Jaguar Night, Mahucutah, True Jaguar, and the Tams and Ilocs: Tulan Zuyua, Seven Caves, Seven Canyons is the name of the citadel. Those who were to receive the gods arrived there.

And they arrived there at Tulan, all of them, countless people arrived, walking in crowds, and their gods were given out in order, the first being those of Jaguar Quitze, Jaguar Night, Mahucutah, and True Jaguar. They were happy:

"We have found what we were looking for," they said. And this one was the first to come out:

Tohil is the name of the god loaded in the backpack borne by Jaguar Quitze. And the others came out in turn:

Auilix is the name of the god that Jaguar Night carried.

Hacauitz, in turn, is the name of the god received by Mahucutah.

Middle of the Plain is the name of the god received by True Jaguar.

And there were still other Quiché people, since the Tams also received theirs, but it was the same Tohil for the Tams, that's the name received by the grandfather and father of the Tam lords, as they are known today.

And third were the Ilocs: again, Tohil is the name of the god received by the grandfather and father of those lords, the same ones known today.

And such was the naming of the three Quichés. They have never let go of each other because the god has just one name: Tohil for the Quiché proper, and Tohil for the Tams and Ilocs. There is just one name for their god, and so the Quiché threesome has not come apart, those three. Tohil, Auilix, and Hacauitz are truly great in their very being.

And then all the tribes came in: Rabinals, Cakchiquels, those of the Bird House, along with the Yaqui people, as the names are today. And the languages of the tribes changed there; their languages became differentiated. They could no longer understand one another clearly when they came away from Tulan.

And there they broke apart. There were those who went eastward and many who came here, but they were all alike in dressing with hides. There were no clothes of the better kinds. They were in patches, they were adorned with mere animal hides. They were poor. They had nothing of their own. But they were people of genius in their very being when they came away from Tulan Zuyua, Seven Caves, Seven Canyons, so says the Ancient Word.

T HEY WALKED IN CROWDS WHEN THEY ARRIVED AT TULAN, AND THERE WAS NO FIRE. Only those with Tohil had it: this was the tribe whose god was first to generate fire. How it was generated is not clear. Their fire was already burning when Jaguar Quitze and Jaguar Night first saw it:

"Alas! Fire has not yet become ours. We'll die from the cold," they said. And then Tohil spoke:

"Do not grieve. You will have your own even when the fire you're talking about has been lost," Tohil told them.

> "Aren't you a true god!
> Our sustenance and our support!
> Our god!"

they said when they gave thanks for what Tohil had said.

> "Very well, in truth,
> I am your god: so be it.
> I am your lord: so be it,"

the penitents and sacrificers were told by Tohil.

And this was the warming of the tribes. They were pleased by their fire.

After that a great downpour began, which cut short the fire of the tribes. And hail fell thickly on all the tribes, and their fires were put out by the hail. Their fires didn't start up again. So then Jaguar Quitze and Jaguar Night asked for their fire again:

"Tohil, we'll be finished off by the cold," they told Tohil.

"Well, do not grieve," said Tohil. Then he started a fire. He pivoted inside his sandal.

After that, Jaguar Quitze, Jaguar Night, Mahucutah, and True Jaguar were pleased.

After they had been warmed, the fires of the other tribes were still out. Now they were being finished off by the cold, so they came back to ask for their fire from Jaguar Quitze, Jaguar Night, Mahucutah, and True Jaguar. They could bear the cold and hail no longer. By now they were chattering and shivering. There was no life left in them. Their legs and arms kept shaking. Their hands were stiff when they arrived.

"Perhaps we wouldn't make ourselves ashamed in front of you if we asked to remove a little something from your fire?" they said when they arrived, but they got no response. And then the tribes cursed in their thoughts. Already their language had become different from that of Jaguar Quitze, Jaguar Night, Mahucutah, and True Jaguar.

"Alas! We left our language behind. How did we do it? We're lost! Where were we deceived? We had only one language when we came to Tulan, and we had only one place of emergence and origin. We haven't done well," said all the tribes beneath the trees and bushes.

And then a person showed himself before Jaguar Quitze, Jaguar Night, Mahucutah, and True Jaguar, and he spoke as a messenger of Xibalba:

"Truly, since you have your god, your nurturer, and he is the representation, the commemoration of your Maker and your Modeler, don't give the tribes their fire until they give something to Tohil. You don't want them to give anything to *you*. You must ask for what belongs to Tohil; to *him* must come what they give in order to get fire," said the Xibalban. He had wings like the wings of a bat.

"I am a messenger of those who made you and modeled you," said the Xibalban. So now they were happy; now they thought all the more of Tohil, Auilix, and Hacauitz. When the Xibalban had spoken he made himself vanish right in front of them, without delay.

And so again the tribes arrived, again done in by the cold.

Thick were the white hail, the blackening storm, and the white crystals. The cold was incalculable. They were simply overwhelmed. Because of the cold all the tribes were going along doubled over, groping along when they arrived in the presence of Jaguar Quitze, Jaguar Night, Mahucutah, and True Jaguar. There was great pain in their hearts; they had covetous mouths and covetous faces.

And now they were coming as thieves before Jaguar Quitze, Jaguar Night, Mahucutah, and True Jaguar:

"Wouldn't you take pity on us if we asked to remove a little something from your fire? Wasn't it found and wasn't it revealed that we had just one home and just one mountain when you were made, when you were modeled? So please take pity on us," they said.

"And what would you give us for taking pity on you?" they were asked.

"Well, we'd give you metal," said the tribes.

"We don't want metal," said Jaguar Quitze and Jaguar Night.

"Whatever might you want, if we may ask?" the tribes said then.

"Very well. First we must ask Tohil, and then we'll tell you," they were told next. And then they asked Tohil:

"What should the tribes give you, Tohil? They've come to ask for your fire," said Jaguar Quitze, Jaguar Night, Mahucutah, and True Jaguar.

"Very well. You will tell them:

' "Don't they want to be suckled on their sides and under their arms? Isn't it their heart's desire to embrace me? I, who am Tohil? But if there is no desire, then I'll not give them their fire," says Tohil. "When the time comes, not right now, they'll be suckled on their sides, under their arms," he says to you,' you will say," they were told, Jaguar Quitze, Jaguar Night, Mahucutah, and True Jaguar, and then they spoke the word of Tohil.

"Very well. Let him suckle. And very well, we shall embrace him," said the tribes, when they answered and agreed to the word of Tohil. They made no delay but said "very well" right away, and then they received their fire.

After that they got warm, but there was one group that simply

"THEY'VE COME TO ASK FOR YOUR FIRE": This is a scepter held by a ruler, one of the forms taken by Tahil, the classic Maya antecedent of Tohil. On his forehead he wears an obsidian mirror with a burning torch emerging from it. Sometimes he is shown with a body of human form, except that one leg is a serpent; only his head and the serpent leg are shown here. The drawing is reconstructed from several stucco reliefs at Palenque.

DRAWING BY THE AUTHOR

stole the fire, there in the smoke. This was the Bat House. Calm Snake is the name of the god of the Cakchiquels, but it looks like a bat. They went right past in the smoke then, they sneaked past when they came to get fire. The Cakchiquels didn't ask for their fire. They didn't give themselves up in defeat, but all the other tribes were defeated when they gave themselves up to being suckled on their sides, under their arms.

And this is what Tohil meant by being "suckled": that all the tribes be cut open before him, and that their hearts be removed "through their sides, under their arms." This deed had not yet been attempted when Tohil saw into the middle of it, nor had Jaguar Quitze, Jaguar Night, Mahucutah, and True Jaguar received fiery splendor and majesty.

WHEN THEY CAME AWAY FROM TULAN ZUYUA, they weren't eating. They observed a continuous fast. It was enough that they watch intently for the dawning, that they

175

watch closely for the rising of the sun, taking turns at watching for the great star named daybringer. This one came first before the sun when the sun was born, the new daybringer.

And there, always, they were facing the east, when they were there in the place named Tulan Zuyua. Their gods came from there. It wasn't really here that they received their fiery splendor and their dominion, but rather there that the tribes, great and small, were subjugated and humiliated. When they were cut open before Tohil, all the peoples gave their blood, their gore, their sides, their underarms. Fiery splendor came to them all at once at Tulan, along with great knowledge, and they achieved this in the darkness, in the night.

And now they came away, they tore themselves away from there. Now they left the east:

"Our home is not here. Let's go on until we see where we belong," said Tohil. He actually spoke to them, to Jaguar Quitze, Jaguar Night, Mahucutah, and True Jaguar.

"It remains for you to give thanks, since you have yet to take care of bleeding your ears and passing a cord through your elbows. You must worship. This is your way of giving thanks before your god."

"Very well," they replied, then they bled their ears. They cried in their song about coming from Tulan. They cried in their hearts when they came away, when they made their departure from Tulan:

> "Alas! We won't be here when we see the dawn,
> when the sun is born, when the face of the earth
> is lit,"

they said.

A ND THEN THEY CAME AWAY, JUST CAMPING ON THE ROAD. People were just camping there, each tribe slept and then got up again. And they were always watching for the star, the sign of the day. They kept this sign of the dawn in their hearts when they came away from the east. In unity they passed beyond the place named Great Abyss today.

And then they arrived on top of a mountain there. All the Quiché people got together there, along with the other tribes, and all of them held council there. The name the mountain has today is from when they took counsel together: Place of Advice is the name of the mountain. They got together and identified themselves there:

"Here am I: I am a Quiché person, and you there, you are Tams, this will be your name," the Tams were told. And then the Ilocs were told:

"You are the Ilocs, this will be your name. The three Quichés must not be lost. We are united in our word," they said when they fixed their names.

And then the Cakchiquels were named: their name became Cakchiquels. So, too, with the Rabinals; this became their name. It hasn't been lost today.

And then there are those of the Bird House, as they are named today.

These are the names they named for each other. When they held council there, they were still waiting for the dawning, watching for the appearance of the rising star, the one that came before the sun when it was born.

"When we came away from Tulan, we broke ourselves apart," they told each other.

This is what kept weighing on their hearts, the great pain they went through: there was nothing to eat, nothing to feed on. They were just smelling the tips of their staffs as if they were thinking of eating them, but they weren't eating at all as they came.

And it isn't clear how they crossed over the sea. They crossed over as if there were no sea. They just crossed over on some stones, stones piled up in the sand. And they gave it a name: Rock Rows, Furrowed Sands was their name for the place where they crossed through the midst of the sea. Where the waters divided, they crossed over.

And this is what weighed on their hearts when they took counsel: that they had nothing to eat. They had one beverage to drink, just one atole, which they brought up on the mountain named Place of Advice. And they also brought Tohil, Auilix, and Hacauitz.

Observing a great fast was Jaguar Quitze, with his wife; Great Seahouse is his wife's name.

Likewise doing it was Jaguar Night, with his wife, named Prawn House.

And Mahucutah was also there at the great fast, with his wife, named Hummingbird House, along with True Jaguar, whose wife's name is Macaw House.

So these were the ones who fasted, there in the blackness, in the early dawn. Their sadness was great when they were there on the mountain named Place of Advice today. And their gods spoke there.

A ND THEN TOHIL, ALONG WITH AUILIX AND HACAUITZ, SPOKE TO THEM, to Jaguar Quitze, Jaguar Night, Mahucutah, and True Jaguar:

"Let's just go, let's just get up, let's not stay here. Please give us places to hide. It's nearly dawn. Wouldn't you look pitiful if we became plunder for warriors? Construct places where we can remain yours, you penitents and sacrificers, and give one place to each of us," they said when they spoke.

"Very well. Let's get out and search the forests," they all replied.

After that they packed each one of the gods on their backs.

And then Auilix went into the canyon named Concealment Canyon, as they called it, into the great canyon in the forest. Pauilix is the name of the place today. He was left there, placed in the canyon by Jaguar Night, coming first in the sequence of placements.

And then Hacauitz was placed above a great red river. Hacauitz is the name of the mountain today, and it became their citadel. So the god Hacauitz remained there, and Mahucutah stayed with his god. This was the second god to be hidden by them. Hacauitz didn't stay in the forest. It was on a bare mountain that Hacauitz was hidden.

THE MOUNTAIN IS CALLED PATOHIL TODAY: A divination in progress on top of Patohil. At left is the client, Lucas Pacheco, himself a daykeeper; the basket and bundle near him contain various sacred stones from his household altar. At right is the paraphernalia of the daykeeper who is divining for him, set up for a counting of days. Burning in the background are offerings of candles and copal; the smoke of the copal may be seen behind the head of don Lucas and at the extreme right.

And then came Jaguar Quitze. He arrived in the great forest there. Tohil was put into hiding by Jaguar Quitze; the mountain is called Patohil today. Then they gave Concealment Canyon an epithet: Tohil Medicine. Masses of serpents and masses of jaguars, rattlesnakes, yellowbites were there in the forest where he was hidden by the penitents and sacrificers.

So they were there in unity: Jaguar Quitze, Jaguar Night, Mahucutah, and True Jaguar. In unity they waited for the dawn, there on top of the mountain named Hacauitz.

Also, a short distance away, was the god of the Tams, together with the Ilocs. Tam Tribe is the name of the place where the god of the Tams was, there at the dawn. Net Weave Tribe is the name of the place where dawn came for the Ilocs. The god of the Ilocs was just a short distance away.

Also there were all the Rabinals, Cakchiquels, those of the Bird House, all the tribes, small and great. In unity they stopped there, and in unity they had their dawning there. In unity they waited there for the rising of the great star named daybringer.

"It will rise before the sun when the dawn comes," they said, and they were in unity there: Jaguar Quitze, Jaguar Night, Mahucutah, and True Jaguar. There was no sleep, no rest for them. They cried their hearts and their guts out, there at the dawning and clearing, and so they looked terrible. Great sorrow, great anguish came over them; they were marked by their pain. They just stayed that way.

"Coming here hasn't been sweet for us. Alas! If we could only see the birth of the sun! What have we done? We all had one identity, one mountain, but we sent ourselves into exile," they said when they talked among themselves. They talked about sorrow, about anguish, about crying and wailing, since their hearts had not yet been set to rest by the dawn.

And these are the ones who did feel settled there: the gods who were in the canyons, in the forests, just out in the bromelias, in the hanging mosses, not yet set on pedestals. At first, Tohil, Auilix, and Hacauitz actually spoke. The greatness of their day and the greatness of their breath of spirit set them above all the other tribal gods. Their genius was manifold and their ways were manifold, their strategies. They were chilling, they were frightening in their very being and in the hearts of the tribes, whose thoughts were calmed by Jaguar Quitze, Jaguar Night, Mahucutah, and True Jaguar. Their hearts did not yet harbor ill will toward the gods who had been taken up and carried away when they all came from Tulan Zuyua, there in the east, and who were now in the forest.

These were the dawning places: Patohil, Pauilix, and Hacauitz, as they are called today. And this is where our grandfathers, our fathers had their sowing, their dawning.

This is what we shall explain next: the dawning and showing of the sun, moon, and stars.

A ND HERE IS THE DAWNING AND SHOWING OF THE SUN, MOON, AND STARS. And Jaguar Quitze, Jaguar Night, Mahucutah, and True Jaguar were overjoyed when they saw the daybringer. It came up first. It looked brilliant when it came up, since it was ahead of the sun.

After that they unwrapped their copal incense, which came from the east, and there was triumph in their hearts when they unwrapped it. They gave their heartfelt thanks with three kinds at once:

Mixtam Copal is the name of the copal brought by Jaguar Quitze.

Cauiztan Copal, next, is the name of the copal brought by Jaguar Night.

Godly Copal, as the next one is called, was brought by Mahucutah.

The three of them had their copal, and this is what they burned as they incensed the direction of the rising sun. They were crying sweetly as they shook their burning copal, the precious copal.

After that they cried because they had yet to see and yet to witness the birth of the sun.

And then, when the sun came up, the animals, small and great, were happy. They all came up from the rivers and canyons; they waited on all the mountain peaks. Together they looked toward the place where the sun came out.

So then the puma and jaguar cried out, but the first to cry out was a bird, the parrot by name. All the animals were truly happy. The eagle, the white vulture, small birds, great birds spread their wings, and the penitents and sacrificers knelt down. They were overjoyed, together with the penitents and sacrificers of the Tams, the Ilocs.

And the Rabinals, Cakchiquels, those of the Bird House.

And the Sweatbath House, Talk House, Quiba House, those of the Yoke House.

And the Yaqui Sovereign—however many tribes there may be

today. There were countless peoples, but there was just one dawn for all tribes.

And then the face of the earth was dried out by the sun. The sun was like a person when he revealed himself. His face was hot, so he dried out the face of the earth. Before the sun came up it was soggy, and the face of the earth was muddy before the sun came up. And when the sun had risen just a short distance he was like a person, and his heat was unbearable. Since he revealed himself only when he was born, it is only his reflection that now remains. As they put it in their own words:

"The sun that shows itself is not the real sun."

And then, all at once, Tohil, Auilix, and Hacauitz were turned to stone, along with the idols of the puma, jaguar, rattlesnake, yellowbite, which the White Sparkstriker took with him into the trees. Everywhere, all of them became stone when the sun, moon, and stars appeared. Perhaps we would have no relief from the voracious animals today—the puma, jaguar, rattlesnake, yellowbite—and perhaps it wouldn't even be our day today, if the original animals hadn't been turned to stone by the sun when he came up.

There was great happiness in the hearts of Jaguar Quitze, Jaguar Night, Mahucutah, and True Jaguar. They were overjoyed when it dawned. The people on the mountain of Hacauitz were not yet numerous; just a few were there. Their dawning was there and they burned copal there, incensing the direction of the rising sun. They came from there: it is their own mountain, their own plain. Those named Jaguar Quitze, Jaguar Night, Mahucutah, and True Jaguar came from there, and they began their increase on that mountain.

And that became their citadel, since they were there when the sun, moon, and stars appeared, when it dawned and cleared on the face of the earth, over everything under the sky.

A ND THERE BEGAN THEIR SONG NAMED "THE BLAME IS OURS." They sang out the lament of their very hearts and guts. In their song they stated:

"Alas!
We were lost at Tulan!
We shattered ourselves!
We left our elder brothers behind!
Our younger brothers!
Where did they see the sun?
Where must they be staying,
now that the dawn has come?"

They were speaking of the penitents and sacrificers who were the Yaqui people.

"Even though Tohil is his name, he is the same as the god of the Yaqui people, who is named Yolcuat and Quitzalcuat. When we divided, there at Tulan, at Zuyua, they left with us, and they shared our identity when we came away," they said among themselves when they remembered their faraway brothers, elder and younger, the Yaqui people whose dawn was there in the place named Mexico today.

And again, there were also the Fishkeeper people. They stayed there in the east; Sovereign Oloman is their name.

"We left them behind," they said. It was a great weight on their hearts, up there on Hacauitz. The Tams and Ilocs did likewise, except that they were in the forest. Tam Tribe is the name of the place where it dawned for the penitents and sacrificers of the Tams, with their god, the same Tohil. There was just one name for the god of all three divisions of the Quiché people.

And again, the name of the god of the Rabinals was the same. His name was only slightly changed; "One Toh" is the way the name of the god of the Rabinals is spoken. They say it that way, but it is meant to be in agreement with the Quichés and with their language.

And the language has differentiated in the case of the Cakchiquels, since their god had a different name when they came away from Tulan Zuyua. Calm Snake is the name of the god of the Bat House, and they speak a different language today. Along with their god, the lineages took their names; they are called Keeper of the Bat Mat and Keeper of the Dancer Mat. Like their god, their language was differentiated on account of a stone,

AND NOW THEY BOWED DOWN BEFORE THEIR STONES, THERE IN THE FOREST: Before a stone image on the mountain of Turcah in Chichicastenango, Andrés Xiloj offers tallow candles.

---

when they came from Tulan in the darkness. All the tribes were sown and came to light in unity, and each division was allocated a name for its god.

And now we shall tell about their stay and their sojourn there on the mountain. The four were there together, the ones named Jaguar Quitze, Jaguar Night, Mahucutah, and True Jaguar. Their hearts cried out to Tohil, Auilix, and Hacauitz, who were now amid the bromelias and hanging mosses.

A ND HERE THEY BURN THEIR COPAL, and here also is the origin of the masking of Tohil.

And when they went before Tohil and Auilix, they went to

184

visit them and keep their day. Now they gave thanks before them for the dawning, and now they bowed down before their stones, there in the forest. Now it was only a manifestation of his genius that spoke when the penitents and sacrificers came before Tohil, and what they brought and burned was not great. All they burned before their gods was resin, just bits of pitchy bark, along with marigolds.

And when Tohil spoke now it was only his genius. When the gods taught procedures to the penitents and sacrificers, they said this when they spoke:

"This very place has become our mountain, our plain. Now that we are yours, our day and our birth have become great, because all the peoples are yours, all the tribes. And since we are still your companions, even in your citadel, we shall give you procedures:

"Do not reveal us to the tribes when they search for us. They are truly numerous now, so don't you let us be hunted down, but rather give the creatures of the grasses and grains to us, such as the female deer and female birds. Please come give us a little of their blood, take pity on us. And leave the pelts of the deer apart, save them. These are for disguises, for deception. They will become deer costumes, and so also they will serve as our surrogates before the tribes. When you are asked:

'Where is Tohil?' then you will display the deer costumes before them, and without revealing yourselves. And there is still more for you to do. You will become great in your very being. Defeat all the tribes. They must bring blood and lymph before us, they must come to embrace us. They belong to us already," said Tohil, Auilix, and Hacauitz. They had a youthful appearance when they saw them, when they came to burn offerings before them.

So then began the hunting of the young of all the birds and deer; they were taken in the hunt by the penitents and sacrificers.

And when they got hold of the birds and fawns, they would then go to anoint the mouth of the stone of Tohil or Auilix with the blood of the deer or bird. And the bloody drink was drunk by the gods. The stone would speak at once when the penitents and sacrificers arrived, when they went to make their burnt offerings.

They did the very same thing before the deerskins: they burned resin, and they also burned marigolds and yarrow. There was a deerskin for each one of the gods, which was displayed there on the mountain.

They didn't occupy their houses during the day, but just walked in the mountains. And this was their food: just the larva of the yellow jacket, the larva of the wasp, and the larva of the bee, which they hunted. As yet there wasn't anything good to eat or good to drink. Also, it wasn't obvious how to get to their houses, nor was it obvious where their wives stayed.

And the tribes were already densely packed, settling down one by one, with each division of a tribe gathering itself together. Now they were crowding the roads; already their roadways were obvious.

As for Jaguar Quitze, Jaguar Night, Mahucutah, and True Jaguar, it wasn't obvious where they were. When they saw the people of the tribes passing by on the roads, that was when they would get up on the mountain peaks, just crying out with the cry of the coyote and the cry of the fox. And they would make the cries of the puma and jaguar, whenever they saw the tribes out walking in numbers. The tribes were saying:

"It's just a coyote crying out," and "Just a fox."

"Just a puma. Just a jaguar."

In the minds of all the tribes, it was as if humans weren't involved. They did it just as a way of decoying the tribes; that was what their hearts desired. They did it so that the tribes wouldn't get really frightened just yet; that was what they intended when they cried out with the cry of the puma and the cry of the jaguar. And then, when they saw just one or two people out walking, they intended to overwhelm them.

Each day, when they came back to their houses and wives, they brought just the same things—yellow-jacket larvae, wasp larvae, and bee larvae—and gave them to their wives, each day. And when they went before Tohil, Auilix, and Hacauitz, they thought to themselves:

"They are Tohil, Auilix, and Hacauitz, yet we only give them the blood of deer and birds, we only draw cords through our ears and elbows when we ask for our strength and our manhood from Tohil, Auilix, and Hacauitz. Who will take care of the death of the tribes? Should we just kill them one by one?" they said among themselves.

And when they went before Tohil, Auilix, and Hacauitz, they drew cords through their ears and elbows in front of the gods. They spilled their blood, they poured gourdfuls into the mouths of the stones. But these weren't really stones: each one became like a boy when they arrived, happy once again over the blood.

And then came a further sign as to what the penitents and sacrificers should do:

"You must win a great many victories. Your right to do this came from over there at Tulan, when you brought us here," they were told. Then the matter of the suckling was set forth, at the place called Staggering, and the blood that would result from it, the rainstorm of blood, also became a gift for Tohil, along with Auilix and Hacauitz.

Now here begins the abduction of the people of the tribes by Jaguar Quitze, Jaguar Night, Mahucutah, and True Jaguar.

A ND THEN COMES THE KILLING OF THE TRIBES. This is how they died: when there was just one person out walking, or just two were out walking, it wasn't obvious when they took them away.

After that they went to cut them open before Tohil and Auilix.

After that, when they had offered the blood, the skull would be placed in the road. They would roll it onto the road. So the tribes were talking:

"A jaguar has been eating," was all that was said, because their tracks were like a jaguar's tracks when they did their deed. They did not reveal themselves. Many people were abducted.

It was actually a long time before the tribes came to their senses:

"If it's Tohil and Auilix who are after us, we have only to search for the penitents and sacrificers. We'll follow their tracks to wherever their houses are," said all those of the tribes, when they shared their thoughts among themselves.

After that, they began following the tracks of the penitents and sacrificers, but they weren't clear. They only saw the tracks of the deer, the tracks of the jaguar. The tracks weren't clear, nothing was clear. Where they began the tracks were merely those of animals. It was as if the tracks were there for the sole purpose of leading them astray. The way was not clear:

It would get cloudy.

It would get dark and rainy.

It would get muddy, too.

It would get misty and drizzly.

That was all the tribes could see in front of them, and their search would simply make them weary at heart. Then they would give up.

Because Tohil, Auilix, and Hacauitz were great in their very being, they did this for a long time, there on the mountain. They did their killing on the frontiers of the tribes when the abductions began; they singled them out and cut them down. They would seize the people of the tribes in the roads, cutting them open before Tohil, Auilix, and Hacauitz.

And the boys hid there on the mountain. Tohil, Auilix, and Hacauitz had the appearance of three boys when they went out walking; these were simply the spirit familiars of the stones. There was a river. They would bathe there on the bank, just as a way of revealing themselves, and this gave the place its name. The name of the river came to be Tohil's Bath, and the tribes saw them there many times. They would vanish the moment they were seen by the tribes.

Then the news spread as to the whereabouts of Jaguar Quitze, Jaguar Night, Mahucutah, and True Jaguar, and this is when the tribes realized how they were being killed.

F IRST THE TRIBES TRIED TO PLAN THE DEFEAT OF TOHIL, AUILIX, AND HACAUITZ. All the penitents and sacrificers of the tribes spoke to the others. They roused and summoned one another, all of them. Not even one or two divisions were left out. All of them converged and presented themselves, then they shared their thoughts. And they said, as they questioned one another:

"What would assure the defeat of the Cauecs, the Quiché people? Our vassals have met their ends because of them. Isn't it clear that our people have been lost because of them? What if they finish us off with these abductions?"

"Let it be this way: if the fiery splendor of Tohil, Auilix, and Hacauitz is so great, then let this Tohil become our god! Let him be captured! Don't let them defeat us completely! Don't we constitute a multitude of people? And as for the Cauecs, there aren't as many of them," they said when all of them had assembled. Then the Fishkeepers spoke to the tribes, saying:

"Who could be bathing every day at the river bank? If it's Tohil, Auilix, and Hacauitz, then we can defeat them ahead of time. Let the defeat of the penitents and sacrificers begin right there!" said the Fishkeepers, and then they spoke further:

"How shall we defeat them?" And then they said:

"Let this be our means for defeating them: since they present the appearance of adolescent boys at the river, let two maidens go there. Let them be in full blossom, maidens who radiate preciousness, so that when they go they'll be desirable," they said.

"Very well. So we'll just search for two perfect maidens," the others replied. And then they searched among their daughters for those who were truly radiant maidens. Then they gave the maidens instructions:

"You must go, our dear daughters. Go wash clothes at the river, and if you should see three boys, undress yourselves in front of them. And if their hearts should desire you, you will titillate them. When they say to you:

'We're coming after you,' then you are to say:

'Yes.' And then you will be asked:

189

'Where do you come from? Whose daughters are you?' When they say that, you are to answer them:

'We are the daughters of lords, so let a sign be forthcoming from you.' Then they should give you something. If they like your faces you must really give yourselves up to them. And if you do not give yourselves up, then we shall kill you. We'll feel satisfied when you bring back a sign, since we'll think of it as proof that they came after you," said the lords, instructing the two maidens.

Here are their names: Xtah is the name of the one maiden, and Xpuch is the name of the other.

ND THEY SENT THE TWO OF THEM, NAMED XTAH AND XPUCH, over to the place where Tohil, Auilix, and Hacauitz bathed. All the tribes knew about this.

And then they went off. They were dressed up, looking truly beautiful, when they went to the place where Tohil bathed. They were carrying what looked like their wash when they went off. Now the lords were pleased over having sent their two daughters there.

And when they arrived at the river, they began to wash. They undressed themselves, both of them. They were on the rocks, on their hands and knees, when Tohil, Auilix, and Hacauitz came along. They got to the bank of the river and just barely glanced at the two maidens washing there, and the maidens got a sudden scare when Tohil and the others arrived. They did not go lusting after the two maidens. Then came the questioning:

"Where do you come from?" the two maidens were asked. "What do you intend by coming here, to the bank of our river?" they were also asked.

"We were sent here by the lords, so we came. The lords told us:

'Go see the faces of Tohil and the others, and speak to them,' the lords told us, 'and also, there must come a sign as to whether you really saw their faces. Go!' is what we were told," said the two maidens, explaining their errand.

But this is what the tribes had intended: that the maidens should be violated by the spirit familiars of Tohil and the others. Then Tohil, Auilix, and Hacauitz spoke, answering the two maidens named Xtah and Xpuch:

"Good. Let a sign of our word go with you. But you must wait for it, then give it directly to the lords," they were told.

And then Tohil and the others plotted with the penitents and sacrificers. Jaguar Quitze, Jaguar Night, and Mahucutah were told:

"You must draw figures on three cloaks. Inscribe them with the signs of our being. They're for the tribes; they'll go back with the maidens who are washing. Give them to the maidens," Jaguar Quitze, Jaguar Night, and Mahucutah were told.

After that, they drew figures for all three of them. Jaguar Quitze drew first: his image was that of the jaguar. He drew it on his cloak.

And as for Jaguar Night, he drew the image of an eagle on his cloak.

And the one who drew next was Mahucutah, who drew the images, the figures of swarms of yellow jackets, swarms of wasps on his cloak. Then the figures were complete; they had drawn all three of them, the threefold figures.

After that, when Jaguar Quitze, Jaguar Night, and Mahucutah went to give the cloaks to those who were named Xtah and Xpuch, they spoke to them:

"Here is the proof of your word. When you come before the lords you will say:

'Tohil really spoke to us, and here is the sign we've brought back,' you'll tell them, and give them the cloaks to try on," the maidens were told when they were given their instructions.

So then they went back, taking the figured cloaks.

And when they arrived, the lords were happy the moment they spotted what they had asked for, hanging from the arms of the maidens.

"Didn't you see the face of Tohil?" they were asked.

"See it we did," said Xtah and Xpuch.

"Very good. You've brought back some sort of sign. Isn't that so?" said the lords, since there seemed to be signs of their sin—

or so thought the lords. So then they were shown the figured cloaks by the maidens: one with a jaguar, one with an eagle, and one with yellow jackets and wasps drawn on the inside, on a smooth surface.

And they loved the way the cloaks looked. They costumed themselves. The jaguar didn't do anything; it was the first figure to be tried on by a lord.

And when another lord costumed himself with the second figured cloak, with the drawing of the eagle, the inside of it just felt good to him. He turned around in front of them, unfurling it in front of all of them.

And then came the third figured cloak to be tried on by a lord; he costumed himself with the one that had yellow jackets and wasps painted inside.

And then he started getting stung by the yellow jackets and wasps. He couldn't endure it, he couldn't stand the stings of the insects. That lord yelled his mouth off over the insects. Mahucutah's figures inside the cloak looked like a mere drawing. It was the third drawing that defeated them.

And then the maidens named Xtah and Xpuch were reprimanded by the lords:

"How did you get these things you brought back? Where did you go to get them, you tricksters!" the maidens were told when they were reprimanded.

Again, all the tribes were defeated because of Tohil. This is what they had intended: that Tohil would be tempted to go after the maidens. It then became the profession of Xtah and Xpuch to bark shins; the tribes continued to think of them as temptresses.

So the defeat of Jaguar Quitze, Jaguar Night, and Mahucutah was not brought about, since they were people of genius.

And then all the tribes plotted again:

"How are we going to beat them? They are truly great in their very being," they said when they shared their thoughts.

"Even so, we'll invade them and kill them. Let's fit ourselves out with weapons and shields. Aren't we a multitude? There won't even be one or two of them left," they said when they shared their thoughts. All the tribes fitted themselves out. There were masses of killers, once the killers of all the tribes had joined together.

And as for Jaguar Quitze, Jaguar Night, Mahucutah, and True Jaguar, they were there on the mountain. Hacauitz is the name of the mountain where they were, and those spirit boys of theirs were hidden there on the mountain. They were not a numerous people then; their numbers were not equal to the numbers of the tribes. There were just a few of them on the mountain, their fortress, so when it was said that the tribes had planned death for them, all of them gathered together. They held a council; they all sent for one another.

AND HERE IS THE JOINING TOGETHER OF ALL THE TRIBES, all decked out now with weapons and shields. Their metal ornaments were countless, they looked beautiful, all the lords, the men. In truth, they were just making talk, all of them. In truth, they would become our captives.

"Since there is a Tohil, and since he is a god, let's celebrate his day—or let's make him our prize!" they said among themselves. But Tohil already knew about it, and Jaguar Quitze, Jaguar Night, and Mahucutah also knew about it. They had heard about it while it was being plotted, since they were neither asleep nor at rest.

So then all the lance-bearing warriors of the tribes were armed.

After that, all the warriors got up during the night, in order to enter our very midst. They set off, but they never arrived. They just fell asleep on the way, all those warriors.

And then they were defeated again by Jaguar Quitze, Jaguar Night, and Mahucutah, since every last one of them fell asleep in the road. Now they couldn't feel a thing. A multitude slept, all of them, and that's when things got started. Their eyebrows were plucked out, along with their beards.

And then the metal was undone from their cloaks, along with their headdresses.

And their necklaces came off too, and then the necks of their staffs. Their metal was taken just to cause them a loss of face, and the plucking was done just to signify the greatness of the Quiché.

After that, they woke up. Right away they reached for their headdresses, along with the necks of their staffs. There was no metal on their cloaks and headdresses.

"How could it have been taken from us? Who could have plucked us? Where did they come from? Our metal has been stolen!" said all the warriors.

"Perhaps it's those tricksters who've been abducting people! But it's not over with. Let's not get frightened by them. Let's enter their very citadel! That's the only way we'll ever see our metal and make it ours again!" said all the tribes, but even so, they were just making talk, all of them.

The hearts of the penitents and sacrificers were content, there on the mountain, but even so, Jaguar Quitze, Jaguar Night, Mahucutah, and True Jaguar were making great plans.

A ND THEN JAGUAR QUITZE, JAGUAR NIGHT, MAHUCUTAH, AND TRUE JAGUAR HAD A PLAN. They made a fence at the edge of their citadel. They just made a palisade of planks and stakes around their citadel.

Next they made manikins; it was as if they had made people. Next they lined them up on the parapet. They were even equipped with weapons and shields. Headdresses were included, with metal on top, and cloaks were included. But they were mere manikins, mere woodcarvings. They used the metal that belonged to the tribes, which they had gone to get in the road. This is what they used to decorate the manikins. They surrounded the citadel.

And then they asked Tohil about their plan:

"What if we die, and what if we're defeated?" They spoke straight from their hearts before Tohil.

"Do not grieve. I am here. And here is what you will use on them. Do not be afraid," Jaguar Quitze, Jaguar Night, Mahucutah, and True Jaguar were told, and then the matter of the yellow jackets and wasps was set out.

And when they had gone to get these insects and come back with them, they put them inside four large gourds, which were placed all around the citadel. The yellow jackets and wasps were shut inside the gourds. These were their weapons against the tribes.

And they were spied upon and watched from hiding; their citadel was studied by the messengers of the tribes.

"There aren't many of them," they said, but when they came to look it was only the manikins, the woodcarvings, that were moving, with weapons and shields in their hands. They looked like real people, they looked like real killers when the tribes saw them.

And all the tribes were happy when they saw there weren't many of them. The tribes themselves were in crowds; there were countless people, warriors and killers, the assassins of Jaguar Quitze, Jaguar Night, and Mahucutah, who were there on the mountain called Hacauitz. This is where they were when they were invaded. Here we shall tell about it.

A ND THESE ARE THE ONES WHO WERE THERE: JAGUAR QUITZE, JAGUAR NIGHT, MAHUCUTAH, AND TRUE JAGUAR. They were in unity on the mountain with their wives and children.

And then all the warriors came, the killers, and it was nothing less than eight hundred score, or even thirty times eight hundred people who surrounded the citadel. They were bellowing, bristling with weapons and shields, rending their mouths with howling and growling, bellowing, yelling, whistling through their hands when they came up below the citadel. But the penitents and sacrificers had no fear; they just enjoyed the spectacle from the parapet of the stockade. They were lined up with their wives and children. Their hearts were content, since the tribes were merely making talk.

And then they climbed up the mountainside, and now they were just a little short of the edge of the citadel.

And then the gourds were opened up—there were four of them around the citadel—and the yellow jackets and wasps were like a cloud of smoke when they poured out of each of the gourds. And the warriors were done in, with the insects landing on their eyes and landing on their noses, on their mouths, their legs, their arms. The insects went after them wherever they were, they overtook them wherever they were. There were yellow jackets and wasps everywhere, landing to sting their eyes. They had to watch out for whole swarms of them, there were insects going after every single person. They were dazed by the yellow jackets and wasps. No longer able to hold onto their weapons and shields, they were doubling over and falling to the ground, stumbling. They fell down the mountainside.

And now they couldn't feel a thing when they were hit with arrows and cut with axes. Now Jaguar Quitze and Jaguar Night could even use sticks; even their wives became killers.

Then the Fishkeepers turned away, and all the other tribes just took off running. The first to be overtaken were finished off, killed, and it wasn't just a few people who died. For those who didn't die the chase was carried into their very midst when the insects caught up with them. There were no manly deeds for them to do, since they no longer carried weapons and shields.

Then all the tribes were conquered. Now the tribes humbled themselves before Jaguar Quitze, Jaguar Night, and Mahucutah:

"Take pity on us! Don't kill us!" they said.

"Very well. Although you were destined to join the dead, you will be payers of tribute for as long as there are days and as long as there is light," they were told.

Such was the defeat of all the tribes by our first mother-fathers. It was done there on the mountain named Hacauitz today. This is where they first began. They grew, they multiplied, they had daughters, they had sons on Hacauitz. They were happy, once they had beaten all the tribes, who were defeated there on the mountain.

In this way they accomplished the defeat of the tribes, all the tribes.

After that, their hearts were content. They informed their sons that their death was approaching. They very much intended to be taken by death.

N OW THIS IS WHERE WE SHALL TELL ABOUT THE DEATH OF JAGUAR QUITZE, JAGUAR NIGHT, MAHUCUTAH, AND TRUE JAGUAR, as they are named. Since they knew about their death and disappearance, they left instructions with their sons. They weren't sickly yet, they weren't gasping for breath when they left their word with their sons.

These are the names of their sons:

Jaguar Quitze begot these two: Cocaib was the name of the firstborn and Cocauib was the name of the second of the sons of Jaguar Quitze, the grandfather and father of the Cauecs.

And again, Jaguar Night begot two. These are their names: Coacul was the name of his first son, and the other was called Coacutec, the second son of Jaguar Night, of the Greathouses.

And Mahucutah begot just one son, named Coahau.

These three had sons, but True Jaguar had no son. They were all true penitents and sacrificers, and these are the names of their sons, with whom they left instructions. They were united, the four of them together. They sang of the pain in their hearts, they cried their hearts out in their singing. "The Blame Is Ours" is the name of the song they sang.

And then they advised their sons:

"Our dear sons: we are leaving. We are going back. We have enlightened words, enlightened advice to leave with you—and with you who have come from faraway mountains, our dear wives," they told their wives. They advised each one of them:

"We are going back to our own tribal place. Again it is the

197

time of our Lord Deer, as is reflected in the sky. We have only to make our return. Our work has been done, our day has been completed. Since you know this, neither forget us nor put us aside. You have yet to see your own home and mountain, the place of your beginning.

"Let it be this way: you must go. Go see the place where we came from," were the words they spoke when they gave their advice.

And then Jaguar Quitze left a sign of his being:

"This is for making requests of me. I shall leave it with you. Here is your fiery splendor. I have completed my instructions, my counsel," he said when he left the sign of his being, the Bundle of Flames, as it is called. It wasn't clear just what it was; it was wound about with coverings. It was never unwrapped. Its sewing wasn't clear because no one looked on while it was being wrapped.

In this way they left instructions, and then they disappeared from there on the mountain of Hacauitz. Their wives and children never saw them again. The nature of their disappearance was not clear. But whatever the case with their disappearance, their instructions were clear, and the bundle became precious to those who remained. It was a memorial to their fathers. Immediately they burned offerings before this memorial to their fathers.

When the lords began their generation of the people, the Cauecs took their start from Jaguar Quitze, the grandfather and father; his sons, named Cocaib and Cocauib, were not lost.

Such was the death of all four of our first grandfathers and fathers. When they disappeared their sons remained there on the mountain of Hacauitz; their sons stayed there for awhile. As for all the tribes, it was now their day to be broken and downtrodden. They no longer had any splendor to them, though they were still numerous.

All those on Hacauitz gathered on each day that was for the remembrance of their fathers. For them, the day of the bundle was a great one. They could not unwrap it; for them it stayed bundled—the Bundle of Flames, as they called it. It was given this epithet, this name when it was left in their keeping by their fathers, who made it just as a sign of their being.

Such was the disappearance and loss of Jaguar Quitze, Jaguar Night, Mahucutah, and True Jaguar, the first people to come across the sea, from the east. They came here in ancient times. When they died they were already old. They had a reputation for penitence and sacrifice.

PART
FIVE

A ND THEN THEY REMEMBERED WHAT HAD BEEN SAID ABOUT
THE EAST. This is when they remembered the instructions of their fathers. The ancient things received from their fathers were not lost. The tribes gave them their wives, becoming
their fathers-in-law as they took wives. And there were three of
them who said, as they were about to go away:

"We are going to the east, where our fathers came from," they
said, then they followed their road. The three of them were representative sons:

Cocaib was the name of the son of Jaguar Quitze who represented all the Cauecs.

Coacutec was the name of the son of Jaguar Night who served
as the sole representative of the Greathouses.

Coahau was the name of the only son of Mahucutah, representing the Lord Quichés.

So these are the names of those who went across the sea.
There were only three who went, but they had skill and knowledge. Their being was not quite that of mere humans. They advised all their brothers, elder and younger, who were left
behind. They were glad to go:

"We're not dying. We're coming back," they said when they
went, yet it was these same three who went clear across the sea.

And then they arrived in the east; they went there to receive
lordship. Next comes the name of the lord with dominion over
those of the east, where they arrived.

A ND THEN THEY CAME BEFORE THE LORD NAMED NACXIT,
the great lord and sole judge over a populous domain.
And he was the one who gave out the signs of lordship, all the
emblems; the signs of the Keeper of the Mat and the Keeper of
the Reception House Mat were set forth.

And when the signs of the splendor and lordship of the Keeper of the Mat and Keeper of the Reception House Mat were set forth, Nacxit gave a complete set of the emblems of lordship. Here are their names:

Canopy, throne.

Bone flute, bird whistle.

Paint of powdered yellow stone.

Puma's paw, jaguar's paw.

Head and hoof of deer.

Bracelet of rattling snail shells.

Gourd of tobacco.

Nosepiece.

Parrot feathers, heron feathers.

They brought all of these when they came away. From across the sea, they brought back the writings about Tulan. In the writings, in their words, they spoke of having cried.

And then, when they got back up in their citadel, named Hacauitz, all the Tams and Ilocs gathered there. All the tribes gathered themselves together; they were happy. When Cocaib, Coacutec, and Coahau came back, they resumed their lordship over the tribes. The Rabinals, the Cakchiquels, and those of the Bird House were happy. Only the signs of the greatness of lordship were revealed before them. Now the lords became great in their very being; when they had displayed their lordship previously, it was incomplete.

This was when they were at Hacauitz. The only ones with them were all those who had originally come from the east. And they spent a long time there on that mountain. Now they were all numerous.

And the wives of Jaguar Quitze, Jaguar Night, and Mahucutah died there. Then they came away, they left their mountain place behind. They sought another mountain where they could settle. They settled countless mountains, giving them epithets and names. Our first mothers and our first fathers multiplied and gained strength at those places, according to what the people of ancient times said when they told about the abandonment of their first citadel, named Hacauitz.

ND THEN THEY CAME TO A PLACE WHERE THEY FOUNDED A CITADEL NAMED THORNY PLACE. They spent a long time there in that one citadel. They had daughters and sons while they were there. There were actually four mountains, but there came to be a single name for the whole town. Their daughters and sons got married. They just gave them away. They accepted mere favors and gifts as sufficient payment for their daughters. They did only what was good.

Then they examined each division of the citadel. Here are the names of the divisions of Thorny Place: Dry Place, Bark House, Culba, Cauinal are the names of the mountains where they stayed.

And this is when they looked out over the mountains of their citadel. They were seeking a further mountain, since all the divisions had become more numerous. But those who had brought lordship from the east had died by now; they had become old in the process of going from one citadel to another. But their faces did not die; they passed them on.

They went through a great deal of pain and affliction; it was a long time before the grandfathers and fathers found their citadel. Here is the name of the citadel where they arrived.

ND BEARDED PLACE IS THE NAME OF THE MOUNTAIN OF THEIR CITADEL. They stayed there and they settled down there.

And they tested their fiery splendor there. They ground their gypsum, their plaster, in the fourth generation of lords. It was said that Conache ruled when Nine Deer was the Lord Minister, and then the lords named Cotuha and Iztayul reigned as Keeper of the Mat and Keeper of the Reception House Mat. They reigned there at Bearded Place. It was through their works that it became an excellent citadel.

The number of great houses only reached three, there at

Bearded Place. There were not yet a score and four great houses, but only three of them:

Just one Cauec great house.

And just one great house for the Greathouses.

And finally, just one for the Lord Quichés.

But the three were housed in just two buildings, one in each of the two divisions of the citadel.

This is the way it was when they were at Bearded Place:

They were of just one mind: there was no evil for them, nor were there difficulties.

Their reign was all in calm: there were no quarrels for them, and no disturbances.

Their hearts were filled with a steady light: there was nothing of stupidity and nothing of envy in what they did.

Their splendor was modest: they caused no amazement, nor had they grown great.

And then they tested themselves. They excelled in the Shield Dance, there at Bearded Place. They did it as a sign of their sovereignty. It was a sign of their fiery splendor and a sign of their greatness.

When it was seen by the Ilocs, the Ilocs began to foment war. It was their desire that the Lord Cotuha be murdered, and that the other lord be allied with them. It was the Lord Iztayul they wanted to persuade; the Ilocs wanted him as their disciple in committing murder. But their jealous plotting behind the back of the Lord Cotuha failed to work out. They just wanted it over with, but the lord wasn't killed by the Ilocs on the first try.

Such were the roots of disturbances, of tumult and war. First they invaded the citadel, the killers were on the move. What they wanted was to obliterate the very identity of the Quichés. Only then, they thought, could they alone have sovereignty, and it was for this alone that they came to kill. They were captured and they were made prisoners. Not many of them ever got their freedom again.

And then began the cutting of flesh. They cut the Ilocs open before the gods. This was in payment for their wrongs against Lord Cotuha. And many others went into bondage; they were made into slaves and serfs. They had simply given themselves up in defeat by fomenting war against the lord and against the canyon and the citadel. What their hearts had desired was the destruction and disintegration of the very identity of the Quiché lord, but it did not come to pass.

In this way it came about that people were cut open before the gods. The shields of war were made then; it was the very beginning of the fortification of the citadel at Bearded Place. The root of fiery splendor was implanted there, and because of it the reign of the Quiché lords was truly great. They were lords of singular genius. There was nothing to humble them; nothing happened to make fools of them or to ruin the greatness of their reign, which took root there at Bearded Place.

The penance done for the gods increased there, striking terror again, and all the tribes were terrified, small tribes and great tribes. They witnessed the arrival of people captured in war, who were cut open and killed for the splendor and majesty of Lord Cotuha and Lord Iztayul, along with the Greathouses and the Lord Quichés. There were only three branches of kin there at the citadel named Bearded Place.

And it was also there that they began feasting and drinking over the blossoming of their daughters. This was the way those who were called the "Three Great Houses" stayed together. They drank their drinks there and ate their corn there, the payment for their sisters, payment for their daughters. There was only happiness in their hearts when they did it. They ate, they feasted inside their palaces.

"This is just our way of being thankful and grateful that we have good news and good tidings. It is the sign of our agreements about the daughters and sons born to our women," they said.

Epithets were bestowed there, and the lineages, the allied tribes, the principalities gave themselves names there.

"We are intermarried: we Cauecs, we Greathouses, and we Lord Quichés," said those of the three lineages and the three great houses. They spent a long time there at Bearded Place, and then they sought again and saw another citadel. They left Bearded Place behind.

AND THEN THEY GOT UP AND CAME TO THE CITADEL OF ROT-
TEN CANE, as the name is spoken by the Quichés. The
Lords Cotuha and Plumed Serpent came along, together with all
the other lords. There had been five changes and five generations
of people since the origin of light, the origin of continuity, the
origin of life and of humankind.

And they built many houses there.

And they also built houses for the gods, putting these in the

AND THEY ALSO BUILT HOUSES FOR THE GODS: Here is one of the pyramids at Iximche, a site whose buildings are far better preserved than those of Rotten Cane. Iximche was built by the Cakchiquels when they ended their allegiance to the Quichés, two generations after the founding of Rotten Cane. On top of the pyramid would have been the temple proper, probably a single room with wood-reinforced adobe walls and a thatched roof. In the background is a long stone-faced platform of the sort that bore palaces. Note the remains of plaster on the pyramid and elsewhere; originally all public buildings, here and at Rotten Cane, were stuccoed and painted, inside and out. Some stucco surfaces bear the traces of polychrome murals.

center of the highest part of the citadel. They came and they stayed.

After that their domain grew larger; they were more numerous and more crowded. Again they planned their great houses, which had to be regrouped and sorted out because of their growing quarrels. They were jealous of one another over the prices of their sisters and daughters, which were no longer a matter of mere food and drink.

So this was the origin of their separation, when they quarreled among themselves, disturbing the bones and skulls of the dead. Then they broke apart into nine lineages, putting an end to quarrels over sisters and daughters. When the planning of the lordships was done, the result was a score and four great houses.

It was a long time ago when they all came up onto their citadel, building a score and four palaces there in the citadel of Rotten Cane. That was the citadel blessed by the lord bishop after it had been abandoned.

They achieved glory there. Their marvelous seats and cushions were arranged; the varieties of splendor were sorted out for each one of the lords of the nine lineages. One by one they took their places:

The nine lords of the Cauecs.

The nine lords of the Greathouses.

The four lords of the Lord Quichés.

The two lords of the Zaquics.

They became numerous. Those who were in the following of a given lord were also numerous, but the lord came first, at the head of his vassals. There were masses, masses of lineages for each of the lords. We shall name the titles of the lords one by one, for each of the great houses.

A ND HERE ARE THE TITLES OF THE LORDS WHO LED THE CAUECS, beginning with the first in rank:

Keeper of the Mat.

Keeper of the Reception House Mat.

Keeper of Tohil.

Keeper of the Plumed Serpent.

Great Toastmaster of the Cauecs.

Councilor of the Stores.

Lolmet Quehnay.

Councilor of the Ball Court.

Mother of the Reception House.

So these are the lords who led the Cauecs, nine lords with

their palaces ranged around, one for each of them. And now to show their faces . . .

A ND NOW THESE ARE THE LORDS WHO LED THE GREAT-HOUSES, beginning with the first lord:
Lord Minister.
Lord Crier to the People.
Minister of the Reception House.
Great Reception House.
Mother of the Reception House.
Great Toastmaster of the Greathouses.
Lord Auilix.
Yacolatam, or Edge of the Zaclatol Mat.
Great Lolmet Yeoltux.
So there were nine lords who led the Greathouses.

A ND NOW THESE ARE THE LORD QUICHÉS. Here are the titles of the lords:
Crier to the People.
Lord Lolmet.
Lord Great Toastmaster of the Lord Quichés.
Lord Hacauitz.
Four lords led the Lord Quichés, with their palaces ranged around.

A ND THERE WERE ALSO TWO LINEAGES OF ZAQUIC LORDS:
Lord Corntassel House.
Minister for the Zaquics.
There was just one palace for these two lords.

Such was the arrangement of the score and four lords, and there came to be a score and four great houses as well.

T HEN SPLENDOR AND MAJESTY GREW AMONG THE QUICHÉ. The greatness and weight of the Quiché reached its full splendor and majesty with the surfacing and plastering of the canyon and citadel. The tribes came, whether small or great and whatever the titles of their lords, adding to the greatness of the Quiché. As splendor and majesty grew, so grew the houses of gods and the houses of lords.

But the lords could not have accomplished it, they could not have done the work of building their houses or the houses of the gods, were it not for the fact that their vassals had become numerous. They neither had to lure them nor did they kidnap them or take them away by force, because each one of them rightfully belonged to the lords. And the elder and younger brothers of the lords also became populous.

Each lord led a crowded life, crowded with petitions. The lords were truly valued and had truly great respect. The birthdays of the lords were made great and held high by their vassals. Those who lived in the canyons and those who lived in the citadels multiplied then. Even so they would not have been numerous, had not all the tribes arrived to give themselves up.

And when war befell their canyons and citadels, it was by means of their genius that the Lord Plumed Serpent and the Lord Cotuha blazed with power. Plumed Serpent became a true lord of genius:

On one occasion he would climb up to the sky; on another he would go down the road to Xibalba.

On another occasion he would be serpentine, becoming an actual serpent.

On yet another occasion he would make himself aquiline, and on another feline; he would become like an actual eagle or a jaguar in his appearance.

On another occasion it would be a pool of blood; he would become nothing but a pool of blood.

Truly his being was that of a lord of genius. All the other lords were fearful before him. The news spread; all the tribal lords heard about the existence of this lord of genius.

And this was the beginning and growth of the Quiché, when the Lord Plumed Serpent made the signs of greatness. His face was not forgotten by his grandsons and sons. He didn't do these things just so there would be one single lord, a being of genius, but they had the effect of humbling all the tribes when he did them. It was just his way of revealing himself, but because of it he became the sole head of the tribes.

This lord of genius named Plumed Serpent was in the fourth generation of lords; he was both Keeper of the Mat and Keeper of the Reception House Mat.

And so he left signs and sayings for the next generation. They achieved splendor and majesty, and they, too, begot sons, making the sons still more populous. Tepepul and Iztayul were begotten; they merely served out their reign, becoming the fifth generation of lords. They begot another generation of lords.

A ND HERE ARE THE NAMES OF THE SIXTH GENERATION OF LORDS. There were two great lords; they were fiery. Quicab was the name of one lord; Cauizimah was the name of the other.

And Quicab and Cauizimah did a great deal in their turn. They added to the greatness of the Quiché because they truly had genius. They crushed and they shattered the canyons and citadels of the tribes, small and great—the ones that had citadels among them in ancient times, nearby:

There was a mountain place of the Cakchiquels, called Above the Nettles today.

And also a mountain place of the Rabinals, Place of Spilt Water.

And a mountain of the Caoques, Plaster House.

And then a citadel of the White Earths, Above the Hot Springs. Under Ten, Before the Building, and Willow Tree.

They all hated Quicab. They made war, but in fact they were brought down, they were shattered, these canyons, these citadels of the Rabinals, Cakchiquels, White Earths. All the tribes went down on their faces or flat on their backs. The warriors of Quicab kept up the killing for a long time, until there were only one or two groups, from among all the enemies, who hadn't brought

A MOUNTAIN OF STONES IS THERE TODAY: A shrine on a flat between San Pedro Jocopilas and Santa Lucía de la Reforma; on the right side of the heap of stones is an altar for burning offerings. This may be the place called Petatayub in the Popol Vuh, where defeated Quiché enemies brought broken stones from their citadels and left them "as a sign of the manhood of Quicab," the mightiest of Quiché kings.

tribute. Their citadels fell and they brought tribute to Quicab and Cauizimah. Their lineages came to be bled, shot full of arrows at the stake. Their day came to nothing, their heritage came to nothing.

Projectiles alone were the means for breaking the citadels. All at once the earth itself would crack open; it was as if a lightning bolt had shattered the stones. In fear, the members of one tribe after another went before the gum tree, carrying in their hands the signs of the citadels, with the result that a mountain of stones

215

is there today. Only a few of these aren't cut stones; the rest look as though they had been split with an axe. The result is there on the flat named Petatayub; it is obvious to this day. Everyone who passes by can see it as a sign of the manhood of Quicab. He could not be killed, nor could he be conquered. He was truly a man, and all the tribes brought tribute.

And then all the lords made plans; they moved to cordon off the canyons and citadels, the fallen citadels of all the tribes.

A FTER THAT CAME THE SENTRIES, to watch for the makers of war. Now lookout lineages were established to occupy the conquered mountains:

"Otherwise the tribes would return to inhabit their citadels," all the lords said when they had all shared their thoughts. Then the assignments were given out:

"Let them be like a palisade to us, and like doubles for our own lineages, and like a stockade, a fortress to us. Let them now become our anger, our manliness," said all the lords. The assignments were given to each of the lineages that were to provide opposition to the makers of war.

And then they were notified, and then they went to their posts, occupying the mountain places of the tribes:

"Go, because these are now our mountains. Do not be afraid. The moment there are makers of war again, coming back among you as your murderers, send for us to come and kill them," Quicab and the Minister and the Crier to the People told them, notifying all of them.

Then they went off, those who are called the Point of the Arrow, Angle of the Bowstring. Their grandfathers and fathers split up then; they were on each of the mountains. They went just as guards of the mountains, and as arrowhead and bowstring guards, and as guards against the makers of war as well. None of them had been there at the dawning nor did any of them have his own god; they just blocked the way to the citadel. They all went out:

Keepers of Above the Nettles, Keepers of Chulimal, White River, Deer Dance Plaza, Plank Place, Eighteen.

Also, Keepers of Earthquake, Meteor, Hunahpu Place.

And Keepers of Spilt Water, Keepers of Cut Rock, Keepers of Plaster House, Keepers of Ziya House, Keepers of Hot Springs, Keepers of Under Ten, of the plains, of the mountains.

The war sentries, the guardians of the land, went out, they went on behalf of Quicab and Cauizimah, Keeper of the Mat and Keeper of the Reception House Mat, and on behalf of the Minister and the Crier to the People. There were four lords who posted messengers and sentries against the makers of war:

Quicab and Cauizimah are the names of the two lords who led the Cauecs.

Quema is the name of the lord who led the Greathouses.

And Armadillo Dung is the name of the lord who led the Lord Quichés.

So these are the names of the lords who posted messengers and couriers. Their own vassals went to the mountains, to each one of the mountains, and as soon as they had gone, spoils kept coming back, and prisoners of war kept coming back to Quicab and Cauizimah, to the Minister and the Crier to the People. The Points of the Arrows and Angles of the Bowstrings made war. They took spoils and prisoners again. There came to be heroes again, among those who were sentries. They were given seats and honored; they were generously remembered by the lords when they came to turn over all their spoils and their prisoners.

After that, when the Lords Keeper of the Mat, Keeper of the Reception House Mat, Minister, and Crier to the People had shared their thoughts, their decision came out:

"When it comes to the ennobling of the lookout lineages, we'll induct only those who are first in rank. I am Keeper of the Mat."

"And I am Keeper of the Reception House Mat."

"The nobility of Keeper of the Mat, which is mine—and that which is yours, Lord Minister—should enter into this. Ministers will be ennobled." And all the lords spoke as they gathered their thoughts. The Tams and Ilocs did just the same; the three divisions of the Quiché were in concord when they carried out the investiture. They titled those of the first rank among their vassals.

In this way the decision was reached. But they weren't inducted at Quiché. The mountain where the first-ranking vassals were inducted has a name; all of them were summoned, from each of the mountains where they were, and they gathered in just one place. Under the Twine, Under the Cord is the name of the mountain where they were inducted, where they entered into nobility. It was done there in Chulimal.

And here are their titles, their honors, and their marks: a score of Ministers and a score of Keepers of the Mat were created by the Keeper of the Mat and the Keeper of the Reception House Mat, and by the Minister and the Crier to the People.

All of these entered the nobility: Ministers, Keepers of the Mat, eleven Great Toastmasters, Minister for the Lords, Minister for the Zaquics, Military Minister, Military Keeper of the Mat, Military Walls, and Military Corners are the titles that came in when the soldiers were titled and named to their seats, their cushions.

These were the first-ranking vassals, watchers and listeners for the Quiché people, Points of the Arrows, Angles of the Bowstrings, a palisade, an enclosure, a wall, a fortress around Quiché.

And the Tams and Ilocs did the same thing; they inducted and titled the first-ranking vassals for each mountain.

So this was the origin of the noble Ministers and Keepers of the Mat that exist for each of the mountains today. The sequence was such that they came out later than the Keeper of the Mat proper and the Keeper of the Reception House Mat, and later than the Minister and the Crier to the People.

A ND NOW WE SHALL NAME THE NAMES OF THE HOUSES OF THE GODS, although the houses have the same names as the gods:

Great Monument of Tohil is the name of the building that housed Tohil of the Cauecs.

Auilix, next, is the name of the building that housed Auilix of the Greathouses.

Hacauitz is the name, then, of the building that housed the god of the Lord Quichés.

Corntassel, whose house of sacrifice can still be seen, is the name of another great monument.

These were the locations of the stones whose days were kept by the Quiché lords. Their days were also kept by all the tribes. When the tribes burned offerings, they came before Tohil first.

After that, they greeted the Keeper of the Mat and Keeper of the Reception House Mat next, then they handed over their quetzal feathers and their tribute to the lords, these same lords.

And so they nurtured and provided for the Keeper of the Mat and Keeper of the Reception House Mat, who had been victorious over their citadels.

They were great lords, they were people of genius. Plumed Serpent and Cotuha were lords of genius, and Quicab and Cauizimah were lords of genius. They knew whether war would occur; everything they saw was clear to them. Whether there would be death, or whether there would be famine, or whether quarrels would occur, they knew it for certain, since there was a place to see it, there was a book. Council Book was their name for it.

But it wasn't only in this way that they were lords. They were great in their own being and observed great fasts. As a way of cherishing their buildings and cherishing their lordship, they fasted for long periods, they did penance before their gods.

And here is their way of fasting:

For nine score days they would fast, and for nine they would do penance and burn offerings.

Thirteen score was another of their fasts, and for thirteen they would do penance and burn offerings before Tohil and their other gods. They would only eat zapotes, matasanos, jocotes; there was nothing made of corn for their meals.

Even if they did penance for seventeen score, then for seventeen they fasted, they did not eat. They achieved truly great abstinence.

This was a sign that they had the being of true lords. And there weren't any women with them when they slept; they kept themselves apart when they fasted. They just stayed in the

GREAT MONUMENT OF TOHIL: This is all that remains of the pyramid of Tohil at Rotten Cane, stripped of its outer masonry during construction in nearby Santa Cruz Quiché. This is the south side; on the east side is an active shrine.

houses of the gods, each day. All they did was keep the days, burn offerings, and do penance. They were there whether it was dark or dawn; they just cried their hearts and their guts out when they asked for light and life for their vassals and their domain. They lifted their faces to the sky, and here is their prayer before their gods, when they made their requests.

ND THIS IS THE CRY OF THEIR HEARTS, here it is:

"Wait! On this blessed day,
thou Hurricane, thou Heart of the Sky-Earth,
thou giver of ripeness and freshness,
and thou giver of daughters and sons,
spread thy stain, spill thy drops
of green and yellow;
give life and beginning
to those I bear and beget,
that they might multiply and grow,

nurturing and providing for thee,
calling to thee along the roads and paths,
on rivers, in canyons,
beneath the trees and bushes;
give them their daughters and sons.

"May there be no blame, obstacle, want or misery;
let no deceiver come behind or before them,
may they neither be snared nor wounded,
nor seduced, nor burned,
nor diverted below the road nor above it;
may they neither fall over backward nor stumble;
keep them on the Green Road, the Green Path.

"May there be no blame or barrier for them
through any secrets or sorcery of thine;
may thy nurturers and providers be good
before thy mouth and thy face,
thou, Heart of Sky; thou, Heart of Earth;
thou, Bundle of Flames;
and thou, Tohil, Auilix, Hacauitz,
under the sky, on the earth,
the four sides, the four corners;
may there be only light, only continuity within,
before thy mouth and thy face, thou god."

So it was with the lords when they fasted during nine score, thirteen score, or seventeen score days; their days of fasting were many. They cried their hearts out over their vassals and over all their wives and children. Each and every lord did service, as a way of cherishing the light of life and of cherishing lordship.

Such were the lordships of the Keeper of the Mat, Keeper of the Reception House Mat, Minister, and Crier to the People. They went into fasting two by two, taking turns at carrying the tribes and all the Quiché people on their shoulders.

At its root the word came from just one place, and the root of nurturing and providing was the same as the root of the word. The Tams and Ilocs did likewise, along with the Rabinals, Cakchiquels, those of the Bird House, Sweatbath House, Talk House.

They came away in unity, having heard, there at Quiché, what all of them should do.

It wasn't merely that they became lords; it wasn't just that they gathered in gifts from nurturers and providers who merely made food and drink for them. Nor did they wantonly falsify or steal their lordship, their splendor, their majesty. And it wasn't merely that they crushed the canyons and citadels of the tribes, whether small or great, but that the tribes paid a great price:

There came turquoise, there came metal.

And there came drops of jade and other gems that measured the width of four fingers or a full fist across.

And there came green and red featherwork, the tribute of all the tribes. It came to the lords of genius Plumed Serpent and Cotuha, and to Quicab and Cauizimah as well, to the Keeper of the Mat, Keeper of the Reception House Mat, Minister, and Crier to the People.

What they did was no small feat, and the tribes they conquered were not few in number. The tribute of Quiché came from many tribal divisions.

And the lords had undergone pain and withstood it; their rise to splendor had not been sudden. Actually it was Plumed Serpent who was the root of the greatness of the lordship.

Such was the beginning of the rise and growth of Quiché.

And now we shall list the generations of lords, and we shall also name the names of all these lords.

A ND HERE ARE THE GENERATIONS, THE SEQUENCES OF LORD-SHIPS, so that all of them will be clear.

Jaguar Quitze, Jaguar Night, Mahucutah, and True Jaguar were our first grandfathers, our first fathers when the sun appeared, when the moon and stars appeared.

And here are the generations, the sequences, of lordships. We shall begin from here, at their very root. The lords will come up two by two, as each generation of lords enters and succeeds the previous grandfathers and lords of the citadel, going on through each and every one of the lords.

And here shall appear the faces of each one of the lords.

A ND HERE SHALL APPEAR THE FACES, ONE BY ONE, OF EACH OF THE QUICHÉ LORDS . . .

Jaguar Quitze, origin of the Cauecs.

Cocauib, in the second generation after Jaguar Quitze.

Jaguar Conache, who began the office of Keeper of the Mat, was in the third generation.

Cotuha and Iztayul, in the fourth generation.

Plumed Serpent and Cotuha, at the root of the lords of genius, were in the fifth generation.

Tepepul and Iztayul next, sixth in the sequence.

Quicab and Cauizimah, in the seventh change of lordship, were the culmination of genius.

Tepepul and Xtayub, in the eighth generation.

Tecum and Tepepul, in the ninth generation.

Eight Cords, with Quicab, in the tenth generation of lords.

Seven Thought and Cauatepech next, eleventh in the sequence of lords.

Three Deer and Nine Dog, in the twelfth generation of lords. And they were ruling when Tonatiuh arrived. They were hanged by the Castilian people.

Tecum and Tepepul were tributary to the Castilian people. They had already been begotten as the thirteenth generation of lords.

Don Juan de Rojas and don Juan Cortés, in the fourteenth generation of lords. They are the sons of Tecum and Tepepul.

So these are the generations, the sequences of lordships for the Keeper of the Mat and Keeper of the Reception House Mat, the lords who have led the Cauecs of Quiché. Next we shall name the lineages.

And here are the great houses of each one of the lords in the following of the Keeper of the Mat and Keeper of the Reception

224

House Mat. These are the names of the nine lineages of the Cauecs, nine great houses. Here are the titles of the rulers of each one of the great houses:

Lord Keeper of the Mat, with one great house. Granary is the name of the palace.

Lord Keeper of the Reception House Mat. Bird House is the name of his palace.

Great Toastmaster of the Cauecs, with one great house.

Lord Keeper of Tohil, with one great house.

Lord Keeper of the Plumed Serpent, with one great house.

Councilor of the Stores, with one great house.

Lolmet Quehnay, with one great house.

Councilor of the Ball Court, Xcuxeba, with one great house.

Sovereign Yaqui, with one great house.

So these are the nine lineages of the Cauecs. Many vassals are counted in the following of these nine great houses.

A ND HERE ARE THOSE OF THE GREATHOUSES, with nine more great houses. First we shall name the genealogy of the lordship. It began, from just one root, at the origin of the root of the day and the light:

Jaguar Night, first grandfather and father.

Coacul and Coacutec, in the second generation.

Cochahuh and Cotzibaha, in the third generation.

Nine Deer next, in the fourth generation.

Cotuha, in the fifth generation of lords.

And Monkey House next, in the sixth generation.

And Iztayul, in the seventh generation of lords.

Cotuha then, eighth in the sequence of lordships.

Nine Deer, ninth in the sequence.

Quema, as the next one was called, in the tenth generation.

Lord Cotuha, in the eleventh generation.

Don Cristobal, as he was called, became lord in the presence of the Castilian people.

Don Pedro de Robles is Lord Minister today.

And these are all the lords who come in the following of the Lord Minister. Now we shall give the title of the ruler of each one of the great houses:

Lord Minister, the first-ranking lord at the head of the Greathouses, with one great house.

Lord Crier to the People, with one great house.

Lord Minister of the Reception House, with one great house.

Great Reception House, with one great house.

Mother of the Reception House, with one great house.

Great Toastmaster of the Greathouses, with one great house.

Lord Auilix, with one great house.

Yacolatam, with one great house.

So these are the great houses at the head of the Greathouses; these are the names of the nine lineages of the Greathouses, as they are called. There are many branch lineages in the following of each one of these lords; we have named only the first-ranking titles.

A ND NOW THESE ARE FOR THE LORD QUICHÉS. Here are their grandfathers and fathers:

Mahucutah, the first person.

Coahau is the name of the lord of the second generation.

Red Banner.

Cocozom.

Comahcun.

Seven Cane.

Cocamel.

Coyabacoh.

Person of Bam.

So these are the lords at the head of the Lord Quichés; these are their generations and sequences.

And here are the lords within the palaces, with just four great houses:

Crier to the People for the Lords is the title of the first lord, with one great house.

Lolmet of the Lords, the second lord, with one great house.

Great Toastmaster of the Lords, the third lord, with one great house.

And Hacauitz, the fourth lord, with one great house.

And so these are the four great houses at the head of the Lord Quichés.

A ND THERE ARE THREE GREAT TOASTMASTERS IN ALL. They are like fathers to all the Quiché lords. They come together in unity, these three Toastmasters. They are givers of birth, they are Mothers of the Word, they are Fathers of the Word, great in being few, these three Toastmasters:

Great Toastmaster for the Cauecs, first.

And Great Toastmaster for the Greathouses, second.

Great Toastmaster Lord for the Lord Quichés, third of the Great Toastmasters.

And so there are three Toastmasters, one representing each of these lineages.

T HIS IS ENOUGH ABOUT THE BEING OF QUICHÉ, given that there is no longer a place to see it. There is the original book and ancient writing owned by the lords, now lost, but even so, everything has been completed here concerning Quiché, which is now named Santa Cruz.

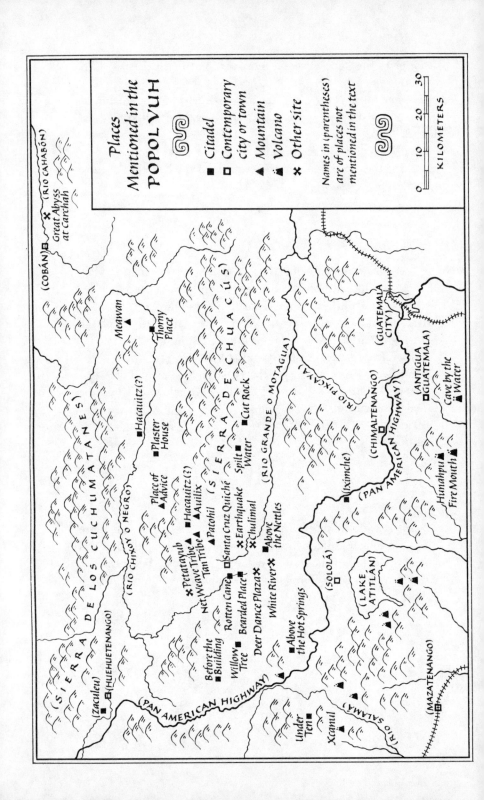

Places
Mentioned in the
POPOL VUH

■ Citadel
□ Contemporary city or town
▲ Mountain
⏑ Volcano
✕ Other site

Names in (parentheses) are of places not mentioned in the text

KILOMETERS
0   10   20   30

(RIO CAHABÓN)
✕ Great Abyss at Carchah
(COBÁN) ■

Meawan ▲

Hacauitz (?) ■
Plaster House ■
Thorny Place ▲

(SIERRA   DE   LOS   CUCHUMATANES)

(RIO CHIXOY O NEGRO)
Place of Advice ■
Hacauitz (?) ■ ▲
Auilix ▲
Patohil ▲
Petatayub ✕
Net Weave Tribe ■ ▲
Tam Tribe ■
Santa Cruz Quiché □
Earthquake ✕
Chulimal ✕
Above the Nettles ✕

SIERRA   DE   CHUACÚS

Spilt Water ■
Cut Rock ■

(RIO GRANDE O MOTAGUA)

Before the Building ■
Willow Tree ■
Rotten Cane ■
Bearded Place ■
Deer Dance Plaza ✕
White River ✕

Above the Hot Springs ■

(HUEHUETENANGO) ■
(Zaculeu) ■

(PAN AMERICAN HIGHWAY)

Under Ten ■
Xcamul ▲

(RIO SALAMÁ)

(SOLOLÁ) □

(LAKE ATITLÁN)

(Iximche) □

(CHIMALTENANGO) □

(PAN AMERICAN HIGHWAY)

(RIO PIXCAYÁ)

(GUATEMALA CITY) ■

(ANTIGUA GUATEMALA) □
Cave by the Water ▲

Hunahpu ⏑
Fire Mouth ⏑

(MAZATENANGO) □

NOTES
AND COMMENTS

Quiché words in brackets are corrections of the spellings in the Popol Vuh manuscript. Popol Vuh is abbreviated P.V. throughout. Sources for the meanings of words, here and in the Glossary, are cited by the following letter code (see the Bibliography for the full citations):

(A.) Miguel Alvarado López, *Léxico médico quiché-español.*

(B.) Domingo de Basseta, "Vocabulario en lengua quiché."

(C.) Lyle Campbell, "Préstamos lingüísticos en el Popol Vuh."

(D.) Alonso de Molina, *Vocabulario en lengua castellana y mexicana.*

(E.) Charles Etienne Brasseur de Bourbourg, *Gramática de la lengua quiché.*

(F.) Floyd G. Lounsbury, "The Identities of the Mythological Figures in the 'Cross Group' Inscriptions."

(G.) Pantaleón de Guzmán, "Compendio de nombres en lengua cakchiquel."

(K.) Terrence Kaufman, "Common Cholan Lexical Items."

(L.) Robert M. Laughlin, *The Great Tzotzil Dictionary.*

(M.) Antonio de Ciudad Real, *Diccionario de Motul.*

(P.) Pedro Morán, "Bocabulario de solo los nombres de la lengua pokoman."

(Q.)   Munro S. Edmonson, *Quiche-English Dictionary.*

(R.)   Adrián Recinos et al., *Popol Vuh.*

(S.)   Linda Schele, *Notebook for the Maya Hieroglyphic Writing Workshop.*

(T.)   Fermín Joseph Tirado, "Vocabulario de lengua kiche."

(V.)   Francisco de Varela, "Calepino en lengua cakchiquel."

(X.)   Gail Maynard and Patricio Xec, "Diccionario preliminar del idioma quiché."

(Z.)   Dionysio de Zúñiga, "Diccionario pocomchí-castellano y castellano-pocomchí."

INTRODUCTION

24–25
My account of Mayan archaeology is based largely on Michael D. Coe, *The Maya,* and Norman Hammond, *Ancient Maya Civilization.*

27
For a general discussion of pre-Columbian books in the Mayan region, see J. Eric S. Thompson, *A Commentary on the Dresden Codex,* chap. 1; the hieroglyphic book now in Dresden is reproduced in color in this same source. For a color reproduction of the fragment that was found more recently in Chiapas, see Coe, *The Maya Scribe and His World;* for a demonstration of the authenticity of this fragment, see John B. Carlson, "The Grolier Codex."

28
For a comparison of the towns of Quiché and Chichicastenango during the colonial period, see Robert M. Carmack, *The Quiché Mayas of Utatlán,* pp. 76, 106, 304, 328.

28–30
For a longer account of the odyssey of the Ximénez manuscript, see Adrián Recinos et al., *Popol Vuh: The Sacred Book of the Ancient Quiché Maya,* pp. 32–45.

30
For the Vienna volume see Francisco Ximénez, *Las historias del origen de los indios de esta provincia de Guatemala;* for the Paris volume, see Charles Etienne Brasseur de Bourbourg, *Popol Vuh: Le livre sacré et les mythes de l'antiquité américaine.* The title chosen by Scherzer for the Vienna volume is the one used by Ximénez; Brasseur was the first to call the alphabetic version of the ancient book by the name of its hieroglyphic predecessor. His version of the Quiché text leaves much to be desired; by far the best version ever published is

that of Leonhard S. Schultze Jena (*Popol Vuh: Das heilige Buch der Quiché-Indianer von Guatemala*). A highly legible facsimile of the manuscript (easier to read than the original) was published in 1973 by the Guatemalan Ministry of Education (Francisco Ximénez, *Popol Vuh*).

For evidence that the manuscript Ximénez worked from contained at least a few hieroglyphs, see the notes to pp. 211 and 224 of the present translation. Maya writing, like Egyptian and Chinese, was both logographic and phonetic, which is to say that a given word could be written with a single sign all its own, but could also be spelled out with glyphs that stood for the sounds of its individual consonants or syllables; see David Humiston Kelley, *Deciphering the Maya Script*, chaps. 6 and 9. The monkey patrons of writing and painting and the close relationship between these arts are discussed in Coe, "Supernatural Patrons of Maya Scribes and Artists."

32
The four corners in question here are not the four cardinal points, but the four places marked out by the solstitial rising and setting points of the sun; see Eva Hunt, *The Transformation of the Hummingbird*, chap. 6.

32–33
See Alfred M. Tozzer, *Landa's Relación de las cosas de Yucatán*, pp. 153–54, for a description of the reading of a hieroglyphic book in Yucatán. At present there are public readings of alphabetic manuscripts in the Yucatec Maya ceremonial center of Xcacal, in Quintana Roo; see Allan F. Burns, "The Caste War in the 1970's," and *An Epoch of Miracles*, pp. 22–23, 71–72.

33
For a further discussion of the Ancient Word and its relation to the preaching of God, see Dennis Tedlock, *The Spoken Word and the Work of Interpretation*, chap. 12.

33
In holding open the possibility that the authors of the alphabetic P.V. had access to the hieroglyphic version I am in agreement with Munro S. Edmonson, *The Book of Counsel: The Popol Vuh of the Quiche Maya of Guatemala*, pp. 6–7. For a discussion of the role of dialogue in the Quiché story of the origin of the world and the contrasting monologue of Genesis, see D. Tedlock, *The Spoken Word*, chap. 11.

34–35
Contemporary Quiché daykeepers and their practices are fully described in Barbara Tedlock, *Time and the Highland Maya*. The 260-day cycle daykeepers divine by is made up of two shorter cycles, one consisting of an endlessly repeating sequence of thirteen day numbers and the other of an endlessly repeating sequence of twenty day

names. Since 13 and 20 have no common factor, the interaction of 13 numbers with 20 names produces a larger cycle consisting of 13 × 20 or 260 days, each with a unique combination of number and name. If we begin with the day that combines the number 1 with the name Queh, the list of successive days proceeds as follows:

QUICHÉ DAY NAMES WITH NUMBERS
(Yucatec names in parentheses)

1 Queh	(Manik)	12 Tihax	(Etznab)
2 3anil	(Lamat)	13 Cauuk	(Cauac)
3 Toh	(Muluc)	1 Hunahpu	(Ahau)
4 4,ii	(Oc)	2 Imox	(Imix)
5 Ba4,	(Chuen)	3 I3	(Ik)
6 E	(Eb)	4 A3abal	(Akbal)
7 Ah	(Ben)	5 4at	(Kan)
8 Ix	(Ix)	6 Can	(Chicchan)
9 4,iquin	(Men)	7 Came	(Cimi)
10 Ahmac	(Cib)	8 Queh	(Manik)
11 Naoh	(Caban)	etc.	etc.

From 8 Queh the count goes on to 9 3anil, 10 Toh, and so forth, returning to 1 Queh after 260 days.

Andrés Xiloj, the daykeeper introduced in the preface to the present work, insists that the period of human pregnancy is the basis for the length of this cycle; medically speaking, 260 days is indeed a sound, average figure for the period lasting from the time when a woman first misses her menses to the time when she gives birth. It should also be noted that the growth cycle of one of the varieties of corn used in highland Guatemala is such that it is harvested 260 days after planting, though it is necessary to hasten the ripening of the ears by bending the stalks over; see B. Tedlock, "Earth Rites and Moon Cycles: Mayan Synodic and Sidereal Moon Reckoning."

35
For more on the ball game, see Theodore Stern, *The Rubber-Ball Games of the Americas*, and Stephan F. de Borhegyi, *The Pre-Columbian Ballgames: A Pan-Mesoamerican Tradition*.

36
For a full exploration of the astronomical dimensions of the P.V., see D. Tedlock, "The Sowing and Dawning of All the Sky-Earth: Astronomy in the Popol Vuh." The sources for the astronomical identifications of Seven Macaw and Chimalmat are given under their names in the Glossary. Claude Lévi-Strauss states that the Big Dipper is identified with the hurricane (rather than opposed to it) in the mythology

of Mesoamerica and the Caribbean (*From Honey to Ashes,* pp. 115–16), but he bases this statement on the work of R. Lehmann-Nitsche, who presents not a single concrete ethnographic example of such an identification and even passes over evidence that would place the stellar aspect of the hurricane close to the ecliptic rather than near the pole star ("La constelación de la Osa Mayor y su concepto como Huracán o dios de la tormenta en la esfera del Mar Caribe").

37
The symbolism of the Pleiades is discussed in B. Tedlock, "Earth Rites and Moon Cycles." The sexual symbolism of the Zipacna story was pointed out by Andrés Xiloj, whose full comments will be found in the notes to p. 98 of the translation.

37
Together, Zipacna and Earthquake probably correspond to the two-headed "Cauac monster" of classic Maya iconography (see Dicey Taylor, "The Cauac Monster").

38
The falcon who serves as the messenger for Hurricane, or Heart of Sky, may correspond to the planet Jupiter, for reasons that are given in D. Tedlock, "The Sowing and Dawning."

38
The Great Abyss at Carchah (see the Glossary) is probably near the town of Cobán; an independent colonial source on that region, Bartolomé de las Casas, has a god named Exbalanquen entering the underworld through a cave near Cobán (*Apologética historia de las Indias,* pp. 330, 619).

39
The movements of the messenger owls, here and elsewhere, fit those of the planet Mercury; see D. Tedlock, "The Sowing and Dawning."

40
The Maya Venus cycle, as given in the Dresden Codex, is discussed at length in Thompson, *A Commentary on the Dresden Codex,* pp. 62–71. A given Venus cycle (lasting 584 days) is divided into four stages, with Venus appearing as the morning star (for 236 days), then disappearing (90 days), then reappearing as the evening star (250 days), and finally disappearing again (8 days). During a given 584-day cycle the 20 day names will repeat fully 29 times, giving 580 days and a remainder of 4; this means that a new Venus cycle will always begin 4 days later in the sequence of 20 day names than the previous cycle. And since 4 divides evenly into 20, giving 5, only 5 of the 20 day names can ever begin a Venus cycle. In the Dresden Codex the chosen days (here given their Quiché names) were Hunahpu, 4at (or "Net"), 3anil, E, and Ahmac, followed by Hunahpu again. Starting from 1 Hunahpu (as the Dresden Codex does) and running through five complete cycles so as to show all of the possible day names, the

beginning dates for the four stages within each Venus cycle work out as follows:

DAY NUMBERS AND NAMES
FOR FIVE SUCCESSIVE VENUS CYCLES

	FIRST CYCLE	SECOND CYCLE	THIRD CYCLE	FOURTH CYCLE	FIFTH CYCLE
Appears as morning star:	1 Hunahpu	13 4at	12 3anil	11 E	10 Ahmac
Becomes invisible:	3 Ahmac	2 Hunahpu	1 4at	13 3anil	12 E
Appears as evening star:	2 Came	1 4,ii	13 Ix	12 Tihax	11 13
Becomes invisible:	5 Ahmac	4 Hunahpu	3 4at	2 3anil	1 E

After five complete cycles totaling 2,920 days, the movements of Venus fill exactly 8 years of 365 days each and come within hours of filling 99 lunar months. At this point Venus is also close to completing 13 of its sidereal periods, which run a little under 225 days each. In the present context this means that when Venus begins its cycle for the sixth time, an event that will fall on 9 Hunahpu, it will have the same relationship to the fixed stars that it had 2,920 days earlier, when its appearance as morning star began on 1 Hunahpu. The date for this appearance will not return to 1 Hunahpu until all five of the possible day names have combined with each of the 13 day numbers, by which time Venus will have passed through precisely 65 cycles of 584 days each, 104 cycles of 365 days each, and 146 cycles of 260 days each.

The divine names One and Seven Hunahpu and One and Seven Came (or "Death") point directly to the Venus calendar, and specifically to the first of its five cycles. Andrés Xiloj pointed out that combining the numbers 1 and 7 with a given day name is a conventional way of indicating all 13 days bearing that name. The reason is that when one traces a single day name through all of its occurrences in a given 260-day cycle, the accompanying numbers fall out in the sequence 1, 8, 2, 9, 3, 10, 4, 11, 5, 12, 6, 13, and 7. This means that if the divine names in question here refer to astronomical events, these should be events whose day names remain constant but whose day numbers are variable, which is indeed the case. By the same argument, the names One Ba4, (or "Monkey") and One Chouen (or "Artisan"), both of which refer to the same day (see the Glossary), point to an event that varies neither as to number nor as to name and must therefore occur each 260 days or a multiple thereof. The only astronomical events that fit this description are those pertaining to Mars, whose synodic period is 780 (3 × 260) days. For example, if Mars made its first appearance in a given cycle on the day 1 Ba4,, the return of this same event would again fall on the day 1 Ba4,.

42
The falcon who serves as the messenger for Xmucane may correspond to the planet Saturn, for reasons that are given in D. Tedlock, "The Sowing and Dawning."

42
It was Andrés Xiloj who pointed out that the ritual performed with the ears of corn in the P.V. is the same as a contemporary ritual; his detailed comments on this and other connections between the P.V. and contemporary practices may be found throughout the notes to the P.V. translation itself. For an account of contemporary sound plays on day names, see B. Tedlock, "Sound Texture and Metaphor in Quiché Maya Ritual Language," and *Time and the Highland Maya*, chap. 5.

43
The macaw's tail and the two fireflies that glowed all night may correspond to the stars Procyon, Castor, and Pollux, for reasons that are given in D. Tedlock, "The Sowing and Dawning."

44
Ideally there should be a total of five test houses, corresponding to the second stage in each of the five types of Venus cycles; these would be Dark House, Razor House, Cold (or Rattling) House, Jaguar House, and Bat House. They may correspond to locations along the Mayan zodiac, since Venus begins to repeat the pattern of its relationship to the fixed stars after five cycles. In the second of two passages naming the houses, the P.V. seems to add a sixth house, a "house of fire," but this may be a secondary elaboration on the part of the narrator (see the notes to p. 143 of the translation).

44
In a given 365-day period the 20 day names repeat themselves completely 18 times, giving 360 days with a remainder of 5; this means that the next solar year will always begin with a day name that comes 5 days later in the cycle of 20 than the name that began the previous year. And since 5 divides evenly into 20, giving 4, only 4 of the 20 day names, evenly spaced within the name cycle, can ever begin a solar year. For the Quiché, these new year's day names were and are Queh or "Deer," E or "Tooth," Naoh or "Thought," and I3 or "Wind," followed by Queh again. As for the new year's day number, the cycle of 13 numbers repeats itself completely 28 times in a given solar year, giving 364 days and a remainder of 1; this means that a given solar year will always begin with a day number that comes a single place later in the cycle of 13 than the number that began the previous year.

The year as a whole is designated by the number and name of its beginning day; starting with a year bearing the name 1 Queh, the reckoning of successive years proceeds as follows:

QUICHÉ YEAR DESIGNATIONS

1 Queh	6 E	11 Naoh
2 E	7 Naoh	12 I3
3 Naoh	8 I3	13 Queh
4 I3	9 Queh	1 E
5 Queh	10 E	etc.

Note that two of these day names, E and I3, also have a potential for events pertaining to Venus (see the Venus calendar in an earlier note). They occur in the fourth and (more markedly) in the fifth and final cycle of Venus, just as the solar dimension of the story of Hunahpu and Xbalanque begins to manifest itself in the final episodes.

44–45

In Mesoamerican iconography the evening-star Venus is a death's head (see Carlson, "The Grolier Codex"). Even the ball game played with the squash fits into place when we consider the report of Ruth Bunzel that in at least one contemporary Quiché town, an excess of large squashes in a field means that the senior male of a family may die, since the squashes are a sign that his head is rotting (*Chichicastenango*, p. 54). The vine shown growing out of the head of a ball-player in one of the ball-court relief panels at Chichen Itza may well be a squash vine; note that the ball in this panel is shown as enclosing a skull (see p. 139 in the present book).

The morning-star and evening-star episodes should total five each, corresponding to the five types of Venus cycles. The morning-star episodes are brought up to five if we count the period when One and Seven Hunahpu were on the surface of the earth as the first episode, with the four above-ground adventures of Hunahpu and Xbalanque following. The first evening-star episode is of course the one in which One Hunahpu's head is placed in the tree at the Place of Ball Game Sacrifice, followed by the three ball games with literal or figurative heads; the fifth head will be Hunahpu's again, when he loses it in a future episode.

45

The appearance of Hunahpu and Xbalanque as catfish recalls that the purported equivalent of Hunahpu among the classic Maya, the god designated G-I in the epigraphic literature on Palenque, has cheeks with appendages that sometimes look like catfish barbels and sometimes like spiny fins (see Floyd G. Lounsbury, "The Identities of the Mythological Figures in the 'Cross Group' Inscriptions at Palenque," and the notes to p. 149 of the present translation). The appearance of the twins as vagabond actors is a further sign, beyond the earlier appearance of the "old man" or possum, that the sun will soon rise. Among the roles of classic Maya year-bearers was that of wandering actors (Thompson, *Maya History and Religion*, p. 277).

46
The similarities between the sun and full moon were also pointed out by the Aztecs (Bernardino de Sahagún, *Florentine Codex*, Book 7, p. 3).

47
Contemporary Quiché mother-fathers are discussed in B. Tedlock, *Time and the Highland Maya*, pp. 74–85.

48
For a general discussion of the subject of Tollan, see Nigel Davies, *The Toltecs*, chap. 2. Tulan (Tulapan in Yucatec sources) and Zuyua (often Holtun Zuyua in Yucatec sources) are mentioned in various Mayan alphabetic writings, including Recinos et al., *The Annals of the Cakchiquels*, pp. 44–53; Ralph L. Roys, *The Book of Chilam Balam of Chumayel*, pp. 74, 132, 139, 153; and Eugene R. Craine and Reginald C. Reindorp, *The Codex Pérez and the Book of Chilam Balam of Maní*, pp. 80, 138, 166, 167.

From a Yucatec point of view (see the Chumayel book), Holtun Zuyua occupied the western position in a four-directional group of towns whose leaders converged on Chichen Itza (a fifth and central town) in order to receive lordship; it may have been at the place now known as Puerto Escondido in Campeche (Thompson, *Maya History and Religion*, p. 23), though Edmonson (without giving any evidence) locates it near Motul in Yucatán (*The Ancient Future of the Itza: The Book of Chilam Balam of Tizimin*, p. 38). As for Tulapan, that was the place where the Tutul Xiu lineage traced its origins; it was even farther west than Zuyua (according to the Maní book), which could mean that it was the primary Toltecan Tollan near Mexico City. The Cakchiquel book uses the name Tulan in this narrow sense when it has the Quichés and Cakchiquels coming to Zuyua from a western Tulan, but it also uses the name in a broader sense that takes in the Yucatec system of directional towns, speaking of a Tulan for each of the four directions and of a convergence on what appears to be a central Tulan. In effect, the authors of the P.V. apply the name Tulan specifically to the western town in the Yucatec system, producing the name Tulan Zuyua. When they say Tulan Zuyua is in the "east," they are reckoning its position not in the context of the Yucatec system but relative to the Tulan or Tulapan that is west of Zuyua in the Maní and Cakchiquel books.

49
The main cave at Teotihuacan and its relationship to a Nahua tradi-

tion concerning seven caves are discussed by Doris Heyden in "An Interpretation of the Cave Underneath the Pyramid of the Sun in Teotihuacan, Mexico." The existence of a god named Tahil at Palenque and his relationship to Tohil have been pointed out by Linda Schele (*Notebook for the Maya Hieroglyphic Writing Workshop*, p. 114) and Floyd G. Lounsbury (personal communication). For more on the Yaqui see the Glossary; they are not to be confused with the Yaqui tribe of Sonora and Arizona.

50
The reference to the body of water crossed by the Quiché forefathers as a "sea" is a hyperbole; it is called both a "lake" and a "sea" in "Historia Quiché de don Juan de Torres," in Recinos, *Crónicas indígenas de Guatemala*, pp. 24–25. The causeways at Potonchan and Tixchel are noted in France V. Scholes and Ralph L. Roys, *The Maya Chontal Indians of Acalan-Tixchel*, p. 81.

51
For more on the Zaki 4oxol or "White Sparkstriker," see the Glossary and B. Tedlock, "El C'oxol: un símbolo de la resistencia quiché a la conquista espiritual."

51
In Quiché theory, at least, the reckoning of the 260-day cycle should have been in synchrony everywhere in Mesoamerica. We do know that Cuauhtemoc, the successor of Moctezuma, surrendered the city of Tenochtitlán to Hernán Cortés on an Aztec day whose name means "One Snake," falling on August 13, 1521, on the Julian calendar (Thompson, *Maya Hieroglyphic Writing*, p. 303). Tracing the contemporary Quiché calendar back to that same Julian date, we come to a day whose Quiché name, Hun Can, also means "One Snake." In other words, when it was One Snake in Tenochtitlán, it was One Snake a thousand road miles away in the town of Quiché. Lounsbury argues, in "The Base of the Venus Table of the Dresden Codex," for a lowland Maya calendar correlation that would move the classic Maya 260-day cycle two days out of synchrony with the Quiché and Aztec calendars, but the astronomical basis of his argument could easily be two days off, according to the astronomer John B. Carlson (personal communication).

52
If the Quichés timed their attacks on their rivals in the same way as the classic lowland Maya, they favored periods when Venus was the evening star (see Lounsbury, "Astronomical Knowledge and Its Uses at Bonampak, Mexico"). The "road" onto which they rolled the head of a sacrifice victim may have been symbolic of the zodiacal path within which Venus is confined, and the head may have been thought of on the model of the severed heads that appeared as the evening-star Venus in the story of Hunahpu and Xbalanque and their fathers.

238

53–54
It took 52 years of 365 days each for all four year-beginning day names to occur in combination with all thirteen day numbers (4 × 13 = 52). The seniority given by the Quiché to Queh or "Deer" among the year-beginning day names is noted in B. Tedlock, *Time and the Highland Maya*, p. 99.

54
Alternative accounts of the names and generational positions of the Quichés who went on the pilgrimage, and of the titles that were given to them, may be found in Adrián Recinos et al., *Title of the Lords of Totonicapán*, pp. 176–79. Tulan, the place where the Quiché founding fathers had spent some time in an earlier episode, may have been left completely empty by the time they and the other tribes mentioned in the P.V. had departed from it. In the Quiché language the word for this place, in the form *tolan*, came to figure in such phrases as *tolanic tinamit*, "abandoned city," and *tolan ha*, "dark, uninhabited house" (B.).

55
A long list of the citadels settled by the Quichés between Hacauitz and Thorny Place is given in Recinos et al., *Title of the Lords of Totonicapán*, pp. 180–83. For a description of Thorny Place, now known as Cauinal (the name given to one of its four divisions in the P.V.), see John W. Fox, *Quiche Conquest: Centralism and Regionalism in Highland Guatemalan State Development*, pp. 243–50, and Alain Ichon, "Arqueología y etnohistoria en Cawinal."

56
For a full discussion of the buildings of ʒumarakah (Rotten Cane) or Utatlán (the Nahua name for the same place), see Carmack, *The Quiché Mayas*, chap. 9.

57
The military exploits of Quicab are discussed in Carmack, *The Quiché Mayas*, pp. 134–37. The citadels that made up the town of Quiché, in addition to Rotten Cane, were Bearded Place to the south, which now belonged to the Tams; Mukuitz Pilocab to the north, belonging to the Ilocs; and Resguardo, or Atalaya, to the east, whose Quiché name and lineage affiliation are unknown (Carmack, *The Quiché Mayas*, chap. 8).

59
For the full story of Alvarado's conquest of the Quiché kingdom, which was resisted by a large military force, see Victoria Reifler Bricker, *The Indian Christ, the Indian King*, pp. 39–41. The events at Rotten Cane itself are further described in Carmack, *The Quiché Mayas*, pp. 143–47. According to Spanish sources, Three Deer and Nine Dog were burned at the stake and it was Tecum and Tepepul who were hanged.

59–60

In dating the writing of the alphabetic P.V., I follow Recinos, *Popol Vuh*, pp. 22–23. For a description of *títulos* contemporary with the P.V., see Carmack, *Quichean Civilization*, pp. 19–71. The calculations correlating a year-beginning day bearing the name One Deer with June 2, 1558 (Julian) are my own. The fact that a calendrical event of the same kind fell on April 10, 1818 (Gregorian), may help explain why the years 1816 to 1820 saw a Quiché revolt against tribute payments to the Spanish crown, climaxing in the coronation of Atinasio Tzul, the mayor of Totonicapán, as King of the Quichés. For a description of this revolt see Bricker, *The Indian Christ*, chap. 7.

60

For more on the Spanish journey of Juan Cortés and the warning sent to Philip II, see Pedro Carrasco, "Don Juan Cortés, cacique de Santa Cruz Quiché."

60

The lineal descendants of Juan de Rojas and Juan Cortés continued to litigate well into the eighteenth century. The Cortés line died out by 1788; the de Rojas line still lives, but its members lost all remaining vestiges of their lordly privileges with the coming of liberal reforms in 1801 (Carmack, *The Quiché Mayas*, pp. 321, 362).

61

In translating the *nim chocohib* of the P.V. as "Great Toastmasters" or "Great Conveners of Banquets" I take my cue from Ximénez, who has "grandes combites" (*Popol Vuh*, p. 265); see also *Great Toastmaster* in the Glossary. For more on contemporary matchmakers (or "road guides"), see B. Tedlock, *Time and the Highland Maya*, pp. 74, 110, 117, 156.

61

The name Cristobal Velasco may be found in Recinos et al., *Title of the Lords of Totonicapán*, p. 195.

62

The Dresden Codex page that begins an otherwise torn-off section is discussed in Thompson, *A Commentary on the Dresden Codex*, pp. 78–80.

62–63

My discussion of the Palenque inscriptions is based on lectures given by Linda Schele in the spring of 1984; their contents are partially available in Schele, *Notebook for the Maya Hieroglyphic Writing Workshop at Texas*.

63–64

For more on the dialectical nature of Quiché thought see B. Tedlock, *Time and the Highland Maya*, pp. 145–46, 176–77. The role of myth in Mayan thinking about history is explored by Bricker in *The Indian Christ*, chaps. 1 and 14.

PART ONE

71

the beginning: This is *uxe,* literally "its base" or "root"; it is as if the writers were starting at the bottom of something vertical and working their way up.

71

this place called Quiché: That "Quiché" is meant as a place name here is confirmed at the very end of the P.V. (p. 227): "everything has been completed here concerning Quiché, which is now named Santa Cruz." See the Glossary for more on Quiché and Santa Cruz.

71

And here: The paragraphing of the present translation is largely based on two considerations. The first is the occurrence of what Dell Hymes calls "initial particles" (*"In Vain I Tried to Tell You",* pp. 318–20). Examples in Quiché are *are 4ut,* "And here" (or "And this is"); *4ate 4ut,* "And next"; and *quehe 4ut,* "And so." The second consideration is the occurrence of quotations. In contemporary Quiché speech there are deliberate pauses both before and after phrases consisting of initial particles, and immediately before quotations. For more details, see D. Tedlock, *The Spoken Word,* chap. 4, and "Hearing a Voice in an Ancient Text."

71

how things were put in shadow and brought to light: This is *euaxibal zaquiribal [zakiribal],* "being-hidden-instrument becoming-light-in-strument." The first word is built on a passive (*-x*) form of *euah,* which V. glosses as "to hide" but then explains that it has to do with shadows or dark places. The second word is built on an inchoative (*-ir*) form of *zak,* "be light," which it shares with *zakiric,* "to dawn." The two words together describe the activities of the gods at a very general level. As will be seen, the gods not only bring things to light but can also darken what was once in the light.

On the other hand, the two words could also be translated as "the hiding place, the dawning place," since *-bal* can either be instrumental or indicate place. The "hiding place" would be *euabal ziuan* or "Concealment Canyon" (see Glossary), where the gods were hidden away before the dawn (p. 178); the "dawning place" would be the place (or places) where the founding ancestors of the ruling Quiché lineages were keeping vigil when the morning star and then the sun rose for the first time (p. 180), places which are referred to as *zaquiribal [zakiribal].*

71

the midwife, matchmaker: This is *iyom, mamom.* Andrés Xiloj immediately identified *iyom* as the modern term for "midwife" (*yom* is given the same meaning in B.). He knew of *mamom* only as a term addressed to a matchmaker in the ceremonial language of a bride-asking ceremony; ordinarily the matchmaker is referred to as *4amal be*, "road guide."

71

defender, protector: This is *matzanel chuquenel*. B. lists *matzanel* (under *matzo*) as "defender," which fits the role of the Quiché day-keeper as the maker of prayers and offerings on behalf of clients. As Andrés Xiloj pointed out, the daykeeper who takes this role today may be called, among other things, by the Spanish word *abogado*, "lawyer, advocate," and may be thought of as presenting the case of the client before a divine tribunal. The translation of *chuquenel* rests on the entry in B. for *chukonal* (under *chu3u*), "protector." The two terms are very similar in their root senses; for *matzo*, B. gives "to shelter after the manner of a hen," and for *chu3u*, "to cover over."

71

as enlightened beings, in enlightened words: "Enlightened" is my translation, for the present context, of *zaquil* [*zakil*], "lightness" or "whiteness." This insistence that the aforementioned Quiché deities and their words have the properties of light is directly juxtaposed to a mention of God and Christendom in the sentence that follows; it can thus be read as a direct and deliberate contradiction of the missionary teaching that the pre-Conquest gods were all devils.

71

amid the preaching of God, in Christendom now: After the *Dios* and *christianoil* in this phrase, there will be no more Spanish or Spanish-derived words until p. 210 (see the note for *the lord bishop*). The "preaching" is *4habal*, literally "manner of speaking" or just plain "talk"; the phrase *u4habal Dios*, "talk of God," came to be the stan-dard Quiché way of referring to Christian doctrine and is still used in that sense by both Quichés and missionaries, but the original choice of these words to translate "la palabra de Dios" must have been made by a Quiché rather than a missionary. The proper Quiché term for an authoritative and abiding "word" was and still is *tzih* rather than *4habal*; the writers of the P.V. refer to their own manuscript as con-taining *oher tzih*, "the Ancient Word," but neither they nor contem-porary Quichés use *tzih* as a way of referring to "la palabra de Dios." In choosing to translate *u4habal Dios* as "the preaching of God" in the present context, I have tried to combine the "Christian doctrine" sense of this phrase with the more general sense of *4habal* as an act of speaking.

71

a place to see it: The original pre-Columbian P.V. is referred to here and much later (p. 219) as an *ilbal re* (written *ibal re* in the later place), "an instrument (or place) for the seeing of something." What was "seen" there included "how things were put in shadow and brought to light" by the gods (p. 71), together with future events such as war, death, famine, and quarrels (p. 219). B. has an entry for *ilbal re* (under *ilo*) glossed redundantly as "figura de dibujos," which could variously mean "figure," "drawing," and even "picture." Today *ilbal* or *ilobal* (without the *re*) refers to crystals used for gazing by diviners and to eyeglasses, binoculars, and telescopes.

71
There is the original book and ancient writing, but he who reads and ponders it hides his face: Edmonson is correct in interpreting the phrase *eual uuach,* "hidden his-face," as pertaining to the reader of the P.V. rather than to the book itself (*The Book of Counsel,* p. 7). "There is" is my translation of *40;* some translators have used the past tense here, the usual treatment for Quiché verbs inflected for the complete aspect, but that would call for *x40.* "He who reads" translates *ilol,* literally "one who sees." B. gives *ilol* as "seer" or "prophet," and *ilol uuh* (literally "book seer") as "reader"; an English translation built on "read" does quite well at covering the full range of *ilol,* since "read" still retains divinatory usages that go all the way back to its Germanic root. "[He who] ponders" translates *bizol,* an agentive form of *biz,* "sad" or "pensive." The emotional dimension of *bizol* is made quite clear in later passages, where we hear again and again how the Quiché forefathers wept at the thought of having left the mythic city of Tulan and having become separated from other tribes.

71–72
performance: This is my translation of *peoxic,* which I read as a passive and nominalized form of *peyoh,* "to hire" (V.), probably meaning something like "service rendered."

72
the fourfold siding, fourfold cornering, / measuring, fourfold staking, / halving the cord, stretching the cord / in the sky, on the earth, / the four sides, the four corners: The "fourfold siding" and "cornering" are *ucah tzucuxic* and *ucah xucutaxic;* the "four sides" and "four corners" are *cah tzuc* and *cah xucut. Xucut* was and is "corner," and *cah xucut* is still in use as a way of referring to the four directions, most frequently in prayers in the line, *cah xucut cah, cah xucut uleu,* "four corners of sky, four corners of earth." *Tzuc* is more difficult to translate. Andrés Xiloj suggested "sides" on the basis of context. B. gives *cahzuc* as "a square thing," and although he gives *cahxucut* as a synonym for *cahzuc* under the entry for the latter, he elsewhere glosses *cahxucut* as "four *angles* of the world." The notion that *tzuc* means "side" in the present context, in contrast with "corner" or "angle," is based on *zu3u-,* "to go somewhere straight, without straying" (B.), and on *zu4um,* "straight" (X.). Under *zucube,* which would mean "straight (direct) road," B. lists *tzucu be* as an alternative spelling;

243

this supports the relationship between the *tzuc* of the P.V., with its *tz*, and the dictionary entries for *zu3* and *zu4um*, with their *z*.

The "fourfold staking" is *ucah cheexic*; Andrés Xiloj understood this to be four sticks or poles driven in the ground at the four corners. The "measuring" is *retaxic*, literally "its-being-measured," translated on the basis of *etah*, "to measure, to mark out" (B.), and the reading offered by don Andrés. The measuring in this passage is done according to a unit still in use among the Quiché, the *4aam* or "cord" (a length of rope). Don Andrés was familiar with the phraseology used here, *umeh camaxic* [*4aamaxic*], "its-folded cording," and *uyuc camaxic* [*uyuk 4aamaxic*], "its-stretched cording." He explained that the "folded" measurement is done with the cord folded back upon itself to halve its length, and that the "stretched" measurement is done with the cord pulled out to its full length. His reading of *4aamaxic* (which has a passive ending) is confirmed by an entry in B., *caamaah* (with an active ending), "to measure lands." He observed that the P.V. describes the measuring out of the sky and earth as if a cornfield were being laid out for cultivation. The Book of Chilam Balam of Chumayel also describes the setting up of the earth and sky as an act of measurement, carried out not only in space (by footsteps in this case) but in time (through twenty consecutive days from the 260-day divinatory cycle) (Roys, *The Book of Chilam Balam of Chumayel*, pp. 116–118). The Chumayel document makes a passing reference to a celestial cord (p. 155); Yucatec Mayas near Valladolid told Alfred M. Tozzer that a cord suspended in the sky once linked Tulum and Coba with Chichen Itza and Uxmal (*A Comparative Study of the Mayas and Lacandones*, p. 153).

The present passage offers one of the clearest examples of parallel verse structure in the P.V.; it may be scanned as follows:

ucah tzucuxic,	fourfold siding,
ucah xucutaxic	fourfold cornering,
retaxic,	measuring,
ucah cheexic,	fourfold staking,
umeh camaxic,	halving the cord,
uyuc camaxic	stretching the cord
upa cah,	in the sky,
upa uleu	on the earth,
cah tzuc	the four sides,
cah xucut	the four corners

Note that the first two lines actually form a quatrain, with a slight variation in the third part; such quatrains occur elsewhere in the P.V.

and in Yucatec texts as well (see D. Tedlock, *The Spoken Word*, chap. 8). Edmonson presented the entire P.V. in couplets (*The Book of Counsel*), ignoring triplets, quatrains, and passages in which the horizontal movement of prose strongly modifies the vertical movement of parallelism (see the fifth note to p. 73). In the present work I have chosen a verse format only where the parallelism is both strongly marked and sustained.

In contemporary Quiché discourse with parallelism like that of the passage under discussion, the formation of lines in oral delivery would depend on considerations of audience. If this were a prayer meant only for the ears of the gods and if the wording were well known to the speaker, the whole thing might be run off on a single breath, with the end of each phrase marked by a slight drop in pitch. In a slower rendition meant to be heard by humans, or near the beginning of a performance, there might be a pause after each of the lines as they are given on p. 72 of the translation, though the opening quatrain might well be run together as a single spoken line rather than divided between two lines (see D. Tedlock, "Hearing a Voice"). In any case, the two parts of a couplet are seldom divided between lines.

72
giver of heart, ... upbringer: These are respectively *4uxlanel* and *4uxlaay*, both built on the stem *4ux,* "heart," which in its *4uxla-* forms has to do with thought in the sense of "memory" and "will." Andrés Xiloj defined *4uxlanel* as follows: "One who raises us and has a good reputation for doing this." In the translation I have tried to preserve the full range of *4uxla-* by staying literal for its first occurrence ("giver of heart") and translating for sense the second time around ("upbringer").

72
in the light that lasts: Here I have tried to preserve in English the relationship that exists between the corresponding words of the text, *zaquil amaquil [zakil amaʒel].* These two Quiché words are linked by assonance and alliteration, giving them a parallel sound, but they are not properly parallel in their morphology—in fact, the latter word *modifies* the former. *Zakil* is composed of *zak,* an adjective meaning "light" or "white," and *-il,* which makes it into an abstract noun; *amaʒel,* on the other hand, whether in classical or modern Quiché, is a unitary, unanalyzable form (at least where proper morphology is concerned). As an adverb it means "always" or "all the time"; as an adjective it means "continuous" or "eternal." In rendering *zakil amaʒel* as "the light that lasts," I change parts of speech as the original phrase does (though not in precisely the same way), while at the same time linking the two halves of the phrase through alliteration.

72
Now it still ripples, now it still murmurs, ripples, it still sighs, still

hums, and it is empty: The full sound pattern of this passage can only be fully appreciated in the original; I have corrected *ca* to *4a*, *-oc* to *-ok*, and *tzini-* and *tzino-* to *4,ini-* and *4,ino-*: *4a ca4,ininok, 4a cachamamok ca4,inonic, 4a cazilanic, 4a calolinic, catolona puch. 4a* is "still, yet"; *ca-* is the incomplete aspect; and *-ok* has the effect of "now"; nevertheless, translators have generally put this passage in the past tense! What we are hearing here is the performer's effort to make the primordial state of the world *present* for his listeners, setting a scene rather than recounting a past event; the mood is a lyric rather than a historical one.

Translators have rendered the first five verbs here with adjectives like "quiet" or "silent"; the problems with such a treatment only begin with the fact that the Quiché words in question are, after all, verbs and not adjectives. To translate these verbs as referring to mere silence and the like misses the fact that the stems *4,inin-*, *chamam-*, *4,inon-*, and *lolin-* all contain reduplicative alliteration (together with reduplicative assonance in two cases) and are therefore onomatopoeic. Colonial and modern dictionary entries for the stems of this passage do indeed include some of the glosses translators have chosen, but B. gives "ring" for *4,ino-*, and V. explains that *zilan-* (under *zilee*) refers to the (audible) process through which windy weather is calmed. Further, Andrés Xiloj identifies *lolin-* as the standard Quiché way of rendering the sound of a cricket. In translating this passage I have chosen quiet sounds that can be expressed as verbs; my "ripples" are derived from the fact that there is nothing but sky and water in this opening scene, as will be seen further on; for the same reason I have avoided obvious animal sounds. The "quiet" in question here is not so much a complete silence as it is a "hush" (note the onomatopoeic quality of this English word), the kinds of sounds one hears when there are no other sounds—or in this case, the "white noise" of the primordial world itself.

72
the first eloquence: Ximénez translates *uchan* as "eloquence," the same gloss given it by B. (under the entry for *chan*).

72
It is at rest; not a single thing stirs: Some translators have made the first half of this sentence negative by joining it to the negative clause that precedes it, but in fact what we have here is the last in a series of three sentences with the same positive-negative clause structure. The negativity of the second clause of the present sentence is marked by *hunta*, "not one thing" (B.), which is not to be confused with *hutak*, "each one." The entire sentence is perfectly intelligible, just as it is, in modern Quiché; Andrés Xiloj gave it the same reading I have.

72
It is held back: This is *camal cabantah*, which is difficult to translate. I

246

find my clue in the entry for *camalo* in B., which is glossed "late, not quick"; the entire phrase might be read as, "it is made to be late (or slow)."

73
a glittering light: This is *zactetoh* [*zaktetoh*], which B. glosses as "the brightness that enters through cracks." If this is the central meaning of this word rather than an illustrative example, then the light in question must be escaping between the feathers with which the Bearers and Begetters are covered (see the next two sentences). Note that the first light in the primordial scene is not up in the sky, but down at (or in) the level of the water. Its "glittering" corresponds, in the sensory domain of light, to the soft and repetitive nature of the primordial sounds described earlier.

73
in their very being: This is *chiqui4oheic*, "at-their-being-there." I have translated it as "in their *very* being" because the writers of the P.V., wherever they add *chiqui4oheic* (or a similar form based on *4oheic*) to a statement in which the verb "to be" is already present or understood, are making a *pointedly* ontological statement. Some translators have softened the ontological abstractness of these statements by using such phrases as "by their nature," but *4oheic* has no aura of the natal or the biological hanging about it the way "nature" does, and in fact I know of no Quiché concept that corresponds to "nature." If I were translating *4oheic* into German, I would choose *Dasein*.

73
the name of the god: The word I have translated as "god" here is *cabauil* [*4abauil*]. The primary reference of *4abauil*, through most of the P.V., is to the patron deities of the ruling Quiché lineages and to the sacred stones that were the material embodiments of these deities. But the present passage—given that *4abauil* is linked specifically to the Heart of Sky, and given that the Heart of Sky will shortly hereafter be described as a trinity—must be read as an allusion to Christian teachings. Note carefully that when the passage is read literally rather than as an allusion, it contains nothing that directly contradicts indigenous Quiché theology; Heart of Sky is among the names uttered before *4abauil* stones in a prayer given much later (pp. 221–222). For a general discussion of biblical allusions in the P.V., see D. Tedlock, *The Spoken Word*, chap. 11.

Looking into the etymology of *4abauil*, we find *4ab*, "to have the mouth open" for example, in admiration and in death (V.). B. and T. have *caba*, "to open," with the mouth given as an example. *4abauil*, then, could mean something like "open-mouthed." The ancient stone *4abauil* were given drinks of sacrificed blood through their mouths; their modern counterparts in the eastern Quiché area, called

4amauil, are given drinks of liquor (and sometimes chicken blood) through their mouths.

73

in the early dawn: This phrase constitutes the P.V.'s first allusion to the day names of the 260-day divinatory calendar. Instead of the ordinary word for "early dawn," *a3abil,* the text has *a3abal,* an archaic form that is also the proper name of a day. Like other day names, A3abal is often given a divinatory interpretation by means of sound play, and one of the words used to play on it today is in fact *a3abil,* an allusion to the fact that the rituals scheduled for days named A3abal are best carried out during the time of day known as *a3abil.* The rituals in question, appropriately enough, involve the first steps toward the negotiation of new social relationships that will last a lifetime (B. Tedlock, *Time and the Highland Maya,* pp. 77–81). One A3abal is an appropriate day for a daykeeper with the office of mother-father to go to the pair of shrines dedicated to the welfare of the human inhabitants of the lands of his patrilineage, in order to discuss (in prayer) the fact that a family in his lineage wishes to propose a marriage between one of its young men and a woman from another lineage. A later day named A3abal may be chosen for the making of the actual proposal at the house of the prospective bride.

On One, Eight, and Nine A3abal a mother-father who has taken on the responsibility of training and installing the successor of his deceased counterpart in a neighboring lineage will go to the shrines of that lineage to discuss the fact that one of its members wishes to become its new mother-father. In both the marriage and the installation the negotiation has two levels: it is not only the living who must give their approval to the bond between husband and wife or between the new mother-father and the foundation shrines (which is thought of as a spiritual marriage), but the ancestors and the gods. In the case of the Heart of Sky's discussion with the Sovereign Plumed Serpent in the P.V., the problem is a more fundamental one. When, by their joint efforts (and those of other gods) they eventually succeed in making four different mother-fathers, each of them married to one of four different women, these will be the first human mother-fathers and the first human married couples who ever existed.

73

He spoke with the Sovereign Plumed Serpent. . . . they joined their words, their thoughts: This passage offers an example of what happens when the Quiché tendency to parallel verse is modified by the forward thrust of prose (see D. Tedlock, "Hearing a Voice"). The result is a diagonal trajectory:

xchau ru4 ri tepeu 4ucumatz
xe4ha cut, ta xenaohinic

ta xebizonic,
xerico quib
xquicuch quitzih
quinaoh

He spoke with the Sovereign Plumed Serpent,
and they talked, then they thought,
then they worried.
They agreed with each other,
they joined their words,
their thoughts.

It is passages such as this that move the action forward in narratives, with the balance sometimes swinging more toward the verticality of verse than in the present example and sometimes more toward the horizontality of prose. The more a passage in contemporary Quiché discourse swings toward this horizontality the less predictable—and, potentially, the more dramatic—its pauses become, except for the paragraphing discussed in the notes to p. 71. As in the present case, I have kept such passages in a prose format in the translation proper.

73
the generation: This is *uinaquiric [uinakiric].* Others have translated this as "creation," but it has to do with such processes as the seasonal rising of springs in places that would otherwise be dry, and the growth or formation of algae or larvae in still water (V.). The word "creation" is too heavily laden with an implied ontological priority of the spiritual over the material to be imported into the present account of origins, which contains no word quite like it.

73
Thunderbolt Hurricane comes first, the second is Newborn Thunderbolt, and the third is Raw Thunderbolt: There may be an allusion to the Christian trinity here, but the pre-Columbian Quiché pantheon did include at least one trinity, whether that trinity was the same as the present Thunderbolt trinity or not. The principal gods *(qabauil)* of the ruling Quiché lineages are listed again and again as Tohil, Auilix, and Hacauitz (beginning on p. 171 and ending on p. 222), though there is occasional mention of a fourth god (pp. 171 and 219). The P.V. never directly links the three Thunderbolts with the three lineage gods, but it is at least suggestive that the dwelling place of the latter threesome is described as shrouded in a rainstorm (p. 188).

On the basis of fieldwork, Barbara Tedlock and I can confirm Lowy's report that *cakulha* not only is the Quiché term for thunderbolt but is also the Quiché name for the *Amanita muscaria* mushroom (Bernard Lowy, "*Amanita muscaria* and the Thunderbolt Legend in Guatemala and Mexico," p. 189). We must hasten to add that although Quichés are indeed what Gordon Wasson would call "mycophiles" rather than "mycophobes"—they are very fond of the *Amanita caesaria*, for example—they generally regard the *muscaria* as a poisonous species best avoided. But we cannot rule out the possible presence of a *muscaria* cult in the P.V., whether in the form of a symbolic residue of something long past or a highly coded allusion to something still under way at the time Europeans first arrived, nor can we rule out the use of *muscaria* by some present-day highland Guatemalan shamans.

As to the stone and pottery mushroom effigies discovered in Guatemalan archaeological sites (Stephan F. de Borhegyi, "Pre-Columbian Pottery Mushrooms from Mesoamerica"), these pertain to the hot Pacific lowlands rather than to the high, cool evergreen forests where the *muscaria* grows, and there is the further problem that the ruling Quiché lineages trace their origins to the Gulf coast rather than the Pacific. Moreover, de Borhegyi dates the effigies no later than a thousand years ago, leaving a gap of several centuries before the Quiché kingdom expanded into the Pacific lowlands during the reign of Quicab. Of all the arguments for a mushroom cult among the highland Maya the archaeological one is the weakest.

The case for *Amanita muscaria* in the P.V. itself is somewhat stronger, though we must begin from the fact that mushrooms *as such* are never mentioned. Far beyond the present passage there occur the words *holom ocox*, literally "head of a mushroom" (p. 186), translated there as "yarrow"), but Duncan MacLean Earle ("La etnoecología quiché en el Popol Vuh") has found this to be the Quiché term for a common herb, named (like a great many other Quiché plants and mushrooms) for its resemblance to an anatomical part of another biological species (see *yarrow* in the Glossary). What is more, the *holom ocox* of the P.V. is not eaten but rather burned as incense, along with another common herb called *iya* (see *marigold* in the Glossary); according to Earle, both these herbs are still used as incense today in the region east of Santa Cruz Quiché, and Andrés Xiloj attested the use of *iya* in Momostenango. The flowers of *iya* are yellow and those of *holom ocox* are white; the P.V. mentions the two plant names in this same order (p. 186), which fits with the yellow/white order of corn colors in the P.V. and the color pairings in the couplets of contemporary prayers (see B. Tedlock, *Time and the Highland Maya*, Appendix B).

Whatever the problems with finding a clear reference to mushrooms in the P.V., the evidence for the *Amanita muscaria* is not limited to the fact that *cakulha* could refer both to a literal thunderbolt and to the mushroom named for the thunderbolt. First of all, the stipe of a mushroom (like the trunk of a tree) is called *rakan*, "its leg," in Quiché, and of course a mushroom with a stipe has only one "leg," which recalls that the name translated "Thunderbolt Hurricane" here could also be glossed as "One-legged Thunderbolt" (see *Hurricane* in the Glossary). This leaves the way open to the *muscaria* but does not settle the matter, since there are plenty of *literal* thunderbolts that also have a single "leg." The rawness (or freshness) and youthfulness ascribed to the *cakulha* in the P.V. work in the same way: there *could* be an allusion to the suddenness of the growth of mushrooms, but these same qualities are also possessed by thunderbolts.

The single most suggestive bit of evidence for the mushroom theory lies in the fact that a later P.V. passage gives Newborn Thunderbolt and Raw Thunderbolt two further names: Newborn Nanahuac and Raw Nanahuac (p. 170). As Schultze Jena pointed out (*Popol Vuh*, p. 187), Nanahuac would appear to be the same as the Aztec deity Nanahuatl (or Nanahuatzin), who throws a thunderbolt to open the mountain containing the first corn. *Nanahuatl* means "warts" in Nahua (D.), which suggests the appearance of the *muscaria* when the remnants of its veil still fleck the cap.

73
"How should it be sown, how should it dawn?": "Sowing" (*auax-*) and "dawning" (*zakir-*) are frequently paired throughout the portion of the P.V. that deals with the predawn world. The meanings of these two words, which run through them several different threads when they are paired, have something of the structure of a Möbius strip. If we start with the literal meaning of sowing in the present context, the reference is to the beginning of plants; but if we trace that idea over to the other side of our strip, the sprouting of those same plants is expressed metaphorically as "dawning." If, on the other hand, we start from the literal meaning of "dawning," the present reference is to the first of all dawns; but if we trace that idea back over to the other side of the strip, the origin of that dawn is expressed metaphorically as a "sowing," referring to the fact that the Quiché gods who eventually become Venus and the sun and moon must first descend into the underworld. The head of one of these gods becomes the fruit of a calabash tree (p. 113), while another has his head replaced by a squash (p. 145)—that is, at least two of them acquire plant characteristics in the underworld before the coming of the first literal dawning.

The pairing of sowing and dawning receives a further meaning when it is taken to refer to human beings, whose perfection is the principal goal of the world-making gods of the present passage. To trace out this meaning, we must have recourse to ethnography. In Momostenango a mother father or patrilineage head "sows" and "plants" an unborn child in certain shrines of his lineage by announcing its mother's pregnancy there (B. Tedlock, *Time and the Highland Maya*, p. 80). On the "dawning" side of this process, the woman who gives birth to the child *cuya ri zak*, "gives it light" (Ibid., p. 211). This particular tracing remains metaphorical on both sides of the "sowing" and "dawning," but it retains a twist in that it is specifically built on the model of the literal sowing and metaphorical "dawning" of vegetation. A second human tracing, also metaphorical on both sides but twisted in that it seems to be built on the model of the metaphorical "sowing" and literal dawning of heavenly bodies, is followed out in death and its aftermath. Here the body is put in the earth, but the deceased "becomes light" or "dawns" (both *zakiric*) in two different senses: the body itself is reduced to plain white (light-colored) bones, but the spirit becomes a spark of light, something like a star.

73
provider, nurturer: This is *tzucul cool* [*tzukul ʒool*]; both words broadly refer to sustenance, but the latter seems to refer more overtly to actual food than the former (at least in B.), and the only word that resembles it today is *ʒobic*, "to get fat" (X.). The providers or nurturers ultimately intended here are human beings, who will one day sustain the gods through prayer and sacrifice, but for the time being the gods will succeed only in making animals. Eventually deer and birds will indeed be among those who nurture the gods with their blood, but only when there are humans to sacrifice them (p. 185); these same sacrificers will also provide their very own blood to the gods, drawing it from their ears and elbows (p. 187), and will ultimately offer the blood and the hearts of human captives (foreordained on p. 175 and carried out beginning on p. 187).

73
But there will be no high days and no bright praise: The paired words here are *uquihilabal* [*uʒihilabal*] and *ucalaibal* [*uʒalaibal*]. The first is literally "its-day-ness-instrument," referring to the keeping or setting aside of a specific day on the calendar for ritual purposes; I chose "high days" because the notion of "holidays" has become so secularized in English (despite the etymology of that word). The second is "its-brightness (or manifestness)-instrument"; it could even be translated as "publicity," but that term, unlike the Quiché one, is strictly secular, includes unfavorable attention, and does not involve a visual metaphor.

73
just like a cloud, like a mist, now forming, unfolding. Then the mountains were separated from the water: The "unfolding" here is *upupuheic*, which for both B. and Andrés Xiloj describes the way in which clouds form around mountains. "Separated" is my translation of *xtape*, tangentially based on *tapo*, "to pick out" (B.). On reading this passage don Andrés immediately commented: "It's just the way it is right now, there are clouds, then the clouds part, piece by piece, and now the sky is clear." It is as if the mountains were there in the pri-

252

mordial world all along and were revealed, little by little, as the clouds parted. But don Andrés complicated this interpretation by saying, "Haven't you seen that when the water passes—a rainstorm—and then it clears, a vapor comes out from among the trees? The clouds come out from among the mountains, among the trees." This lends a cyclical movement to the picture: the clouds come from the mountains, then conceal the mountains, then part to reveal the mountains, and so on.

73

By their genius alone, by their cutting edge alone: The paired terms here are *naual* and *puz.* The former term, although it is a Nahua borrowing, does not have the narrow meaning in Quiché that it has in central Mexico, but rather covers a very broad notion that may be glossed as "spirit familiar" (see *genius* in the Glossary for more detail). The latter term, *puz,* carries one central literal meaning from its Mixe-Zoque (and possibly Olmec) origins right down to its use in modern Quiché: it refers to the cutting of flesh with a knife (see D. Tedlock, *The Spoken Word,* p. 265). At the time of the conquest it was the primary term for sacrifice. In the present context, it implies that "the mountains were separated from the water" through an act resembling the extraction of the heart (or other organs) from a sacrifice. As if to confirm this allusion, the text goes on to refer to the earth as the "mountain-plain," or *huyub tacah* [*taȝah*], which is today the principal Quiché metaphor for the human body.

When don Andrés read these lines, he shifted away from the idea that the preceding lines about cloud formation and dispersal referred to something happening in the atmosphere around the mountains, moving toward the idea that this process was a simile for the formation and differentiation of the mountains themselves. That the mountains under discussion were made by means of *naual* rather than physical labor suggested a certain insubstantiality to him, and he commented: "Then these mountains are for no other reason than *representing* that there are hills or volcanoes." That is to say, he interpreted the mountains not as hard realities but as mere "signs" (*retal*), unfolding themselves "just like a cloud, like a mist."

75

it was brought forth by the Heart of Sky, Heart of Earth, as they are called, since they were the first to think of it: Andrés Xiloj took this to mean that the formation of the earth was an act of self-revelation on the part of the Heart of Sky and Heart of Earth. He compared them to the present-day *uȝux puuuk* or "Heart of Metal (or silver or money)," which reveals itself to the fortunate. As he explained it, "When one has luck, one picks up some kind of rock, but in the form of an animal; this is the Heart of Metal. When the moment comes, suddenly it appears." Such rocks may be volcanic concretions that happen to resemble animals, or they may be ancient stone artifacts. They are properly kept in the indoor half of a pair of patrilineage shrines called the *mebil*, which consists of a wooden box placed on a family altar (B. Tedlock, *Time and the Highland Maya*, p. 81). Don Andrés continued, "This is where one prays, this is where the fortune, the money, abounds. Here in the Popol Vuh, the Heart of Sky and the Heart of Earth appeared, and this is where the earth was propagated." The objects in a *mebil* should multiply of their own accord, and that, as don Andrés would have it, is what happened to the object or objects from which the earth began.

The notion of a "Heart of Sky" might seem out of place where something as substantial as earth or stone is concerned, but don Andrés' interpretation is supported by a much later passage in which the names Heart of Sky and Heart of Earth are both addressed to gods whose bodies have been petrified. The connection between these gods and the sky lies in the fact that they were petrified when the sun first rose and burned them. The objects called "Heart of Metal" today also have their celestial dimensions: volcanic concretions with animal shapes are said to have been formed at the first sunrise, just as the stone gods of the P.V. were, while ancient stone artifacts are said to have been formed where thunderbolts struck the ground. The P.V. does not mention the latter process, but it does include thunderbolts among the attributes of the Heart of Sky. The Book of Chilam Balam of Chumayel takes the question of celestial stoniness home to the sky itself, declaring that the "Heart of Heaven" is a bead of precious stone (Roys, *The Book of Chilam Balam of Chumayel*, p. 91).

76

all the guardians of the forests: Andrés Xiloj commented: "The animals are the caretakers of the woods. They [the gods] thought, 'There is a need for animals, so that people won't be able to enter the woods. The animals will frighten them.' " For the contemporary Quiché, wild animals are (in effect) the domestic animals of the Mundo, or earth deity. One cannot take a deer in the hunt without first asking permission of the Mundo. When a family is in arrears in its offerings, the Mundo may send a predator from out of the woods to raid its flocks or herds.

76

deer, birds, . . . yellowbites: On the basis of meaning this list might be organized into couplets and triplets:

quieh,	deer,
tziquin,	birds,
40h,	pumas,
balam,	jaguars,

cumatz,	serpents,
zochoch,	rattlesnakes,
canti	yellowbites

But whatever the groupings according to meaning, a list of this kind would be orally delivered today without any more marking of the transition between jaguars and serpents than that between pumas and jaguars; each individual word would retain its integrity, as marked by a stress on its final (or only) syllable, but there would be no pause until the run of parallel nouns came to a halt, or until the breath of the speaker ran out. On this basis I have chosen not to break such lists into lines of verse in the translation, but have run them on as prose.

76
"Why this pointless humming?": The "humming" and "rustling" referred to in this passage are the *lolin-* and *tzinin-* sounds discussed earlier (see notes for p. 72). What the gods are ultimately looking for here is the sound of articulate human speech, but they will not succeed in hearing it until p. 165. In the present scene, all they can hear on the earth is sounds that are indefinitely repetitive or vibratory and therefore without meaning, just as sounds were without meaning when there was only the sea.

78
"You, precious birds": This is *ix ix 4,iquin*, in which the second *ix* might be treated as a scribal error, but it is essential to the full understanding of the phrase. The first *ix* is plainly enough "you," in the familiar and in the plural, but the second one has a double meaning. At one level it is diminutive, making the whole phrase translatable as "You, precious (or little) birds," but at another level it is the day name Ix, which immediately precedes 4,iquin or "Bird" in the sequence of twenty day names. These are the two days devoted to the contemporary rites of the patrilineage shrine called the *mebil*, specifically Seven Ix and Eight 4,iquin; indeed, this shrine is often referred to simply by naming these two days.

78
a place to sleep: This is *uarabal*, and it alludes to patrilineage shrines, which are called *uarabalha*, "foundation of the house" or, literally, "sleeping (or resting) place of the house" (see the illustration on p. 256 for a present-day shrine of this kind). The animals that are given places to sleep in this passage, *queh* or "deer" and *4,iquin* or "birds," give their names to two of the days used for *uarabalha* rites today. The human mother-father or patrilineage head uses a low-numbered day bearing the name Queh or "Deer" to go to the parts of the *uarabalha* dedicated to people in order to announce that a woman married into his lineage is pregnant and to pray for the child she bears. This ritual is called a "sowing," just as is the long process in

SLEEPING PLACE OF THE HOUSE: A foundation shrine belonging to a patrilineage in Momostenango. The stone slab that covers the shrine marks it as a place of worship that is private rather than open to the public; only the head of the patrilineage that owns this particular shrine may pray and burn copal here.

which the divine mother-fathers of the P.V. speak of making humans and prepare for their coming long before they actually succeed in making them a reality. Deer result from one of their four attempts to make humans; these animals are, in effect, an approximation of real humans, their fault being that they walk on all fours and lack articulate speech. The implication here is that in visiting his shrines to announce a child on the day named after the deer, the human mother-father commemorates the process whereby properly walking and talking humans were spoken of and approximated by the divine mother-fathers (the Maker and Modeler) before they were realized.

The most startling link between shrines and deer—deer as animals rather than days named Deer—manifests itself in dreams. On this point I can give firsthand testimony. During the period of my formal apprenticeship as a daykeeper in Momostenango, I told Andrés Xiloj of dreaming that I was followed along a path by a series of large deer. After a laugh of immediate recognition he told me that I had been followed by shrines! He explained that outdoor shrines have spirit familiars that frequently take the form of deer—and, these days, of horses and cattle. The path, of course, was that of the days of the calendar, along which each shrine had its proper place in a sequence. The deer were following me in anticipation of the time when I would end my apprenticeship and feed them—that is, make offerings of my own.

78

"Talk, speak out. Don't moan, don't cry out.": Here again (as on p. 76) the gods express their desire for articulate human speech, this time contrasted with moans and cries rather than humming and rustling. Not only that, but they want to hear their own names and praises, and they ask the animals to "keep our days." This last idea is expressed by *cohiquihila* [*cohiʒihilaa*], literally, "to-us-you (plural familiar) day (transitive imperative)," analogous to the form rendered as "high days" on p. 73. If English permitted "day" to be a verb, one could translate *cohiʒihilaa* as "dayify us," with the pun on "deify" being appropriate enough. A less direct translation would be "calendrify us."

78

they just squawked, they just chattered, they just howled: New sounds have been added to the world here. They are not yet the sounds of speech, but neither are they like the rippling, murmuring, and humming of the world that had only a sea (see p. 72). Those sounds tended toward vowel harmony and repeated consonants—*-4,inin-* and *chamam-*, for example—whereas the verb stems here retain vowel harmony but do not repeat their consonants: *uachela-, carala-,* and *uoho-*.

78

It wasn't apparent what language they spoke: The text has *maui xua-chinic uuach quiʒhabal*, literally, "not faced-out its face their-talk-instrument." The active verb *uachinic*, built on *uach*, "face," is used primarily with reference to the bearing of fruit by plants. The implication is that the sounds made by the animals contained a potential for articulate speech, but that this potential was never realized.

79

It talked at first, but senselessly: The person of mud is unique among all the creatures made by the gods in that it not only lacks sensible speech, but is not even quoted by means of onomatopoeia. Note also the correlate lack of articulation of its body. But the subtlest point here is that the only creature made of mud is also the only one made in the singular, which makes this episode an allusion to the Adamic myth. What the writers of the P.V. have to say about Adam, in their indirect way, is that a singular creature of mud could neither have

made sense nor walked nor multiplied. If there ever was such a creature, there is no way it could have left a trace of itself; it must have
dissolved.

80
"a counting of days, a counting of lots": This is *uquihixic* [*uȝihixic*]
ubitaxic, "its-being-dayed (or timed) its-being-modeled (or shaped)."
As daykeepers, Xpiyacoc and Xmucane will divine by means of
counting the day numbers and names of the 260-day divinatory cycle,
dividing or "shaping" a fistful of seeds of the coral tree (see the Glossary) into lots.

80
the human mass: "Mass" is *anom*, which is given this gloss in B.

81
master craftsman: This is *ahtoltecat*, in which *ah-* is occupational; the
rest is from Nahua *toltecatl*, "master of mechanical arts" (D.).

81
*"Run your hands over the kernels of corn, over the seeds of the coral
tree"*: The verb stem here is *mala-*, "to run the hand over something"
(V.). The contemporary Quiché daykeeper first pours the seeds out of
a small bundle into a pile on a table and mixes them, moving the right
hand over them with palm down flat and fingers spread, and then
grabs a fistful. The remaining seeds are then set aside; those from the
fistful are sorted into lots of four seeds each, arranged in parallel rows
so that the days can easily be counted on them, one day for each lot.
When seeds are left over from the division into fours, a remainder of
three seeds is made into two additional lots (with two seeds in one and
one seed in the other), while a remainder of one or two seeds counts
as one additional lot. Once the clusters are complete the diviner
begins counting the days of the 260-day cycle, starting in the present
(the day of the divination itself), the past (the day the client's problem began), or the future (the day of an action contemplated by
the client). The augury is reckoned from the character or portent
of the day that is reached by counting through to the final lot of
seeds.

The alphabetic P.V. does not give the numbers and names of the
days counted by Xpiyacoc and Xmucane in this earliest of all divinations, but the ancient P.V. may have been like the Chilam Balam
book from Chumayel, which treats the first counting of days as nothing less than the origin of the 260-day calendar itself and gives not
only numbers and names but day-by-day interpretations, running
through twenty consecutive days (Roys, *The Book of Chilam Balam of
Chumayel*, chap. 13).

81
the borrowing: This is *ukahic*, a term that Andrés Xiloj, as a daykeeper, recognized immediately. When today's daykeeper speaks the

opening prayer for a divination, invoking the sheet-lightning, clouds, mists, and damp breezes of the world, he or she is said to be "borrowing" these forces from the days themselves, each of which is ruled by a lord, and from the mountains of the world, each of which has a spirit familiar (B. Tedlock, *Time and the Highland Maya*, pp. 155, 157, 162). Xpiyacoc and Xmucane are not as modest as this human daykeeper in their own borrowing of lightning, moisture, and air currents: they name the Heart of Sky, whose electrical aspect ultimately manifests not as far-off and silently flickering sheet-lightning but as close-up thunderbolts, and who is also known as Hurricane, the bringer of rains and winds of world-destroying proportions. Meteorological forces, large or small, serve to connect the cosmos at large, both temporally and spatially, with the microcosmic scene of the divination, transmitting information about distant places or times through the counting of days and through lightninglike sensations that occur in various parts of the diviner's own body.

81

the lots: This is *bit*, possibly the same as the stem in the name *bitol*, "Modeler" (see *Maker, Modeler* in the Glossary). My guess is that it refers to the clusters of seeds that are made up from the random fistful taken up by the diviner (as described above); in effect, the diviner is giving shape to a chaotic mass. I translate *bit* as "lots" because that word both fits the groups of seeds, which are arranged in lots of four, and figures in English-language divination terminology. "Diviner" (on p. 83) is a translation of *ahbit*, in which *bit* has the occupational prefix.

82

who stands behind others: This is *chiracan*, which Andrés Xiloj identified as part of a phrase used today by daykeepers: *chirakan uȝab*, "at-his/her-legs his/her-arms" (in which "legs" and "arms" include "feet" and "hands"). To be at someone's feet and hands means to give assistance, as a daykeeper does when praying and giving offerings on behalf of a client, or a midwife does when assisting a birth.

83

"may you succeed, may you be accurate": Like Xpiyacoc and Xmucane, the contemporary daykeeper speaks to the seeds while arranging them, asking for a clear outcome.

83

"Have shame, you up there, . . . attempt no deception": Andrés Xiloj was not surprised to hear the Heart of Sky addressed in this manner. He pointed out that today's daykeepers (including himself) also ask that the gods not deceive their divinatory clients. The praying diviner may say, for example, *ma ban la ri mentira*, "Do not make a lie." In the case of the P.V. the client in question is none other than the god Sovereign Plumed Serpent.

259

83
manikins, woodcarvings: Andrés Xiloj remarked, "Then these will only be *representations* of humans."

83
They just went and walked wherever they wanted: Andrés Xiloj commented: "Then they're like animals." In Quiché thinking one of the major differences between animals and humans is that humans must ask permission of the gods to go abroad in the world. To pray that nothing bad happen to one in the road is to ask permission to pass; the need for such permission is more acute in the case of visits to powerful shrines or distant towns. In prayers that prepare the way for a long trip, one asks not only that there be no robbers in the road, but that policemen, soldiers, and customs officials look the other way.

84
The man's body was carved from the wood of the coral tree: The body of the god presently called Maximon in the Tzutuhil Maya town of Santiago Atitlán is made of this wood (Michael Mendelson, "Maximon: An Iconographical Introduction," p. 57).

84
the pith of reeds: This is *zibac;* B. gives *ziba3* as "the pith or insides of a small reed."

84
a rain of resin: Andrés Xiloj commented: "This was turpentine that fell, and it was burning as it fell."

84
the black rainstorm: This is *quecal hab* [*3ekal hab*]. As Andrés Xiloj explained, this does not mean that the rain itself was black, but refers to the darkness created by a very intense rainstorm.

84
Into their houses came: This is *xoc ula* [*xoc ulaa*], "entered as visitors." Today any invasion of the house (including its patio) by a wild animal is viewed as a sign sent by the earth deity, whether it is a fox or possum that attacks domestic animals or, say, a bird that happens to fly indoors. Andrés Xiloj pointed out that such animals do not speak (*4hauic*) but rather give signs (*retal*) by their cries or movements. Note that even under the cataclysmic conditions of the present episode the speaking is done by domestic animals and by artifacts; it is not attributed to wild animals.

84
turkeys: This is *ac* [*a4*], which became the term for the Old World chicken during colonial times. A number of colonial dictionaries give the term for turkey as *kitzih a4,* "true *a4*" (T. and V.), or *mazeual a4,* "Indian *a4*" (G.), which makes it plain enough that the pre-Hispanic term for turkey was *a4*. Today the turkey is called *nooz* (X.), a term

that had already appeared by the seventeenth century (listed in B. as *noz*).

85

r-r-rip, r-r-rip, / r-r-rub, r-r-rub: This is *holi, holi, huqui, huqui*, onomatopoeic for the sound of a handstone (mano) rubbing against a grinding stone (metate). If the performance of the present Quiché story was anything like that of North American Indian tales, these lines were probably sung. It must be kept in mind that *h* in Quiché is rough, like Spanish *j* or German *ch*. This roughness would probably be exaggerated in a dramatic oral rendering, hence my suggestion in the translation that the *r* be trilled. When judged by the fact that the verb for "rub together" is *hukunic* (X.), *huqui, huqui* should probably be *huki, huki*. Andrés Xiloj immediately heard a sound play in these lines, which he rendered as follows:

> *hoo ali, hoo ali,*
> *hukuuic, hukuuic*

meaning something like this:

> Let's go girl, let's go girl,
> rubbing together, rubbing together.

85

their hearthstones were shooting out: Andrés Xiloj remarked: "It's like a cataract of stones from a volcano!" This incident may be the origin of the stars Alnitak, Saiph, and Rigel in Orion; today these three stars are said to be the three hearthstones of the typical Quiché kitchen fireplace, arranged to form a triangle, and the cloudy area they enclose (Great Nebula M42) is said to be the smoke from a fire (B. Tedlock, "Earth Rites and Moon Cycles").

86

wood alone was used for their flesh: Andrés Xiloj remarked, "They lacked blood, or quickening, which is what corn gives." As it turns out later, real human beings are indeed made of corn.

86

"I am their sun . . . their months": "Sun" is *quih* [*ȝih*] here, which could either be "sun" or "day," but "months" is *iquil* [*iȝil*], which is definitely "months," rather than *iȝ*, "moon."

86

"I am the walkway and I am the foothold of the people": "Walkway" is *binibal* and "foothold" is *chacabal; -bal* is an instrumental suffix. Andrés Xiloj explicated Seven Macaw's statement as follows: *"Binibal* is to give light for walking, or to go out on a somewhat clear road; and *chacabal*—now we say *chacanibal*—is the same. These words are in the prayers we say at the *uarabalha* [patrilineage shrines], to ask permission for anyone who goes out of the house to whatever place. They

can walk, they can crawl—*chacanibal* is to crawl on all fours. Seven Macaw is saying that he is a person's feet, since he knows that he has light [to show a person where to step], but in fact the person sees darkly, it isn't very clear."

86

"they stand out": This is *cauacoh*, translated on the basis of *cauaquic*, "to have big teeth (so as to be unable to close the mouth)" (X.).

86

the scope of his face lies right around his own perch: Seven Macaw, as the Big Dipper, is restricted to a path that lies close to the pole star, unlike the sun and moon (see Glossary and D. Tedlock, "The Sowing and Dawning of All the Sky-Earth"). The classic Maya equivalent of Seven Macaw is shown perched atop a northern tree at Palenque, in the central panel of the Tablet of the Cross and on the lid of the sarcophagus beneath the Temple of the Inscriptions (Linda Schele, *Notebook*, pp. 66–67).

PART TWO

89

the mountains . . . are softened by him: "Softened" is my translation of *nebonic*; X. glosses this as "overcooked," but Andrés Xiloj read it as "soaked." He commented: "When the earth is completely soaked it can be destroyed by the water. When there are rains of forty-eight or sixty hours, there may be destruction. Landslides are the work of such rains."

92

Then he went up over the tree and fell flat on the ground: When birds are shot they fly upward in a spasm before falling from a tree. But Seven Macaw's movement here also suggests that of the Big Dipper; assuming that his head and body correspond to the bowl of the Big Dipper and his tail to its handle, his climbing of the tree to eat his nances, his going up over the tree when shot, and his fall to the ground all follow the pattern of the Big Dipper, which rises with its handle down, goes up over the North Star (counterclockwise) in a momentarily horizontal position, and then sets with its bowl end down. The period when all seven stars may be seen in ascendancy, from mid-October to mid-May, corresponds approximately to the dry season; the period when the Big Dipper is already in steep descent by twilight and when all seven stars may become invisible for as much as half the night, from mid-July to mid-October, corresponds to the hurricane season.

92

"tricksters": This is *4axto4*; it is glossed as "the devil" or "liar" in colonial dictionaries (B. and V.), but that is a missionary view of the

matter. In the P.V., where the word is used ten different times, it is usually obvious from context that the person or persons labeled by it have done something tricky or are accused of trickery. In the present case Hunahpu and Xbalanque have ambushed Seven Macaw while he was at his meal. In other cases the Four Hundred Boys suspect Zipacna of being tricky, which he indeed turns out to be (p. 95); Xmucane accuses Blood Woman of trickery (p. 118), but (ironically) Blood Woman's ability to work magic apparently comes from the fact that she carries Xmucane's own grandchildren in her womb; Hunahpu and Xbalanque accuse a toad of trickery (p. 133), and sure enough it turns out that the toad never swallowed what he claimed was in his belly; Xtah and Xpuch are accused of trickery when painted wasps turn into real ones (p. 192); and the Quichés are called tricksters by their enemies for making it look as though the people they've seized for sacrifice were attacked by wild animals (p. 194). Except for the cases of Zipacna and the toad, the trickery works on the side of the protagonists in a given story. Translating *4axto4* as "trickster" rather than "devil" puts the matter in a more general American Indian context, where the exploits of trickster figures are simultaneously disapproved and enjoyed.

92
"they've dislocated my jaw": This is obviously the origin of the way a macaw's beak looks, with a huge upper mandible and a much smaller and retreating lower one.

92
"All my teeth are just loose": "Loose" is *chu*, translated on the basis of a reduplicated form in B., *chuyucha*, "to rattle."

92
" 'Do forgive us' ": The addition of " 'Do' " to this phrase is my way of translating *qui* [*ki*], which, according to V., carries a sense of exaggerated politeness.

93
with great effort: This is *nimac ua chih* [*nimak uaa 4hih*], "great this effort," in which *4hih* is translated on the basis of *4hihinic*, "the strength to do something" (X.).

93
"What sweets can you make, what poisons can you cure?": The "sweets" and "poisons" are both *qui* [*quii*], a word that carries both these meanings to this day (for an explanation see *sweet drink* in the Glossary).

93
"We just pull the worms out of teeth": There is a contemporary Mopán Maya myth in which Lord Kin ("Sun" or "Day") causes the chief of the vultures to have a toothache and then is begged to come and cure it (Thompson, *Ethnology of the Mayas*, pp. 129–32). But in

this case the motive of the trickery is the protagonist's desire to get his wife back from the vultures.

93
"we just cure eyes": As a medical specialty, the curing of eyes fits under the same heading as bones and teeth because the Quiché language classifies the eyes as bones. Eyes are *ubac [ubak] uuach*, literally "its-bones (or pits) his/her-eyes," in the P.V.; today they are *uba3uach*. Andrés Xiloj himself covers a medical territory similar to that of Hunahpu and Xbalanque: in addition to being a bonesetter and healer of sprains, he knows how to make eyedrops.

93
"It's a worm, gnawing at the bone": The present-day Quiché retain the notion that a toothache is caused by a worm gnawing at the bone. According to T. J. Knab (personal communication), there is a Mesoamerican parasite that takes up residence in the gums.

93
a coating: This is *cu [3u]*, "covering" (X.).

93
When his eyes were trimmed back: The verb stem here is *cholic [4holic]*, "to cut or pull out hair or feathers" (X.), or "flay, skin, take off crust" (V.). This is clearly meant to be the origin of the large white eye patch and very small eyes of the scarlet macaw (see *Seven Macaw* in the Glossary). I take it that Seven Macaw sported two large metal discs where the patches of the scarlet macaw are now.

94
What they did was simply the word of the Heart of Sky: In a similar fashion the Zunis sometimes portray the Ahayuuta warrior heroes— who, like Hunahpu and Xbalanque, are tricksters—as simply carrying out the word of the Sun Father, though they may appear to be acting on their own (see D. Tedlock, *Finding the Center*, pp. 234–48).

94
a post for their hut. . . . the lintel of their hut: This passage is self-contradictory as to what use the Four Hundred Boys intend for their log. The "post" is *acan [akan]*, literally "leg"; Andrés Xiloj explained that this would be a vertical post with a fork at the top. The "lintel" is *uapalil (apalil* today), which he specified as a term for a horizontal beam over a door or window.

94
"We'd like some help": This is *cacachaquimah [cakacha3imah] tana*, in which *caka-* is "incomplete-we" and *tana* indicates supplication; the verb stem, *cha3imah*, is given by V. as "ask to borrow."

95
"we'll throw him down": The verb stem here is *tzac [tzak]*, "fling, cast" (X.). This is mere bravado; it is not what the Four Hundred Boys actually end up doing.

95
" 'Why are you spilling dirt in the hole?' ": The verb stem here is written *macaha*, but with the stem of the *h* crossed off to make it into an *n*. I translate it "spill" on the basis of *ma4anic*, "to spill or scatter" (X.). Here the Four Hundred Boys are proposing to make a sarcastic statement to Zipacna, but once again, as when they talked about throwing him into the hole, they are indulging in bravado.

95
"wedged": This is *pachal*, translated on the basis of *pa4hinic*, "be between two walls or in a crack" (X.).

95
"we'll wham a big log": The verb stem here is *tarih*, "give a blow that makes a sound" (X.). In effect the Four Hundred Boys are planning to put a major vertical post for their hut into place, resting its butt end on a sacrifice victim.

95
he dug a separate hole to one side: Edmonson notes here that in digging a hole for the present-day Flying Pole Dance, Quichés place offerings in a hole dug to one side from the post hole proper (*The Book of Counsel*, p. 45). Speakers of the Achí dialect of Quiché tell a story in which a character now known as Zipac carries a log the narrator compares with the pole used in the Monkey Dance (Mary Shaw, *According to Our Ancestors*, p. 48).

95
"on another level, or two levels away": "Level" is my translation of *elebal;* literally this would be "place of egress," but I take my cue from Burgess and Xec, who decided on "elevation" (*Popol Wuj*, p. 42), a solution that fits with the general Mesoamerican notion of a stratified underworld.

96
to dedicate: This is *lacabebal*, with an instrumental suffix (*-bal*), translated on the basis of *la3abeh*, "to inhabit some place, occupying it" (B.).

96
Having taken their pickings: The verb stem here is *culun*, translated on the basis of *3ulunic*, "to pluck, devastate, strip" (X.).

97
a play on words: This is *zacbal tzih*, "play-instrument words"; B. gives *zaquibal* as "instrument for playing." The authors of the P.V. seem uncertain as to whether the Four Hundred Boys actually became the Pleiades (see *Hundrath* in the Glossary), in which case *motz* (the Quiché term for these stars) would mean the same thing as *omu4h*, "four hundred," or whether the supposed connection between the Four Hundred Boys and the Pleiades is merely a matter of a pun between *omu4h* and *motz*.

97
counterfeiting: This is *haluachixic,* translated on the basis of *halua-chir,* "change one thing for another" (V.).

97
the forearms: This is *xul,* translated on the basis of an entry in V. that is missing its heading but falls between *xulbak* and *xulu;* the gloss is "little arms of crabs or shrimps."

97
where they opened: This is *pa hac; pa* is "in" and *hac* is translated on the basis of the entry for *hak* in V., "to open things" (such as curtains or eyelids).

97
the claws: This is *ucoc* [*ucooc*] *3ab,* "its-carrying-device arm," in which *cooc* is translated on the basis of an entry in X.

97
They used a flagstone for the back of the crab, which clattered: Andrés Xiloj commented: "A crab is just like a wristwatch: it has the meat inside and it's pure bone outside."

97
they put the shell beneath an overhang: Andrés Xiloj pictured this as a spot beneath a waterfall.

97
"By now I can't stand the hunger": "Hunger" is a Quiché metaphor for sexual appetite; that the metaphorical level is intended here becomes more obvious as the story unfolds.

98
"please come point her out, boys": Andrés Xiloj chuckled as he read this and then said, "This Zipacna is abusing the boys here, he's saying they shouldn't be afraid. It says here, *quibe ta iuaba,* which could be *quibe ta iuabaa,* 'If only you would come along to *iuabaa*—to point it out,' but it could also be, *quebe ta iuabah,* 'If only *iuabah*—your stones, your balls—would come along.' Today, when someone runs from a fight, the saying is *queeme ta iuabah,* 'Don't hide your balls.' So Zipacna is saying, 'Don't you have any balls, boys?' They're still young." Since the puns in this passage cannot be preserved in English I have tried to make its sexual dimension more obvious by using feminine pronouns for the crab (though Quiché pronouns do not have gender), since the crab is the object of Zipacna's "hunger."

98
"But won't you please": This sentence begins with *la qui* [*ki*]; *la* makes it a yes/no question and *ki* (according to V.) indicates exaggerated politeness.

98
"I'll show you a place where there are plenty of birds": Continuing along the lines of the above comment, Andrés Xiloj said, "There it is

again, only now it's *nuuaba,* 'I show you something,' or else *nuabah,* 'my balls'—he's got balls." As for the "birds" (*4,iquin*), the primary metaphor for penis is "bird" in Quiché; Q. dates this metaphor to the late post-Hispanic period, but it is already present in a colonial dictionary for Pokoman Maya (P.), a Quichean language.

98

"We were entering": The verb stem here is *oc-,* translated (literally) as "enter" throughout this passage, a simple solution that keeps the same double meaning going in English that is present in the original.

98

"facedown . . . on our back": These two opposite body positions are given throughout the present episode as *hupulic* and *pacalic,* respectively. Although they seem to have caused difficulties for some translators, they are spelled correctly in the MS., are glossed in B. in the same way I have translated them, and were perfectly transparent to Andrés Xiloj.

98

her shell is gleaming red there: Some translators have complained about the color of this crab, but there are species of crab that are red before they are cooked.

98

"perhaps I'd better enter on my back": By this time Andrés Xiloj had already begun snickering as he read, but now he burst into laughter. Explaining himself, he said: "Clearly, the crab is a woman. As you already know, a woman does it on her back, but here it's in reverse: the man is on the bottom and the crab will go on top. These are trial runs. In ancient times, I think, they didn't know what sin was. They were looking for a way to understand everything."

98

only his kneecaps were showing now: At this point don Andrés sat back and said, "My God! All the way to the knees!"

98

He gave a last sigh and was calm: The "sigh" here is *biquitahic,* translated as suggested by don Andrés; X. gives *biჳbitic,* "sigh." Don Andrés translated *xlilob* as "was calm"; V. gives *lilot* as "tranquil." Of Zipacna's state don Andrés commented: "Nothing will bother him now." The story of Zipacna and the crab prompted him to tell a story that has been translated elsewhere (see D. Tedlock, *The Spoken Word,* pp. 317–20). There is a contemporary Achí story about a character named Zipac that makes the sexual dimension more overt than it is in the P.V. (Shaw, *According to Our Ancestors,* pp. 48–51).

99

"Lure this Earthquake into settling down": "Lure" is *bochiih,* translated on the basis of *bochih,* "allure" (B.); "settling down" is *cuubic,* "to sit" (X.). I have supplied "this Earthquake" in order to clarify the

sense of the sentence, setting it apart from the plural reference of the previous sentence.

99

"in the course of the days, in the course of the light": *chi be quih* [*zih*], *chi be zac* [*zak*], "in-road day (or sun), in-road light." According to Andrés Xiloj, this means "for all time. Just the way we in my family are weavers. All the time, and for all time, we are weavers." For an alternative translation of this line and a further comment by don Andrés, see *"as long as there is day"* in the notes to p. 170.

100

"Lead the way": This is *chicama cabe* [*chiʒama kabe*], literally "imperative-you-take our-road," a common Quiché idiom which I have translated into the equivalent English idiom.

100

they just blow at the birds when they shoot: Andrés Xiloj remarked: "When people go out hunting today with guns, and when they see that an animal is coming, they do this: [blows a quick puff of air]. It is like magnetism, they pull it, the animal stops—it feels, it thinks there is a person hidden. When the animal has stopped for a moment, the person shoots, and there it is. The animal stopped to see what this noise was."

101

made fire with a drill: This is *xquibac cu quicac* [*xquibak ʒu quiʒaʒ*], "they-drilled then their-fire." An example of the same idiom is given by B. as *canubaʒ caʒ*, "I start a fire"; V. gives *bak* as "to drill."

101

"the one to be made and modeled": The reference is to humankind, and the problem is the same one the twins discuss on pp. 89–90. Like so many other American Indian hero twins, they are monster slayers, making the earth habitable for humans.

101

"the human heart": I have supplied "human" here, assuming that the subject of the discussion has not changed since the previous sentence.

101

"a bite of meat, a meal of flesh": The parallel items here are *tiic* and *chacuxic*, which have been translated in many different ways; my version is based on *tiinic*, "to eat meat" (X.), and *ʒhacuh*, "to eat meat" (V.).

101

his ankles were bound to his wrists: The "ankles" and "wrists" are *ucul racan ucab* [*rakan uʒab*], literally "its-necks his-legs his-arms"; as Andrés Xiloj explained, the "neck" of a leg or arm is its "ankle" or "wrist" in Quiché.

PART THREE

105

let's just drink to the telling: The verb stem for "drink" here is *camuh;* I follow Edmonson in reading it as a variant of *kumuh,* "to drink" (*The Book of Counsel,* p. 58). Andrés Xiloj liked this reading and pictured the narrator as seated on the tomb of One Hunahpu and Seven Hunahpu, on a day bearing the name Hunahpu. On many such days contemporary Quiché cemeteries look like crowded picnic grounds; whole families come to the graves of their ancestors, sprinkling flower petals, burning offerings, reciting prayers, and eating and drinking, all this in a respectful but festive mood.

105

One Hunahpu and Seven Hunahpu, as they are called: The MS. leaves out Seven Hunahpu here; I assume that this is an error, given that everything else in the sentence is in the plural, and given that One and Seven Hunahpu are named together two sentences later.

105

a partner: This is *laquel [laȝel].* V. gives an example of the use of this term in which a woman may refer to another woman who shares the same man with her as *nulaȝel (nu-* is "my").

105

flautists, singers, and writers; carvers, jewelers, metalworkers: Note that in these two sets of three skills each, writing is grouped with the performing arts rather than with handicrafts. Whatever writing system or systems were employed by the Quiché, the grouping of writing with flute playing and singing points to its close association with oral recitation (see also the notes to p. 71). "Writers" is my translation of ahtzib *[ahɥ,ib],* "person-who-does-writing," in which *ɥ,ib* also covers painting.

105

The four ballplayers: These words are supplied; the text only indicates "they."

106

"They're really determined to run right over us!": This is *xax quehiquic uloc [ulok] pacaui [pakaui],* literally "certainly they-cut-straight hither above-us."

107

to draw blood from people: Andrés Xiloj commented: "When there is strife, when people begin to fight, they strike one another. The blood comes out, and Xibalba receives this blood. We see that it fell, but it fell into the flasks of the evil ones. It is like their food."

107

to make pus come out of their legs, to make their faces yellow, to cause jaundice: "Jaundice" is *ʒanal,* "yellowness." This passage could refer not only to hepatitis but to yellow fever (if yellow fever was present in pre-Columbian times), whose symptoms include jaundice. The pus in the legs would be sores spread out along the lymphatic system.

107

to reduce people to bones ... until they die from emaciation and edema: The first of these ailments is *ziiah bac* [*bak*], in which the first word may be a form of *ziy,* "extended" (E.), and the second is "bone"; B. gives *ziyah bak* as "skeleton" and *ziyah bakil* as the name of an unspecified illness; X. gives *bakil,* literally "bony," as "thin, weak." The second ailment is *xupan,* "dropsy" (V. and G.), better known today as "edema," swelling caused by excess fluid in the tissues or cavities of the body. According to Andrés Xiloj, the contemporary shamans called *ahmesa,* "keepers of the table," sometimes go bad and practice a ritual called *chakih mesa,* "dry table," in which they ask Xibalba to cause emaciation: "They put bones into the body of a person by means of prayers, in order to dry him up. They put a skull into the body of a person. They dry up the whole body." He told of a recent case in Momostenango in which a man was brought to court because "there were skulls, and bones of the arms and legs, in the place where this man burned his offerings. It was by means of these things that he screwed people up." Edema is caused by a separate ritual, called *rax mesa,* "fresh (or unripe, sudden, strong) table." Don Andrés continued: "This, too, is done with bones. They put the bone in water, or whatever they put it in, and this same bone comes to be left in the body of the person, then he swells up. It's like an injection, but the evil is contained by this bone. The moment it is put in the body, the evil befalls one."

107

to catch up with people: The verb here is *culuachih* [*ʒuluachih*], "to come about" (B.), "to strike with misfortune" (V.).

107

whenever they have filth or grime in the ... house: According to Andrés Xiloj, the best way to keep the agents of Xibalba out of one's house is to keep the place swept out and not allow trash to accumulate. See the story in the first note to p. 109 for a case in which a house is cleaned out as a way of ending the deeds of a Xibalban.

107

in the doorway of the house, in the patio of the house: This is *chirih ha,* "at the back of the house," and *chuua ha,* "at the face of the house." In Quiché terminology, as Andrés Xiloj explained, the "back" of a house is the side that has a door or entrance way giving access to a public road or path, while the "face" is the side that gives onto a patio (whether enclosed on all four sides or not).

107

that people should die in the road, just "sudden death": This affliction
is *rax camical,* "fresh (or unripe, sudden, strong) death." According to
Andrés Xiloj, it is like edema (see the third note to p. 107) in that it is
caused by practices that come under the heading of *rax mesa:* "They
come to frighten one in the road, and now one doesn't arrive home.
Suddenly one may fall in the ditch, *rax camical.* As it says here in the
Popol Vuh, 'Blood comes to the mouth,' it is as if one had pneumonia,
suddenly one begins to vomit blood, and one dies in a moment. It is a
matter of the *rax mesa.* They put a bone in the lung, and it is damaged
in a moment. One begins to vomit pure blood. They carry their materials on their shoulders, as it says here: 'The load on his shoulders.'
When they are encountered in the road, they can kill one. But it isn't
the *ahmesa* directly, but rather his genius [see the Glossary] or *uin*
[were animal]." See the third note to p. 107 for more about the *ahmesa.*

109

Such are those who shared their thoughts: At this point Andrés Xiloj
was reminded of a story, which he told on the spot. It is about a young
man who gets aggravated with his wife almost to the point of taking a
machete to her, all because an emissary of Xibalba keeps sneaking
hairs or bits of rag or even bugs into the food she prepares. Moving in
for the kill, the Xibalban tells the young man he has just seen his wife
serving lunch to another man. Sure enough, when he gets home for
lunch and asks his wife to give him the breast of the chicken she has
prepared, she cannot find it in the pot. Later the young man is seized
with the idea of climbing a tree; the earth rumbles and he suddenly
finds himself looking down on the spot where the lords of Xibalba regularly assemble to banquet on blood that has been spilled by violence.
He sees Blood Gatherer (the head lord) come out, and the last one to
arrive, named Jodido (a Spanish word roughly translatable as
"screwed-up"), turns out to be the very Xibalban who has been plotting against him. Jodido brags about how he sneaked the chicken
breast out of the pot and tells the others they will soon enjoy the
blood of the poor woman who was cooking it. After the Xibalbans
leave, the young man returns home and throws boiling water in each
corner of his house. Returning to the banquet spot in time to see the
Xibalbans reassemble, he sees Jodido come in very late, barely able to
move because of the scalding he has received. After this no more for-
eign objects appear in the young man's food.

109

they were piqued and driven: This is *xetzaixic,* "they were salted
(spiced)" (X.), and *xecotobax,* "they were pursued" (B.).

109

And these messengers of theirs are owls: Andrés Xiloj remarked: "At times an owl suddenly arrives near the house and begins to sing. This is a warning. Yes, it is a warning from Xibalba."

109–110

repeated their words, reciting the exact words: This is *ta xquizac* [*xquitzak*] *cut* [*4ut*] *quitzih xaui xere ucholic utzih.* B. gives *tzaconizah ri tzih* as "to fulfill words," and V. gives *tzakantic* as "deliver up, render, regurgitate"; *xaui xere* is "yet the same," and *ucholic* is "to say in an ordered way" (V.).

110

"Don't the lords . . . speak truly?": That this line is part of the dialogue rather than part of the narrative is made obvious by the next line, which is clearly a reply.

110

"We're going, . . . even though we've just arrived": "Even though" is my translation of *xaet,* which B. gives as "in vain, uselessly." Antitheses are rather frequent in the speech of Hunahpu and Xbalanque.

110

"just play and just sing": The playing here (*tzuan-*) is specifically on the flute.

110

where the rapids cut through: This is *chuchi halha ziuanub,* in which the first word is "at-its-mouth"; the second is "rapid, violent river" (B.); and the third may be an error for *ziuanuh,* "to open a ditch" (V.).

111

"Morning": This is *calah* [*3alah*], literally "clear, bright, plainly visible," used as a morning greeting in classical Quiché. Today the preferred greeting for the morning is *zakiric,* "it is getting light (or dawning)."

111

they got no relief: This is *maui xeyacamaric,* in which *maui* is negative; B. gives *yacamaric* as "be relieved, alleviated."

111

the laughter rose up like a serpent in their very cores: Cumatz or "serpent" is a term for various kinds of disabling cramps (see B. Tedlock, *Time and the Highland Maya,* pp. 54, 56). Concerning the present case of "serpent," Andrés Xiloj said the following: "There are people who begin to make an uproar when one passes by, they die laughing. This is because those of Xibalba are among them; it is as if they had been ordered to do this. This is a work of Xibalba, and this is what the Popol Vuh is talking about. People get a serpent (*cumatz*) here in the breast [indicates a diagonal through his trunk, from one shoulder to the opposite hip] for having laughed so hard. Now one can't bear laughing because of the pain of the serpent; now it doesn't let one breathe. We could go out in the street right now. There could be a group of people there. They could begin to make an uproar, killing themselves laughing, and we couldn't hear what they were laughing about. But Xibalba would know what they were saying."

111

down to their blood and bones: This is *chi quiqui [quiqui4] quib, chi quiba [quibak] quib,* literally, "that they-blooded themselves, that they-boned themselves." That is, they became nothing but blood and bones, having laughed their flesh away; in idiomatic English, "they laughed themselves sick."

112

This ball of theirs is just a spherical knife: This is *are cu [4u] ri quichah [chaah] xa coloquic cha,* "this-is then the their-ball just rounded knife." *Chaah* often means "ball game" in the P.V.; wherever it is used for the ball itself, as it is here, it refers to the ball of Xibalba, whereas the ball used by One and Seven Hunahpu (and later by Hunahpu and Xbalanque) is always called *quic [qui4],* literally "blood (or sap)," but "rubber [ball]" in the context of the ball game. I suspect that *chaah* was a generic term and therefore translate it (wherever it refers to the ball) as just plain "ball," as contrasted with "rubber ball."

112

their torch was brought: The torch is *chah,* literally "pine"; in the present context it is the Quiché term for what is more widely known in Mesoamerica as *ocote* (a Nahua-derived term), a split-off stick of extremely resinous pine wood, still widely used for torches and kindling.

112

they were cowering: The verb here is *chocochoh,* which means to crouch "in a cowering manner" (B.).

112

whistling with drafts, clattering with hail: This is *zac [zak] xuruxuh, zac caracoh [4aracoh],* in which *zak* may be shortened from *zakbach,* "hail." The first verb is similar to *xururic,* "the penetration of cold" (into a house) or "a sharp whistling" (X.); the second is similar to *4ararem,* "the sound of hail falling" (X.). My translation retains the drafts and the hail while at the same time preserving the onomatopoeia.

112

The blades are moving back and forth: "Back and forth" is *zacleloh,* which B. gives as "in alternation."

113

"Put his head in the fork of the tree that stands by the road": Andrés Xiloj read *xol che [chee]* as "in the fork of a tree," as did Ximénez long before him. Given that the head of One Hunahpu is Venus as evening star (see D. Tedlock, "The Sowing and Dawning"), the form of the tree has two different astronomical interpretations. On the one hand,

it could represent the forked or crossed sticks that Mesoamerican astronomers used for sighting heavenly bodies; on the other hand, it could be part of a tree constellation lying somewhere along the zodiac. Once the calabash tree of the story bears fruit, the head of One Hunahpu cannot be told apart from the fruit, which suggests a conjunction between Venus (as evening star) and a number of closely grouped stars. For example, it could be that this particular evening star spent part of its period of visibility between the horns of Taurus, which point upward when Taurus is on the western horizon.

114

" ' "*Its fruit is truly sweet!" they say,' I hear.*": The words "they say" translate *cacha* [*cachaa*], whose use following a statement in Quiché marks that statement as general hearsay. A more literal translation would be "it says" or "it is said," but I have chosen "they say" because that is what a speaker of English would be likely to use when citing hearsay. Blood Woman is repeating something that was already marked as hearsay by the time she heard it, so she adds a further layer of quotation with "I hear." As Andrés Xiloj pointed out, the hearsay in question here is misinformation, since the fruit referred to is not only not sweet, but is not even edible (see *calabash tree* in the Glossary). For a general discussion of how the writers of the P.V. address the epistemological questions raised by their text, see D. Tedlock, *The Spoken Word*, chap. 12.

114

"*Stretch out your right hand here*": Andrés Xiloj explained that the right side of the body (whether that of a male or female) is symbolically male, while the left is female. Further, the hands unite the fingers, which symbolize the living members of a family, graded from babies (the little finger of each hand) on up to the elderly (thumbs). The fact that Blood Woman receives the sign from the head of One Hunahpu in her right hand already points toward the bearing of a male child; in fact she will bear male twins.

114

"*It is just a sign I have given you, my saliva, my spittle*": Because of the mention of "sign" (*retal*) here, Andrés Xiloj remarked, "Then this is a dream." Asked what would be augured by being spit on in a dream, he said, "This is two matters. It depends on whether the saliva is good or bad. When it is good it has a lot of foam; when it is just clear water it is bad. But here in the Popol Vuh, one isn't told which kind of saliva it is."

115

"*Keep the word*": The stem of the verb here is *oc-*, which can carry the sense of "keeping to something" (V.).

115

they were of one mind: This is *xaui quinaoh*, "same their-thoughts."

115
"It's just a bastard": "Bastard" is *hoxbal*, literally "fornication-instrument," glossed as "bastard" by B.

115
"Get her to open her mouth": This is *chacoto uchi* [*uchii*], literally "Dig it out of her mouth," an idiom for close questioning. In terms of the somatic mapping of actual or potential speech, as conceived by Quichés, this implies that she knows perfectly well what her father wants her to say; if her word were "in her belly," on the other hand, it would mean that she could not readily articulate a response even if she wanted to. See also the notes to pp. 128 and 132.

115
"there is no man whose face I've known": This statement is not only true in its figurative reference to Blood Woman's sexual innocence, but in its literal sense: she has never known the (fleshly) face of the man responsible for her miraculous pregnancy. For the importance of a man's "face" (and personal identity) in sexual encounters, see pp. 190–191.

116
"take it in their hands": This is *quicololeh* [*qui4ololeh*], a reduplicative form of *4oleh*, "have something round in the hand" (V.); B. gives *colola* as "revolve, turn around."

116
"So please stop": The verb here is *queque*; B. gives *quequeba* as "stop, detain."

116
"they will make themselves familiar with its composition": This is *xchiquihunam uachih utzaquic* [*u4,akic*], "will-they-compare appearance its-being-made (or constructed)"; X. gives *hunamanic* as "compare" and B. gives *hunamah uach* as "to make friends."

116
"nor will your homes be here": In the biological sense, this means that future owls will be free to move around the surface of the earth. If I am right in suspecting that the messenger owls of Xibalba correspond to the planet Mercury, the astronomical sense of this same statement would be that Mercury appears above the horizon on more days than it remains below (the average ratio for a given Mercury cycle is 76:40).

116
"only blood": "Blood" is a literal translation of *quic* [*qui4*], which also refers to gums and resins from trees (including latex), in this case the blood-red resin of the cochineal croton (see *croton* in the Glossary).

116
"use the fruit of a tree": This is a figurative reference to nodules of sap

275

from the cochineal croton.

116

it formed a surface like blood: This is *quehe cu [4u] ri quic [qui4] rih xuxic,* "like then the blood its back (or upper or outer surface) became."

116

"nodules of blood": This is *quic [qui4] holomax.* For a discussion of "blood" in this context, see the notes to the previous page. *Holomax* would seem to be composed of a verbal form of *holom,* "head," with a passive suffix (*-x*); in the present context it would mean something like "headed-up," hence "nodules."

117

and when he lifted it up with his fingers: This is *ta xuchuieh cu [4u] acanoc [a3anok],* "when he-lifted-with-fingers and upward"; B. gives *chuieh* as "to lift with the fingers."

117

they leaned over it intently: This is *xechique [xechike] chuui,* in which *xe-* is "complete-they" and *chuui* is "over (or on top of)"; V. gives *chiker* as "to be inclined pensively."

117

the mother of One Monkey and One Artisan: In fact the mother (in the literal sense) of One Monkey and One Artisan has already died by this time (see p. 109); in the present passage the term "mother" is being used in its role-designating sense rather than in its genealogical sense. One Monkey and One Artisan are living alone with Xmucane, their father's mother, at this point; she is the only person they have who could fill the role of "mother."

117

"mother, madam": This is *lal chichu,* in which *lal* is "you (singular polite)," here translated as "madam." I cannot locate *chichu* in any dictionary, colonial or modern, nor did Andrés Xiloj know it, but it resembles *chuch,* "mother." It is not the ordinary term for mother-in-law; that is *alib,* which is used by Blood Woman later on in this same dialogue (p. 117).

117

"I'm your daughter-in-law and I'm your child": The use of "child" here is metaphorical. A Quiché daughter-in-law takes up residence with her husband's family; in offering herself not only as a daughter-in-law but as a "child," Blood Woman both seeks the kind of acceptance a daughter would have and makes an offer of loyalty.

117

"my lastborn children": Given that Xmucane is never mentioned as having had any children other than One and Seven Hunahpu, she may be using *chipa [4hipa]* or "lastborn (youngest)" endearingly, in

effect calling her sons, who were adults when they left home, "my little babies."

117

"They have merely made a way for the light to show itself": "A way ... to show itself" is *ucutbal* [*u4utbal*] *rib*, literally "its-showing-instrument." The immediate reference, as the rest of the sentence makes clear, is to the symbolic survival of the dead through their offspring (see also p. 114), "light" being a metaphor for birth. But "light" may also be taken literally here: Blood Woman's twin sons will account for Venus (in some of its cycles) and, in time, the sun and moon (or at least the full moon) (see D. Tedlock, "The Sowing and Dawning").

118

"Truly, what I say to you is so!": I take it that this sentence belongs to Blood Woman rather than Xmucane, given that it is followed with *utz bala*, "Very well," which signals the beginning of a reply and definitely belongs to Xmucane.

118

"since you are already my daughter-in-law": The grandmother isn't so much accepting Blood Woman's claim to kinship here as she is saying (with sarcasm) something like, "If you *say* you're my daughter-in-law, then *act* like one." Quiché daughters-in-law, who live with the families of their husbands, are subject to the commands of their mothers-in-law, who give them heavy household tasks to do.

118

she went to the garden: "Garden" is *abix*, often translated "milpa." Maize is the principal plant in the highland Mayan milpa, but it is interplanted with beans and squash. Each of these crops has different characteristics in its response to wet or dry conditions at various points in its growth cycle; interplanting assures that when one crop suffers during a given season, another part will prosper.

118

but there was only one clump: In Mesoamerica corn is properly grown in thick clumps, not stalk by stalk in single file; clumps survive high winds better.

118

"Come thou, rise up, come thou, stand up": This is *tatul ualoc tatul tacaloc*. In *tatul, ta-* suggests Cakchiquel "you" (singular familiar in V.) and *-at-* suggests Quiché "you" (singular familiar), while *-ul* would be "come" in either language. For the rest, *ual-* is "get up" (B.) and *tacal-* is "stand up, present oneself" (B.), while *-oc* [*-ok*] carries an urgent or imperative force. Throughout the P.V., I translate the first person singular familiar pronoun as "thou" in prayers but as "you" in conversation.

they were rowdyish and flushed with jealousy: For these two qualities the MS. has *quichaquimal* and *qui3a3* [*quicak*] *uachibal,* in which *qui-* is "their." B. gives *chaquimal* as "tumult, clatter, fuss, disturbance; clamor of boys." X. gives *quiak* [*cak*] *uachinic,* which would literally be "red in appearance," as "zeal, jealousy."

120

the successors: This is *quexel* [*4exel*], "substitute." This may be a reference to the fact that Mars, the planet of One Monkey and One Artisan, sometimes serves as morning star in the absence of Venus, which in one of its five cycles is the planet of One and Seven Hunahpu (see D. Tedlock, "The Sowing and Dawning"). When Venus and Mars appear in the east together Mars remains long after Venus has descended into the underworld, just as One Monkey and One Artisan remained on the face of the earth when One and Seven Hunahpu went to Xibalba.

120

The anger in their hearts came down on their own heads: Andrés Xiloj remarked, "We see a person; we speak behind his back and he doesn't hear what we are murmuring. Then this murmur doesn't fall upon that person, but we are the ones who pay for it." A daykeeper, taking on the task of defending a person who has been the victim of witchcraft, asks in prayer that "the one who did this work should be the one to receive it."

120

They were decoyed: The verb here is *poizaxic* [*poyizaxic*]; if English "doll" were a verb, this could be translated literally as "to be dolled"—that is, to be misled by a doll. Today *poyizaxic* is most commonly employed with reference to the use of scarecrows in fields.

120

"but our birds just got hung up in a tree": When birds are shot they sometimes close their feet around the branch where they were sitting and then hang there, dead.

120

"We'll just turn their very being around": The verb here is *catzolcomih,* which Andrés Xiloj read as *catzol3omih,* "to turn around."

121

"Just as they wished us to be slaves here": This is *quehe ri ala xohpe ui uloc* [*ulok*] *chiqui4ux,* "like the slaves we-came location here in-their-hearts," in which I take *xohpe chiqui4ux* to be an idiom analogous to the one given in B. as *chi nucux* [*4ux*] *petinac* [*petinak*], literally "in-my-heart come-from-perfect" but glossed as "of my own will." *Ala* ("slaves") is shortened here from *alabil,* which is the form given in a later and similar passage (translated "slaves" on p. 124).

278

121
"How can we grab hold?": The verb stem here is *chanic*, translated on the basis of *chanih*, "keep in the fist" (B.). The tree is too thick for One Monkey and One Artisan to use their hands in coming down.

121
"simply shameless": This is *rax quiuach*, "fresh (or raw or green) their-faces"; B. gives *rax uach* as "shameless."

122
"Will you please not laugh": Among the contemporary Jacaltec Maya there are myths in which the hero tricks his elder brother or his mother's brothers into going up a tree that grows taller and maroons them, after which they turn into monkeys. The hero's mother then tries to reverse this transformation but fails (Morris Siegel, "The Creation Myth and Acculturation in Acatán, Guatemala," pp. 122–24; Oliver La Farge, *Santa Eulalia*, pp. 53–56), in one case because she disobeys an admonition not to laugh (La Farge, pp. 51–53).

122
the patio of the house: See the notes to p. 107 for a discussion of the parts of a house.

122
the skinny little things below their bellies: This is *chi xiriric xe quipam;* Ximénez translated *xiriric* as "that which is thin," and Andrés Xiloj read it as "round little thing," chuckling as he did so. This refers not to the "bellies" of the monkeys (*quipam*) but to what is "below" or "at the bottom of" (*xe*) their bellies.

122
and their tails wiggling in front of their breasts: This is *chi chilita he pu chuchi quiɋux*, "that wag tails and at-edge-of their-breasts." Andrés Xiloj read *chuchi* as "up against" in this context. Spider monkeys and howler monkeys both have very long prehensile tails; howlers are seldom observed, but spider monkeys are given to winding their tails around to the front of their bodies and all the way up to their chins.

123
thin red lips: This is *caɜ [cak] ruxruh uchi [chii]*, "red thin his-mouth (or lips)"; *ruxruh* may be a reduplicative form of *ruxaa*, "thin" (X.).

123
with faces blank: "Blank" is my translation of *tac [taɜ]*, "deafened" (B.) or "fool" (X.) or "flat" (various sources).

123
puckering their lips: "Puckering" is my translation of *mutzumac [mutzumak]*, based on the gloss offered by Andrés Xiloj: "to make small, like a trumpet." This passage reminded don Andrés of the contemporary Monkey Dance in Momostenango: "These monkeys, when

they come out here in the fiesta, they scratch themselves, and do their mouths this way [touches himself all around the mouth], as if they had fleas and lice." They also climb a high pole and do acrobatics on a tightrope above the plaza.

123

wiping their mouths and faces: The verb stem here is *mal;* B. gives *mala-* as "to touch lightly" and Andrés Xiloj read it as "to clean."

123

suddenly scratching themselves: This is *macama* [*makama*] *chiquiho-quih chique;* Andrés Xiloj read *hoquih* as *ho3oh,* "to scratch"; *chique* is "to them," possibly referring to the mouths and faces of the monkeys.

124

their mattock, their hoe: These tools are *mixquina* and *xoquem,* respectively; I have rendered the former word as "mattock" because B. glosses it as a "large" hoe.

125

leveling . . . the trees: "Leveling" is my translation of *3a3chacachoh,* based on *cakchachoh,* "thrown down by the wind" (V.).

125

stalks and brambles: "Stalks" is my translation of *tum,* based on *tun,* "shoot (of a plant)" (V.); "brambles" translates *quixic,* based on *4ix,* "spine (or thorn)" (X.).

125

dumps wood chips on his head: The verb here is *puquih,* translated on the basis of *pu4unic,* "dunk" or "throw" (X.); the "wood chips" are *uuebalche* [*uuebalchee*], glossed as such by B.

125

they massage, they stretch their legs, their arms: Andrés Xiloj, who is a *uikol bak* or "bonesetter" in addition to being a daykeeper, remarked here that he uses a combination of massage and stretching to treat sprains.

125

fox, coyote: The fox is *yac* in Quiché; it is sometimes called *gato del monte* or "mountain cat" in rural Guatemalan Spanish, which has caused much confusion among speakers of English. Foxes are more like cats than like dogs in their fur and in their graceful leaps. But in Quiché, as in English, the fox is nevertheless thought of together with the coyote (*utiu*), as in the case of the present list, whereas cats are covered by the "puma, jaguar" pair of terms occurring earlier in the list.

128

"Arise, conjoin, you trees!/Arise, conjoin, you bushes!": This is *iac lin che* [*chee*] *iac lin caam* [*4aam*], in which *iac* is "for inciting someone" (V.) and is probably related to *yacalic,* "be up high" (X.); *lin* is "to

squeeze, press together" and is used for tamping the weft in weaving (B.).

128

"My word is in my belly": Here and in a later passage (p. 132) the animal who makes this statement is assigned its characteristic food in exchange for a message. For the contemporary Quiché diviner, words that are "in the belly" of a person are words that person is unable to bring to consciousness and articulate; words that are higher up, in the chest or the head, are more likely to be spoken, and those that are in the throat or mouth or on the tongue are at the very point of actually being said. As for animals, their utterances are regarded as clear to other members of the same species but very difficult for a human to understand. The fact that the animals in the P.V. have their word in their bellies is not only an indication of their interest in being given food but an indication of the difficulties of understanding what animals have to say. They may be able to make sounds, but the meaning of these sounds is as hidden as are the crucial facts a human client may find difficult to articulate when a diviner asks probing questions. See also the notes to pp. 115 and 132.

128

"up under the roof of the house": This is *chuui ha*, "at-its-top house," which, as Andrés Xiloj explained, means the attic. He pointed out that this is the part of the house where tools are kept today, along with the stored harvest.

129

"But what will your grandmother say if she sees me?": Andrés Xiloj commented: "When the rat speaks it isn't understood what he says, '*Ui4,, ui4,, uit4,.*' When a boy is born, then the rat doesn't cry, 'tis said. He is content, because the boy is the one who sows the garden. Now, if a woman is born, then the rat cries, 'tis said, because when the rat is near a woman in the kitchen she grabs a stick to kill him."

129

they were just fooling: "Fooling" is *michbal* [*mi4hbal*], literally "means of plucking," an idiom for deception. Note that in a later story the victims of deception are *literally* plucked (p. 193).

129

loosening the ball: The verb here is *colon*, translated on the basis of *colo*, "to free" (B.).

130

These were taken away: The verb stem here is *mahix*, "be-taken," translated on the basis of *mahinic*, "to take" (X.).

131

a louse fell on her elbow: I read *chucayac* as "elbow" on the basis of *4hucah*, the entry for "elbow" in X., and picture Xmucane with her head buried in her arms. The louse, of course, falls from her head.

131
"My word is contained": "Contained" is *4oba*, translated on the basis of *coba*, "to contain" or "keep to oneself" (B.).

131
"bent over": This is *pe*, translated on the basis of *pe4elic*, "to sag" (X.).

131
when he had been united with the toad: The verb here is *xrictaxic*, a complete and passive form of the verb given by B. as *riquitahic*, "to join."

132
on the rim of the ball court: "Rim" is *zutzil* (in which *-il* is adjectival), translated on the basis of *tzutz*, "to finish weaving" (E.) or "to finish weaving by filling out the space at the edge" (V.). I take it that the falcon alighted at the top of the wall enclosing the ball court.

132
"Wak-ko! Wak-ko!": This is *uac co, uac co* in the MS. The bird in question, the *uac* or laughing falcon (see Glossary), makes two different sounds: a long call consisting of a single, rapidly repeated syllable, resembling laughter, and a short song that makes use of two different syllables. L. Irby Davis transcribes a typical phrase of the song as *woo-o ka-woo* (*A Field Guide to the Birds of Mexico and Central America*, p. 25), which is close to the way the P.V. has it. Michael Coe has called my attention to the fact that the Aztecs, like Hunahpu and Xbalanque in the present passage, took the sounds of this falcon (called *oactli* in Nahuatl) to be portentous. The call, which they heard as uncontrolled laughter, was a bad omen, but the song was good (Sahagún, *Florentine Codex*, book 5, pp. 153–55). Hunahpu and Xbalanque, in a move the original hearers of their story may have found humorous, take the matter of the omen into their own hands, bringing the bird down and demanding to know exactly what message it carries. The song would seem to be a good omen for them, despite the dangers implied by the message that lies behind (or inside) it; they are like the twin heroes of North American Indian myths in fearlessly taking immediate action whenever a new adventure presents itself. But their grandmother, like her own North American counterpart, is filled with apprehension.

132
their blowgun shot: The "shot" of the blowgun is *ubac* [*ubak*], literally "its bone" or "its pit" (in the sense of the pit of a fruit).

132
"My word is contained in my belly": See the notes to p. 128 for a discussion of the meaning of words in bellies. What is notable in the present context, where the hawk contains the snake that contains the toad that contains the louse who has the message, is a symbolic acting

out of the structure of the speech of messengers. Again and again the messengers of the P.V. deliver their news in the form of multiply embedded quotes; in the present episode each animal corresponds, as it were, to a pair of quote marks, one pair inside the next.

133
he just sort of drooled: This is *xa quehe chucaxh,* "just like that-he-drooled"; I translate the verb stem, *caxh,* on the basis of *caxahinic,* "to drool" (B.).

133
they kicked him: The verb stem here is *iic,* translated on the basis of *yicbal,* "kick with the foot" (B.). I have spared the reader the redundancy of the original phrasing, which goes on to specify that the kicking was indeed done with the foot.

133
they crushed the bones: The verb stem here is *cah [4ah],* translated on the basis of *4ahinic,* "to crumble" (X.).

133
it was right there in his mouth: In terms of the somatic mapping of speech, as conceived by Quichés, this implies that the toad knew perfectly well what the message was; it was not buried in his belly, a realm of the unconscious or the dimly perceived, but right up front in his mouth (see the notes to pp. 128 and 132).

133
Each of us will plant an ear of corn: These are not kernels (*ixim*) but ears (*ah*) that are planted (*tic*), and as will be made clear on p. 159, they are "planted" not in the earth but above it, in the attic of the house, where harvested corn is stored. Andrés Xiloj recognized this as one of the rituals he carries out in his capacity as a mother-father (see also the notes immediately below and for p. 158, as well as the Introduction).

133
When the corn dries up: "Corn" has been supplied here; the original sentence does not specify what is drying (*chakihic*). It might be the ears of corn Hunahpu and Xbalanque left in the center of their house, but Andrés Xiloj took it to be the ripening of a corn crop in their field, which would coincide with the arrival of the dry season.

133
when the sprouting comes: This is *ta chipe utux,* "when there-comes its-shoot." It would not be the sprouting of the ears of corn left in the center of the house by Hunahpu and Xbalanque, but of a new crop in the field (see the notes to p. 158).

133
Hunahpu planted one and Xbalanque planted another: This makes it sound as though there were two ears of corn, but today it would be

four: one yellow, one white, one spotted, and one blue. Note that the
ears planted by Hunahpu and Xbalanque, however many of them
there may have been, are later given four different names (p. 159).
134
where the earth is damp: This is *rax uleu,* literally "green (or raw)
earth," in contrast with the *chaquih* [*chakih*] *uleu* or "dry earth"
mentioned in this same sentence; my translation follows the reading
offered by Andrés Xiloj.
134
in the middle of the inside of their house: This is *chunicahal*
[*chuni4ahal*] *upa cochoch,* "at-its-middle its-inside their-house."
Andrés Xiloj was quite definite that this could only mean indoors, not
in the patio. See the notes to p. 107 for further information on the
parts of a house.
134
the roads of Xibalba: Apparently all four roads eventually lead to or
through Xibalba, but in an earlier passage "the" Road of Xibalba, and
specifically of its lords, is the Black Road (see p. 111 and Glossary).
135
"What is it, Wing?": "Wing" has been provided.
136
*each one named by the one ranking above him, and naming in turn
the name of the one seated next to him:* This is *huhun chiholoman
ubixic cumal are chibiin ubi hun ri cubul chuxucut,* "each-one from-
ahead being-named by-them this-one naming his-name one that
seated at-his-side." I interpret *chiholoman* as referring to differences
in rank, with *chi-* as prepositional and *holom* as "head" in the sense of
leadership (a sense given by V. under the entry for *ui*). In the dialogue
that follows each lord is indeed named by the one ranking immediately above him and in turn names the next one down the line; the
only exception is One Death, who has no one above him and must
therefore be named by Seven Death.
136
"These aren't lords! These are manikins, woodcarvings!": Strictly
speaking this remark refers to the two manikins, or woodcarvings,
who are seated first in the sequence, but may also be taken as slyly
referring to the entire group of lords. They are waiting for a good
laugh, like the one they had earlier at the expense of One Hunahpu
and Seven Hunahpu (p. 111), but instead the joke is on them.
137
"here's our rubber ball," said the Xibalbans: This is one of the few
points at which *qui4,* "rubber ball," is used with reference to the ball
belonging to Xibalba, which is otherwise called *chaah,* a generic term
for "ball" (see the notes to p. 112), or else by its proper name, White
Dagger (see Glossary). Given the general air of duplicity in the pres-

ent passage, we may assume that the Xibalbans are falsely using the term *qui4*.

138

"just a decorated one": This is *xa huchil* [*hu4hil*], in which I take *hu4hil* to be an adjectival form of *hu4hunic*, "to stripe, put on a design" (X.). The ball of Xibalba (see *White Dagger* in the Glossary) is fundamentally different from the rubber ball used by Hunahpu and Xbalanque, but the Xibalbans are claiming that it is merely decorated.

138

"just a skull": The ball of Xibalba is surfaced with crushed bone (see *White Dagger* in the Glossary).

138

"We've said enough!": This is *coh4hachic*, "we-stop-talking," translated on the basis of forms like *chach* and *chachachi* in B., which have to do with the cessation or hushing of talk. Others have treated *coh* as a separate word here, in which case it would mean "puma," but that leaves *4hachic* hanging.

139

"Death is the only thing you want for us! Wasn't it you who sent a summons to us?": This is an ironic reference to the names of One and Seven Death. To put it in other words, "Given that you are named *came* (Death), no wonder you want our *camic* (death)!" Hunahpu and Xbalanque play on the name *came* again in a later episode (p. 153). See *One Death, Seven Death* in the Glossary for a discussion of their name.

139

"One bowl of red petals": "One bowl" is my translation of *huticab*, in which I take *-ticab* to be a numeral classifier for counting by the bowlful, similar to *-tuc* in *hutuc*, "one jarful" (T.); the bowls in question here (*zel*) are mentioned just before this. "Petals" translates a word given as *muchih* the first time and *muchit* thereafter, which Andrés Xiloj read as *muchic*, referring to the "undoing" of flowers to get their petals off, rather than as *mu4h*, which is an herb (known as *chipilín* in Spanish) whose leaves are used as a seasoning in beans. Today flower petals are sprinkled on tombs and may be used to adorn shrines before offerings are burned.

141

"Whip-poor-will!" and *"Poor-willow!"*: The bird calls here are *xpurpuuec* and *puhuyu*, respectively. Andrés Xiloj recognized *xpurpuuec* as the call of the bird named *perpuuak*, which he described as a ground-dwelling bird that calls out at night. This is obviously a whippoorwill; phonetically the Quiché rendition of its call is not that different from the English version, except for the final consonant (for an ornithologist's technical description of the call see Davis, *A Field*

Guide to the Birds of Mexico and Central America, pp. xiii–xv). I interpret *puhuyu* as a similar but somewhat simpler call, belonging to a related species, and translate it as "poorwill" when it is used (on this same page) as a species name rather than as a call.

141

the nibbling at their own tails, . . . wings: This may be a reference to the fact that the tails and wings of whippoorwills and poorwills are marked with bands, bars, and spots that give them a mottled appearance.

141

an acrobatic performance: This is *tiquitoh,* translated on the basis of *tiquita,* "to dance audaciously in front of others" (B.).

141

all the Xibalbans looked sick, they paled: The key forms here are *zaccahe* [*zakcahe*], "be discolored in sickness" (V.), and *zacbu* [*zakbu*], "pallid" (B.).

141

their mouths were split wide: Whippoorwills and poorwills are nightjars (*Caprimulgidae*), all of which have small bills but mouths that gape very wide.

142

countless drafts, thick-falling hail: For more about the drafts (*teu*), see the notes to p. 112. The hail is *zacbocom* [*zakbokom*], based on glosses offered by B. and by Andrés Xiloj.

143

a house of fire: This is *hun ha chi 3a3,* a descriptive phrase not constructed in the same way as the proper names given the other houses—*balami ha,* "Jaguar House," for example. It is omitted from the earlier list of five test houses (p. 112) and is the most briefly described of the houses in the present sequence; it may be a secondary elaboration, based on the immolation undergone by Hunahpu and Xbalanque in a later episode (p. 149). That would leave five proper test houses in both passages, probably corresponding to segments of five different kinds of Venus cycles (see *Bat House* in the Glossary and D. Tedlock, "The Sowing and Dawning").

143

"Can you see how long it is till dawn?": "How long" is my translation of *hanic,* "How much?" (B.).

143

"What's going on?": This is my reading of *huchalic,* based on *hucha,* "How?" or "What's this?" (B.).

144

Xbalanque despaired: The verb stem here is *quixbih,* translated on the basis of *4ixbeh,* "to have shame" (V.) and considerations of context.

144

"Alas!": This is *acaroc* [probably *akarok*], which Ximénez translates as "Ay! Ay!" Elsewhere *akarok* begins a song of lament (p. 183), where I again translate it as "Alas!" But when it begins prayers (pp. 169, 221) I render it as "Wait!" on the basis of *akar,* "wait" (V.) and the apparent imperative suffix (*-ok*). A person at prayer is said to "cry" (*o3ic*) and "call out" (*zi4ih*); to translate *akarok* as "Alas!" emphasizes the emotional tone, while "Wait!" emphasizes the attempt to get attention.

145

He brought a squash: What the coati brings is written as *coc,* which must be *303,* "squash," rather than *cooc,* "turtle." As Edmonson has pointed out (*The Book of Counsel,* p. 124), turtles do not have seeds (see p. 147), and I would add that a turtle would not burst open when hitting the floor of a ball court.

145

then brains came from the thinker, from the sky: I follow Edmonson (*The Book of Counsel,* p. 124) in reading *tzatz* as *tzatz 3or,* "brains" (literally "thick dough"). According to the riddling "language of Zuyua" in the Book of Chilam Balam of Chumayel, the "brains" of the sky consist of copal (Roys, *The Book of Chilam Balam of Chumayel,* pp. 90, 96). That raises the possibility that "thinker," which is *ahnaoh* (*ah-* is occupational) in the present passage, could be a pun on *naoh* [*nooh*], which is a variety of copal (X.). For a discussion of punning in the language of Zuyua, see Brian Stross, "The Language of Zuyua."

145

His strength was just the same: "Strength" is *chuuc* here, translated on the basis of *chu3a,* "strength" or "force" (V.).

145

"Possum is making streaks": This is *caxaquin uuch* [*caxakin uu4h*], "he-is-making-black-streaks possum." V. has an entry for *xakin uu4h,* "a darkness before dawn," which confirms that *uuch* should be *uu4h,* "possum"; Ximénez translated "vulture," as if the text had read *4uch.* Andrés Xiloj read the verb stem as *xakin,* "make black stripes"; V. has "stripe with carbon" as a gloss for *xakih.* Don Andrés commented: "At four-thirty in the morning it is as if black clouds were placed there at the end of the sky [the horizon], they are like a sea, they are in grades or levels, alternating yellow and black. Then, according to the hour, as it clears up, the black becomes blacker, blacker, blacker, and what was yellow becomes redder, as the sun comes nearer. Then it changes, these black clouds are no longer there, now there is only the light of the sun. These black clouds appear to be over the earth, they go far [to the left and right], all the way to wherever. The stripes signal that the sun is already shining; they are a reflection. When one

gets up at four or four-thirty in the morning, *cak chuui xecah*, 'it is red over the end of the sky.' At first only one black band is there, then it divides up. One can see all this in the dry season, but not at this time of year" (as he said this his voice was almost drowned out by the sound of rain). The possum who made the black streaks or bands in the P.V. is called *mama*, "old man (or grandfather)," which identifies him as one of the so-called "year-bearers" (see the Introduction). The year-bearers announce the coming of a new solar year, just as the black streaks announce the coming of a new day.

145
"You should just make lots of threats": The verb stem here is *yecuh*, "be in a threatening attitude" (under the entry for *yecoh* in B.).

145
"Stay there in the oaks": These are *pixc*, "oaks" or "acorns" (V., G.), not *pix*, "tomatoes."

147
having recovered the ball from among the oaks: "Oaks" has been supplied here. I picture Hunahpu and Xbalanque standing among the oaks, pretending they have found the ball when in fact they have traded it for a squash.

147
The squash was wearing out: The verb stem here is *pucabin* [*puჳabin*], translated on the basis of *puჳ*, "wear down" (V.).

147
bringing to light its light-colored seeds, as plain as day: This is *zaquiram cu ri uzaquilal* [*zakiram ჳu ri uzakilal*], literally "becoming-light (or white) then the its-lightness-own." *Zakir*- is also "to dawn," and *zakil* is the term for squash seeds; in the translation I have added the word "seeds" and the phrase "as plain as day" in order to make these dimensions more obvious to the reader. Further, *zakir*- is a metaphor for the sprouting of plants, but the phrase "bringing to light its light-colored seeds" turns that metaphor inside out. When the squash bursts and causes a "dawning" of seeds, it is a "dawning" that comes from the harvested fruit of a plant rather than from the planted seeds. To put it another way, the seeds burst forth rather than being sown.

This passage probably has an astronomical dimension as well. Keeping in mind that Hunahpu and Xbalanque, in their Venus or ballplayer aspect, cannot stray from the zodiac, we may speculate that the splattered squash seeds correspond to a constellation, and that this constellation is closer to being "in bounds" with respect to the zodiac than the oaks (or acorns) discussed in the notes for p. 145. The Pleiades are within the zodiac, but they would seem to be accounted for by the Four Hundred Boys. But the seeds of the burst squash could at least be somewhere near the Pleiades, since the Four

Hundred Boys may be rabbits (see under their name in the Glossary) and since it is a rabbit who leads the Xibalbans away from the ball court.
148
if we dumped their bones in the canyon: T. J. Knab informs me that in the lore of contemporary Nahuatl speakers in the Sierra de Puebla, this is precisely the procedure that would be used to put a permanent and complete end to a person. On the other hand, grinding the bones and putting them directly into water (which is what is finally done with Hunahpu and Xbalanque) would ensure continued life in some form.
148
since you would see their faces: This is an allusion to what happened when the head of One Hunahpu was put in a tree.
148
sprinkle them: The verb stem here is *icah,* "sprinkle" (B.).
149
"You'll never put that one over on us": The verb stem here is *mich* [mi4h], "pluck," but in the present context a literal translation would not make sense in English (see the notes to p. 193 for a case in which deception involves *literal* plucking of the victim).
149
They grabbed each other by the arms and went head first into the oven: Hunahpu and Xbalanque do not ascend as the sun and moon until p. 159, but their self-immolation here is obviously the act that opens the way to that event. In Aztec mythology the sun and moon are again a pair of males, Nanahuatzin and Tecuciztecatl, though apparently not brothers. They do not jump into the flames arm in arm; instead, the former jumps in because the latter is afraid to, and then the latter follows out of shame. At first they rise as two identical suns, but then Tecuciztecatl is dimmed and becomes the moon (Sahagún, *Florentine Codex,* Book 7, pp. 2–7).
149
raising their shouts, raising their cheers: Andrés Xiloj remarked, "It's like they held a fiesta, complete with a marimba."
149
The two of them looked like channel catfish: For the identification of the fish, see the Glossary. There is a classic Maya vase on which a figure that has been positively identified as Hunahpu by Floyd Lounsbury ("The Identities of the Mythological Figures in the 'Cross Group'") is shown in profile with a barbel growing out of his cheek (see the illustration on p. 156). The scene depicted takes place not far beyond the one in the present passage (see the notes for p. 153). It should be noted that among the Pokomchí Maya Xbalanque gave his

name to a fish of the perch and bass family (see *Xbalanque* in the Glossary), whose members lack the barbels that characterize catfish and (unlike catfish) have spiny fins. It may be that for speakers of Quichean languages (who include the Pokomchí) Hunahpu manifested as a catfish and Xbalanque as a perch or bass, but it remains to be seen whether their classic counterparts might be sorted out between two different fish.

Taking our cue from the fact that other P.V. episodes involve the establishment of customs by Hunahpu and Xbalanque, we may guess that the casting of their bones in the water (an event they themselves planned) may have established a fishing ritual. Many fishing cultures—on the northwest coast of North America, for example—have rituals in which the casting of fish bones back in the water results in the reincarnation of the fish to which they belonged. When we combine this possibility with the fact that Hunahpu and Xbalanque also established a ritual for the perpetuation of the life of corn plants, it brings to mind the raised-field complex among the classic lowland Maya, who harvested fish from the same ditches that drained their cornfields (see Hammond, *Ancient Maya Civilization*, pp. 160–63). Contemporary Quichés do not link corn with fish, but the founders of the leading Quiché lineages came from the Gulf-coast lowlands, and a later generation of lords obtained the hieroglyphic P.V. from the lowlands.

149

vagabonds: This is my translation of *meba*, given by B. and X. as "poor person"; I have chosen "vagabonds" because Hunahpu and Xbalanque later disclaim any attachment to a particular place (p. 87). At this point in their career they probably correspond to the so-called "year-bearers" or "possum actors" of the lowland Maya, and this is probably the point at which they earned the epithets Hunahpu Possum, Hunahpu Coyote (see Glossary).

149

They seemed unrefined: This is *mana chibananta quiuach*, literally "not-yet that-get-to-be-done their-faces"; *ban uach* is an idiom meaning "polished, adorned" (B.).

150

Now Xibalba was full of admiration: The "admiration" is *cayic*, translated on the basis of *cai₃*, "watch admiringly" (B.).

150

Next they would sacrifice themselves, one of them dying for the other: This would seem to indicate that either of the twins could assume either role in this act. When the P.V. describes the act, it is Xbalanque who sacrifices Hunahpu (p. 153), but the classic Maya vase that portrays this scene shows it the other way around (see the illustration on pp. 156–157). In terms of consistency within the P.V. the former arrangement makes more sense, since the sacrifice includes decapitation and since it is otherwise Hunahpu who gets dismembered; by this time he has already suffered a decapitation by a snatch-bat, having previously lost his arm to Seven Macaw.

151
had to keep coming back: The verb stem here is *machcay*, translated on the basis of *machcai3*, "to come and go repeatedly" (B.).

151
Feigning great humility: This is *quemochochic*; B. gives *mochochic* as "to humble oneself hypocritically."

151
they bowed their heads all the way to the ground: This is *chiquixulela quiuach*, in which the second word is "their faces"; B. gives *xulela* as "throwing the face on the ground."

151
down to the rags, to the tatters: The "rags" are *mayoquih*, translated on the basis of *maquih*, "to throw out"; the "tatters" are *atziac* [*a4,iak*], which carries this meaning in both classical and modern Quiché.

151
their mountain: This is *quihuyubal*, "their-mountain-place." *Huyubal* is a metonym for almost any settlement, but especially a fortified town or "citadel" (*tinamit*), located on a defensible elevation.

152
And they showed its roundness: This is *xquicoloba cut* [*xqui4oloba 4ut*] *chiquiuach*, "they-positioned-round-thing then to-their-faces."

153
his legs, his arms were spread wide: The verb here is *xperepoxic*, apparently a complete (*x-*), passive (*-xic*), and reduplicated form of *pere-*, "to put a wide thing somewhere" (V.); B. has an entry for *per-repic*, "wide." The limbs of Mesoamerican sacrifice victims were indeed spread wide.

153
was smothered in a leaf: This is *xcheque* [*xcheke*] *chuuach tzalic* [*4,alic*], "stanched in-face-of leaf-wrapping." X. gives *4hekelic* as "stop the flow of" and *4,alic* as "leaves for wrapping." This line has caused much confusion, but Andrés Xiloj found it crystal clear. He commented that *4,alic* refers to any leaves used to wrap tamales, of which there are several different kinds.

153
"Do it to us! Sacrifice us!": Here Andrés Xiloj remarked, "It didn't please them that they were perfectly well; what pleased them was to be butchered."

153
"After all, aren't you Death?": Edmonson has pointed out the irony of

291

this statement (*The Book of Counsel*, p. 138). "Death" is *cam* here, lacking any suffixes, which leaves it open to various interpretations: *caminak*, "dead person"; *camical*, the ordinary term for "death"; or *came*, "Death" as the proper name of a day on the calendar and of the two highest lords of Xibalba, One and Seven Death. Hunahpu and Xbalanque also played on the name *came* in an earlier passage (see the notes to p. 139).

153
heart sacrifice: The stem here is *xaraxo-*; B. gives *xaraxoh* as "cut or open the chest and take out the heart."

155
countless ants: This may or may not be metaphorical; if not, it may be that the fate of the vassals of the lords of Xibalba was to become the ants of today. In any case it is very unusual for "vassals" to come downward to get to where their lords are; it would seem that the domain of Xibalba is the reverse of earthly domains, where lords are situated in citadels rather than at the bottoms of canyons.

157
no cleanly blotted blood for you: This is *chahom quic* [*4hahom qui4*], literally "washed blood." I take this to be a reference to autosacrifice, in which the blood that flowed from self-inflicted pricks and wounds was blotted up with paper or leaves. This is no longer done today, but Andrés Xiloj pointed out that it is still said of the Xibalbans that they collect blood that is spilled on the ground—that is, dirty blood.

157
just griddles, just gourds, just brittle things broken to pieces: The "griddles" are *xot*, for toasting tortillas; the "gourds" are *acam*, translated on the basis of *akem*, "gourd" (V.); the "brittle things" are *chuch*, which B. glosses as "delicate, thin"; and "broken to pieces" is *xheraxic*, translated on the basis of *hera-*, "crumble" (V.). This list suggests the contemporary ritual of the days Seven 4,ii and Eight Ba4, (Seven Dog and Eight Monkey) at Momostenango, in which novice daykeepers are initiated. On the eve of Eight Monkey, the novice is visited at home by his or her teacher, who breaks a large and previously unused jar and burns copal incense in the shards; the ashes of the copal are put in a small gourd. The next day the shards and the gourd are taken to a shrine called 4huti Zabal or "Little Place of Declaration" and deposited there (see B. Tedlock, *Time and the Highland Maya*, pp. 65–66 for more details). But this ritual is dedicated primarily to the Mundo (earth deity) and the ancestors; there is no mention of Xibalba in its liturgy. Perhaps the Quiché elite of pre-Columbian times was given to defaming the indigenous highland Guatemalan religion as Xibalban in the same way that Christian missionaries have since defamed it as Satanic.

157
born in the light, begotten in the light: Andrés Xiloj pointed out that
only human beings can be referred to in this way; note the contrast
with "creatures of the meadows and clearings" in the previous sentence. The point is that the lords of Xibalba will henceforth be denied
proper human sacrifices.

158
the blame is clear: The idiom here is *chac umac,* "to make clear one's
sin" (B.).

158
And you will hear petitions over headed-up sap: This is *quixtaon puch
chuui ri quic [qui4] holomax,* "you-listen and over the blood (sap)
headed-up." Elsewhere I have translated *qui4 holomax* as "nodules of
sap." What this sentence means is that henceforth, when people pray
to the Xibalbans, they will burn nodules of the sap of croton trees (see
croton in the Glossary) as offerings.

158
they are inciters to wrongs and violence: Andrés Xiloj commented:
"They are the ones who send one to do evil. It is as if, in spirit, they
enter us, into the head. I think, 'I'm going to do such-and-such a
thing,' but I don't know who put this bad idea into me."

158
masters of perplexity: This is *ahlatzab,* consisting of *ah-,* "person or
owner of"; *latz,* "embarrassed, perplexed" (B.); and *-ab,* plural.

158
crying and calling out: What the grandmother of Hunahpu and Xbalanque does is *coquic caziquin [co3ic cazi4in],* translated literally
here, but in both classical and contemporary Quiché the combination
of the verb stems *o3-* ("cry") and *zi4-* ("call out"), used in that order,
refers to the act of praying. This is generally done in a mildly insistent
tone rather than a sorrowful one, but the petitioner is nevertheless
thought of as seeking pity; the amplitude of the voice is generally low
to moderate, but those who are addressed by a prayer are thought of
as being summoned from a distance.

158
the corn ears they left planted: These are the corn ears Hunahpu and
Xbalanque dedicated when they left for Xibalba (pp. 133–134). "They
left planted" is *xquitic canoc [canok],* "they-plant left," an idiom referring to the establishment of a ritual obligation. Andrés Xiloj recognized one of the obligations of the contemporary mother-father
(patrilineage head) in this passage: "What was 'left planted' was a
custom. They left it 'planted' that because of the corn, they would
never be forgotten. Now, this is the *uinel* [a pair of shrines located
near a cornfield, one above it and the other below]. When the corn is

ripe one has to give thanks, to burn copal in the *uinel.* One gives thanks so that the seeds will have to sprout again; one carries the corn there to have it at the burning place, and when one is finished praying one passes the ears through the smoke of the copal, saying *are 4u ua ru4ux* [this here is that which is its heart]. This is what their grandmother must have done in the Popol Vuh. And after the ears are passed through the smoke they are placed in the center of the house, in the middle of our crop. They are not eaten until another crop is ripe." Although these dedicated ears are not used as seed corn, they are thought of as alive, and it is because "the heart of the corn has not died" that the seed corn is able to sprout and that even the stored corn is able to continue multiplying.

It would seem that Hunahpu and Xbalanque, in addition to their aspects as Venus, year-bearing vagabond actors, and (eventually) the sun and moon, are also maize deities. The rites of the *uinel* are performed on two successive days bearing the names Queh and 3anil, "Deer" and "Yellowness (or Ripeness)," with the latter being the principal day (B. Tedlock, *Time and the Highland Maya*, pp. 77, 80). There are fixed rites each 260 days on Seven Deer and Eight Yellowness; planting rites are carried out on the Deer and Yellowness days nearest the actual planting time, and harvest rites are carried out on the days nearest the actual harvest. The day corresponding to Yellowness (named Lamat in Yucatec) also figures prominently in the Venus table of the Dresden Codex, where it is the first day of the morning star that begins the third of five full Venus cycles and the first day of disappearance for both morning and evening stars during the fourth Venus cycle. It may be that at least portions of these Venus cycles symbolize the life cycle of the maize plant; indeed, the lowland Maya maize god is actually depicted at the bottom of the page dealing with the third cycle.

158
And this was when their grandmother burned something: That is, when the corn dried up (ripened), coinciding with the burning of Hunahpu and Xbalanque in the oven.

158
the ears were deified by their grandmother: "Were deified" is *xca-bauilax* [*x4abauilax*], "complete-deify-passive," which could also be translated "made into an idol," not in the sense of an image but as an object of adoration.

159
the corn ears had been placed up above an earthen floor: This is *chuui chata* [*4hata*] *uleu quitic ui ah,* "above bed (or slab or table) earth they-plant to corn-ear," which makes it quite clear that the corn was not "planted" in any ordinary sense of the word—not that one would plant corn *ears* in the first place.

159

their father: Note that the term for father (*kahau*) is extended to Seven Hunahpu in this passage; he is the younger brother of One Hunahpu, who is the actual father of Hunahpu and Xbalanque. In a sense One Hunahpu (or at least his head) has long since come back to life, but Seven Hunahpu, whose head and body were *both* buried at the Place of Ball Game Sacrifice (see p. 113), has been dead all this time. Therefore Hunahpu and Xbalanque's attempt at a revival of the dead is directed at Seven Hunahpu.

159

he was asked to name everything: The notion here is that articulate speech, with clearly enunciated words, is analogous to a clearly recognizable human face. Seven Hunahpu is not able to articulate the names of all the parts of his face because he has very few parts beyond the ones he does name, having been reduced to bones. The "meat" of his face is irreversibly lost, just as One Hunahpu had said the meat of a dead man's face would be lost (see p. 114).

159

each of his former parts: This is *ri uhunal puil*, "the its-each formerness"; I translated *puil* on the basis of *puhil*, "antiquity" (B.).

159

"You will be prayed to here": Andrés Xiloj saw this as the beginning of the veneration of the dead. He explained that when there is a death in the patrilineage, the funeral rites are not complete until the mother-father goes to the lineage shrines on a Hunahpu day that falls after the actual death. There he prays that the lingering soul of the deceased, which is a spark of light, might pass on into the cool, dark room of the underworld, from which it may later have the good fortune to rise into the sky. The number of the Hunahpu day is chosen according to the age and importance of the deceased, with a very low number for a small child and a high one for a very old person who occupied important offices. With or without a recent death Hunahpu days are appropriate for visiting the graves of relatives, where prayers are said and offerings are burned in much the same way as at lineage shrines, except that the entire family can go along and make a day of it, taking along a picnic lunch and strong drink.

159

"you will be the first to have your day kept": This may refer specifically to the day Seven Hunahpu, but it probably means Hunahpu days in general, regardless of their number prefix.

159

"your name will not be lost": Andrés Xiloj, who is the mother-father for his own patrilineage, remarked: "This is just the way it is with our family. The first man who lived in this place was named Gaspar Xiloj, but we are still remembering him right now. Gaspar is the first gen-

eration, the second is Juan, the third is Sabino, the fourth is Antonio, the fifth is ourselves, but we are still remembering all of them. That's what it's talking about here in the Popol Vuh." He added that ideally, a mother-father would be able to call upon nine or even thirteen generations of predecessors, all of them having lived on the same lands (see the Introduction for a discussion of the naming of predecessors within the P.V. itself). The list of people invoked in prayers should also include the spouses of all these men (with their maiden names); the writers of the P.V. name the women only for the first generation (p. 167).

160

the sun belongs to one and the moon to the other: This is *hun cu [4u] quih [3ih] hun nai pu ic [i4] chique,* "one then sun one also and moon to-them." The text does not say that they literally *became* the sun and moon. From the general order of mention of Hunahpu and Xbalanque and the order of mention of the sun and moon in the present passage, it would appear that the sun pertains to Hunahpu and the moon to Xbalanque. But Thompson noted that except for this passage and a contemporary Cakchiquel myth, all the sources on Mayan peoples (including the contemporary Quiché) cast the moon as a woman, and he argued that the male moon of the P.V. was the result of an influence from outside Mayan culture (*Maya History and Religion,* pp. 234, 368). Lounsbury, following Thompson, argues that Xbalanque in particular is properly a solar rather than a lunar deity, one of his principal pieces of evidence being that among the contemporary Kekchí Maya, one of the names of the sun god is Xbalam3e, in which 3e is "day" and once meant "sun" ("The Identities of the Mythological Figures in the 'Cross Group' "). As for Hunahpu, Thompson associates him with both the sun (*Maya History and Religion,* p. 234) and Venus (p. 368), whereas Lounsbury casts Xbalanque as "the" Maya sun god and assigns Hunahpu (or the equivalent of Hunahpu at Palenque) to Venus alone.

There are at least three major problems with any attempt to give unambiguous astronomical assignments to Hunahpu and Xbalanque—or to their counterparts at Palenque, the gods designated G-I and G-III. The first is that a single celestial light need not be assigned to a single god; in the P.V., at least, one of the five Venus cycles, the first, is assignable neither to Hunahpu nor Xbalanque but to their father, One Hunahpu (see the Introduction), and Thompson notes that the classic Maya personification of the sun takes several different forms (*Maya History and Religion,* pp. 237, 239, 281). The second problem is the converse of the first, which is that a single god need not be limited to a single astronomical assignment. The P.V. treats a given celestial phenomenon as a "sign" (*retal*) or (in the case

296

of the rising sun) a "reflection" (*lemo*) of a past event; given that
Hunahpu and Xbalanque undergo various transformations and take
on various disguises in the course of their adventures, there is no reason to suppose that if the sun and moon (or aspects thereof) are signs
or reflections of their past actions, all other celestial phenomena are
thereby eliminated.

A third major problem with giving simple assignments to Hunahpu
and Xbalanque is that Quichés do not limit the use of *3ih*, "sun" or
"day," to words or expressions for solar phenomena, and the same
may have been true of writers who used glyphic elements meaning
"sun" in classic inscriptions. In the P.V. the morning star is called
iko3ih, "day (or sun) bringer" (see the Glossary), and contemporary
Quichés use *3ih* as a figure of speech for the full moon (see the Introduction). A colonial source reports an occasion on which the Quichés
"saw three suns in one day" (Carmack, *The Quiché Mayas*, p. 129);
this was probably a day that began with Venus as the morning star
and ended with the rising of the full moon. Returning to the P.V., the
fact that Xbalanque (or Xbalan3e) may have "sun" in his name need
not mean that he is "the" Maya sun god, nor does it disqualify him
from having a lunar aspect. And given that *balan* can mean "hidden"
in classic inscriptions and is used to designate human lords who have
passed into the underworld at death (Schele, *Notebook*, p. 118), it
could be that Xbalanque was specifically responsible for the nighttime sun (the one in the underworld), and that he became visible on
the surface of the earth once a month as the full moon. That would
leave the daytime sun open to Hunahpu.

160
They became the sky's own stars: Earlier we were told that the Four
Hundred Boys correspond specifically to the Pleiades (p. 97).

PART FOUR
163
they sought and discovered: The root of the latter verb is *canaizah*,
translated on the basis of *caneizah*, "discover, find" (B.).
163
the animals who brought the food: Andrés Xiloj pointed out that all
four of these animals eat corn. Of the birds he said, "There are birds
that take the kernels from the crop and carry them off to hide them.
When the time comes they still know where they are and go to eat
them. When they don't find where they left them, a garden is created
there."
163
Xmucane did the grinding nine times: Andrés Xiloj commented: "The

first time corn is ground it is broken open. The second time, it is somewhat fine. The third time is finer." He indicated that ordinarily corn would not be ground nine times; that would be very fine indeed.
164
the water she rinsed her hands with: This is *ha ropenal* in the MS.; Andrés Xiloj read it as the *haa* (water) a woman uses to wash off *rupenal*, which is the corn meal that sticks to the hands during grinding.
164
with yellow corn, white corn alone for the flesh: This reminded Andrés Xiloj of a saying used today: *uhral 3anuach, xolob,* "We are the children [specifically a woman's children] of yellow-faced corn, spotted corn."
165
They walked, they worked: The second verb here is *xechapanic,* literally "they grasped," but Andrés Xiloj suggested "worked," since work is done with the hands. Quichés think of the extremities together; walking and using the hands are the physical counterparts of articulate speech. Note that the linking of speech and walking is made explicit in the statement "Isn't your speech good, and your walk?" (p. 165).
167
It was as if they were asleep: Note that this passage seems to allude to Genesis, but that it disagrees with Genesis on four crucial points. First, it was only "as if" (*quehe*) the men were asleep when the women were made, and they were "wider awake" afterward—*qui xe4aztahic,* "really (or very) they-got-to-be-alive (or awake)." Second, there were four men and then four women, not one and one. Third, the women were not made from parts of men but were made separately from men. Fourth, sexual differences already existed among the gods.
167
ladies of rank: This is *xoccohauab* [*xokohauab*], literally "women-lords."
167
penitents and sacrificers: This is *ahquix* (sometimes *ahquixb*) *ahcahb* [*ah4ixb ah4ahb*], in which *ah-* is occupational; V. gives *4ixb* as "shame" and E. gives *4ahb* as "sacrifice, idolize." *4ixb* is probably a verbal form of *4ix,* "spine," and *4ahb* probably has the same root as *4ahinic,* "punish" (X.). The reference is to the penitential autosacrifice of blood, a widespread practice in pre-Columbian Mesoamerica.
168
thirteen allied tribes, thirteen principalities: This is *oxlahuh uca amac* [*ama3*] *oxlahuh tecpan,* in which *oxlahuh* is "thirteen" and *ama3* is "tribe." *Tecpan* is Nahua for "royal house or palace" or "put something in order" (D.); in the Quiché context it seems to be a term for a

tribe that is organized under a recognized noble house, but a house that is tributary (at least ideally) to the larger Quiché state. The *tecpan* list in this passage contains fifteen names rather than thirteen; some of the names may be subdivisions of larger entities, or some may be synonyms, or else the number thirteen is simply an ideal figure rather than a literal count.

That leaves the question of how to translate *uca*, which requires appeal to the only other passage in the entire P.V. that combines *ama3* and *tecpan* in parallel construction (p. 207): *uuc amac [ama3] quib quiticpan [quitecpan] quib*, in which *quib* is "themselves." It stands to reason that *uca* in the first passage should be the same as *uuc* in the second passage. By itself the latter form might be read as *uukub*, "seven," but that is disconfirmed by the fact that there are thirteen *uca ama3* in the earlier passage. I translate both *uca* and *uuc* as "allied" on the basis of two entries in B.: *uuquih* [probably *uu4ih*], "to make a friend," and *uuq* [probably *uu4*], "friend"; these forms are probably related to the prepositional root *-u4*, "with."

168
each one a division in that citadel: This is probably a reference to Tulan Zuyua, a place that will not be properly discussed until later (see pp. 172 ff.).

168
And there were mountain people: Here the P.V. follows the lines of Toltecan myths of national origin, exemplified by the claim of the powerful Aztecs (or Mexicans) to a humble past as Chichimec hunters and gatherers. The ancestors of the Quichés and related tribes will later be described as being "adorned with mere animal hides" (p. 172), and the Quiché ancestors in particular will be described as hunters of deer, birds, and larvae who stay apart from more populous tribes (pp. 185–186).

169
for all the mountain people there was just one language: I have supplied "mountain people" here; the intent seems to be to separate the mountain people (including the Quiché ancestors) from others who were in the east, including "people of many languages" (p. 168).

169
They did not yet pray to wood and stone: That is, they had not yet received the objects whose spirit familiars would become their tribal gods.

169
lifting their faces to the sky: Andrés Xiloj explained: "When one prays, as here, asking for things, one looks to heaven; afterwards, when waiting for the blessing, one looks to earth."

170
"as long as there is day, as long as there is light": This is an alternate

translation of the line discussed in the notes to p. 99 ("in the course of the days"). In the present context Andrés Xiloj commented: "Today one says *kabe 3ih, kabe zak* [our-road day, our-road light]. This is the time that goes forward; it is the road of time, the number of years one is going to live, or the number of times there will be until the end of the world."

170
"will it be": This line has been translated as a question because it begins with *quita*, which B. gives as "what" or "how."

170
"a good life and beginning": Andrés Xiloj commented: "These words would be used in prayer when someone was setting up a new household."

170
they made their fasts: The verb stem here is *quilonic,* translated on the basis of *3ilonic,* "avoid, abstain" (X.).

170
watching intently: This is *zelauachin,* translated on the basis of *zelauachih,* "to view with close attention" (listed under *zeleuachih* in B.).

173
He pivoted inside his sandal: The verb phrase here is *xubac uloc* [*xubak ulok*], "he drilled hither"; V. gives *bak* as "to drill." Just as he promised, Tohil gave his followers fire even when others had lost theirs; his "sandal" was presumably the platform of a fire drill. The classic Maya antecedent of Tohil, who also possesses fire, is the personage designated only as G-II or God K in the past literature, but whose name at Palenque is now known to have been Tahil, "Torch Mirror" or "Obsidian Mirror" (Linda Schele and Floyd G. Lounsbury, personal communications); he is typically shown with a burning torch sticking out of the mirror he wears on his forehead. As Michael Coe had previously pointed out (*The Maya Scribe,* pp. 16, 116), God K is the Mayan cognate of the Nahua god named Tezcatlipoca or "Smoking Mirror." The Tohil of the P.V. is like Tezcatlipoca in demanding human sacrifice; it remains to be seen if the same was true of Tahil at Palenque. Tahil often takes the form of the "manikin scepter" (Thompson, *Maya History and Religion,* pp. 225–26), an object carried by classic rulers (see the illustration on p. 175). In this form he is like Tezcatlipoca in having only one leg (the other "leg," when present, takes the form of a serpent). This suggests that Tohil may be a manifestation of Hurricane or Hurakan (literally "One Leg"); see also the notes to p. 223.

173
they got no response: The verb here is *xeculaxic,* "they were [not] answered"; B. glosses *cula* as "respond."

173

place of emergence: This is *tzuquibal* [*4,uquibal*], in which *-bal* is "place of"; V. glosses *4,uc* as "spring forth, sprout."

173

And then a person showed himself: At this point in the MS. Ximénez, who otherwise confines his own parenthetical remarks to the Spanish translation in the right-hand column of each page, inserts a remark into the left-hand column, otherwise reserved for the Quiché text. As if avoiding an impropriety, he uses Latin, writing *"Demonio loquens eis."* The writers of the P.V. probably intended their own allusion to Christian demonology in this passage, since they describe the person under discussion as having the wings of a bat and as coming from Xibalba (the underworld), but note that they make this allusion at the expense of the Cakchiquels, the principal rivals of the Quichés, whose god, they say, "looks like a bat" (p. 175). To this day a great many Cakchiquel men wear jackets with a bat motif on the back.

173

the representation: This is *quexuach* [*4exuach*], literally "substitute-face," which B. glosses as "resemblance" (under the entry for *quexel*); Andrés Xiloj offered the same reading.

174

They were simply overwhelmed: This is *xa quiculu*, in which *xa* is "just" and *qui-* is "they"; *culu* is translated on the basis of *culum* [*4ulum*], "dismay" (B.).

174

groping along: The verb stem here is *chacchot*, translated on the basis of *chacacha*, "to go like a blind person" (B.).

174

they had covetous mouths and covetous faces: This is *chiquimah qui-chi* [*chii*] *chiquimah quiuach*. The combination of *mah* ("rob") with *chii* ("mouth") and *uach* ("face") is an idiom meaning "to be pained by not having something to trade with or something one has need of" (under *mah* in V.). A more literal translation of the present example would be something like "They had thieving mouths and thieving faces."

174

"Wasn't it found and wasn't it revealed": This is a divinatory phrase, much like the one used by Xpiyacoc and Xmucane at the beginning of their divinatory question concerning the making of humans from wood (p. 83). The verb stems in both cases are *culu* [*4ulu*] and *rico* [*riko*], "encounter" and "find." In the present context the implication is that those who want fire claim a kinship with those who already have it on the basis of some past divinatory reading rather than on the basis of a clear genealogy. This is what anthropologists call "fictive kinship"; it may have been standard practice in highland Guatemala

to include divinatory readings in the negotiation of such relationships.

174

"Don't they want to be suckled?": Throughout this passage I follow Edmonson in translating *tunic* [*tuunic*] as having to do with suckling (*The Book of Counsel*, p. 168), a meaning found in both classical and modern Quiché. In the present context the suckling is a metaphor for sacrifice by removal of the heart, as is made quite explicit on p. 175. It may be the horror of this metaphor that has caused translators to pass over it heedlessly; even Edmonson's note on the subject suggests that mere sacrifice by self-bleeding is meant. The place where Tohil desires to do his suckling is "on their sides and under their arms," which fits with what is known about Mesoamerican heart sacrifice: the incision ran all the way to the sides of the chest (Francis Robicsek and Donald Hales, "Maya Heart Sacrifice"). The next sentence, "Isn't it their heart's desire to embrace me?" is not only a statement about motivation but a further reference to heart sacrifice. Tohil is no mere suckler of breasts; what he wants from those who embrace him is deep inside the breast, and he wants the whole thing.

174

They made no delay: The text has *maui xquiquiyaluh*, in which I take the second word to be an error for *xquiyaluh; yaluh* is "to delay oneself" (B.), giving "not complete-they-delay" for the whole phrase.

175

This deed had not yet been attempted: The verb stem here is *tihou*, translated on the basis of *tihouic*, "try, practice" (X.).

176

the new daybringer: "New" is my translation of *raxa*, which could also be "raw"; I assume that the reference is to the first appearance of Venus as morning star after a period of invisibility.

176

they left the east: The verb stem here is *canah*, "to leave" (B.).

176

"where we belong": This is *cohtique ui*, "incomplete-we-stop"; B. glosses *tequeic* as "to stop."

176

"bleeding your ears and passing a cord through your elbows": The verbs here are *hutic*, "to let blood" (B.), and *ziza*, translated on the basis of *tzizo*, "to sew a seam, to string [like beads]; formerly, to let blood for sacrifice to idols" (B.). The "ears" and "elbows" are *xiquin* and *chuc* [*4huc*]. Ears are well attested throughout Mesoamerica as sites for the drawing of blood in rites of self-sacrifice, but elbows are mentioned only for the Quiché, in both the P.V. and in B. (under the entry for *tzizo*). Michael D. Coe has pointed out to me that the penis

was a primary site for the drawing of blood among the classic Maya. In the present passage *chuc* (if it is not *4huc*) could conceivably be related to *chu3a* or *chu3ab*, "strength, energy, vigor" (V. and X.), and thus allude to the penis, but this seems unlikely, given that B. confirms the elbow as a site for drawing blood.

176
camping on the road: This is *xucanahibeh ri pa be*, literally "it was left in the road."

177
In unity: This is *chiquihunam uach*, "in-their-one face," an idiom given in X. as *hunam quiuach*, "in agreement," and in B. as *hunamah uach*, "to make friends."

177
They were just smelling the tips of their staffs: Andrés Xiloj commented: "Perhaps these staffs had some secret. Perhaps they were of a wood like cherry, which has the odor of the fruit."

178
packed . . . on their backs: The verb stem here is *eca* [*eka*], "to carry on the shoulders or back" (B.).

178
above a great red river: This is *chuui hun nima ca3ha* [*cakhaa*], "on-top one great red-river." Given that the writers of the P.V. usually transcribe both "house" (*ha*) and "water (or river)" (*haa*) as *ha*, this could also be "great red house." Red was perhaps the commonest color for the stuccoed exteriors of Mayan public buildings, going all the way back to the pre-classic.

178
on a bare mountain: This is *zaqui* [*zaki*] *huyub*, literally "white mountain," but *zaki* is sometimes used to mean "plain" (in the sense of unadorned). I take it that the writers mean to contrast the situation of Hacauitz with that of Auilix and Tohil, both of whom seem to be "in a great forest" even though the latter, like Hacauitz, is on a mountain.

179
Masses of serpents . . . jaguars, rattlesnakes, yellowbites were there in the forest where he was hidden: Today in Momostenango the shrines on the high mountains that bound the community, together with the shrine (atop a very high waterfall) used by those who organize and play parts in the Monkey Dance, are all said to be haunted by dangerous animals. Such animals appear to those whose ritual office does not entitle them to visit a particular shrine; they also appear to those who have a right to visit but have failed to abstain from sexual or violent acts (whether verbal or physical) on the day of their arrival at the shrine.

180
they stopped there: The verb stem here is *tacotob,* translated on the basis of *taʒatobic,* "to stop and not move forward" (under *taʒaba* in B.).

180
They cried their hearts and their guts out: Asked why, Andrés Xiloj said, "They were sad in the darkness, there was no light, no day, no night, all the time it was dark." The Quiché do not think of night as simply "dark" as opposed to "light" (see *in the early dawn* in the notes to p. 73). The conditions before the first dawn of the P.V. were so bad that one could not even speak properly of night, with its moon and stars and even a faint trace of dawn, to say nothing of the full light of day.

180
the gods who were . . . just out in the bromelias, in the hanging mosses, not yet set on pedestals: Today bromelias and hanging mosses (see Glossary) are standard materials in the construction of temporary outdoor arbors or archways for saints; the present passage would seem to mean that the gods were put beneath such arbors, not that they were put up in the trees where bromelias and hanging mosses actually grow. Only later were the gods "set on pedestals," presumably in the "houses" at the tops of pyramids (see pp. 218–219).

180
their strategies: This is *quichacabal* [*qui4hacabal*], "their-win-instrument."

180
Their hearts did not yet harbor ill will: This is *mana chilic cayal ta qui4ux,* in which *mana* is "not yet," *ta* is a further marker of the negative, and *qui4ux* is "their hearts." B. glosses both *chilic* and *cayal* as "ill will, anger."

181
they incensed: The verb stem here is *zacbiza,* translated on the basis of *zaʒbizah,* "to incense" and "to wag [a tail]" (B.). In the next sentence I have translated the same verb as "they shook." A pottery censer of the kind used in Mesoamerica must be shaken or swayed back and forth to keep the incense burning.

182
it is only his reflection that now remains: What might lie behind this statement is revealed by a contemporary Mopán Maya tale in which Lord Kin (the sun) goes from his home in the east to the center of the sky and then back to the east again; it appears that he goes clear across the sky because he has placed a mirror at its center (Thompson, *Ethnology of the Mayas of Southern and Central British Honduras,* p. 132). To interpret the movements of the sun in this manner is to

model it on Venus as morning star, which both rises and sets in the east.

182

Tohil, Auilix, and Hacauitz were turned to stone, along with the idols of the puma, jaguar, rattlesnake, yellowbite, which the White Spark-striker took with him into the trees: The "idols" here are *ucabauilal* [*u4abauilal*], "its-god-own," *4abauil* being translated elsewhere as "god." The White Sparkstriker is named immediately after the yel-lowbite and could be included in the list of beings who are turned to stone, but in terms of what is known about him (or her) today (B. Tedlock, "El C'oxol: un símbolo de la resistencia quiché") it makes much more sense to treat the name as the subject of the sen-tence that follows it, *xa xuchap chi uca* [*u4ah*] *rib pa che* [*chee*], "just he/she took that to-accompany him/herself into trees." Today the White Sparkstriker is the keeper of volcanic concretions and ancient artifacts that resemble animals; these objects, which are said to have been petrified when the sun first rose, are called *mebil* (the same as the name of the shrine in which they are kept) in Momostenango and *4amauil* in the eastern Quiché area.

Andrés Xiloj commented on the passage at hand as follows: "When all the birds, animals were converted into stone, they remained as *mebil.* When the moment comes and one is able to acquire one of these, this is the *mebil.* Birds, rabbits, in sum, all the different kinds of stones. Now the *4oxol* [Sparkstriker], this one, yes, he has money, 'tis said. When one has luck, the *4oxol* presents himself. If he takes off his shoe and leaves it thrown away, then there is the money; or his little bag—because he has a little bag, and if he leaves it thrown away, there is the money. This is the *mebil* of a person; it is the luck." Lucas Pacheco said that the *4oxol* lost his/her shoe when the sun first rose; the *4oxol* escaped petrification by running into the trees, but the shoe did not.

182

Perhaps we would have no relief from the voracious animals today— the puma, jaguar, rattlesnake, yellowbite— . . . if the original animals hadn't been turned to stone: "Voracious animals" is *tionel chicop,* "biting (or meat-eating) animals." The MS. erroneously adds the White Sparkstriker to the list of animals in this sentence; apparently Ximénez (or a copyist) interpreted the previous naming of the White Sparkstriker (see above) as part of a list of animals and then assumed that the name must be missing from the present list. Andrés Xiloj commented: "The *4oxol* [Sparkstriker] has to take care of the animals; he doesn't allow them to go out, because they are harmful. He keeps them, he has them in a corral." This is the Sparkstriker in his role as gamekeeper (see B. Tedlock, *Time and the Highland Maya,* pp.

181–87); today the dangerous animals only attack people who have failed in their ritual duties. According to Lucas Pacheco, the corral where the Sparkstriker keeps his animals is located deep within a branch of the cave beneath the ruins of Rotten Cane; in that context they take the form of small stones. The fortunate may be allowed to take some of these; the unfortunate fall into a great, wide mouth.

183
And the language has differentiated in the case of the Cakchiquels: In this passage (beginning on p. 183) the P.V. presents a theory that linguistic differentiation correlates with differences in the names originally assigned to tribal gods. The linguistic observations are themselves quite accurate (see the Introduction).

184
their stay: This is *quiabulic,* translated on the basis of *yabulic,* "to stop" (B.).

184
the masking of Tohil: The "masking" is *cohbal,* "mask-instrument," apparently referring to the deer costumes discussed on p. 185.

185
they bowed down: The verb here is *uonouoh,* "contract, as in joining the chin with the knees" (B.).

185
Now it was only a manifestation of his genius that spoke when the penitents and sacrificers came before Tohil: That is to say, the words came not from the stone itself but from an apparition of its spirit familiar, which in this case would be a youth.

185
All they burned before their gods was resin, just bits of pitchy bark, along with marigolds: That is to say, they burned things gathered in nature rather than proper copal (see Glossary). The resin is *3ol,* which may be gathered in gummy nodules from the trunks of various trees. The bits of pitchy bark are *rachak nooh,* literally "leavings of pine resin," pieces of bark on which a hard red resin has been formed as a result of the holes bored by worms. The species of marigold in question is a common roadside herb (see Glossary). According to Andrés Xiloj, all of these things are burned as offerings today in Momostenango, but they constitute a poorer offering than copal. Earle reports the use of marigolds in the eastern Quiché area as well ("La etnoecología quiché"), and I have seen the unburned remains of bits of bark at a shrine near Chichicastenango.

185
Do not reveal us to the tribes: Andrés Xiloj compared this hiding of the gods (or the stones that contain their geniuses) to the proper treatment of the valuable objects that are called *mebil* in the Quiché dialect of Momostenango: "These stones are like *mebil.* When one

finds one, one must not show it to another person, because it's for one-self directly. There are persons who find some little things; they may show them to others, but this *mebil* won't allow it, now it won't give good fortune to the person who found it. It withdraws. If there is some little thing, an ancient coin found in the woods, or a stone, then one must guard it." See also the notes to p. 73.

185
"they search for us": This is *coh3a3anih rumal*, "us-watch-closely by-them"; the verb stem is translated on the basis of *3a3alinic*, "am-bushed, surveyed closely" (Q.).

185
"don't you let us be hunted down": This is *maui cohiralahobizah*, "not incomplete-us-you-hunt (or trap)-cause."

185
"female deer and female birds": "Female" is *xnam* here; V. gives *xnam* as "female deer," but in the present passage *xnam* appears as an adjective with both "deer" and "birds": *xnam queh xnam 4,iquin.*

185
"deer costumes": These are *u queh* at the first mention and *cu queh* thereafter. B. gives *cuu* as "clothing"; it should probably be *4uu* on the basis of its resemblance to *4ul*, which several other sources gloss as "clothing."

185
"They belong to us already": This is a reference to the long-standing promise the tribes made in order to get fire, namely, that they would allow themselves to be "suckled"—that is, to have their hearts cut out (see p. 175).

185
they would then go to anoint the mouth of the stone of Tohil or Auilix with the blood of the deer or bird: In the eastern Quiché area today, the mouths of stones (now called *4amauil* rather than *4abauil* as here) are more commonly given drinks of distilled liquor than of blood, but the blood of sacrificed chickens is sometimes given in the area of Chi-chicastenango. Drinks of liquor are also put into the mouths of saints. Ideally the liquid offered should quickly disappear, as if actually swallowed by the stone or saint; in the words of the P.V., "And the bloody drink was drunk by the gods."

186
just the larva of the yellow jacket, the larva of the wasp, and the larva of the bee: Andrés Xiloj described these insects, the *uonon, zital,* and *akah,* as follows: "The *uonon* is large and striped yellow and black; there is honey in its hive, and it stings. The *zital* is bigger and has red stripes. Its bite is more serious than that of the *uonon;* it causes a large swelling and one could even die. It, too, has honey. The *akah* is small, a little bigger than a fly, and stings. It makes a nest, with thousands of

akah. If one can get it down with a stick the *akah* stay up there, then one can get whatever pieces of honey there are." At present the larvae are eaten only in the case of the *akah*.

187

"Your right": This is *icolbal iuib*, in which *i-* is "you" and *iuib* is "yourselves" (both plural familiar); B. gives *colbalib* as "liberty." This is a reference to the agreement the tribes made to allow themselves to be sacrificed (see p. 175 and the next note).

187

the suckling: This is *ri 4,um;* some have taken it to be "pelt," but I translate it on the basis of tzumah [*4,umah*], "to suckle" (B.), and take it to be a further reference to the "suckling" (heart sacrifice) pledged by the tribes (see the previous note).

188

the tracks were merely those of animals: This is *cacan [cakan] ri xa quipich,* "their tracks that just their feet," in which "feet" (*pich*) is specifically "the feet of quadrupeds" (V.).

188

dark and rainy: This is *quecal [ʒekal] hab,* literally "black rain," but referring (according to Andrés Xiloj) to a storm that is so intense that the sky gets very dark. This supports the notion that Tohil is an aspect of Hurricane (see the notes to p. 173), who caused a "black rain" when he destroyed the wooden people. In the view of Lounsbury (personal communication), Tahil, the classic equivalent of Tohil at Palenque, was also a rain god.

188

misty and drizzly: This is *muzmul hab,* "misty rain." Andrés Xiloj explained: "These are days when it doesn't rain strongly; instead the drops are small, little bits of water fall. It is *muzmul.*"

188

they singled them out and cut them down: The MS. has *echalamicat,* in which the only certainty is *e,* "they." My reading is based on *chala,* "to pick out among many" (B.), and (following Edmonson, *The Book of Counsel,* p. 192) *4at,* "cut" (in the sense of "reap").

189

"in full blossom": This is *chaom,* "blossom," a "metaphor meaning beauty" according to B.

189

"radiate preciousness": This is *zaclocoh [zakloʒoh],* a combination of "light" (*zak*) and "valuable" or "precious" (*loʒoh*). Andrés Xiloj pictured the maidens as twelve to fifteen years old.

190

on their hands and knees: This is *chacachaxinac [chacachaxinak],* with passive and perfect suffixes (*-xinak*), which I translate on the basis of *chacachotic,* "go on all fours" (B.).

190

Tohil and the others: Here and elsewhere in this story I have supplied "and the others"; the name Tohil is often used to mean all three gods and may be combined with a plural verb prefix.

190

there must come a sign as to whether you really saw their faces: Note that when Blood Woman went before the head of One Hunahpu, he gave her a "sign" by spitting in her hand, which made her pregnant (p. 114); in this case the signs will be quite different, intended not for the women but for their fathers.

191

they spotted: This is *xil quiuach*, in which *x-* is complete and *qui-* is "they," translated on the basis of *ilauachih*, "to look with attention" (B.).

192

on a smooth surface: This is *chiyulinic uuach*, "on-smooth its-face"; B. gives *yulunic* as "a smooth thing." The paintings were on "the inside" (*upam*) of the cloaks, and it was this side that went next to the body of the lord who was then stung by wasps, despite the "smooth surface."

192

He turned around: The verb stem here is *zolouic*, translated on the basis of *zololic*, "to give turns" (B.).

192

unfurling it: This is *catzonon ucuxic* [*uȝuxic*], literally "he-undresses his-being-covered"; B. gives *tzonolic* as "undressed." I take it that this lord opened up his cloak so that everyone could see the eagle on the inside of it.

192

It then became the profession of Xtah and Xpuch to bark shins: "Bark shins" is my translation of *hoxol chec* [*ȝhek*], based on the comments of Andrés Xiloj: "*ȝhek* is the shin bone. *Hoxol* is 'one who wounds.' It is the wound that they [the girls] gave them. A girl or a boy comes to know how the world is [laughs]. Let's suppose we are now old people. We can deceive a girl of fifteen or sixteen years, and there is the wound. The violence. And so a woman can deceive a boy of fifteen or fourteen years, then there it is. The old woman wounded the boy [laughs]. This is *hoxol ȝhek*, 'the wounder of shins.' Only now we say *xuporo rakan*, 'she burned his legs.' "

193

those spirit boys: I have supplied "spirit" to make it clearer that the reference is to Tohil, Auilix, and Hacauitz.

193

their fortress: Ximénez translates *catem* as "fortification" here; B. gives *cateh* as "to block passage."

193
Their eyebrows were plucked out, along with their beards: The "plucking" here is *mich* [*mi4h*], which is elsewhere a metaphor for deception; this time plucking carries both its literal and metaphorical meanings.

194
made a fence: The "fence" is *coxtun*, "wall, castle, fence" (B.). In the next paragraph I translate this same word as "parapet" on the basis of context.

194
They just made a palisade of planks and stakes: The materials for this structure are *tzalam* and *chut*, respectively glossed as "board" and "stake" by B.; the verb for the making of the palisade is *quehbeh*, translated on the basis of *quehom che*, "palisaded" (B.). This was definitely not stonework.

194
around their citadel: This is *rih quitinamit*, which is misleading when translated literally as "its-back their-citadel." *Rih*, when applied to a house, means the side or sides that face the outside world, whereas *uuach*, "its-face," means the side or sides that face the patio; I assume that the same scheme was analogously applied to a citadel. That is to say, a citadel turned its "back" to the outside world and its "face" inward. This interpretation is confirmed by the entry for *cotoh chirih tinamit* in B., literally "surround at-its-back citadel" but glossed (following European reckoning) as the "face of a fortress."

194
They surrounded the citadel: The verb stem here is *cotcomih*, a reduplicated form meaning "surround" (B.).

195
eight hundred score, . . . thirty times eight hundred: This is my attempt to translate Mayan numbers into English without completely converting them from the vegesimal system to the decimal one; "score" in English is of course a remnant of vegesimal reckoning. The numbers in the text are *cachui* and *oxchui*, "2 × 8,000" and "3 × 8,000," 8,000 being the third power of 20 and filling the same place in a vegesimal system that 1,000 fills in a decimal system.

195
they just enjoyed the spectacle: The verb stem here is *cai*, "to watch admiringly, like watching dances" (listed under *cai3* in B.).

195
their legs, their arms: As Andrés Xiloj pointed out, this is an idiom meaning "all over their bodies."

195
they were doubling over: The verb stem here is *uon*, translated on the

basis of *uonih,* "to be doubled over so that the knees meet the chin"
(B.).
196
stumbling: The verb stem here is *lahahic,* a reduplicated form, translated on the basis of *lahab,* "snare" (B.).
196
they were hit: Edmonson has *qiyaq* [*kiyak*], "poisoned," here (*The
Book of Counsel,* p. 208), but the MS. has *cac,* which I translate on the
basis of *ca3o,* "hit with stones" (B.).
197
gasping for breath: This is *quehilouic quepolou,* probably an idiom for
heavy or laborious breathing; *hilouic* is "sigh of tiredness" and *polou*
is "breath" (both in B.).
197
"our own tribal place": This could be all the way back at the place
where they were before arriving at Tulan Zuyua.
197–198
"Again it is the time of our Lord Deer": "It is the time" is my translation of *cholan,* "order" (in the sense of sequence). "Our Lord Deer" is
a reference to one of the twenty day names of the 260-day divinatory
cycle. At present a day addressed in prayer is always prefaced with
the title "Lord," but the number prefix of the day is specified—for
example, *ahau hun queh,* "Lord One Deer." One of the few contexts
in which days may be addressed or referred to by name alone is that
of prayers to or stories about the *mam,* the only four day names that
can serve to mark a new solar year. Deer is one of these days, and it
seems likely that the present passage refers to the day named Deer in
its capacity as a *mam.* For speculation that the specific day in question was One Deer, see the Introduction.
198
"Go see the place where we came from": Given that Jaguar Quitze
and the others have already said that they themselves are going to
"our own tribal place," it is difficult to interpret their instructions to
their sons. Perhaps the answer is that the fathers are going in spirit,
whereas their sons will make a pilgrimage in the flesh. Also, the sons
will not go until some time later. In any case, the irreducible difference between the journey of the fathers and that later undertaken by
the sons is that the former are never seen again.
198
"for making requests": This is *tanabal* [*taanabal*], "asking-instru-
ment." Andrés Xiloj remarked, "It's like a place to burn offerings.
But this word is only used for places that are open to the public,
not for shrines that only a mother-father [patrilineage head] can
visit."

198
"fiery splendor": This is my translation of *3a3al*, "fire-ness" or "hot-ness," a frequent metaphor for the glories and splendors of lordly dominance over others.

198
downtrodden: This is *yocotahinac*, translated on the basis of *yo3o*, "step on" (B.).

198
All those on Hacauitz: This phrase has been supplied in order to distinguish the inhabitants of the citadel of Hacauitz from the "broken and downtrodden" tribes.

198
the day of the bundle: This may have been the day named Deer, mentioned by the departing Quiché ancestors on the same occasion as the presentation of the bundle. Today this day is associated, above all others, with mother-fathers, the priest-shamans who perform rites for lineages, cantons, and an entire town (according to their rank). All mother-fathers, as well as the ordinary daykeepers who rank just below them, possess a sacred bundle, but this bundle contains divining paraphernalia and is opened frequently.

PART FIVE

203
who represented all the Cauecs: This is *rech ronohel cauiquib*, literally "of (or belonging to) all the Cauecs." There are similar phrases in the sentences dealing with the Greathouses and Lord Quichés in this same passage.

203
judge: This is *catol* [*3atol*] *tzih*, at present *3atal tzih* (X.) or (in the dialect of Momostenango) *3atbal tzih*, "reap-instrument [of] words."

204
From across the sea, they brought back the writings about Tulan. In the writings, in their words, they spoke of having cried: The MS. reads as follows: *xquicam* [*xqui4am*] *ula ri chaca* [*chaka*] *palo utzibal* [*u4,-ibal*] *tulan utzibal xe4ha chire quioquinac* [*quio3inak*] *chupan chupan quitzih.* The repetitions of *utzibal* and *chupan* make no sense unless we assume a scribal transposition; moving the second *utzibal* to a position immediately after the first *chupan* gives the following reading: "they-brought back the from-across sea its-writings Tulan, they-talked about having-cried inside its-writings, inside their-words." The writers of the P.V. do not specify whether the "writings about Tulan" and the Council Book (P.V.) itself were one and the

same, but it seems likely, given that one of the epithets of the Council Book is "The Light That Came from Across the Sea."

205

There were actually four mountains: "Mountains" (*huyub*), in referring to settlement, could mean prominences in close proximity and of any size; for symbolic purposes even a small mound can be called "mountain" in Quiché.

205

they examined: This is *xeico chiri chuui*, literally "they passed there above," but Andrés Xiloj read it as an idiom meaning "to look over."

205

But their faces did not die: This is *mana xucam quiuach*, translated almost literally. The reference is to the eschatology set forth by One Hunahpu in his lecture to Blood Woman, in which he says, "Neither dimmed nor destroyed is the face of a lord" (p. 114).

205

pain and affliction: This is *caxcol [4ax4ol] rail*, translated on the basis of entries in B., where the two words are treated as synonyms, and on the basis of the entry for *4ax4ol* in X.

205

They ground their gypsum, their plaster: This seems to be a metonym for major construction. It may not mean that previous Quiché sites lacked gypsum plaster, but in the present context it combines with such phrases as "excellent citadel," "the root of fiery splendor," and "lords of singular genius" (pp. 205, 206, 207) to indicate that the building of Bearded Place represented a whole new level in the rise of the Quiché lords.

206

one in each: This is my interpolation.

206

and that the other lord be allied with them: This is *xa cu [4u] hun ahau xrah cu [cuu] quib*, "just then one (other) lord was-wanted to-keep themselves," in which the translation of *cuu* is based on B. The lord in question here is Iztayul, as the next sentence makes clear; in the present sentence he is being distinguished from Cotuha.

206

the Ilocs wanted him as their disciple: This is *xrah tihox cumal ilocab*, "was-wanted disciple by-them Ilocs"; B. gives *tihoxel* as "disciple."

206

First they invaded the citadel: This is *xcoquibeh nabe tinamit*, literally "they-entered first citadel"; B. gives *oquibeh tinamit* as "scale a fortress."

206

This was in payment: The "payment" is *tohbal*, "pay-instrument," which in this context is a sound play on Tohil, the principal god before whom the Ilocs were sacrificed, and on the day name Toh, which was the day of Tohil. This day is still interpreted by diviners as having to do with the payment of debts; in making this interpretation they utilize a sound play on the day name similar to the one used here, moving from *toh* as a proper name to the verb *tohonic*, "pay" (see B. Tedlock, *Time and the Highland Maya*, p. 155).

207
the canyon and the citadel: This is the first of a number of joint appearances of *ziuan*, "canyon," and *tinamit*, "citadel"; taken together, they seem to encompass both a citadel proper (see Glossary), in the sense of a high, fortified place with temples and palaces, and what lies around or below that citadel as well. The effect is to extend the sense of settlement or community beyond its fortified core, with temples and palaces, to the surrounding population, creating a compound concept meaning something like "town" or "city." T. J. Knab (personal communication) suggests that this expression might be the Quiché equivalent of the Nahua term for town or city, which also involves a juxtaposition of the low with the high (in that order): *altepetl*, compounded of *al* (from *atl*), "water," and *tepetl*, "mountain" (D.). The Quiché also use a water-mountain pairing, but it is applied not to towns but to outdoor shrines, which (ideally) exist in low-high pairs (see B. Tedlock, *Time and the Highland Maya*, pp. 76, 80). In sum, the Quiché and Nahua terms for "town," along with the Quiché pairing of shrines, all involve a juxtaposition of the low and the high, in that order. Both languages construct their term for town by pairing complementary metonyms for a town rather than by reducing the complexity of a town to a unitary abstraction.

207
lords of singular genius: "Singular" is *humah*, translated on the basis of *hunah*, "make oneself unique" (B.).

207
nothing happened to make fools of them: "To make fools" is my translation of *alachinak*, which is given by B. as "joke."

207
or to ruin the greatness: This is *xaui banol rech nimal*, in which *xaui* indicates "the same as the aforesaid" and links this clause to the negative one preceding it; *banol* is translated "to ruin" on the basis of *banoh*, "disaster" (V.); *rech* is "of their"; and *nimal* is "greatness."

207
the blossoming of their daughters: The verb stem here is *ziih*, "to flower" (X.), and fits with an earlier floral metaphor for young women (see the notes to p. 189).

207
ate their corn: The verb here is *uech*, which refers specifically to the eating of foods made of corn, and what I have translated "corn" is *ua*,

which refers to these same things, primarily to tamales (which are often made of nothing but corn dough in Guatemala).

207

our way of being thankful and grateful: The former is *camouabal* [*4amouabal*], "thanks-instrument," and the latter is *pacubal*, translated on the basis of *pa3uh*, "be thankful for" (B.).

207

allied tribes . . . principalities: See the notes to p. 168 for a discussion of these terms.

208

The Lords Cotuha and Plumed Serpent: The Cotuha mentioned here is probably not the one who ruled as Keeper of the Mat at Bearded Place, but the Cotuha who was Keeper of the Reception House Mat when Plumed Serpent was Keeper of the Mat.

208

There had been five changes and five generations: This is *xroquexoc xrolea puch*, in which *x*- is complete, *ro*- is "five," and *puch* is "and." The rest is translated on the basis of *quexoc*, "change, return," and *le*, "generation" (both in B.).

210

their separation, when they quarreled among themselves, disturbing the bones and skulls of the dead: The scribe got into a tangle here, writing as follows (the items in parentheses were written in the margin with their places of insertion marked by daggers): *quihachouic quib ta xqui (tzolbeh quib) tzol (cacbeh) bac uholom caminac xquicacbeh quib.* The only way I can make sense of this is to assume that the scribe meant to cross out the final *xquicacbeh quib* and move it (except for *xqui-*) to a position immediately following the dangling *xqui* he had already written, and to insert a missing *beh* after *tzol.* In the process he unnecessarily repeated *tzol* before *-beh* and then inverted the order of *cacbeh* and *tzolbeh*, meanwhile forgetting to cross out the final *xquicacbeh quib.* If I am right, the text should read, *quihachouic quib ta xquicacbeh* [*xquicakbeh*] *quib tzolbeh bac* [*bak*] *uholom caminac* [*caminak*], "their-sorting-out themselves when they-quarreled themselves turning-over bone its-head dead-person."

210

the lord bishop: This is *Sr. obicpo*, the first Spanish to appear in the text since p. 71. The person referred to here is Francisco Marroquín, who blessed the ruins of Rotten Cane in 1539, fifteen years after the place had been burned by Alvarado.

211

And now to show their faces: This is *cate* [*4ate*] *chic chiuachin uuach*, "next now that-show his-face," singular in Quiché in order to agree with "each of them" in the previous sentence. The notion of "face" is intimately tied up with personal identity in Quiché; a person's day of birth, for example, is called *uuach u3ih*, "its-face his/her-day," and a number of Quiché lords were named after the days of their birth (see p. 226). A later passage mentioning the "faces" of lords precedes a list of the names of individual lords (p. 224). I have put dots following both of these mentions of faces to indicate that graphic elements might be missing here, something that was in the manuscript Ximénez discovered but which he did not reproduce. If that manuscript was like the Book of Chilam Balam of Maní, there may have been a graphic device, at least partially based on hieroglyphic writing, corresponding to each lord. In the Maní book the device is a line drawing of a face with a European crown, a latter-day version of the much more stylized face that composes the glyph meaning *ahau* or "lord," but the individual name of each lord is written in block letters on a scroll beneath the head rather than rendered hieroglyphically (Eugene R. Craine and Reginald C. Reindorp, *The Codex Pérez and the Chilam Balam of Maní*, pp. 79–86).

212

a crowded life, crowded with petitions: "Crowded" translates *molomox*, a passive form of *molomanic*, "many join together" (B.). "Petitions" translates *utabal tzih*, in which the stem of *utabal* is *taba*, "supplicate" (B.), and *tzih* is "words."

212

The birthdays: This is *uquih [u3ih] ralaxic*, "its-day his-being-born," the phrase still used for "birthday."

212

On one occasion: This is *hu uuc*, a phrase most translators have taken to be *hu uuk* and to mean "one seven" (literally) and "seven days" (idiomatically). But "seven" should be *uukub*, not *uuk*, and there is nothing in the colonial dictionaries of Quichean languages that would allow for its combination with *hu*. The solution I offer is based on considerations of context and on *uu3ul*, a form that refers to pauses or interruptions in the normal course of events (V.); I take the present phrase to be *hu uu3* and to mean something like "during one interval," or (idiomatically) "one time" or "on one occasion."

212

serpentine.... aquiline ... feline: At some moments this passage claims that Plumed Serpent became an "actual" (*quitzih*) serpent (*cumatz*) or eagle (*cot*) or jaguar (*balam*), but at other moments it would seem that he took on the *qualities* of these animals. Wherever I translate with English words ending in -ine, the MS. has *cumatzil*, *cotal*, and *balamil*, each of which has a suffix meaning something like "-ness."

213

The news spread: This is *xpaxin rib utaic*, "it-scattered itself its-being-heard."

213
he became the sole head: "Sole" here is *huquizic,* translated on the basis of *hu4izic,* "only" (V.).

214
went down on their faces or flat on their backs: This is *xuleic, xpacaic,* translated on the basis of *xuleic,* "throw face down" (B.), and *pa4alic,* "face up" (X.).

215
Their lineages came to be bled, shot full of arrows at the stake: This is *xeoc chinamit xelotzic xecacquic chiche* [*chichee*], in which *xeoc* is literally "they-entered" but idiomatically "it was their time," and *chichee* is "at-tree" or "at-pole." *Xelotzic,* in which *xe-* is "complete-they," is translated on the basis of *lotzo,* "to let blood" (B. and V.). *Xecacquic* (with a passive suffix) is translated "they were shot with arrows" by Ximénez; B. has *cacoqueh* (with an active suffix), "hunt with arrows." This passage confirms that Quiché rituals included arrow sacrifice, a practice better known from central Mexico.

215
Projectiles alone were the means for breaking the citadels: The weapon here is *4ha* [sometimes *4hab*] in the MS., "arrow" and (judging from V.) the spear thrown by an atlatl (spear-thrower). *4ha* or *4hab* is distinct from *cha* or *chaa,* which is the term for any lithic projectile point or cutting instrument and (today) for glass (see *4ha* and *chaa* in V., *chab* and *cha* in B., and *4hab* and *cha* in X.). In Mixtec codices, towns (or citadels) are identified by place signs whose basic element is a mountain; the conquest of a town is signified by showing its place sign pierced with a projectile (Mary Elizabeth Smith, *Picture Writing from Ancient Southern Mexico,* p. 33 and fig. 51). The present passage sounds like a literal reading of a codex of this style. It may also be that such codices depict a ritual practice in which the very earth or native stone of a conquered citadel was actually pierced or broken. Whatever the case with codices, people from the towns conquered by the Quiché came to Petatayub, "carrying in their hands the signs of the citadels," which "look as though they had been split with an axe."

215
one . . . after another: This is *libah chi,* given by B. as "step by step."

215
the gum tree: I follow Edmonson in reading *col che* as *3ol chee,* "gum (or resin) tree" (*The Book of Counsel,* p. 236), rather than as a place named "Colche," partly because the name of the place under discussion in this passage is otherwise accounted for.

215
carrying in their hands: This is *chelah,* translated on the basis of *4he-lenic,* "to carry with the hands" (X.).

cut stones: I have supplied "stones" here, assuming that they are still the subject of the discussion; "cut" is my translation of *xcatatahic* [*xʒatatahic*], "complete-cut-result-passive." Reading the verb stem as *ʒata,* "cut," fits with *xchoi chi icah,* "split with an axe," later on in this same sentence, and with the general sense of the paragraph up to this point.

there on the flat: Ximénez translates *tacah* [*taʒah*] as "the coast," meaning the long Pacific coastal plain of Guatemala, but this term can refer even to very small flats. See *Petatayub* in the Glossary for a further discussion.

"and like doubles for our own lineages": This is *quehe pu cacachinamit,* which I read as *quehe pu kacacab chinamit,* "like and our-pair lineages."

"send for us to come and kill them": Here the text has both *nu,* the first person singular, and *ca* [*ka*], first person plural. The text reads *chulibiih chibe nu ca camizah,* in which *ca* is written somewhat above the line, just after *nu;* for this reason, and because the statement quoted here is attributed to three people, I take *nu* to be an error the scribe forgot to cross out when he added *ca.*

nor did any of them have his own god: That is to say, those who were sent to occupy the conquered citadels did not have stone gods (*ʒabauil*) of the kind that were brought from Tulan Zuyua. We do not know whether the previous lords of these citadels had such stones or what might have been the fate of their stones. It is interesting to note that the present-day term *ʒamauil,* which covers large stones found in outdoor shrines, is used only in the region around the ruins of Rotten Cane. Shrines in the western Quiché area lack such stones, and the small stone objects collected for household altars are called by a different term, *mebil.*

"the ennobling of the lookout lineages": The "ennobling" is *quecalem* [*quekalem*], in which *qu-* is "their"; B. gives *ecalem* as "dignity" or "nobility." The root *eka-* has to do with taking a load on the shoulders; it is used today in various expressions having to do with the taking on of responsibilities, such as those of mother-fathers for people they train as daykeepers, or those of daykeepers for the clients they are currently praying for.

"we'll induct": This is *cachapa* [*kachapa*], literally "we-take-hold-of," but V. notes that *chapa* is also an idiom for "putting into lordship."

217

"which is mine . . . which is yours": This translates *ue,* "of mine," and *aue,* "of yours (singular familiar)"; others have missed the sense of this sentence, trying to make these two pronouns agree; Edmonson has *ui* for the *ue* of the MS. (*The Book of Counsel,* p. 240).

217

in concord: This is *hunam uach,* literally "equal face," an idiom meaning "to be in concord" (under the entry for *hun* in B.).

218

a fortress around Quiché: In effect, the entire Quiché state was conceived as a gigantic fortress, an enlargement of the citadel at its center.

219

house of sacrifice: This is *cahbaha,* which I take to be composed of *cahb,* "sacrifice" (see the notes to p. 167), and *ha,* "house." Some have taken *cahbaha* to be a reference to the place called Sajcabajá today, but that is written *zacabaha* or *zaccabaha* in the P.V. (see *Plaster House* in the Glossary) and combines *ha* with *zakcaba,* "plaster."

219

they nurtured and provided for the Keeper of the Mat and Keeper of the Reception House Mat: The gods are spoken of at various points as needing nurturers and providers (beginning on p. 73); the present passage means that the relationship between lords and vassals was conceived in the same terms as that between gods and humans. Note here that the text goes right on to emphasize the greatness of the lords under discussion.

219

everything they saw was clear to them: That is to say, they were able to recover the clairvoyance that the first humans had before "they were blinded as the face of a mirror is breathed upon" (p. 167).

219

there was a place to see it, there was a book: The "place to see it" is *ibal re,* earlier written as *ilbal re.* With the book the lords are able to recover the full vision of the first humans; such vision, as this passage makes clear, reached into future time.

219

a way of cherishing: This is *locbal [loʒbal],* "love (or desire or value) instrument." Andrés Xiloj suggested "something that shows esteem or expresses a sense of value."

219

For nine score days they would fast: "Nine score" is *beleh uinac [uinak];* Edmonson is correct in reading this as 9 × 20 rather than "nine persons" (*The Book of Counsel,* p. 243). As he has observed, 180 is half a *tun,* the 360-day cycle (distinct from the solar year) used by the lowland Maya in reckoning chronologies. The "thirteen score" (or

260) mentioned next is the length of the so-called divinatory cycle, while the "seventeen score" (or 340) is the combined length of the 90- and 250-day segments of the Venus cycle (see the notes to the Introduction).

219
They would only eat zapotes, matasanos. . . . : For identifications of the tropical fruits listed here, see the Glossary. Of this kind of diet, Andrés Xiloj said, "This was so that they would have strength. This Tecum Umam [hero of Quiché resistance to the Spanish] didn't eat cooked things, only raw [or green] things. Because of this, the people of that time were muscular. Whatever place they went, whatever kind of fruit they found, they ate in place of tamales."

219
abstinence: This is *auazinic*, translated on the basis of *auazim*, "forbidden" (in B. under *auatz*).

219
there weren't any women with them when they slept: This does not mean that women were not present at all. When people "keep the days" at present, the abstinence always includes sexual contact but never avoidance of all interaction with the opposite sex. If the fasts described here were like those of the first four Quiché ancestors, it was not only the lords who fasted but their wives as well (see p. 178).

221
"On this blessed day": This is *atoob uquih* [u3ih], in which *u3ih* is "its-day"; B. gives *atob* as "good."

221
"ripeness and freshness": literally *3anal*, "yellowness," and *raxal*, "greenness." Andrés Xiloj commented: "When one prays, *3anal* means to have corn, to have money, to do business. Yes, it is like 'yellow' but it isn't yellow, but rather that it *ripens. Raxal* is like a plant that is green, it is developing to give fruit. *3anal* is when it ripens."

221
"spread thy stain, spill thy drops/of green and yellow": This is a fairly literal translation of *chatziloh, chamaquih uloc* [cha4,iloh, chama4ih ulok] *araxal, a3anal.* Andrés Xiloj commented: "*4,iloh* is to use [sexually]; now they are going to have a family. *Ma4ih* is the sin. The man looks for his companion, there it is. And there is that liquid [semen]. And the green [*raxal*], there it is, it is the son or daughter, and the yellow [*3anal*]; and they, in turn, have to produce again. Here it is like a plant, the sowing of a plant, and its ripening."

221
"that they might multiply" [chipo3tah]: Andrés Xiloj commented: "*Po3tah* is that it produces. Like a seed: when we cast it, we say to it,

capo3 la, 'Come out [sprout], produce more.' " Commenting on the prayer as a whole (pp. 221–222), he said, "We're using this now; it's just that the language has changed somewhat."
222
"may they neither be snared nor wounded, / nor seduced, nor burned, / nor diverted below the road nor above it": "Burned" is paired with "seduced" here because, as Andrés Xiloj pointed out, the act of seducing an innocent person may be expressed in the phrase *xuporo rakan,* "He (or she) burned her (or his) legs." He suggested that a contemporary prayer for safety in the road might include the following lines:

> Do not let us fall into the hands
> of this person, this neighbor,
> who has a pistol, who has a dagger,
> who has a knife, who has a revolver;
> keep away the legs and arms
> of people at the corners, on the streets.

Contemporary prayers also include numerous passages with lists of negative requests; here is an example from a prayer by Esteban Ajxub, a professional *ahbix* or "singer":

> May there be no pain,
> may there be no trouble,
> may there be no jail,
> may there be no prison,
> may there be no weakness,
> may there be no feebleness,
> may there be no stiffness,
> may there be no lies and gossip.

222
"secrets or sorcery of thine": This is *acuil auitzmal,* in which *a-* is "your (singular familiar)." Andrés Xiloj read *cuil* as *4uyil,* "hidden"; *itzmal* is translated on the basis of *itzim,* "witched" (X.). Don Andrés commented, "God gives all the good and all the evil."
222
"before thy mouth and thy face": Placement "before" someone's "face" is the commonest Quiché way of saying something like English "in" someone's "presence"; sometimes this is elaborated, as here, by adding "mouth" to "face," in which, if "face" is a metonym for the whole front of the body, "mouth" is a metonym for the whole face. In the present context "mouth" has an additional connotation, given that it refers in part to Heart of Earth, the deity called Mundo today.

This is the great Mesoamerican earth deity, the ultimate swallower of all living things, depicted in classic Maya art (in the Palenque relief panels, for example) as an enormous pair of jaws upon whose lips even the feet of great lords must rest in precarious balance, and into whose throat even great lords must fall. Turning to the contemporary scene, daykeepers who visit the cave beneath the ruins of Rotten Cane, the last Quiché capital, speak of the danger of falling into "the open mouth of the Mundo" there, which is said to be more than four yards wide.

222
carrying the tribes and all the Quiché people on their shoulders: This is *rezalaxic* [*rekalaxic*] *amac* [*ama3*] *ru4 ronohel queche uinac* [*uinak*], "its-being-carried (on the shoulders) tribe, with all-of Quiché people."

223
they became lords: The verb stem here is *ahauaric*, "to make oneself a lord" (B.).

223
gathered in gifts: This is *xquicac cochih*, in which *xqui-* is "complete-they"; the rest is translated on the basis of *4a4*, "to gather" (E.), and *cochih*, "to receive a gift." (B.).

223
food and drink: This is *uain ucaha*, translated on the basis of the reading offered by Andrés Xiloj, who uses the phrase *uaim o4aha*, "food, drink," in his own prayers.

223
falsify: This is *tzuba*, translated on the basis of *tzubu*, "deceive" (B.).

223
drops . . . that measured the width of four fingers or a full fist across: "Drops" is my translation of *racan* [*rakan*], literally "its leg" but also a term for the large drops of rain that begin or end a thunderstorm (see *Hurricane* in the Glossary). The measurements are *cahcab* [*cah3ab*], translated on the basis of *cah3a*, "measured with the four fingers together" (under *3a* in V.), and *tuic*, translated on the basis of *tuuic*, "measurement of the fist with the thumb out" (B.).

223
green and red featherwork: This is *raxon cubulchactic*. *Raxon*, literally "greened," is a synonym for *3u3*, "quetzal feather." *Cubulchactic* is a "thing made of feathers" (G.) or a "garland" (R.); B. lists *chactic* as "a species of red bird."

223
rise and growth: The MS. has *unimaric ri unimaric puch*, in which the second *unimaric* is probably an error for *uuinakiric*, giving "its-big-becoming its-growth and."

223

two by two: In the list of Cauec lords that follows, the pairing of lords will not actually begin until the fourth generation.

223

succeeds: This is *camiheic,* which Ximénez translates this way; B. has *4amibeh,* "continue" (listed after *camibeh*).

224

the faces . . . of each of the Quiché lords: Again, as on p. 211, it would seem that something is missing here; perhaps the MS. Ximénez copied had name glyphs for the lords in the list that follows this statement.

226

Great Reception House: The MS. repeats this title after Mother of the Reception House and leaves out Great Lolmet Yeoltux, the final name on an earlier list of titles belonging to the Greathouses (p. 211).

227

great in being few: This is *nim zcaquin u4oheic,* "great few (or little bit) its-being-there."

227

the original book and ancient writing: This is simply *nabe oher,* "original (or first) ancient" in the MS., abbreviated from a phrase near the opening of the P.V., *nabe uuhil, oher tzibam [4,ibam] puch,* translated as "the original book and ancient writing" on p. 71. I have repeated the full phrase here to make the echo of the opening more obvious. In general the closing paragraph is rather terse, as if the hand that wrote it were running downhill toward the finish.

GLOSSARY

ABOVE THE HOT SPRINGS *Chuui miquina* [*miʒinaa*], "above (or on top of) hot water." The town known today as San Miguel Totonicapán, capital of the Department of Totonicapán, formerly located on one of the hilltops above the present site. Once a citadel of the White Earths (Mam Mayas), conquered by the Quiché lords during the reign of Quicab. Today the inhabitants speak Quiché.

ABOVE THE NETTLES *Chuui la*, "above (or on top of) the nettles." The town more widely known today as Chichicastenango, a Nahua name meaning "Nettles Citadel." Formerly a Cakchiquel citadel, conquered by the Quiché lords during the reign of Quicab. Today the inhabitants speak Quiché.

ACUL PEOPLE *Acul uinac* [*uinak*], in which *uinak* is "people." A people belonging to a group of thirteen allied tribes the Quichés regarded as having come (like themselves) from the east.

ANCIENT WORD *Oher tzih*, also translatable as "Prior Word." A word, whether in the narrow sense of a single word or in the broad sense of an extended discourse, that carries the authority of tradition rather than being mere hearsay. At the beginning the writers of the P.V. claim this authority for their entire work, though they occasionally assign their later statements to hearsay.

ANONAS *Cauex* [*ʒauex*]. A tropical fruit (*Anona spp.*), sometimes called "cherimoya" or "custard apple" in English. Heart-shaped, green outside and creamy inside, segmented, and incredibly sweet.

ARMADILLO *Yboy*. The name of a dance done by Hunahpu and Xbalanque in their guise as vagabonds.

ARMADILLO DUNG *Achac* [*achak*] *iboy*, "dung armadillo." Crier to

325

the People for the Lord Quichés when Quicab was Keeper of the Mat; possibly a nickname for one of the Lord Quiché lords listed on p. 211.

ARM GUARD *Pachcab* [*pa4h3ab*], composed of *pa4h*, "tighten, fasten" (X.), and *3ab*, "arm." Part of the equipment necessary for the ball game played in the P.V. (see *gaming equipment*). The players of the pre-Columbian ball game are usually depicted with a wrapping on the lower arm (often the right arm only).

ATOLE *A ixim*, "water corn-kernel," is the Quiché term for the corn-gruel drink more widely known in Mesoamerica by its Nahua name, atole.

AUILIX Often *aulix* in the MS. Patron deity of the Greathouse lineage, given to Jaguar Night at Tulan Zuyua and eventually placed in Concealment Canyon, "the great canyon in the forest" (p. 178), in a location that came to be named Pauilix, literally "At Auilix"; the Greathouses were there when the dawn first came. Auilix was also the name of the temple that housed the god Auilix in the citadel of Rotten Cane, at the east side of the main plaza. It consisted of a pyramid with a single stairway (on the west side) and topped by a single thatch-roofed room with its door facing west across the plaza, toward the temple that housed the god Tohil; at present its ruins are the site of an active shrine. And finally, Auilix or Lord Auilix was the title of the priest of the god Auilix; he was seventh in rank among the lords of the Greathouses and headed one of the nine great houses into which their lineage was divided after the founding of Rotten Cane.

BALL COURT *Hom.* The I-shaped courtyard in which the Mesoamerican ball game was played. The playing field was paved with stone and bounded by stone walls; the side walls of the narrow part (connecting the two ends of the I) sloped upward in opposite directions from the playing surface, resembling grandstands in appearance but in fact constituting part of the area where the ball was in play. The ball court at Rotten Cane (see *Councilor of the Ball Court*) ran east-west, but many Mesoamerican ball courts ran north-south. Today *hom* is the Quiché term for "graveyard," which suggests the deadly nature of the game described in the P.V., at least when it is played in the underworld court of the lords of Xibalba (see also *Place of Ball Game Sacrifice*). It should be noted that the playing fields of the ball courts in Mesoamerican archaeological sites typically lie on a lower plane than that of the nearby plazas or courtyards.

BARK HOUSE See *Thorny Place*.

BAT HOUSE *Zotzi* [*zo4,i*] *ha.* One of the tests of Xibalba, fourth (p. 112) or sixth (p. 143) in the sequence of tests. If the test of fire that comes fifth in the later list (p. 143) is discounted as a redundant elaboration based on the eventual immolation of Hunahpu and Xbalanque (which does not take place in a house), then Bat House would come fifth in the later sequence and both sequences would total five houses. These houses may correspond to the five different kinds of complete Venus cycles plotted out in the Maya calendar; each cycle includes a ninety-day period during which Venus has disappeared as the morning star and has not yet reappeared as the evening star. Bat House is also the name of a lordly Cakchiquel lineage whose founders steal fire from the Quichés rather than pledge themselves as sacrifice victims.

BEARDED PLACE *Chi izmachi,* "at bearded." Citadel of the Quiché lords after they left Thorny Place and before they built Rotten Cane, founded by Jaguar Conache. When the Cauecs, Greathouses, and Lord Quichés left for Rotten Cane, Bearded Place was left to the Tams. The ruins are located one kilometer south of Rotten Cane, separated from the latter by a canyon.

BEARER, BEGETTER *Alom, 4aholom,* "one who bears children, one who begets sons," sometimes pluralized (*e alom, e 4aholom*). Names or epithets for the gods who make the earth, plants, animals, and humans. The bearing and begetting is metaphorical, since these gods do their work by means of words, genius, and sacrifice rather than through procreation. The same gods are also called Maker, Modeler, and they include Sovereign Plumed Serpent.

BEFORE THE BUILDING *Chuua tzac* [*4,ak*], "in-front-of building (of earth or stone)." The town more widely known today as Momostenango, a Nahua name meaning "Citadel of Shrines," formerly located five kilometers northwest of its present site. Conquered by the Quiché lords during the reign of Quicab.

BIRD HOUSE *Tziquina* [*4,iquina*] *ha.* The palace, at Rotten Cane, of the Keeper of the Reception House Mat, second in rank among all the Quiché lords. Not to be confused with the *ah4,iquina ha,* "those of the Bird House," a people known today as the Tzutuhil. They speak a language of the Quichean family and are located south and west of Lake Atitlán. They belong to a group of thirteen allied tribes the Quichés regarded as having come (like themselves) from the east.

BLACK ROAD *Quecabe* [*3ekabe*]. One of four cosmic roads (see *Crossroads* and *Road of Xibalba*).

"BLAME IS OURS, THE" *Camacu* [*kamacu*], "our blame or wrong." A song sung by Jaguar Quitze, Jaguar Night, Mahucutah, and True Jaguar, in which they lamented being separated from the other peoples who were together at Tulan Zuyua before the first dawn. They especially lamented leaving the Yaqui people behind, presumably Nahua speakers of the Gulf coast.

BLOOD GATHERER *Cuchuma quic* [*qui4*], "gathering (or uniting) blood." Fourth-ranking lord of Xibalba; by this same name he figures in present-day Quiché tales, in which he heads the banquet table where the other lords of Xibalba bring together all human blood that has been lost by violence or illness since their previous banquet.

BLOOD RIVER *Quia* or *quiquia* [*qui4 yaa*], "blood water." A river that crosses the road to Xibalba (the underworld). This name, along with Pus River, might have been an actual toponym, referring to a large, muddy river of the kind that originates in the Guatemalan highlands and flows into the northern lowlands. For today's Quiché the region that drops off toward the Atlantic in the vicinity of Cobán is still an abode of evil.

BLOOD WOMAN *Xquic* [*xqui4*], composed of *x-*, archaic in Quiché but "she of" or "small" in Cholan (K.), and *qui4*, "blood"; by way of sound play the name also suggests *i4*, "moon." Daughter of Blood Gatherer, one of the lords of Xibalba, and mother of Hunahpu and Xbalanque. She is probably the moon but perhaps not the full moon (see *Xbalanque*).

BLOODY TEETH, BLOODY CLAWS *Quic* [*qui4*] *re, quic rixcac* [*rix4ak*], "blood his teeth, blood his claws." These two lords of Xibalba are omitted from earlier lists (pp. 106–107) but appear as the eleventh- and twelfth-ranking lords in later lists (p. 136). The situation is just the opposite for Trash Master and Stab Master, who appear only in the earlier lists and may be these same two lords under different names.

BONE FLUTE, BIRD WHISTLE *Zubac* [*zubak*], in which *zu* is "flute" and *bak* is "bone," and *chamcham*, possibly a reduplicated form derived from *4hanin*, referring to the trilling and warbling of birds (V.). Among the emblems of lordship given out by Nacxit.

BONE SCEPTER, SKULL SCEPTER *4hamia bac* [*bak*], *4hamia holom*, "staff bone, staff skull (or head)." Seventh- and eighth-ranking lords of Xibalba.

BRACELET OF RATTLING SNAIL SHELLS *Macutax tot tatam*, in which *macutax* is probably from Nahua *mahcuetlax*, "bracelet" (C.); *tot* is "snail"; and *tatam* may be related to *totaanic*, "shake" (X.). One of the emblems of lordship given out by Nacxit.

BROKEN PLACE, BITTER WATER PLACE *Pan paxil, pan cayala* [*cayalaa*], in which *pan* is an archaic or non-Quiché form of *pa*, "at" or "in"; *paxil* probably has the same root as *paxinic*, "to break" (used with pottery); and *cayal* may be like modern *4ayil*, "bitter," combined with *-aa* for "water." A mountain or citadel where the Makers and Modelers got the corn and water needed to make the bodies of the first true humans; its interior was filled not only with corn but with a variety of tropical fruits. The name

Broken Place suggests the Nahua myth in which a mountain containing the corn needed for human flesh was split open by a thunderbolt.

BROMELIAS   *Ec* [*e4*]. *Tillandsia spp.*, air plants abounding in the trees of highland Guatemala, except in arid regions. In some species the flowers have pointed petals and grow at the ends of stiff stalks that jut out from the rest of the plant; hence their use by Hunahpu and Xbalanque in constructing the arms and claws of an artificial crab. Today, bromelias and Spanish moss are among the principal materials used in constructing outdoor arbors for saints.

BUNDLE OF FLAMES   *Pizom 3a3al*, "wrapped fieriness or heat." A sacred relic left to the Quiché lords by Jaguar Quitze. Like the sacred bundles of the North American Indians, a sort of cloth-wrapped ark with mysterious contents.

CACAO   *Caco. Theobroma cacao*, a higher grade of cacao than pataxte. The seeds of cacao, which is native to the New World, were and are used by Mesoamerican Indians to make cocoa and chocolate.

CAKCHIQUELS   *3a3chequeleb* or *ca3chiqueleb*, in which *che* is from *chee*, "tree"; the first syllable would be "fire" (*3a3*), judging by the spelling in the P.V., but in the etymology offered by the Annals of the Cakchiquels it is *cak*, "red." This is the name (still used today) of a people who border the Quichés on the south and east; they speak a language of the Quichean family. They belong to a group of thirteen allied tribes the Quichés regarded as having come (like themselves) from the east. One of the Cakchiquel citadels, Above the Nettles, was conquered by the Quiché lords during the reign of Quicab.

CALABASH TREE   *Zima* [*tzimah*]; *tzimah* is Cholan for "gourd" (K.), but in Quiché this is a term for a lowland tree with fruit resembling gourds (*Crescentia cujete*). It did not bear fruit until the head of One Hunahpu was placed in a fork of its branches. According to Andrés Xiloj, the "gourds" of this tree are indeed the size of a human head; they have a woody or bonelike rind and are halved to make bowls.

CALM SNAKE   *Chamalcan*, in which *chamal* may be derived from *chaman*, "calm" (V.), and *can* is Yucatec for "snake." That the writers of the P.V. were aware of the meaning of *can* is hinted at by the fact that they comment, after mentioning the name *chamalcan*, "but it looks like a bat" (p. 175). The name of the god of the Bat House lineage of the Cakchiquels.

CANOPY, THRONE   *Muh*, "canopy" (literally "shade"), and *3alibal*, "presiding chair" (G.). Among the emblems of lordship given out by Nacxit. The Keeper of the Mat was entitled to have four can-

329

opies over him, the Keeper of the Reception House Mat three, the Lord Minister two, and the Crier to the People one.

CAOQUES *Caoqueb*, an untranslatable proper name with a plural suffix (*-b*). A tribe whose citadels once included Plaster House, which was among the places conquered by the Quiché lords during the reign of Quicab. Possibly the Caoques are the ancestors of the people who speak the Quichean language called Uspantec today and whose present territory begins only ten kilometers north of Plaster House.

CAUATEPECH A Nahua name of uncertain translation. Keeper of the Reception House Mat in the eleventh generation of Cauec lords.

CAUECS *Cauiquib* [*cauikib*], singular *cauec* [*cauek*]. First-ranking Quiché lineage, founded by Jaguar Quitze and divided into nine segments or great houses after the founding of Rotten Cane.

CAUINAL See *Thorny Place*.

CAUIZIMAH Keeper of the Reception House Mat in the seventh generation of Cauec lords.

CAUIZTAN COPAL *Cauiztan pom*, in which *pom* is "copal incense" and the rest is a Nahua name of uncertain translation. The kind of copal used by Jaguar Night to incense the direction of the rising sun.

CAVE BY THE WATER *Pecul ya;* V. gives *rupecul* as "cave at the edge of a river or lake," and *ya* is "water." One of the volcanoes made by Zipacna. It may be the Volcán de Agua, eleven kilometers south of Antigua Guatemala, which once had a lake at its summit.

CELEBRATED SEAHOUSE *Caha* [*ʒaha*] *paluna*, from *ʒahar*, "be famous"; *palu*, an archaic or non-Quiché form of *plo* or *palo*, "sea"; and *na*, Yucatec for "house." One of the first four human females; wife of Jaguar Quitze.

CHANNEL CATFISH *Uinac* [*uinak*] *car*, "person fish," identified by G. as the *bagre* or channel catfish. One of the forms assumed by Hunahpu and Xbalanque. Catfish barbels are shown coming out of the cheeks of the classic Maya equivalent of Hunahpu.

CHIMALMAT A Nahua-derived name in which *chimal* is from *chimalli*, "shield." The word *chimalli* also entered Yucatec; M. gives *chimal* as "shield" and *chimal ek* ("shield stars") as "the guards of the north (Ursa Minor)," but the constellation in question might well have included Draco (to form the border of the shield). Chimalmat is the wife of Seven Macaw and the mother of Zipacna and Earthquake. Her astronomical identification fits with Seven Macaw's (he is the Big Dipper).

CHULIMAL A place three kilometers north of Chichicastenango, occupied by vassals of the Quiché lords during the reign of Quicab.

CHURNING SPIKES, RIVER OF *Halha ha* [*haa*] *zimah;* B. has *halha ha* as "waters that join and revolve"; *zimah* is "sharpened or pointed things." One of the rivers that crosses the road to Xibalba (the underworld).

CITADEL *Tinamit*, from Nahua *tenamitl*, "enclosure, or wall of a city" (D.). A town in a defensible position, whether on top of a hill or mountain or between two canyons; any points of easy access were walled or stockaded. Under Spanish rule most such towns were relocated to weaker sites as a matter of colonial military policy; today *tinamit* (or *tinimit*) is the general Quiché term for "town," regardless of location.

CO- *4O-* or *co-* in the MS., probably related to the *co-* in two forms given in B.: *cobic*, "to have an epithet," and *cobizah*, "to praise." Co- begins the names of a large number of Quiché lords (see below), especially the earlier ones, and probably has an honorific effect.

COACUL First-ranking lord in the second generation of Greathouse lords.

COACUTEC Second-ranking lord in the second generation of Greathouse lords. He represented the Greathouses on the pilgrimage to the lord Nacxit.

COAHAU *Co-*, an honorific prefix, with *ahau*, "lord." First-ranking lord in the second generation of Lord Quiché lords. He represented the Lord Quichés on the pilgrimage to the lord Nacxit.

COATI *Tziz. Nasua narica*, an omnivorous, tree-dwelling, raccoon-like mammal with a long, flexible nose and a long, erect tail, ranging from southern Arizona to South America; confined to the lowlands in Guatemala.

COCAIB *Co-*, an honorific prefix, with *caib*, "two." First-ranking lord in the second generation of Cauec lords. He represented the Cauecs on the pilgrimage to the lord Nacxit. According to the Title of the Lords of Totonicapán, his generation was already the fourth one (starting with Jaguar Quitze) rather than the second.

COCAMEL Crier to the People for the Lords in the seventh generation of Lord Quiché lords.

COCAUIB Second-ranking lord in the second generation of Cauec lords and brother of Cocaib. According to the Title of the Lords of Totonicapán, the generation of these brothers was already the fourth one (starting with Jaguar Quitze) rather than the second. While Cocaib was on the pilgrimage to the Lord Nacxit, Cocauib fathered a child, Jaguar Conache, with Cocaib's wife. On his return, Cocaib nevertheless recognized Jaguar Conache as his own legitimate successor in the first-ranking Cauec lordship.

COCHAHUH First-ranking lord in the third generation of Greathouse lords.

331

COCHINEAL   See *croton*.

COCOZOM   Crier to the People for the Lords in the fourth generation of Lord Quiché lords.

COHAH   A people belonging to a group of thirteen allied tribes the Quichés regarded as having come (like themselves) from the east.

COLD HOUSE   *Teuh ha*. One of the tests of Xibalba, also called Rattling House; it is second (p. 112) or third (p. 142) in the sequence of test houses. These houses may correspond to the periods when Venus is invisible between its appearances as morning and evening star (see *Bat House*).

COMAHCUN   Crier to the People for the Lords in the fifth generation of Lord Quiché lords.

CONACHE   See *Jaguar Conache*.

CONCEALMENT CANYON   *Euabal ziuan*, "hiding place (or place of putting into shadow) canyon." A great canyon in a forest; location of Pauilix, where Jaguar Night placed the god Auilix. After Jaguar Quitze had placed the god Tohil on a mountain in this same vicinity, Concealment Canyon received the epithet Tohil Medicine.

COPAL   *Pom*, from proto-Mixe-Zoque (C). The Quiché term for a type of incense widely used in Mesoamerica to this day, better known as copal (from Nahua *copalli*). The basic ingredient is the resin from the bark of the *palo jiote* tree (*Hymenaea verrucosa*).

CORAL TREE, CORAL SEEDS   *Tzite [4,ite]*. A tree known in Spanish as *palo pito* (*Erythrina corallodendron*), or its hard, red, beanlike seeds. The seeds are used by Xpiyacoc and Xmucane in performing calendrical divination for the gods who seek the proper materials for the human body; the wood of the tree is then used in making an experimental male figure.

CORNTASSEL HOUSE   *Tzutuha [4,utuha]*, composed of *4,utuh*, "tassel of the maize plant," and *ha*, "house." Temple of the patron deity of the Zaquic lineage, who was probably called *4,utuh*, at Rotten Cane or perhaps at a site now known as El Resguardo, one kilometer to the east. Lord Corntassel House was the title of the first-ranking lord of the Zaquic lineage, who headed one of the two great houses into which that lineage was divided; he must have been the priest of the Corntassel god.

CORTÉS, DON JUAN   Lord Keeper of the Reception House Mat in the fourteenth generation of Cauec lords, alive when the P.V. was written. His title was recognized by the Spanish, but he was unsuccessful in his attempt to restore the full powers of the Cauec lords to don Juan de Rojas (Keeper of the Mat) and himself, an effort that took him all the way to Spain.

COTUHA   *Co-*, an honorific prefix, probably with *tuh*, "sweatbath," and *ha*, "house." Keeper of the Mat in the fourth generation of

Cauec lords. There were two plots against his life, in the second of which he was ambushed at his sweatbath, according to the Title of the Lords of Totonicapán; the latter source does not make it clear whether this second plot succeeded, but the P.V. implies that it did (p. 206). A second Cotuha was Keeper of the Reception House Mat in the fifth generation of Cauec lords, helping Plumed Serpent to found Rotten Cane. Still other Cotuhas served as Lord Minister in the fifth, eighth, and eleventh generations of Greathouse lords.

COTZIBAHA *Co-*, an honorific prefix, probably with *4,iba*, "write, paint," and *ha*, "house." Second-ranking lord in the third generation of Greathouse lords.

COUNCIL BOOK *Popo uuh* or *popol uuh*, in which *pop* is "mat," *-ol* has the effect of "-ness," and *uuh* (or *vuh*) is "paper" or "book." In classical Quiché, *popol* occurs in many phrases in which it has the effect of "public" or "in common"; *popoh*, a verb built on the same root, was "to hold a council" (V.), and the pronouncements of a council were *popol tzih*, in which *tzih* is "word." *Popol*, literally "matness," would be a metonymic reference to a council, referring to the mat on which a council sat; at the very same time it could be a metaphor for the way councils were structured, weaving diverse interests together. Alternative readings of *popol uuh* would be "Common Book" or "Council Paper."

COUNCILOR OF THE BALL COURT *Popol uinac* [*uinak*] *pahom tzalatz*, "council person in-courtyard long-and-narrow"; the second time this title is mentioned (p. 210) the name Xcuxeba is added (untranslatable). Title of the lord who was eighth in rank among the Cauecs and head of one of the nine great houses into which their lineage was divided after the founding of Rotten Cane. The ball court at Rotten Cane ran east-west and was located immediately south of the Great Monument of Tohil, with its east end forming part of the west side of the main plaza. The north wall of the ruins of the ball court is at present the site of an active shrine.

COUNCILOR OF THE STORES *Popol uinac* [*uinak*] *chituy*, "council person at-stack"; in B., *tuyuba* is "put one thing on top of another." Title of the lord who was sixth in rank among the Cauecs and head of one of the nine great houses into which their lineage was divided after the founding of Rotten Cane.

COYABACOH Crier to the People for the Lords in the eighth generation of Lord Quiché lords.

CRIER TO THE PEOPLE *Ahtzic uinac* [*ahtzi4 uinak*], "person who [or person whose occupation is] calling out to people"; G. gives *ahzi4* as "crier" (in the sense of "town crier"), and *tzi4* could be an archaic form of *zi4*, "to call out." Crier to the People or Crier to the People for the Lords was the title of the lord who ranked first among the Lord Quichés and headed one of the four great houses into which their lineage was divided after the founding of Rotten Cane. He ranked fourth among the four lords who jointly ruled the Quiché state from Rotten Cane, with the Keeper of the Mat, Keeper of the Reception House Mat, and the Lord Minister above him. A title with a slightly different wording, Lord Crier to the People, pertained to the lord who ranked second among the Greathouses and headed one of the nine great houses of that lineage.

CRISTOBAL, DON   Lord Minister in the twelfth generation of Greathouse lords, still in office by September of 1554.

CROSSROADS   *Cahib xalcat be*, "four junction roads"; *xalcat* refers to any joining or forking of roads, and *cahib* makes this junction a "crossroads." There are two lists of the names of the four roads that lead away from this junction. The earlier list has Red, Black, White, and Yellow roads (p. 111); it seems consonant (in terms of both sequence and colors) with the lowland Maya color-directional scheme, in which red is east, black west, white north, and yellow south. The later list has Black, White, Red, and Green roads (p. 134); this may be a separate scheme for which the Milky Way (rather than the sun's path) is the key. In the P.V. the Black Road is also the Road of Xibalba, which corresponds to the cleft in the Milky Way. Whenever the cleft is visible, the opposite end of the Milky Way is undivided where it intersects the horizon; the undivided part is called White Road (see below), which could explain why Black and White (rather than Red and Black) are paired in the later list of roads. Since characters corresponding to Venus (One and Seven Hunahpu and later Hunahpu and Xbalanque) travel a path that intersects the Black Road, the Crossroads would seem to be the point at which the cleft is crossed by the zodiac. Note that both the Milky Way and the zodiac shift positions with respect to the horizon; we are not dealing so much with a system of cardinal points fixed to the terrestrial plain as with a complex system of navigation.

CROTON   *3a3che* [*cakchee*] or *chuh 3a3che*, "red tree" or "cochineal red tree." A croton called *sangre de dragón* in Spanish (*Croton sanguifluus*). Cochineal is a red dye made from scale insects that feed on the prickly pear cactus; in the present context the Quiché word for this dye is used simply as a color term. When the "cochineal red tree" is cut open, the sap that flows looks like blood and dries in scabrous nodules. A large nodule of this sap is passed off as the heart of Blood Woman by the messengers of Xibalba, and the burning of such nodules is established as an appropriate offering to the lords of Xibalba.

CRUNCHING JAGUAR   *Cotzbalam* [*co4,balam*], composed of *co4,ih*, "grind" (V.), and *balam,* "jaguar." One of the monsters who ends the era of the wooden people.

CULBA   See *Thorny Place.*

CUT ROCK   *Xay* (or *xoy*) *abah,* possibly composed of *choy,* "cut," and *abah,* "rock." The town known today as Joyabaj, occupied by vassals of the Quiché lords during the reign of Quicab.

CUTTING ANTS, CONQUERING ANTS   *Chai zanic, chequen [4hequen] zanic; chai* refers to cutting instruments made of stone. Ants summoned by Hunahpu and Xbalanque to help them cut the flowers of Xibalba; possibly two names for the same species. V. lists *he chay* as ants that go in swarms; Andrés Xiloj identified *4hequen zanic* as very large leaf-cutting ants seen only in the lowlands, called *zampopo* in Guatemalan Spanish.

DARK HOUSE   *Que3uma [3ekuma] ha.* One of the tests of Xibalba, first in the sequence of test houses. These houses may correspond to the periods when Venus is invisible between its appearances as morning and evening star (see *Bat House*).

"DAWN OF LIFE, THE"   *Zac [zak] 4azlem,* "light (or dawn) life." An epithet for the P.V., referring to the period after the first light of dawn and of the sun itself, as contrasted with the previous period, which is referred to by the epithet, "Our Place in the Shadows." An alternative reading of the present epithet would be "The Life in the Light."

DAYBRINGER   *Icoquih [iko3ih* in both T. and V.], composed of *iko-* (or *eko-*), "to carry a burden," and *3ih,* "sun" or "day." The morning star.

DAYKEEPER   *Ahquih [ah3ih],* "keeper (or person of) day (or sun)," referring to diviners who count the days of the 260-day calendar using coral seeds (see above). The daykeepers in the P.V. are the husband and wife Xpiyacoc and Xmucane.

DEER DANCE PLAZA   *Xahba quieh,* "dance-place deer." A place six kilometers northwest of Chichicastenango, occupied by vassals of the Quiché lords during the reign of Quicab.

DRY PLACE   See *Thorny Place.*

EARTHQUAKE   *Cabracan [cabrakan],* "earthquake" in both classical and modern Quiché. This name has been etymologized as *cab-,* "two," *-r-,* "his," and *-akan,* "leg," but "two" is *caib* in classical Quiché and Cakchiquel and takes the form *cabi-* as a prefix. The Cakchiquel equivalent of this name, *cabarakan,* makes it even harder to read "two" and instead suggests *caba,* "pile up a quantity of earth" (V.). In that case *-rakan,* which can mean not only "leg" but "trunk" or "pillar," suggests that the body of *cabarakan* provides the pillar (or pillars) that hold up the earth, and that earthquakes are caused by his movements. Earthquake is the second son of Seven Macaw and the younger brother of Zipacna.

335

He gives his name to a place nine kilometers southeast of Rotten Cane, occupied by vassals of the Quiché lords during the reign of Quicab.

EIGHT CORDS *Uahxaqui caam* [*uahxaquib 4aam*]. Keeper of the Mat in the tenth generation of Cauec lords.

EIGHTEEN *Uaxalahuh.* A place of unknown location, occupied by vassals of the Quiché lords during the reign of Quicab.

EMBLEMS OF LORDSHIP *Uuachinel rahauarem,* "its-face-agentive his-lord-inchoative-substantive." The symbols of Toltecan lordship given by Nacxit to Cocaib, Coacutec, and Coahau, listed as bone flute, bird whistle; bracelet of rattling snail shells; canopy, throne; gourd of tobacco; head and hoof of deer; nosepiece; paint of powdered yellow stone; parrot feathers, heron feathers; and puma's paw, jaguar's paw (see also under each of these headings).

FALCON *Uoc,* a bird that probably resembles the laughing falcon (*uac*) listed elsewhere. A divine name paired with Hunahpu in a prayer (p. 170). *Uoc* is also the term used for the bird that serves as a messenger for Heart of Sky, flying over One and Seven Hunahpu, as well as One Monkey and One Artisan, while they play ball (p. 105, translated as "falcon"); *uac* is the term for the bird that later brings a message to Hunahpu and Xbalanque at the same ball court (p. 132). The two falcons may be the planets Jupiter and Saturn; given that the *uoc* seems to be given greater importance, he may be Jupiter, which is brighter than Saturn.

FIRE MOUTH *Chicac* [*chi3a3*], "mouth fire." One of the volcanoes made by Zipacna. Generally thought to be the Volcán de Fuego, nineteen kilometers southwest of Antigua Guatemala.

FISHKEEPERS *Chah* [*4hah*] *car,* "guard fish." A people, also known as Sovereign Oloman, who stayed in the east when the Quiché ancestors left, but who later participated in a plot against them while they were settled in the citadel of Hacauitz.

FOUR HUNDRED BOYS *Omuch* [*omu4h*] *4aholab,* "four-hundred boys (or sons of a male)." The boys who attempt to kill Zipacna but are killed by him instead, eventually becoming the Pleiades (see *Hundrath*). They die while in a drunken stupor, just as the four hundred rabbits of Nahua mythology do, and like those rabbits they were probably the patron deities of an alcoholic beverage (see *sweet drink*) and of drunkenness.

GAMING EQUIPMENT *Etzabal* [*e4,abal*], "play-instrument." The gear used by One and Seven Hunahpu and by their sons, Hunahpu and Xbalanque, in the Quiché version of the Mesoamerican ball game. The items mentioned in the P.V. include a kilt, yoke, arm guard, panache, headband, and rubber ball (see also under each of these headings).

GENEROUS WOMAN, HARVEST WOMAN, CACAO WOMAN, CORNMEAL
WOMAN *Xtoh, xcanil [x3anil], xcacau, ix pu tziya,* in which the
x- or *ix* is archaic in Quiché but "she of" or "small" in Cholan
(K.); *toh* may be related (given the horticultural nature of the accompanying names) to *tohohohenic,* "to give in abundance" (X.);
3anil is "yellow" or "harvest"; *cacau* is "cacao"; and *tziya* is
"corn flour." Apparently these are all names or epithets for the
single goddess who guards the crops of One Monkey and One
Artisan.

GENIUS *Naual.* From a Nahua term (usually written *nagual*) referring to the animal alter ego of a person. In Quiché usage *naual* is
much broader, referring to the spiritual essence or character of a
person, animal, plant, stone, or geographical place; this corresponds to English "genius" in its older sense as "spirit familiar."
In the P.V. *naual* is sometimes paired with *puz,* a word of Mixe-
Zoque and possibly Olmec origins (C.) that refers to the cutting
open of flesh with a knife and is the primary term for the act of
heart sacrifice. When used together, *puz* and *naual* are metonyms for shamanic power, referring to the ability to make genius or spiritual essence visible or audible by means of ritual.

GODLY COPAL *Cabauil [4abauil] pom,* "god copal." The kind of
copal incense used by Mahucutah to incense the direction of the
rising sun.

GOUGER OF FACES *Cotcouach [4ot4ouach],* composed of *4ot4o,* a reduplicated form of *4oto,* "to carve out," and *uach,* "face." One of
the monsters that ends the era of the wooden people. Andrés
Xiloj gave the modern name as *4ot quiuach,* "gouges out their
faces," and identified it as a kind of animal, commenting that
"they still exist, but I don't know whether in the sky or the forest. They stay in the darkness, and when the sun doesn't shine
they come out." In the P.V. the Gouger of Faces accompanies a
great, dark rainstorm.

GOURD OF TOBACCO *4uz buz,* from Yucatec *cuz* or *cutz,* "tobacco,"
and *buz,* referring to a small gourd used for keeping tobacco (R.).
One of the emblems of lordship given out by Nacxit.

GRANARY *Cuha,* "granary for maize." The palace, at Rotten Cane,
of the Keeper of the Mat, first in rank among all the Quiché
lords.

GRANDMOTHER OF DAY, GRANDMOTHER OF LIGHT *Ratit quih [3ih],
ratit zac [zak],* "its-grandmother day (or sun), its-grandmother
light." Epithets for Xpiyacoc and Xmucane, despite the fact that
Xpiyacoc is described in other contexts as a grandfather (*mama*).
Andrés Xiloj explained that a grandmother of "day" and "light"
would be a grandmother from the beginning of light "until the
end of the world," that is, for as long as light lasts. In this con-

text, then, "day" and "light" are a dyadic and less direct way of referring to what Indo-European languages reduce to the unitary concept of "time."

GREAT ABYSS AT CARCHAH *Nim xob carchah* (p. 109) or *nim xol* (p. 177). If these two forms both referred to the same place, and if *xob* were correct, then the translation of *nim xob* would be "great respect (or shame)." But if *xol* were correct, then the translation would be something like "great insertion"; *xolobachan* is given as "abyss" by B. Finally, *carchah* suggests the town called San Pedro Carchá, located eight kilometers east of Cobán on a river that descends rapidly into a canyon and thence to the lowlands. *Nim xob carchah* is the ball court where One and Seven Hunahpu played (followed later by Hunahpu and Xbalanque) before they were summoned by the lords of Xibalba. The route from this ball court to Xibalba is described as descending very steeply; perhaps it was poised at the edge of the "great abyss." *Nim xol* (translated "Great Abyss" on p. 177) refers to a place located somewhere between Staggering and Place of Advice on the Quiché route of migration. Note that San Pedro Carchá is located far to the east of the area presently inhabited by the Quichés—that is, in the direction from which the P.V. says the Quichés came—and that One and Seven Hunahpu are responsible for the morning star, which appears and disappears in the east.

GREAT HOUSE *Nim ha.* A term for a formally organized and named lineage segment (within a larger patrilineage) with a person of lordly rank at its head, and for the palace that served as headquarters for that segment (see also *lineage*).

GREATHOUSES *Nihaib*, composed of *ni-* from *nima*, "great"; *ha* or *hai*, "house"; and *-ib* or *-b*, plural. Second-ranking Quiché lineage, founded by Jaguar Night and divided into nine segments or great houses after the founding of Rotten Cane.

GREAT LOLMET YEOLTUX See *Lolmet.*

GREAT MONUMENT OF TOHIL *Nima tzac [4,ak] tohil*, literally "great building [specifically of stone or earth] Tohil." The temple that housed the god Tohil in the citadel of Rotten Cane, on the west side of the main plaza. It consisted of a pyramid with stairways on three sides (all but the west) and topped by a single thatch-roofed room with its door facing east across the plaza, toward the temple of Auilix; at present its ruins are the site of an active shrine. It is not clear whether the Great Monument of Tohil housed the original Tohil stone brought from Tulan Zuyua by Jaguar Quitze or whether that stone was left on the mountain of Patohil (see *Tohil*) and was represented by some secondary object in Rotten Cane. In today's ritual practice, one can use a shrine close at hand to summon up a deity whose proper residence is another and quite distant shrine. The diviners of El Palmar, a community whose inhabitants emigrated from Momostenango, have named their local shrines after those of their parent town but address the shrines of Momostenango itself from a distance; they try to make a pilgrimage to the parent shrines once each 260 days. In a like manner, the priest of Tohil at Rotten Cane might have addressed the mountain named Patohil while he was actually on the pyramid of Tohil, making periodic pilgrimages to the mountain itself.

GREAT RECEPTION HOUSE *Nima camha* [*4amha*], "great receive-house." Title of the lord who was fourth in rank among the Greathouses and head of one of the nine great houses into which their lineage was divided after the founding of Rotten Cane.

GREAT TOASTMASTER *Nim chocoh,* "great convener of banquets." E. gives *choc-* as "invite to a banquet"; G. and V. give *chocola* a similar meaning, with V. specifying a banquet in which a drink prepared from cacao was consumed. Each of the three ruling Quiché lineages had a lord with this title, and each one of these lords was the head of one of the great houses of his respective lineage. The Great Toastmaster ranked third among the Cauec lords, sixth among the Greathouses, and third among the Lord Quichés; these three Great Toastmasters came together for meetings. They are described as being like fathers and like "givers of birth" to the other lords, and as being Mothers of the Word, Fathers of the Word (see below); they may be the authors of the Popol Vuh. During the reign of Quicab the title of Great Toastmaster was bestowed upon the heads of eleven vassal lineages.

GREAT WHITE PECCARY, GREAT WHITE TAPIR *Zaqui* [*zaki*] *nim ac* [*ak*], *zaqui nima tziz,* "white great peccary, white great tapir (or coati)" (p. 92); in abbreviated form, "Great White Peccary, Tapir" (p. 71) or "Great Peccary, Great Tapir" (p. 80). These are epithets for Xpiyacoc and Xmucane, respectively. That the *ak* is "great" and "white" identifies it as the white-lipped peccary (*Tayasu pecari*), which has white jowls and is markedly larger than the collared peccary (*Tayasu tajacu*); the white-lipped peccary is strictly a lowland species, *ak* being the Cholan term for the male (K.). That the *tziz* is "great" and "white" identifies it as the tapir (*Tapirella bairdii*), which is enormously larger than the coati and has white hair all over its jowls, cheeks, and chest; no Quiché term for the tapir has been reported in dictionary sources, but *tzimin* is "tapir" in Cholan (K.). Like the white-lipped peccary, the tapir is a lowland species. What the coati or *tziz* (see *coati*) and the tapir or *tzimin* have in common, in addi-

339

tion to the first syllable of their names, is a very long and very flexible snout. What the tapir and peccary have in common, in addition to long, flexible snouts, is that they are ungulates.

GREEN ROAD   *Raxabe.* In a prayer quoted in the P.V. (p. 222), the petitioner asks for the Green Road and does not mention roads of any other color (see also the "greening road" in the prayer on p. 170). The Green Road also appears in the later of two lists of the four cosmic roads (p. 134), where it replaces the Yellow Road mentioned earlier (p. 111). In the lowland Maya color scheme green did not correspond to any of the four directions, but to the center, a sort of fifth direction. The Green Road of the P.V. may be a paradoxical fifth road, synthesizing the other four roads or passing vertically through the spot where they cross. See also *Crossroads.*

GUARDIANS OF THE SPOILS   *Canchaheleb [can4haheleb]*, composed of *can-* from *canab*, "spoils of war" (B.); *4hahel*, "guardian"; and *-eb*, plural. A people belonging to a group of thirteen allied tribes the Quichés regarded as having come (like themselves) from the east.

HACAUITZ   *Uitz* is Cholan for "mountain" (K.) and the rest is of uncertain derivation. Patron deity of the Lord Quiché lineage, carried by Mahucutah from Tulan Zuyua and eventually placed "above a great red river" on a mountain that then took the name Hacauitz. The Lord Quichés were there when the first dawn came, and the same mountain was the site of the first Quiché citadel, built by Jaguar Quitze, Jaguar Night, Mahucutah, and True Jaguar and abandoned after their deaths. Hacauitz was also the name of the temple that housed the god Hacauitz in the citadel of Rotten Cane, with its back marking the south side of the main plaza. It consisted of a pyramid with a single stairway (on the south side) and topped by a single thatch-roofed room with its door facing south onto a courtyard considerably smaller than the main plaza. Lord Hacauitz was the title of the priest of the god Hacauitz; he was fourth in rank among the lords of the Lord Quichés and headed one of the four great houses into which their lineage was divided after the founding of Rotten Cane.

HANGING MOSSES   *Atziyac [a4,iak]*, literally "clothing." *Dendropogon usneoides*, an air plant commonly called Spanish moss in English. See *bromelias* for a discussion of its use.

HEAD AND HOOF OF DEER   *Holom pich queh*, "head (or skull) hoof deer." Among the emblems of lordship given out by Nacxit.

HEADBAND   *Uach zot*, in which *uach* is "face" and *zot* is "to make circular, like a crown or ring" (V.). Part of the gear needed by players of the ball game in the P.V. (see *ball court* and *gaming equipment*), probably corresponding to the wreaths or turbans worn at forehead level by the players in the ball-court reliefs of Chichen Itza.

HEART OF SKY, HEART OF EARTH *U4ux cah, u4ux uleu*, "its-heart sky, its-heart earth." Heart of Sky, sometimes followed by Heart of Earth (which never appears by itself), is an epithet for the god or gods otherwise named Hurricane, Newborn Thunderbolt, and Raw Thunderbolt. These epithets are no longer used in Quiché prayers, but Andrés Xiloj compared the notion of *u4ux uleu* to that of *u4ux puuak*, "Heart of Metal," which is applied to found objects that are either ancient artifacts or stones that happen to resemble life forms. Some of these objects (especially artifacts shaped by flaking) are said to have been formed where lightning struck the ground, which suggests that it was lightning that provided the conceptual link between the Hearts of Sky and Earth for the Quichés of the P.V.

HEART OF THE LAKE, HEART OF THE SEA *U4ux cho, u4ux palo*, "its-heart lake, its-heart sea." These are epithets that may cover all the gods who were in or on the sea before the raising of the earth; they are also known as Maker, Modeler and as Bearer, Begetter, and they include Sovereign Plumed Serpent. Their counterparts, with whom they cooperate in making the earth, are covered by a contrasting pair of epithets: Heart of Sky, Heart of Earth.

HOT SPRINGS See *Above the Hot Springs*.

HOUSE CORNER *Xiquiri pat;* in Pokomchí Maya (a language of the Quichean family), *xiquin pat* is "corner of a house" (Z.). Third-ranking lord of Xibalba. According to Andrés Xiloj, it is at the corners of a house that the evil influences of Xibalba enter. When a house is under construction in Momostenango, eight skulls are painted on the outside walls (two at each corner); they are something like scarecrows.

HULIZNAB One of the volcanoes made by Zipacna; location uncertain.

HUMMINGBIRD HOUSE *Tzununiha [4,ununiha]*, in which *4,unun* is "hummingbird" and *ha* is "house." One of the first four human females; wife of Mahucutah.

HUNAHPU Composed of *hun*, "one"; *ah-*, occupational; and *pu*, from *pub*, "blowgun" (B.); thus the name as a whole could be read as "One Blowgunner." This is one of the twenty day names of the 260-day divinatory calendar; since a speaker of Quiché no more takes note of the "blowgunner" contained in Hunahpu than a speaker of English takes note of the "Thor" in Thursday, the name has been left untranslated in the body of the present work. The *hun* is so embedded in the name that in both classical and modern Quiché, the particular Hunahpu day that bears the num-

341

ber one is called *hun hunahpu*, literally "One One-blowgunner." In the P.V., Hunahpu without any number prefix is the name of the elder brother of Xbalanque; the two of them are twins, the sons of One Hunahpu and Blood Woman and nephews of Seven Hunahpu. Hunahpu and his twin succeed their father and uncle at controlling the morning-star aspect of Venus, playing ball at an eastern site on the brink of Xibalba. Hunahpu is most like his father in losing his head (twice) in Xibalba; as in the case of his father, his detached head is probably the evening-star aspect of Venus. Ultimately he becomes the sun, or at least the sun belongs to him. Hunahpu is also the name of one of the volcanoes made by Zipacna; this could be the Volcán de Amatenango, five kilometers north of the Volcán de Fuego (Fire Mouth in the P.V.), since the Annals of the Cakchiquels describes Hunahpu as standing beside Fire Mouth.

"HUNAHPU MONKEY" *Hunahpu coy [4oy]*. Title of a tune played on the flute by Hunahpu and Xbalanque; One Monkey and One Artisan, having been turned into monkeys, danced and did acrobatics to it, climbing up over their grandmother's house instead of using the door. Today there are numerous Guatemalan Indian towns whose fiestas include a Monkey Dance. The version done in Momostenango seems to confirm the celestial aspect of One Monkey and One Artisan: two monkeys, with stars on their costumes, climb a high pole and do acrobatics on a tightrope.

HUNAHPU PLACE *Chi hunahpu*, "at Hunahpu." A place of unknown location, occupied by vassals of the Quiché lords during the reign of Quicab.

HUNAHPU POSSUM, HUNAHPU COYOTE *Hunahpu uuch [uu4h]*, *hunahpu utiu*. Epithets for Hunahpu and Xbalanque in their guise as vagabond dancers and magicians. The year-bearers of the lowland Maya are the so-called possum actors, strolling players who appear at the transition point between two solar years. Hunahpu and Xbalanque do not assume their guise as performers until shortly before Hunahpu becomes the sun. In the Venus tables of the Dresden Codex, day names with solar implications do not appear until the last two divisions in a series of five Venus cycles, reaching a crescendo in the fifth cycle. In this last cycle, the descent of the morning star into the underworld on a day associated with a year-bearing possum actor (the day Eb in Yucatec and E in Quiché) would correspond to the appearance of the vagabond Hunahpu and Xbalanque before the lords of Xibalba.

HUNDRATH *Motz*, the Pleiades; the astral form of the Four Hundred Boys. *Motz* appears to be an archaic form of *omu4h*, "four hundred"; for that reason it is translated here as "Hundrath," the archaic (Old Norse) source of English "hundred." In today's

Quiché thought the Pleiades symbolize a fistful of seeds. The planting season for high-altitude maize, in March, is marked by evening settings of the Pleiades, which leave them invisible for most of the night; by May, when low-altitude maize is planted, the Pleiades enter a period of complete invisibility. In the P.V., the Pleiades' first fall into the earth corresponds to Zipacna's defeat of the Four Hundred Boys.

HURRICANE *Huracan [hurakan]*. The god who causes the rain and flood that end the era of the wooden people; his aspects include thunderbolt gods (see *Newborn Thunderbolt, Raw Thunderbolt*) and the first-ranking patron deity of the Quiché people (see *Tohil*), and his epithets include Heart of Sky, Heart of Earth (see above). The name can be read as *hu[n]rakan*, "one-his-leg," but Andrés Xiloj pointed out that it could also mean "one out of a group" or "one of a kind," since *-rakan* is a numeral classifier used in counting things that belong to collectivities. V. gives *rakan hab* as "the drops of a rainstorm when it begins or ends," apparently referring to the very large drops that precede or follow a thunderstorm; thus *hurakan* could be an abbreviated form of a phrase meaning "one large raindrop." All of these readings point to the classic Maya god who is one-legged when he takes the form of the so-called manikin scepter, whose names include Hunab Ku or "Solitary God," and who is sometimes referred to as the *itz* or "drop of liquid" (M.) of the sky, though he causes torrential rainstorms. Another name for this classic god is Tahil, "Torch Mirror" or "Obsidian Mirror" (see *Tohil*). This name, together with his one-leggedness and his rains, make him cognate, in turn, with the Nahua god named Tezcatlipoca or "Smoking Mirror," who was (among other things) a god of the hurricane. Whatever the etymology of the word *hurakan*, it may well have included the meaning "hurricane" in the Mayan language spoken in the Gulf coast region where the Quichés came from, a region susceptible to frequent hurricanes. Throughout the West Indies and along the north coast of South America, especially among Carib and Arawakan peoples, there is a god of the hurricane and thunderbolt whose name is cognate with *hurakan;* in the Guianas he is one-legged. Dictionary compilers favor a Taino (Arawakan) origin for the word "hurricane" (which came into English from Spanish or French) over a Mayan origin, but the Taino word itself could have been borrowed from the Quiché homeland, which was a center of far-reaching maritime trade.

ILOCS *Ilocab* (singular *iloc*). One of the allied groups of lineages called "the three Quichés," the other two members being the Quiché proper (comprising the Cauecs, Greathouses, and Lord Quichés) and the Tams.

343

IZTAYUL   Sometimes *ztayul* or *ztayub* in the MS.; from Nahua *izta*, "white, salt," and *yol*, "heart" (C.). Keeper of the Reception House Mat in the fourth generation of Cauec lords, with Cotuha as Keeper of the Mat. A second Iztayul was Keeper of the Reception House Mat in the fifth (p. 210) or sixth (p. 224) generation of Cauecs, with Tepepul as Keeper of the Mat. A third Iztayul was Lord Minister in the seventh generation of Greathouse lords. See also *Xtayub*.

JAGUAR CONACHE   *Balam conache* or simply *conache*. The first to rule with the title of Keeper of the Mat, coming in the third generation of Cauec lords; a contemporary of Nine Deer, who was Lord Minister in the fourth generation of Greathouse lords. According to the Title of the Lords of Totonicapán, Jaguar Conache was the son of Cocaib's wife but was fathered by Cocaib's brother Cocauib while Cocaib was on his pilgrimage to the Lord Nacxit. Nevertheless Cocaib officially recognized Jaguar Conache as his legitimate successor in the first-ranking Cauec lordship. But after Jaguar Conache's death the descendants of Cocauib were shifted to the second-ranking lordship, supplying Keepers of the Reception House Mat (beginning with Jaguar Conache's own son Iztayul), while the first-ranking title of Keeper of the Mat reverted to the direct descendants of Cocaib.

JAGUAR HOUSE   *Balami ha*. One of the tests of Xibalba, third (p. 112) or fourth (p. 142) in the sequence of test houses. These houses may correspond to the periods when Venus is invisible between its appearances as morning and evening star (see *Bat House*). Jaguar House is also the name of a people belonging to a group of thirteen allied tribes the Quichés regarded as having come (like themselves) from the east.

JAGUAR NIGHT   *Balam acab* [*aȝab*]. One of the first four human males and founder of the Greathouse lineage.

JAGUAR QUITZE   *Balam quitze* in the MS.; *balam* is "jaguar" and *quitze* (or better *4itze*) could well be an archaic form of *4iche*, "Quiché." One of the first four human males and founder of the Cauec lineage.

JAGUAR ROPES   *Balam colob*, composed of *balam*, "jaguar"; *colo*, "rope" (B.); and *-b*, plural. A people belonging to a group of thirteen allied tribes the Quichés regarded as having come (like themselves) from the east.

JOCOTES   *Quinom* [*ȝinom*], also meaning "richness." A tropical fruit (*Spondias purpurea*), yellow in color and resembling small plums.

KEEPER OF THE BAT MAT   *Ahpo zotzil* [*zo4,il*], "keeper-mat bat-ness." A Cakchiquel lineage whose god was Calm Snake.

344

KEEPER OF THE DANCER MAT *Ahpo xa* [*xahil* in other sources], "keeper-mat dancer." A Cakchiquel lineage.

KEEPER OF THE MAT *Ahpop*, "person of [or person whose occupation is] mat," a woven mat being a metonym for a council (whose members sat on a mat or mats) and probably, at the same time, a metaphor for a council (whose members might have been thought of as being interwoven like a mat or as serving to interweave those whom they represented). Keeper of the Mat or Lord Keeper of the Mat was the title of the lord who ranked first among the Cauecs and headed one of the nine great houses into which their lineage was divided after the founding of Rotten Cane. He also ranked first among the four lords who jointly ruled the Quiché state from Rotten Cane, with the Keeper of the Reception House Mat, the Lord Minister, and the Crier to the People for the Lords coming below him. The signs or emblems that accompanied these four titles (or at least the first two of them) were given out by Nacxit, the lord of a "populous domain" located in "the east" (see p. 203); the Keeper of the Mat was entitled to have four superimposed canopies over his head, with the others having three, two, and one, respectively. During the reign of Quicab, the title of Keeper of the Mat was conferred upon the heads of twenty vassal lineages, presumably lineages that were specifically vassals of the Cauecs.

KEEPER OF THE PLUMED SERPENT *Ahcucumatz* [*ah3ucumatz*], "person of [or person whose occupation is] quetzal serpent." Title of the priest of the god Sovereign Plumed Serpent at Rotten Cane; he was fourth in rank among the lords of the Cauecs and headed one of the nine great houses into which their lineage was divided after the founding of Rotten Cane. The temple of Sovereign Plumed Serpent was a round tower near the center of the main plaza, halfway between the temples of Tohil and Auilix. Its circular foundation, whose outline is still visible in the pavement of the plaza, is the site of an active shrine.

KEEPER OF THE RECEPTION HOUSE MAT *Ahpop camha* [*4amha*], "person of [or person whose occupation is] mat receive-house." That the *cam-* of the MS. should be *4am-*, "receive," rather than *3am-*, "stairway," is indicated by V. and G., both of whom list an analogous Cakchiquel title as *4amahay*. The Keeper (or Lord Keeper) of the Reception House Mat ranked second among the Cauec lords and was the head of one of the nine great houses into which the Cauecs were divided after the founding of Rotten Cane. He ranked second among the four lords who jointly ruled the Quiché state from Rotten Cane, coming below the Keeper of the Mat and above the Lord Minister and the Crier to the People for the Lords. If there was a council connected with the "Reception House Mat," it might have consisted of the Keeper of the Reception House Mat himself (representing the Cauecs), the two Mothers of the Reception House (one each for the Cauecs and Greathouses), and the Minister of the Reception House and the Great Reception House (both representing the Greathouses). If these lords were like the Cakchiquel *4amahay*, their business was the collection of tribute.

KEEPER OF TOHIL   *Ahtohil*, "person of [or person whose occupation is] Tohil." Title of the priest of the god Tohil at Rotten Cane; he was third in rank among the lords of the Cauecs and headed one of the nine great houses into which their lineage was divided after the founding of Rotten Cane.

KILT   *4,uum*, "hide." The protective kilt worn by players of the ball game in the P.V. (see *ball court* and *gaming equipment*); this kilt is clearly shown to be a hide in classic Maya art of the lowlands.

LAKE-SEA   *Chopalo*, composed of *cho*, "lake," and *palo*, "sea," but pronounced as a single word. In this context "lake" and "sea" are complementary metonyms that together produce a term for all pooled water, but without any final reduction of the difference between lakes and seas. This composite term is used in contemporary Quiché prayers.

LAMACS   *Lamaquib*, in which *-ib* is plural. A people belonging to a group of thirteen allied tribes the Quichés regarded as having come (like themselves) from the east.

LAUGHING FALCON   *Uac;* its cry is *uac co, uac co* in the text. In Tzotzil Maya, the laughing falcon is *vakos* and its cry is *vakvon* (L.). That *vakos* and *uac* are the same bird is confirmed by the fact that Hunahpu and Xbalanque patch the wounded eye of the *uac* with gum (p. 132); the laughing falcon has a black patch around the eye. It is amusing to note that the *uac* of the P.V. catches a snake; the scientific name of the laughing falcon is *Herpetotheres cachinnans.* This bird is obviously closely related to the *uoc* mentioned elsewhere (p. 105); both birds are messengers, and there are reasons for thinking the *uoc* corresponds to Jupiter and the *uac* to Saturn (see *Falcon*).

"LIGHT THAT CAME FROM ACROSS THE SEA, THE"   *Zac petenac chaca palo* [*zak petenak 4haka palo*], "light come-from-perfect other-side sea." An epithet for the P.V., alluding to the fact that the sons of the first Quiché lords, returning from a pilgrimage to the great lord named Nacxit, "brought back the writings about Tulan" from "across the sea" (p. 204). "Sea" is probably a hyperbole for "lagoon" here; other Quiché documents call the body of water in question both a "lake" and a "sea."

LINEAGE   *Chinamit*, from Nahua *chinamitl*, "hedge or enclosure of cane plants" (D.). In Quiché this refers to an organized and named patrilineage (or segment thereof) or to its lands; in the P.V. *chinamit* seems to be synonymous with *nim ha* or "great house" in most contexts.

LOLMET   Each of the three ruling lineages of the Quiché included one lord whose title incorporated this word; in G., *lolmay* is "he who is sent on business," suggesting "emissary" as a possible translation of Lolmet. Lolmet Quehnay was the title of the lord who ranked seventh among the Cauecs and headed one of the nine great houses into which their lineage was divided after the founding of Rotten Cane. Great Lolmet Yeoltux was the title of the lord who ranked ninth among the Greathouses and headed one of their nine great houses; this title is omitted in the second of the two lists of Greathouse lords (p. 225). Lord Lolmet or Lolmet of the Lords was the title of the lord who ranked second among the Lord Quichés and headed one of their four great houses.

LORD QUICHÉS   *Ahau quiche* [*4iche*]. Third-ranking Quiché lineage, founded by Mahucutah and divided into four segments or great houses after the founding of Rotten Cane.

MACAMOB   Possibly from *macamo,* "to do something suddenly" (V.). One of the volcanoes made by Zipacna; location uncertain.

MACAW HOUSE   *Caquixaha* [*cakixaha*]. One of the first four human females; wife of True Jaguar.

MACAW OWL   *Caquix* [*cakix*] *tucur,* in which *cakix* is specifically the term for the scarlet macaw. Third-ranking Military Keeper of the Mat for the lords of Xibalba, a messenger. This is clearly the so-called Moan bird of classic Maya vase paintings, who seems to have the head and wings of an owl but the tail of a macaw. Along with three other owl messengers, he may correspond to the planet Mercury (see *Shooting Owl*).

MAHUCUTAH   Possibly *ma,* "not," with *hucotah,* "right away, in a moment" (B.), giving something like "nonmomentary." One of the first four human males and founder of the Lord Quiché lineage.

MAKER, MODELER   *Tzacol bitol* [*4,akol bitol*], consisting of an agentive suffix, *-ol,* added to two different verb stems. In both classical and modern Quiché, *4,ak-* has to do with making things out of clay, plaster, cement, or stone; the objects made range through bricks, walls, monuments, mounds of earth, and buildings of all sizes. *Bit-,* on the other hand, has to do with making definite shapes out of a pliable and otherwise formless material, as when vessels are shaped out of clay. Andrés Xiloj said of *4,ak-* (whose agentive form would be *4,akal* today), "This is to make or construct, like a building, a wall." Of *bit-* he said, "This *bitic* is to form, as when we were small and played with mud; we made forms. *Kabitic*, 'we form it'." He saw *4,akol* and *bitol* as referring, respectively, to the amassing of clay and then its shaping into forms such as vessels or figures. In the P.V. these two words are names or epithets for the gods who make the earth, plants, animals, and humans. The same gods are also called Bearer, Begetter, and they include Sovereign Plumed Serpent.

MAKER OF THE BLUE-GREEN PLATE, MAKER OF THE BLUE-GREEN BOWL *Ahraxa la3* [*lak*], *ahraxa tzel*, "person-of-blue-green plate, person-of-blue-green bowl." First used as an epithet for Xpiyacoc and Xmucane; later appears in a list of the arts and crafts practiced by their grandsons, One Monkey and One Artisan. The plate and bowl may refer ultimately to the earth and sky; the term *raxa* covers both the green of a verdant landscape and the blue of the sky. Andrés Xiloj pointed out that when the head of a contemporary patrilineage (who is always a diviner) dies, his successor must be installed in office by the head of a neighboring lineage, who is hired as an *ah4hahbal lak, ah4hahbal tasa*, "washer of the plate, washer of the cup." Before the new lineage head can take office, the "washer" must go to all that lineage's shrines and clean out the ashes of all the offerings burned by the deceased lineage head. Such shrines are lined and covered with slabs of stone and pieces of pottery, which are spoken of as "plates" and "cups." In the P.V., Maker of the Blue-Green Plate, Maker of the Blue-Green Bowl would refer to Xpiyacoc and Xmucane in their general roles as those who look after (and even create) shrines, or it might refer to pottery vessels used for burning incense rather than to shrines as such.

MARIGOLD *Yia* [*iya*]. A species of marigold called *pericón* in Guatemalan Spanish (*Tagetes lucida*), a common roadside herb in the highlands, with all-yellow flowers. In the P.V. (as among today's Quiché) the burning of marigolds, together with yarrow (see below), constitutes a more modest offering than the burning of copal incense.

MATASANOS *Ahache* [*ahachee*]. A tropical fruit (*Casimiroa edulis*), large, pulpy, thin-skinned, yellow inside and chartreuse outside; called *matasanos* in Guatemalan Spanish.

MEAUAN The mountain beneath which Hunahpu and Xbalanque defeated Earthquake. Possibly located within the great bend of the Río Negro or Chixoy, north of Rabinal.

METEOR *Cabicac* or *chabicac* [*4habi3a3*], "globe of fire" (T.), literally "arrow fire"; a comet, by contrast, is *uhe 4humil*, "star's tail." A place of unknown location, occupied by vassals of the Quiché lords during the reign of Quicab.

MIDDLE OF THE HOUSE, MIDDLE OF THE HARVEST, LIVING CORN, EARTHEN FLOOR *Nicah* [*ni4ah*] *ha, nicah bichoc* [*bichok*], *cazam [4azam] ah, chatam [4hatam] uleu,* "middle house, middle shucked-corn, living corn-ear, bed (or slab) earth"; the gloss of *bichoc* is from B. When Hunahpu and Xbalanque left their grandmother to go to Xibalba, they "planted" ears of corn in the middle of their house, up above its earthen floor. For their grandmother, the drying (or ripening) and renewed sprouting of corn served as a sign of their death and rebirth, and she burned copal incense before ears of corn as a memorial to them. As Andrés Xiloj pointed out, her act corresponds to the present-day customs of a patrilineage shrine called the *uinel,* located near a cornfield.

MIDDLE OF THE PLAIN   *Nicacah tacah [ni4ah ta3ah],* "middle plain." Name of the god received by True Jaguar at Tulan Zuyua.

MIDMOST SEERS   *Nicuachinel [ni4uachinel],* composed of *ni4,* "middle"; *uachin,* "see with one's own eyes" (V.); *-el,* agentive. A term for diviners, applied both to Xpiyacoc and Xmucane and to Xulu and Pacam. It could mean that a diviner sees into the middle of things, or it could mean that a diviner recovers the vision that the first humans had when they could see everything from the spot where they were, without having to walk around.

MILITARY KEEPER OF THE MAT   *Rahpop achih,* "its-keeper-mat soldier." Title held by the four owls who served as messengers for the lords of Xibalba. One of the titles conferred upon the heads of vassal lineages during the reign of Quicab.

MILITARY MINISTER   *U3alel achih,* "its-minister soldier." One of the titles conferred upon the heads of vassal lineages during the reign of Quicab.

MILITARY WALLS, MILITARY CORNERS   *Rahtzalam [rah4,alam] achih, utzam [utzaam] achih,* "his-keeper-wall soldier, his-corner (or angle) soldier." *4,alam* is "wall" in V., while other sources give "plank"; the "walls" and "corners" here are undoubtedly those of a stockade. Military Walls and Military Corners are among the titles conferred upon the heads of vassal lineages during the reign of Quicab; they seem analogous to the "sides" and "corners" of the sky-earth, suggesting that a fortified town was seen as a microcosm.

MINISTER   *3alel,* possibly from *3alunel,* "one who holds something in his arms." Lord Minister was the title of the lord who ranked first among the Greathouses and headed one of the nine great houses into which their lineage was divided after the founding of Rotten Cane. He also ranked third among the four lords who jointly ruled the Quiché state from Rotten Cane, coming below the Keeper of the Mat and the Keeper of the Reception House Mat and above the Crier to the People for the Lords. During the reign of Quicab, when Quema was Lord Minister of the Greathouses, the title of Minister was conferred upon the heads of twenty vassal lineages, presumably lineages that were specifically vassals of the Greathouses.

MINISTER FOR THE LORDS *ʒalel ahau,* "minister lord," with *ahau* referring, as it does when it ends other titles, to the Lord Quiché lineage. One of the titles conferred upon the heads of one or more vassal lineages during the reign of Quicab, when Armadillo Dung was Lord Crier to the People for the Lord Quichés. Presumably these would have been vassals of the Lord Quichés in particular, although Minister is not listed as one of the titles actually held by their lineage.

MINISTER FOR THE ZAQUICS *ʒalel zaquic.* Title of the lord who ranked second among the Zaquics and headed one of the two great houses into which their lineage was divided after the founding of Rotten Cane. The Zaquics may not have acquired this title until the reign of Quicab, two generations after the founding of Rotten Cane, since it is elsewhere listed (p. 218) as one of the titles conferred on the heads of vassal lineages during the reign of Quicab. It could also be that the Zaquics themselves ennobled one or more lineages subordinate to themselves, titling them Ministers for the Zaquics in order to distinguish them from the Ministers created by the Greathouses at this same time.

MINISTER OF THE RECEPTION HOUSE *ʒalel ʒamha,* "minister receive-house." Title of the lord who ranked third among the Greathouses and headed one of the nine great houses into which their lineage was divided after the founding of Rotten Cane.

MIXTAM COPAL *Mixtam pom,* in which *pom* is "copal incense" and the rest is a Nahua name of uncertain translation. The kind of copal incense used by Jaguar Quitze to incense the direction of the rising sun. Andrés Xiloj suggested that this might be Ixtahuacán *pom,* a kind of copal from the area of Ixtahuacán and Cuilco (Mam towns) that is highly valued by the Quiché today.

MONKEY HOUSE *Batza [baʒ,a],* composed of *baʒ,,* "howler monkey," and *ha,* "house." Lord Minister in the sixth generation of Greathouse lords.

MOTHER-FATHER *Chuchcahau [chuchkahau],* composed of *chuch,* "mother," and *kahau,* "father," but pronounced as a single word. In this context "mother" and "father" are complementary metonyms that together produce the sense of "parent," but without any final reduction of the difference between motherhood and fatherhood. In the P.V., the composite term thus produced is used as a metaphor for the gods called Maker and Modeler and less figuratively for the first four human males, three of whom become founders of patrilineages. In several present-day Quiché towns the heads of patrilineages, who are daykeepers and are also responsible for lineage shrines, are called mother-fathers even though they are all males (see also *Mothers of the Word, Fathers of the Word*).

MOTHER OF THE RECEPTION HOUSE *Uchuch camha [4amha]*, "its-mother receive-house." Title of the ninth in rank among the Cauec lords (also titled Sovereign Yaqui) and head of one of the nine great houses into which their lineage was divided after the founding of Rotten Cane. The fifth-ranking lord of the Greathouses, who headed one of the nine great houses of their lineage, was also titled Mother of the Reception House.

MOTHERS OF THE WORD, FATHERS OF THE WORD *Uchuch tzih, ucahau [ukahau] tzih.* An epithet of the Great Toastmasters, suggesting that they were ritual heads of patrilineages (see *mother-father*) and that they may have been responsible for the Word (see *Ancient Word*) that is set forth in the Popol Vuh itself.

MOUNTAIN-PLAIN *Huyubtacah [huyubta3ah]*, composed of *huyub*, "mountain (or hill)," and *ta3ah*, "plain (or flat)," but pronounced as a single word. In this context "mountain" and "plain" are complementary metonyms that together produce the sense of "earth," but without any final reduction of the difference between mountains and plains. In modern Quiché ritual language, at least, *huyubta3ah* (or *huyub* by itself) is a common metaphor for the human body. In the P.V. the gods conceive humans at the same time they conceive the earth, but a great deal of time passes before they succeed in actually making humans.

NACXIT From Nahua *naui*, "four," and *ikxitl*, "foot" (C.). In Nahua sources this is a title held by the king named Quetzalcoatl; in the Book of Chilam Balam of Chumayel, a lord named Nacxit Xuchit is mentioned in connection with events that sound like part of the Nahua legend of Quetzalcoatl. In the P.V. Nacxit gives out the emblems of lordship to Cocaib, Coacutec, and Coahau, who come to him on a long pilgrimage.

NANCE *Tapal.* A tropical fruit (*Byrsonima crassifolia*), small, yellow and purple.

NECK CANYON *Cu [ku] ziuan*, "neck, narrow place" (from *kul*) "canyon." A canyon crossed by the road to Xibalba (the underworld).

NET WEAVE TRIBE *Amac [ama3] uquin cat [4at]*, composed of *ama3*, "tribe"; *u-*, "its"; *quin*, "do the warp in weaving" (B.); and *4at*, "net." Place where the Ilocs gave a home to their patron deity, not far from where the Tams, Cauecs, Greathouses, and Lord Quichés did the same; also the place where the Ilocs were when the dawn first came.

NEWBORN NANAHUAC, RAW NANAHUAC *Chipi [4hipi] nanauac, raxa nanauac*, in which *4hipi* is "youngest child"; *raxa* is "green, blue" or "raw, fresh"; and *nanahuac* seems to be the Quiché equivalent of Nanahuatzin, who in Nahua mythology throws the thunderbolt that opens up the mountain filled with the corn needed to make human flesh (see *Broken Place*). In the P.V., Newborn Nanahuac and Raw Nanahuac are alternative names for Newborn Thunderbolt and Raw Thunderbolt.

NEWBORN THUNDERBOLT, RAW THUNDERBOLT *Chipa* [*4hipa*] *caculha* [*cakulha*], *raxa caculha*, in which *4hipa* is "youngest child"; *raxa* is "green, blue" or "raw, fresh"; and *cakulha* is specifically a bolt of lightning (with the accompanying thunder), as contrasted with *coyopa*, which is sheet lightning (seen in the distance and without distinguishable bolts or audible thunder). Gods who are included under the Heart of Sky, Heart of Earth rubric and make up a threesome when combined with the name Hurricane. Lucas Pacheco recognized their names and said that in today's prayers they also go under the names of two archangels, Michael and Gabriel.

NINE DEER *Beleheb queh.* Lord Minister in the fourth generation of Greathouse lords, when Jaguar Conache was Keeper of the Mat. Another Nine Deer was Lord Minister in the ninth generation. At least the first of these two was apparently born on the day Nine Deer on the divinatory calendar; the second was probably named after the first. Today such a birth date would augur a domineering, articulate, and masculine character with shamanic inclinations, and because of the relatively high number these qualities should be obvious.

NINE DOG *Beleheb tzi* [*4,ii*]. Keeper of the Reception House Mat in the twelfth generation of Cauec lords, apparently born on the day Nine Dog on the divinatory calendar. Today, such a birth date would augur confusion, weakness, promiscuity, and ill fortune. According to the P.V. Nine Dog was hanged by the Castilians; other sources have him burned at the stake. In any case he and Three Deer were executed by Alvarado in 1524, immediately following the fall of Rotten Cane.

NOSEPIECE *Caxeon,* possibly derived from *kaxah* [*3axah*], "to run through, as with an arrow" (T.); *-on* could be the substantive suffix or it could be related to *onih,* "to nail" (E.). One of the emblems of lordship given out by Nacxit; the Annals of the Cakchiquels mentions that noses were pierced when the emblems were given out but does not refer to the ornament itself. Of the various names given to the emblems in the P.V., *caxeon* is the most likely candidate as a term for this particular item.

ONE DEATH, SEVEN DEATH *Hun came, uucub* [*uukub*] *came,* in which *hun* and *uukub* are "one" and "seven." *Came* is one of the twenty day names of the divinatory calendar; it shares the same root with such forms as *camel,* "dead person," but it is not the ordinary term for "death" (that would be *camic* or *camical*). One and Seven Death rank first and second among the lords of Xibalba. They are treated in the narrative as two persons, as are One and Seven Hunahpu (see below), but their numbers show that they represent all thirteen possible days bearing the name *came,* as Andrés Xiloj pointed out (see the notes to the Introduction).

ONE HUNAHPU, SEVEN HUNAHPU *Hun hunahpu, uucub [uukub] hunahpu.* The sons, elder and younger respectively, of Xpiyacoc and Xmucane; One Hunahpu is the father (by Xbaquiyalo) of One Monkey and One Artisan, later becoming the father (by Blood Woman) of Hunahpu and Xbalanque. One and Seven Hunahpu, as their numbers show, represent all thirteen possible days bearing the name Hunahpu (see the notes to the Introduction). They are responsible for Venus in its aspect as a morning star that first rises on a day bearing the name Hunahpu; such a morning star appears at the start of each fifth Venus cycle. One Hunahpu's severed head, when placed in the fork of a tree by the lords of Xibalba, becomes Venus in its aspect as an evening star that first rises on a day bearing the name *Came* or "Death"; this is the particular evening star that follows after a Hunahpu morning star.

ONE-LEGGED OWL *Huracan [hurakan] tucur,* "one-his-leg owl." As Andrés Xiloj pointed out, owls stand on only one leg at a time. Second-ranking Military Keeper of the Mat for the lords of Xibalba, a messenger. Along with three other owl messengers, he may correspond to the planet Mercury (see *Shooting Owl*).

ONE MONKEY, ONE ARTISAN *Hun batz [ba4,], hun chouen,* in which *hun* is "one"; *ba4,* is "howler monkey"; and *chouen* is Yucatec for "artisan" and archaic Yucatec for "howler monkey." The sons of One Hunahpu and Xbaquiyalo; patron deities of flautists, singers, writers, carvers, lapidaries, jewelers, sawyers, carpenters, incense makers, and metallurgists. Hunahpu and Xbalanque (their younger half-brothers) leave them marooned in a tall tree, where they become monkeys; this is also the beginning of their celestial career (see *"Hunahpu Monkey"*). They probably correspond to the planet Mars.

ONE TOH *Hun toh,* a day on the divinatory calendar. The god of the Rabinals, declared by the writers of the P.V. to be equivalent to the Tohil of the Cauecs, Ilocs, and Tams.

"OUR PLACE IN THE SHADOWS" *Camuhibal [kamuhibal],* "our-being-shaded-place." An epithet for the P.V., referring to the period (lasting about two-thirds of the book) before the first sunrise is seen; the following period is referred to by another epithet,

"The Dawn of Life." The implication of "shadows" in the present epithet is that the light of dawn and of sunrise were really there (somewhere) all along, but that "our" position as humans with respect to this light was such that we remained in darkness.

PAINT OF POWDERED YELLOW STONE   *Tatil canabah* [*ȝanabah*]; *tatil* may be the same as *titil*, "bright powder" (B.); *ȝanabah* is an unidentified "yellow stone" (V.) and a paint applied to the body (R.). One of the emblems of lordship given out by Nacxit.

PANACHE   *Iachuach;* B. gives *yachuachibeh* as "to crown." Part of the gear needed by players of the ball game in the P.V. (see *ball court* and *gaming equipment*), probably corresponding to the long bunch of feathers shown attached to the crowns of the heads of the players in the ball-court reliefs of Chichen Itza.

PARROT FEATHERS, HERON FEATHERS   *Chiyom*, "parrot feathers" (R.), and *aztapulul*, which is partly derived from *aztatl*, a Nahua term for a white heron (D.). Among the emblems of lordship given out by Nacxit.

PATAXTE   *Pec. Theobroma bicolor*, a lower grade of cacao than cacao proper (or *caco* in Quiché), more widely known in Mesoamerica by its Nahua name, pataxte. The seeds of pataxte and cacao, which are native to the New World, were and are used by Mesoamerican Indians to make cocoa and chocolate.

PATOHIL   See *Tohil*.

PAUILIX   See *Auilix*.

PERSON OF BAM   *Uinac* [*uinak*] *bam*, "person," followed by an untranslatable proper name. Crier to the People for the Lords in the ninth generation of Lord Quiché lords.

PETATAYUB   Partly from Nahua *petatl*, "mat" (C.). A flat place (*taȝah*) where a "mountain" (*huyub*) of shattered stones from conquered citadels was piled up during the reign of Quicab. Ximénez takes this flat to be the south coastal plain of Guatemala, but *taȝah* can refer to any level place, down to the size of a cornfield. Petatayub may be the spot known today as Altar Place (*chi mumuz*), a prominent pile of broken stones on an otherwise stoneless flat eight kilometers northwest of San Pedro Jocopilas. On the south side of this pile is an active shrine (see the illustration on pp. 214–215).

PLACE OF ADVICE   *Chi pixab*, "at advice (or counsel)." A mountain where the Quichés and other tribes held a council during their migrations. It is a peak, still known by this name, of the Montaña los Achiotes, about seven kilometers west of San Andrés Sajcabajá.

PLACE OF BALL GAME SACRIFICE   *Pucbal chah* [*puzbal chaah*]; B. gives *puzbal* as "place of sacrifice," and *chaah* is "ball game." The place where the decapitated body of One Hunahpu and the complete body of Seven Hunahpu were buried by the lords of Xibalba. Probably not a place name, but rather a name for the altar where losing ball players were sacrificed. That such altars were in or near ball courts is indicated by the fact that the classical Quiché term for a ball court, *hom*, is today the term for a graveyard. Hunahpu and Xbalanque, addressing the remains of Seven Hunahpu (their paternal uncle), tell him, "You will be prayed to here" (p. 159); today, as Andrés Xiloj pointed out, people visit graveyards on days bearing the name Hunahpu.

PLACE OF SPILT WATER See *Spilt Water.*

PLANK PLACE *Chitemah,* "at-plank"; *tema* is a bench or a roofing beam. A place of unknown location, occupied by vassals of the Quiché lords during the reign of Quicab.

PLASTER HOUSE *Zaccabaha* [*zakcabaha*], composed of *zakcaba,* "plaster" (B.), and *ha,* "house." The town known today as San Andrés Sajcabajá. Formerly a Caoque citadel, conquered by the Quiché lords during the reign of Quicab. Today the inhabitants speak Quiché.

PLUMED SERPENT *Cucumatz* [*3ucumatz*], from *3u3,* "quetzal bird" or "quetzal feathers," and *cumatz,* "serpent." Keeper of the Mat in the fourth (p. 213) or fifth (p. 224) generation of Cauec lords, named after the god listed elsewhere as Sovereign Plumed Serpent. The P.V. mentions Cotuha (not the same Cotuha who preceded Plumed Serpent as Keeper of the Mat) as the Keeper of the Reception House Mat who corresponded to Plumed Serpent in a number of places (pp. 208, 219, 224), but elsewhere states that Plumed Serpent served as both Keeper of the Mat and Keeper of the Reception House Mat (p. 213); perhaps Cotuha died during the reign of Plumed Serpent and was not replaced until after the latter's death. However that might be, it was Plumed Serpent and Cotuha who together founded Rotten Cane (p. 208). Both of them were regarded as lords of genius—that is, as lords with powerful spirit familiars—and Plumed Serpent in particular put on miraculous demonstrations of shamanic power. Here, as in the case of his central Mexican counterpart (Quetzalcoatl), it is difficult to separate Plumed Serpent as king from Plumed Serpent as deity.

POINT OF THE ARROW, ANGLE OF THE BOWSTRING *Uchi 4ha, uchi cam* [*4aam*], "its mouth arrow, its mouth cord"; Andrés Xiloj pointed out that in Quiché, the "mouth" of an arrow is its tip, while the "mouth" of a bowstring is the point at which the butt end of the arrow is pulled back against it. Epithets for the vanguard lineages sent out to occupy conquered citadels during the reign of Quicab.

POORWILL, DANCE OF THE *Xahoh puhuy,* "dance poorwill." The name of a dance done by Hunahpu and Xbalanque in their guise as vagabonds.

POPOL VUH   See *Council Book.*

PRAWN HOUSE   *Chomiha,* composed of *chom,* "shrimp" (B.), and *ha,* "house." One of the first four human females; wife of Jaguar Night. The "prawn" etymology—as opposed, for example, to *4humil* or "star"—lets the four women's names fit together in a pattern, making for two with maritime names (Celebrated Seahouse and Prawn House) and two with avian names (Hummingbird House and Macaw House).

PUMA'S PAW, JAGUAR'S PAW   *Tzicuil [4,icuil] coh, tzicuil balam;* V. gives *4,ic* as "heel of hand," and *coh* and *balam* are "puma" and "jaguar." Among the emblems of lordship given out by Nacxit.

PUS MASTER, JAUNDICE MASTER   *Ahal puh, ahal 3ana,* "owner pus, owner yellowness." Fifth- and sixth-ranking lords of Xibalba.

PUS RIVER   *Puhia [puhiaa],* "pus water." A river that crosses the road to Xibalba (the underworld). This name, along with Blood River, might have been an actual toponym, referring to a large, muddy river of the kind that originates in the Guatemalan highlands but flows into the northern lowlands. For today's Quiché the regions that drop off toward the Atlantic, especially in the area of Cobán, are an abode of evil.

QUEHNAY   See *Lolmet.*

QUEMA   Also spelled *queema* in the MS. Lord Minister in the tenth generation of Greathouse lords. Yet he is also mentioned (p. 217) among the contemporaries of the Keeper of the Mat named Quicab, who ruled in the sixth or seventh generation of Cauec lords.

QUENECH AHAU   From Yucatec Kinich Ahau, "sun-eye lord" (C.), one of the names of the lowland Maya sun god. In the P.V. this is the name of a people belonging to a group of thirteen allied tribes the Quichés regarded as having come (like themselves) from the east.

QUETZAL   *Cuc [3u3];* according to G., *raxon,* literally "blued" or "greened" (and translated "blue green" on p. 73), is a synonym for *3u3.* "Quetzal," the name by which this bird is best known, is from Nahua *quetzalli. Pharomachrus mocinno,* the most spectacular bird in the New World, confined to localized cloud forest habitats scattered from Chiapas to Panama; red breast but otherwise mostly green (with blue iridescence). The two-foot-long tail coverts were a major item of tribute and a major feature of lordly regalia throughout Mesoamerica.

QUIBA HOUSE, THOSE OF   *Ahquibaha,* in which *ah-* is "persons from" and *ha* is "house." A people belonging to a group of thirteen allied tribes the Quichés regarded as having come (like themselves) from the east.

QUICAB   Possibly *4i*, "many," with *3ab*, "hand" or "arm." Keeper of the Mat in the sixth (p. 213) or seventh (p. 224) generation of Cauec lords. Quicab greatly expanded the Quiché state, destroying the citadels of neighboring peoples and occupying them with vassal lineages drawn from the immediate vicinity of Rotten Cane. He ennobled the heads of many vassal lineages, including those who had served him well in his conquests, but members of this new nobility later perpetrated a revolt (as described in both the Title of the Lords of Totonicapán and the Annals of the Cakchiquels but not in the P.V.). They failed in an assassination attempt, but the lineages with military titles (see under *Military*) gained in power.

QUICHÉ   *Quiche* [*4iche*] and sometimes *queche* [*4eche*], possibly from *4i*, "many," and *chee*, "trees," thus carrying approximately the same meaning as Cuautemallan, the Nahua name for what is now called Guatemala. Quiché is used in several different senses in the P.V. As a people, the Quiché proper consist of those who descend from Jaguar Quitze, Jaguar Night, and Mahucutah— that is to say, the Cauec, Greathouse, and Lord Quiché lineages—and who worship the gods Tohil, Auilix, and Hacauitz. "The three Quichés" include the Quiché proper, as just described, together with two further lineages whose god was Tohil, the Tams and Ilocs. This Quiché threesome is said to have been inseparable since its members were all at Tulan Zuyua together, and to have shared the same language—a language which is also called Quiché. Late in the narrative Quiché becomes a toponym referring to the vicinity of Rotten Cane, covering Rotten Cane itself, the modern site of Santa Cruz (three kilometers to the east of Rotten Cane), and probably also Bearded Place (half a kilometer to the south of Rotten Cane). By metonymic extension, Quiché also becomes the name for the conquest state formed by the Quiché threesome after the founding of Rotten Cane.

QUITZALCUAT   Equivalent to Nahua Quetzalcoatl, "quetzal serpent." One of the names of the god of the Yaqui people, who is said by the writers of the P.V. to be the same as Tohil.

RABINALS   *Rabinaleb*, in which *-eb* is plural. The people known today as the Achí, whose principal town is Rabinal. Their language, Achí, may be considered either a dialect of Quiché or a separate language of the Quichean family; its speakers are located to the northeast of the speakers of Quiché proper. They belonged to a group of thirteen allied tribes the Quichés regarded as having come (like themselves) from the east. One of the Rabinal citadels, Spilt Water, was conquered by the Quiché lords during the reign of Quicab.

RATTLING HOUSE   *Xuxulim ha;* B. gives *xuxulim* as a continuous

357

buzzing or humming. This is one of the tests of Xibalba, also called Cold House; it rattles because of continuous drafts and hail. This test comes second (p. 112) or third (p. 142) in the sequence of test houses. These houses may correspond to the periods when Venus is invisible between its appearances as morning and evening star (see *Bat House*).

RAZOR HOUSE   *Chaim ha; chay* or *cha* refers to cutting instruments or projectile points made by percussion techniques, probably obsidian blades in the present context. One of the tests of Xibalba, fifth (p. 112) or second (p. 140) in the sequence of test houses. These houses may correspond to the periods when Venus is invisible between its appearances as morning and evening star (see *Bat House*).

RED BANNER   *Ca3lacan* [*cakla3an*], with *cak*, "red"; B. gives *la3am* as "banner." Crier to the People for the Lords in the third generation of Lord Quiché lords.

RED ROAD   *Cacabe* [*cakabe*]. One of four cosmic roads (see *Crossroads*).

ROAD OF XIBALBA   *Ri be xibalba*, "the road Xibalba," also called Black Road (see *Crossroads*). The road that beckoned to One and Seven Hunahpu when they were on their way to Xibalba and led to their deaths (p. 111). At present *ube xibalba*, "its-road Xibalba," is the Quiché term for the black cleft in the Milky Way. From the identity of One and Seven Hunahpu (or their rubber ball) as Venus, and from the fact that they go down to Xibalba from a ball court located far in the east, it may be deduced that they descended at a time when Venus was ending its period of visibility as the morning star in a sidereal position that was in or near the Milky Way cleft. Venus takes five complete cycles to repeat its sidereal position, which is the same number of cycles it takes for its periodic reappearance as a morning star to return to a day bearing the name Hunahpu.

ROBLES, DON PEDRO DE   Lord Minister in the thirteenth generation of Greathouse lords, in office when the P.V. was written. Since his predecessor was still in office in September of 1554, the P.V. must have been written after that time.

ROCK ROWS, FURROWED SANDS   *Cholochic abah, bocotahinac* [*bocotahinak*] *zanaieb*, composed of a reduplicated form of *cholo-*, "to order, put in a row"; *abah*, "rocks"; *boco-*, "uproot"; *tahii-*, "cultivate, plough"; *-nak*, perfect; and *zanaieb*, "sands." The place where Jaguar Quitze, Jaguar Night, Mahucutah, and True Jaguar crossed through a *palo* or "sea" on their migration from Tulan Zuyua. The name is, in effect, a description of a lowland Maya causeway.

ROJAS, DON JUAN DE   Lord Keeper of the Mat in the fourteenth generation of Cauec lords, in office when the P.V. was written. His title was recognized by the Spanish; he retained his serfs, was given a reception room in the Royal Palace at Santiago Guatemala, served as a sort of minister of native affairs, and attempted to regain jurisdiction over the towns that had been conquered by the Quiché state before the arrival of the Spanish. He was still in office in 1554; since he was no longer signing documents by November of 1558, the P.V. must have been written before that date.

ROTTEN CANE   *Cumaracaah* [*ȝumarakah*], "rotten-plural-cane plant." The citadel built by the Quiché lords after they left Bearded Place, founded by the Keeper of the Mat named Plumed Serpent. At Bearded Place there had been only three great houses or lordly lineages, but after the founding of Rotten Cane the Cauecs divided into nine parts, the Greathouses into nine parts, the Lord Quichés into four parts, and there were also two divisions of Zaquics (not mentioned at Bearded Place). Except for the two divisions of the Zaquics, which shared a single palace, each of these lineage segments apparently had a separate palace, making twenty-three palaces in all. It was from Rotten Cane that Quicab greatly expanded the Quiché state, and it was Rotten Cane that was burned by Pedro de Alvarado in 1524. The ruins, better known by their Nahua name, Utatlán, are located three kilometers west of Santa Cruz Quiché (see also *Great Monument of Tohil, Auilix, Hacauitz, Keeper of the Plumed Serpent, Councilor of the Ball Court, Granary,* and *Bird House*).

RUBBER BALL   *Qui4*, literally "blood" but also referring to rubber, rubber balls in particular. Europeans saw rubber balls for the first time in the West Indies and Mesoamerica. In the P.V. a rubber ball is part of the gaming equipment (see under that heading) used by One and Seven Hunahpu and by their sons, Hunahpu and Xbalanque. The ball used by their opponents in Xibalba is not called *qui4* (except by a falsehood that fails to deceive Hunahpu and Xbalanque) but is rather referred to by its proper name (see *White Dagger*) or by the term *chaah*, which is also a term for the ball game itself (whatever kind of ball it is played with).

SANTA CRUZ   Bishop Francisco Marroquín gave this name to Rotten Cane in 1539 (the event referred to on p. 210), but the town that came to be known as Santa Cruz Quiché was not built on the ruins of Rotten Cane itself but three kilometers east of there.

SERPENTS   *Cumatz.* A people belonging to a group of thirteen allied tribes the Quichés regarded as having come (like themselves) from the east.

SEVEN CANE   *Uucub* [*uukub*] *ah*, "seven cane plant." Crier to the

People for the Lords in the sixth generation of Lord Quiché lords. Apparently born on the day Seven Cane on the divinatory calendar; today such a birth date would augur good luck in all the affairs of life and a potential career as a dutiful priest-shaman or official.

SEVEN CAVES, SEVEN CANYONS   *Uucub [uukub] pec, uucub ziuan.* An epithet for Tulan Zuyua, the citadel where the ruling Quiché lineages acquired their patron deities. *Uucub pec* is a Quiché translation of Chicomoztoc, the "seven caves" of the mythic Nahua place of origin. The ruins of both Teotihuacan and Xochicalco have natural caves beneath them; Rotten Cane has an artificial cave that penetrates to a point beneath the main plaza.

SEVEN MACAW   *Uucub caquix [uukub cakix],* in which the term for macaw is composed of *cak,* "red," and perhaps *quiix,* "feathers." A lord who falsely claimed to be both the sun and moon during the era of the wooden people, causing offense to Hurricane; husband of Chimalmat and father of Zipacna and Earthquake. From his red feathers and from his nose that "shines white" (p. 86), the macaw in question could only be the scarlet macaw (*Ara macao*), which displays more red feathers than the military macaw (*Ara militaris*) and contrasts with the latter in having a white beak. The P.V. does not specify Seven Macaw's actual astronomical identification (as contrasted with his false claim to be the sun), but A. gives it as Ursa Major, whose prominent stars (comprising the Big Dipper) number seven. In West Indian Carib myths the Big Dipper has a feathered headdress that shows by day as the rainbow, which suggests that Seven Macaw might also have a rainbow aspect. What the Big Dipper has in common with the rainbow is that its appearance marks the end of storms, only it does so seasonally. In the latitudes of Mesoamerica and the Caribbean, the hurricane season (mid-July to mid-October) begins with nights on which the Big Dipper is already in steep descent at twilight and disappears entirely for as much as half the night, and it ends with the first nights on which all seven stars of the newly ascending Big Dipper appear before dawn. To put this in terms of the P.V., when Hunahpu and Xbalanque (acting on behalf of Hurricane) bring Seven Macaw down out of his tree (or below the horizon), they open the way for the great rain that destroys the people for whom Seven Macaw was the sun.

SEVEN THOUGHT   *Uucub noh [uukub naoh].* Keeper of the Mat in the eleventh generation of Cauec lords, apparently born on the day Seven Thought on the divinatory calendar. Today, such a birth date would augur an ability to solve problems, potential leadership, and a markedly masculine character.

SHIELD DANCE   *Pocob,* "shield," not only an implement of war but "an ancient dance" (B.). A dance performed by the Quiché lords while they were settled at Bearded Place.

SHOOTING OWL   *4habi tucur,* in which *tucur* is "owl"; *4ha* is "arrow," but better yet, B. gives *chabih* as "stoop like a hawk." First-ranking Military Keeper of the Mat for the lords of Xibalba, a messenger. The four owls of Xibalba are able to reach the eastern ball court used by One and Seven Hunahpu and by One Monkey and One Artisan, but in contrast with Falcon, the messenger of the Heart of Sky, or Hurricane, they are not described as being able to reach the place where the Heart of Sky is located. They may correspond to the planet Mercury, with perhaps one pair of owls for its morning star aspect and the other for its evening star aspect.

SKULL OWL   *Holom tucur,* "head (or skull) owl." Fourth-ranking Military Keeper of the Mat for the lords of Xibalba, a messenger. Along with the other three owl messengers, he may correspond to the planet Mercury (see *Shooting Owl*).

SKY-EARTH   *Cahuleu,* composed of *cah,* "sky," and *uleu,* "earth," but pronounced as a single word. In this context "sky" and "earth" are complementary metonyms that together produce the sense of "world," but without any final reduction of the difference between sky and earth. This composite word is used in contemporary Quiché prayers.

SNATCH-BATS   *Camazotz [4amazo4,],* composed of *4ama,* "take," and *zo4,,* "bat." The bats that inhabit the Bat House of Xibalba. B. lists *camotzoh* as "an animal that eats the moon." Andrés Xiloj commented, "These are not animal bats, but the bats of Xibalba." Today in Rabinal the dance-drama of San Jorge includes a character of this same name.

SORREL GUM   *Lotz quic [qui4],* in which *qui4* (literally "blood") is the term for latex or other plant products of a gummy consistency.

SOVEREIGN OLOMAN   *Tepeu oloman* or *oliman,* from Nahua *tepeuani* (see *Sovereign Plumed Serpent*) and *ollomani,* "ballplayer" (D.). A people, also called Fishkeepers, probably from the Gulf coast of Tabasco or eastern Veracruz. They stayed in the "east" when the Quiché ancestors left there, but later, during the time the Quichés were settled in the citadel of Hacauitz, they participated in a plot against them.

SOVEREIGN PLUMED SERPENT   *Tepeu 4ucumatz [3ucumatz],* in which *tepeu* is an honorific title and the second word is composed of *3u3,* "quetzal bird or quetzal feathers," and *cumatz,* "snake." *Tepeu* is from Nahua, in which *tepeuani* is "conqueror or victor in battle" (D.); Quiché *tepeual,* a participial form (marked by *-al*), is translated by B. as "majesty, dignity." *3ucumatz* is the equivalent in Quiché of Yucatec Kukulcan and Nahua Quetzal-coatl, both of which names mean "quetzal-plumed serpent." As a god, the Plumed Serpent is nearly always prefixed with *tepeu* in the P.V.; he numbers among the gods who are covered by the names or epithets Maker, Modeler; Bearer, Begetter; and Heart of the Lake, Heart of the Sea. In the primordial scene these gods, unlike the god or gods called Heart of Sky, Hurricane, Newborn Thunderbolt, and Raw Thunderbolt, are on or in the sea. Just as the Nahua Quetzalcoatl cooperates with Tezcatlipoca in making the present earth in the midst of the sea, so the Quiché Sovereign Plumed Serpent cooperates with Hurricane; the difference is that the Nahua earth in question was the fifth, whereas the P.V. seems to have it as the first. By the time Rotten Cane was founded, Sovereign Plumed Serpent numbered among the most important of Quiché gods, judging from the fact that the Keeper of the Plumed Serpent was among the five heads of lordly lineages who were priests, the others being priests of Tohil, Auilix, Hacauitz, and Corntassel. But the writers of the P.V. neither give the story of Sovereign Plumed Serpent's origin nor elaborate his divine attributes, and scarcely a trace of him remains in today's Quiché oral narratives.

SOVEREIGN YAQUI   Title of the lord who was ninth in rank among the Cauecs and head of one of the nine great houses into which their lineage was divided after the founding of Rotten Cane; he was also called Mother of the Reception House.

SPILT WATER   *Maca* [*ma4aa*] or *pamaca* [*pama4aa*], composed of *pa*, "at" or "in"; *ma4*, "spill or fall"; and *aa*, "water." The town known today as Zacualpa, formerly located two kilometers southeast of its present site. Once a Rabinal citadel, conquered by the Quiché lords during the reign of Quicab. Today the inhabitants speak Quiché.

STAGGERING   *Zilizib; zilizab* is "sway, swing, stagger" (B.). The place where the tribes (other than the Cakchiquels) pledged themselves to be "suckled" (or to have their hearts cut out) by Tohil in exchange for fire (p. 175); the name of this place is not mentioned until later (p. 187).

STAR HOUSE, THOSE OF   *Ahchumilaha* [*ah4humilaha*], "persons-from-star-house." A people belonging to a group of thirteen allied tribes the Quichés regarded as having come (like themselves) from the east.

SUDDEN BLOODLETTER   *Camalotz*, probably composed of *cahmah*, "fright, surprise attack" (V.), and *lotz*, "to let blood." One of the monsters that ends the era of the wooden people.

SUN-MOON   *Quihic* [*3ihi4*], composed of *3ih*, "sun," and *i4*, "moon," but pronounced as a single word. In this context "sun" and "moon" are complementary metonyms that together produce an abstraction encompassing major heavenly bodies (and major markers of time), but without any final reduction of the difference between sun and moon. The composite concept of sun-moon would include Venus as morning star as well, since the latter has *3ih* in its Quiché name (see *daybringer*).

SWALLOWING SWORDS   *Xtzul* [*x4,ul*], a proper name of uncertain etymology. The name of a dance done by Hunahpu and Xbalanque in their guise as vagabonds. B. describes it as a dance in which masked performers with tortoise-shell rattles put sticks or daggers in their mouths. V. (who specifies *4,*, the glottalized *tz*), describes the masks as small and says that the dancers are two in number (as they are in the P.V.), wear the tails of macaws down their backs, put sticks down their throats and bones into their noses, and give themselves hard blows on their chests with a large stone.

SWEATBATH HOUSE   *Tuhalha.* The people who inhabit the area around Sacapulas today, belonging to a group of thirteen allied tribes the Quichés regarded as having come (like themselves) from the east; they speak a highly distinctive dialect of Quiché. One of the four sections of the town of Sacapulas still bears the name Tuhal.

SWEET DRINK   *Qui* [*quii*], "sweet," "poison," and (according to G.) "wine or chicha," chicha generally being an alcoholic beverage made by fermenting corn. It is not known for certain what went into the making of *quii;* the pulque of Mexico (made from maguey) is not reliably reported for indigenous Guatemala, nor is the drink the Yucatec Maya called *balche* (partly made from honey). What is known about *quii* is that it required cooking at some stage, that it took three days to ferment, and that the Four Hundred Boys went "out of their senses" drinking it (pp. 96, 148). The making of *balche* does not involve cooking, but at least one kind of pulque does (a variety in which maguey cuttings are boiled together with honey prior to fermentation). Pulque and *balche* are both sweet to the taste before fermentation and bitter afterward; perhaps the seemingly contradictory meanings of *quii* reflect the paradox of a drink that started out sweet and harmless and ended up bitter and (in sufficient quantities) sickening.

TALK HOUSE.   *Uchabaha* [*u4habaha*], "its-talk-place-house." A people belonging to a group of thirteen allied tribes the Quichés regarded as having come (like themselves) from the east.

TAMAZUL   From Nahua *tamazolin*, "toad" (C.); the Quiché term for this animal is *xpek*. The name of the toad that swallowed the louse that carried the message of Xmucane.

TAMS   *Tamub* (singular *tam*). One of the allied groups of lineages called "the three Quichés," the other two members being the Quiché proper—comprising the Cauecs, Greathouses, and Lord Quichés—and the Ilocs.

TAM TRIBE   *Amac* [*ama3*] *tan*, composed of the term for "tribe" and an archaic pronunciation of *tam*. Place where the Tams gave a home to their patron deity, not far from where the Ilocs, Cauecs, Greathouses, and Lord Quichés did the same; also the place where the Tams were when the dawn first came.

TEARING JAGUAR   *Tucumbalam*, probably composed of *tucun*, "scratch" (V.), and *balam*, "jaguar." One of the monsters that ends the era of the wooden people.

TECUM   A Nahua name of uncertain translation. Keeper of the Mat in the ninth generation of Cauec lords; a second Tecum held the same position in the thirteenth generation. The latter Tecum was taken hostage when Rotten Cane fell to the Spanish in 1524; he was the son of Three Deer, the Keeper of the Mat who was executed by Alvarado. Tecum's accession to his father's title was later recognized by Alvarado, who made that position subordinate to himself, but Tecum plotted rebellion and was eventually hanged. He is not to be confused with the warrior named Tecum Umam, who died in a battle with Alvarado's forces before the attack on Rotten Cane took place.

TEPEPUL   From Nahua *tepe*, "mountain," and *pol*, "big" (C.). Keeper of the Mat in the fifth (p. 213) or sixth (p. 224) generation of Cauec lords; taken prisoner in an attack on the Cakchiquels. Another Tepepul was Keeper of the Mat in the eighth generation of Cauec lords, and still others were Keepers of the Reception House Mat in the ninth and thirteenth generations of Cauec lords. This last Tepepul, along with the last Tecum, was taken hostage when Rotten Cane fell to the Spanish in 1524; he was the son of Nine Dog, the Keeper of the Reception House Mat who was executed by Alvarado. Tepepul's accession to his father's title was later recognized by Alvarado, who made that position subordinate to himself, but Tepepul plotted rebellion and was hanged in 1540.

THORNY PLACE   *Chiquix* [*chi4ix*], "at thorns." Citadel of the Quiché lords after they left Hacauitz and before they built Bearded Place. It was divided into four parts or "mountains": Dry Place, Bark House, Culba, and Cauinal. Dry Place is *chichac* [*chichak*], "at dryness"; Bark House is *humetaha*, composed of *humeta*, "bark," and *ha*, "house." Thorny Place doubtless corresponds to the archaeological site known today as Cauinal (beneath a mountain of the same name), on the Río Blanco near its confluence with the Río Negro or Chixoy, about twenty kilometers northwest of Rabinal. The site has four main plazas, two on each side of the Río Blanco; it is located in a dry region dominated by xerophytic vegetation, in which it contrasts with most of the area occupied by the Quichés today.

THREE DEER *Oxib quieh.* Keeper of the Mat in the twelfth generation of Cauec lords, apparently born on the day Three Deer on the divinatory calendar. Today such a birth date would augur a domineering, articulate, and masculine character, with possible shamanic inclinations, but because of the low number, these qualities would be present in only moderate quantity. According to the P.V. Three Deer was hanged by the Castilians; other sources have him burned at the stake. In any case he and Nine Dog were executed by Alvarado in 1524, immediately following the fall of Rotten Cane.

THRONG BIRDS *4,iquin molai,* "birds joined together." Possibly a mythic species, or possibly referring to a flock rather than a species. One of the obstacles on the road to Xibalba (the underworld).

TOHIL Patron deity of the Cauec, Tam, and Iloc lineages; the name sometimes covers the patron deities of the Greathouse and Lord Quiché lineages as well, Auilix and Hacauitz. Apparently the name is composed of Toh, one of the twenty day names of the 260-day calendar, and *-il,* "having the quality of"; Toh may be related to Cholan *tohokna,* "the way in which clouds join," and *tohmel,* "thunder" (C.), but the classic Maya predecessor of Tohil at Palenque carries the name Tahil, meaning "Torch Mirror" or "Obsidian Mirror" (S.). Tahil is shown with a burning torch sticking out of the mirror on his forehead; Tohil is a giver of fire, pivoting inside his own sandal like a fire drill. The one-leggedness suggested by the fire drill, together with the fact that Tohil can cause great rainstorms, identify him as an aspect of Hurricane (see above). The stone whose genius or spirit familiar was Tohil was carried in a backpack by Jaguar Quitze, founder of the Cauecs, when he left Tulan Zuyua. He placed this stone on a mountain that came to be called Patohil, literally "At Tohil," apparently located above or near Concealment Canyon, where the god Auilix was placed. A temple dedicated to Tohil was later built at Rotten Cane (see *Great Monument of Tohil*); those bringing tribute to Rotten Cane, which was probably payable on days named Toh, gave offerings to Tohil before they made their presentations to the Quiché lords. The present character of the day Toh seems to reflect its past connection with tribute. One of the divinatory mnemonics for the meaning of this day is *tohonic,* "to pay," indicating that the client owes offerings to the gods and the ancestors. In visits to shrines, daykeepers use Toh days to make up for delinquent ritual obligations.

TOHIL MEDICINE *Cunabal tohil,* "cure-instrument Tohil." An epithet given to Concealment Canyon after Tohil was placed nearby on the mountain called Patohil. This epithet may be based on a bilingual pun on the place name Patohil; Nahuatl *patli* means "medicine" (D.).

TOHIL'S BATH *Ratinibal tohil,* "his-bathing-place Tohil." During the time when the Quiché lords occupied the citadel of Hacauitz, the spirit familiars of Tohil, Auilix, and Hacauitz were regularly seen bathing at this place (location unknown).

TONATIUH *Donadiu,* a Nahua word meaning "sun." This was the name given by the Indians of central Mexico to Pedro de Alvarado before he came to Guatemala.

TORTILLA GRIDDLE *Xot.* A round and slightly concave pottery griddle, used in toasting tortillas; better known in Mesoamerica as the comal, from Nahua *comalli.*

TRASH MASTER, STAB MASTER *Ahal mez, ahal tocob* [*to3ob*], "owner filth (or trash), owner puncture wound." These lords of Xibalba rank ninth and tenth in earlier lists (pp. 107, 110) but are omitted from later ones. See also *Bloody Teeth, Bloody Claws.*

TRUE JAGUAR *Iquibalam,* with *balam,* "jaguar," possibly prefixed with *iki-* (V.) or *iqui-* (X.). This prefix can be combined with *a3ab,* "hand," to give "right hand," and with *tzih,* "word," to give "truth" (V.); it is probably present in the expression of affirmation given by B. as *iquiquih.* True Jaguar was one of the first four human males, but he had no son and therefore did not found a lineage.

TULAN From Nahua *tollan,* "Place of Reeds (or Cattails)." A term widely used in Mesoamerica to prefix the names of places where the investiture of Toltecan lords could take place. The P.V. states that the Quichés, Cakchiquels, and various other tribes were assigned their patron deities at Tulan, before the first sunrise; it locates Tulan in the east, perhaps recalling the direction from which the Quichés happened to be moving immediately before coming into the region of their present home rather than the absolute spatial relationship between that home and Tulan. Tulan is nearly always joined to the name Zuyua in the P.V. (see below).

UNDER TEN *Xelahuh,* "under (or below) ten"; the full name (not given in the P.V.) is *xelahuh queh,* "Under Ten Deer." This town is still called Xelaju or Xela in everyday Guatemalan speech, whether in Spanish or in an indigenous language, but in government documents and on maps it is known by a slightly altered form of its Nahau name, Quezaltenango (it should be spelled Quetzaltenango, meaning "Quetzal Citadel"). Its former location, when it was truly a citadel, must have been on one of the hilltops in the vicinity of the present town, but the exact site is not known. It was among the citadels conquered by the Quiché lords during the reign of Quicab.

UNDER THE TWINE, UNDER THE CORD *Xebalax, xecamac*, in which *xe-* may be "under" but could also be a verb prefix indicating completed action and the third person plural; *balax* may be a passive form of *bal*, "to make or twist a cord" (V.), and *camac* may be *4aamak*, a perfect form of *4aamah*, "to cord (measure land with a cord)." A place in Chulimal or perhaps an epithet for Chulimal. This is where the heads of vassal lineages were elevated to lordship and assigned to conquered territories during the reign of Quicab; the name may allude to the setting of boundaries for these territories.

VASSALS *Al4ahol*, "children," a composite term made up of *al*, "child (of a woman)," and *4ahol*, "son (of a man)." The term for members of commoner lineages owing fealty to lordly lineages. Vassalage was a sort of kinship by adoption, but note that the term clouds or averts the issue of lineality by including the term for a woman's children. During the reign of Quicab the first-ranking male members of many vassal lineages were elevated to lordship.

WALKING ON STILTS *Chitic*, "to go on stilts" (B.). The name of a dance done by Hunahpu and Xbalanque in their guise as vagabonds.

WEASEL, DANCE OF THE *Xahoh cux*, "dance weasel." The name of a dance done by Hunahpu and Xbalanque in their guise as vagabonds. B. mentions a dance (*cux*) done with weasel skins.

WHITE CORNMEALS *Zacahib* [*zak4ahib*], "white-cornmeal-plural." A people belonging to a group of thirteen allied tribes the Quichés regarded as having come (like themselves) from the east. They must have settled in the area of the present town of Salcajá, which is called *zak4aha* in Quiché.

WHITE DAGGER *Zaqui toc* [*zaki to3*]; V. gives *to3* as "knife" or "stab"; it is the Cholan term for implements of flaked stone (K.), which are *cha* in Quiché. The name of the sacrificial knife belonging to the lords of Xibalba and of the ball (containing this knife) they are anxious to use in their game with Hunahpu and Xbalanque.

WHITE EARTHS *Zaculeuab* [*zakuleuab*], "white-earth-plural." A tribe named after the citadel of Zakuleu (located five kilometers west of the present town of Huehuetenango) and comprising part or all of the speakers of the Mayan language known today as Mam. The P.V. does not claim that the Quiché lords conquered Zakuleu itself, but rather a separate citadel belonging to the White Earths, named Above the Hot Springs.

WHITE RIVER   *Zaqui ya* [*zaki yaa*], "white water." A place four kilometers west of Chichicastenango, occupied by vassals of the Quiché lords during the reign of Quicab.

WHITE ROAD   *Zaquibe* [*zakibe*]. One of four cosmic roads (see *Crossroads*). Today, at least, this is the term for the solid white portion of the Milky Way, as opposed to the Road of Xibalba (see above), which is the portion divided by a dark cleft.

WHITE SPARKSTRIKER   *Zaqui coxol* [*zaki 4oxol*], composed of *zaki*, "white"; *4oxo*, a verb stem used for the act of striking stones together "to start a fire" (V.); and *-l*, agentive. In the P.V. this being escapes into the shelter of the woods when the sun first rises, taking along the animals that were petrified by the sun; in the present-day Quiché dance-drama of the Conquest, he or she (the sex is ambiguous) escapes into the woods to avoid Spanish domination. In the drama the White Sparkstriker appears as a dwarf dressed entirely in red, but may have silver clothing in dreams and visions. When the sun rose and petrified the first animals, the White Sparkstriker escaped into a tree and is now the keeper of the petrified animals (iron concretions that resemble animals) and may be encountered in caves, in deep woods, and at night. In some manifestations the White Sparkstriker carries a stone hatchet—the one he-she used to strike sheet lightning into the bodies of the first daykeepers, according to Vicente de León Abac.

WHITE VULTURE   *Zac cuch* [*zak 4uch*]. The king vulture (*Sarcoramphus papa*), a lowland species which has a naked red head and black flight feathers but is otherwise white.

WILLOW TREE   *Tzolohchee*, "willow tree." The town known today as Santa María Chiquimula. One of the citadels conquered by the Quiché lords during the reign of Quicab.

WING, PACKSTRAP   *Xic* [*xi4*], *patan*, "wing, packstrap," the latter referring to a strip of hide used to protect the forehead when a load is carried with a tumpline. These lords of Xibalba rank eleventh and twelfth in earlier lists (pp. 107, 110) and ninth and tenth in later ones (pp. 135, 136).

XBALANQUE   The younger brother of Hunahpu and the son of One Hunahpu and Blood Woman; the full meaning of his name remains uncertain. X- is archaic in Quiché but means "she of" or "small" in Cholan (K.); *balan* is from *balam*, "jaguar"; *que* could be from *queh*, "deer," or it could be like *3e* in the Kekchí Maya term for "sun," *zak3e*, which is composed of *zak*, "light," and *3e*, "day" (F.). It has been reported that one of the names of the sun god among the contemporary Kekchí is *xbalam3e* (F.), which recalls the fact that Hunahpu and Xbalanque become the sun and moon in the P.V. If the name Xbalanque literally means "Little

Jaguar Sun" in the P.V., it could refer specifically to the full moon, which is metaphorically called "sun" by contemporary Quichés; that would leave other phases of the moon to his mother, Blood Woman. In Pokomchí Maya, *xbalanque* or *xba-lamque* is the term for species of fish of the family that includes perch and bass (Z.), which recalls the fact that Hunahpu and Xbalanque are described as taking the form of channel catfish after their ground bones are thrown in water; perhaps it was specifically Hunahpu who became a catfish, whereas Xbalanque became a bass.

XBAQUIYALO   The *x-* is archaic in Quiché but "she of" or "small" in Cholan (K.); the rest is of uncertain derivation but could include *bak*, "bone" or "pit (of a fruit)." The wife of One Hunahpu and the mother of One Monkey and One Artisan.

XCANUL   [*X4anul*], in which the *x-* is archaic in Quiché but "she of" or "small" in Cholan (K.). In the P.V. this is a proper name for what is now called the Volcán Santa María (note the feminine gender), nine kilometers south of Quezaltenango, but in the present-day vocabulary of the western part of the Quiché-speaking region it is a generic term for volcano.

XCUXEBA   See *Councilor of the Ball Court.*

XIBALBA   Probably derived, in part, from the same root as *xibih*, "frighten"; the *-al* might have been participial and the final *-ba* could have been *-bal*, "place of." The underworld, located below the face of the earth (*uuach uleu*) but at the same time conceptualized as being accessible by way of a road that descends cliffs and canyons, probably in the general direction of the lowlands that lie to the Atlantic side of the Guatemalan highlands. In Yucatec Maya, Xibalba is one of the names for the lord of the lowest underworld. See also *Road of Xibalba.*

XPIYACOC, XMUCANE   Divine grandparents, probably older than all the other gods; parents of One and Seven Hunahpu; patrons of the diviners known as daykeepers (see above). Their epithets include Grandmother of Day, Grandmother of Light (though Xpiyacoc is male); Maker of the Blue-Green Plate, Maker of the Blue-Green Bowl; Great White Peccary, Great White Tapir; and Bearer twice over, Begetter twice over (as if to make them even older than the gods who are simply called Bearer, Begetter). They are also described (respectively) as a midwife and matchmaker, which are specialized subfields of contemporary daykeepers (female and male respectively). That Xpiyacoc is named first, reversing the normal feminine-masculine order of Quiché phrasing, may reflect the fact that the two of them are the Quiché counterparts of Cipactonal and Oxomoco, an old divining couple named in masculine-feminine order in Nahua. The meaning of the Quiché names is unclear, except that the initial *x*-, though archaic in Quiché, means "she of" or "small" in Cholan (K.). The feminine aspect of Xpiyacoc recalls the fact that contemporary daykeepers (of either sex) are symbolically androgynous, female on the left side of the body and male on the right. Andrés Xiloj suggested that the *-pi-* in Xpiyacoc might be *-pe-*, "to come," and he derived *-yac-* from *yequic* (*yaquic* in some dialects), "to be put in order, to be lifted up," a verb diviners use with reference to the problems of clients. In classical Quiché *yaco* is a numeral classifier for counting tribute (B.); the *yaco* in Xpiyacoc could refer to the counting (and manipulation) of the divining seeds (described on p. 81) rather than to the "lifting up" of the client. In the case of Xmucane, Xiloj derived *mucane* from *moconic*, "to do something requested" or "to do a favor"; he pointed out that a diviner who has ascertained the cause of a problem may then be hired to make prayers and offerings on behalf of the client. To this day, a daykeeper ideally has a spouse who is also a daykeeper, and the divinations with the clearest outcomes are the ones they do together.

XTAH, XPUCH The *x*- is archaic in Quiché but "she of" or "small" in Cholan (K.). The two women sent (by tribes hostile to the Quichés) to seduce Tohil, Auilix, and Hacauitz. On the positive side, *-tah* could be read as "goods, riches, gifts" (V.), and *xpuch* could be read as a borrowing from Nahua *ichpuchtli*, "maiden" (D.). On the other hand, *tahih* is "to sin many times" (V.), and *puchu* is "to smash, disembowel" (B.).

XTAYUB Possibly a variant spelling of Iztayul (see above). Keeper of the Reception House Mat in the eighth generation of Cauec lords.

XULU, PACAM Names of the diviners consulted by the lords of Xibalba on the question of how to dispose of the remains of Hunahpu and Xbalanque. V. describes *xulu* as "[spirit] familiars appearing alongside rivers"; an *ahxulu*, or "keeper of Xulu," is a curer (V.) or a diviner (B.). Pacam could be composed of *pa*, "at" or "in," and *cam*, "bridge" (B.).

YACOLATAM, OR EDGE OF THE ZACLATOL MAT *Yacolatam, utzam pop zaclatol; yaco-* is "to lift," and V. gives *yac* as a particle for counting tribute; *utzam pop* is "its-edge (possibly fringe) mat"; *zac* is likely *zak*, "white" or "light"; the rest is untranslatable. Yacolatam is listed by itself the second time it is mentioned. Title of the lord who ranked eighth among the Greathouses and was head of one of the nine great houses into which their lineage was divided after the founding of Rotten Cane.

YAQUI PEOPLE *Yaqui uinac* [*uinak*], in which *yaqui* is Nahua for "gone, departed" (C.) and *uinak* is Quiché for "people." This refers to Nahua speakers who were present in the citadel of Tulan Zuyua at the same time the Quichés, Rabinals, Cakchiquels, and those of the Bird House (Tzutuhils) were there; according to the P.V., their god (called Yolcuat and Quitzalcuat) was equivalent to Tohil. See also *"The Blame Is Ours."*

YAQUI SOVEREIGN Probably the same as the Yaqui people (see above).

YARROW *Holom ocox,* "head of mushroom." A common aromatic herb in the Guatemalan highlands, named for the shape of its composite flower head, which consists of numerous tiny, closely spaced white blossoms; probably *Stevia eupatoria,* called *pericón blanco* in Spanish. In the P.V. (as among today's Quiché) the burning of this herb, together with marigolds (see above), constitutes a more modest offering than the burning of copal incense.

YELLOWBITE *Canti* [ʒanti], in which ʒan is "yellow" and ti is from the same root as *tiinic,* "to eat (meat)." The snake commonly known as the fer-de-lance, which has a yellow zone around the mouth.

YELLOW ROAD *ʒanabe.* One of four cosmic roads (see *Crossroads*).

YELLOWWOOD *Cante* [ʒante], in which ʒan is "yellow" and te is Cholan for "wood" or "tree" (C.). A. gives ʒante as the *madre cacao* (*Gliricidia sepium*), a large tree that is planted to provide shade in cacao plantations. Hunahpu and Xbalanque send One Monkey and One Artisan up this tree in order to transform them into monkeys.

YOKE *Bate,* from Cholan *bat,* which is today "ax, shovel, blade," and *te,* "wood, tree" (C.). Part of the equipment necessary for the ball game played in the P.V. (see *gaming equipment*). Each player in the Mesoamerican ball game had a yoke-shaped object of wood riding on his hips; it was with this yoke that he returned the ball, which could not be touched with the hands while it was in play. The upper, outer rim of this yoke is often depicted with a mildly sharpened edge. Among all the words for the gaming equipment in the P.V., *bate* is the best candidate as a term for the yoke. First of all, *bate* is used as a term for the game itself over wide areas of Mesoamerica; since the yoke is one of the most distinctive features of the game, it could well have given its name to the game itself at some remote point in the past. Second, it was the *bate* with which Hunahpu and Xbalanque received and returned the ball when they played the game against the lords of Xibalba.

YOKE HOUSE, THOSE OF *Ahbatenaba,* "person-from-yoke-plural-house." A people belonging to a group of thirteen allied tribes the Quichés regarded as having come (like themselves) from the east.

YOLCUAT From Nahua *yol*, "heart," and *coatl*, "snake" (C.). One of the names of the god of the Yaqui people, who is said by the writers of the P.V. to be the same as Tohil.

ZAPOTES *Tulul*. A tropical fruit (*Lucuma mammosa*), sometimes called "sapota" in English. The tan skin resembles suede; the flesh is chocolate-colored.

ZAQUIC A lordly lineage divided into two great houses after the founding of Rotten Cane; not mentioned as having come from the east with the lordly Quiché lineages or as having been present at Tulan. The Zaquics may have been indigenous to the area around Chinique, and they may have been adopted by the Cauecs, Greathouses, and Lord Quichés to fill out an ideal foursome that was left short by the fact that True Jaguar (one of the first four human males) had no sons.

ZAQUICAZ V. gives *zakiȝaz* as "a very thick snake that flees when it sees people, making a noise with its belly." This is the snake that swallows the toad that swallows the louse that carries the message of Xmucane.

ZIPACNA Derived from the same source as Nahua *cipactli*, referring to a mythological animal, with the features of a crocodile and sometimes those of a shark, that gives its name to the Nahua day corresponding to Imox on the Quiché calendar. That Zipacna hunts fish and crabs from a position on shore fits the crocodile identification, but the Quiché term for crocodile, *ayin*, does not occur in the P.V. Zipacna is the son of Seven Macaw and Chimalmat and the elder brother of Earthquake; he claims to be the maker of mountains and even of the earth in general.

ZIYA HOUSE *Ziyaha*, in which *-ha* is "house." A place of unknown location, occupied by vassals of the Quiché lords during the reign of Quicab.

ZUYUA In the P.V. this name (sometimes rendered as *zuua*) always appears as part of the compound name Tulan Zuyua, referring to the town where the Quichés and related peoples are said to have been given the stones containing the spirit familiars of their patron deities (see also *Tulan*). Zuyua was probably on the system of lakes, lagoons, and estuaries that stretches from southwestern Campeche through Tabasco to eastern Veracruz, known in Nahua as Nonoalco. The etymology of the name remains unsolved.

BIBLIOGRAPHY

Alvarado López, Miguel. *Léxico médico quiché-español*. Guatemala: Instituto Indigenista Nacional, 1975.

Aveni, Anthony F. *Skywatchers of Ancient Mexico*. Austin: University of Texas Press, 1980.

Basseta, Domingo de. "Vocabulario en lengua quiché." Manuscript (1698?) in the Bibliothèque Nationale, Paris. Typescript paleography by William Gates (1921), in the J. P. Harrington collection at the National Anthropological Archives, Smithsonian Institution, Washington, D.C.

Borhegyi, Stephan F. de. *The Pre-Columbian Ballgames: A Pan-Mesoamerican Tradition*. Milwaukee Public Museum Contributions in Anthropology and History 1. Milwaukee, 1980.

———. "Pre-Columbian Pottery Mushrooms from Mesoamerica." *American Antiquity* 28 (1963): 328–38.

Brasseur de Bourbourg, Charles Etienne. *Gramática de la lengua quiché*. Translated into Spanish by Jorge Luís Arriola. Guatemala: José de Pineda Ibarra, 1961.

———. *Grammaire de la langue quichée*. Collection de Documents dans les Langues Indigenes de l'Amérique Ancienne, 2, pt. 1. Paris: Arthus Bertrand, 1862.

———. *Popol Vuh: Le livre sacré et les mythes de l'antiquité américaine*. Collection de Documents dans les Langues Indigenes de l'Amérique Ancienne, 1. Paris: Arthus Bertrand, 1861.

———. *Rabinal-Achi ou le drame-ballet du tun*. Collection de Documents dans les Langues Indigenes, 2, pt. 2. Paris: Arthus Bertrand, 1862.

Bricker, Victoria Reifler. *The Indian Christ, the Indian King: The His-*

torical Substrate of Maya Myth and Ritual. Austin: University of Texas Press, 1981.

Bunzel, Ruth. *Chichicastenango: A Guatemalan Village.* Seattle: University of Washington Press, 1959.

Burgess, Dora M. de, and Patricio Xec. *Popol Wuj.* Quezaltenango: El Noticiero Evangélico, 1955.

Burns, Allan F. "The Caste War in the 1970's: Present-Day Accounts from Village Quintana Roo." In *Anthropology and History in Yucatán,* edited by Grant D. Jones, 259–73. Austin: University of Texas Press, 1977.

———. *An Epoch of Miracles: Oral Literature of the Yucatec Maya.* Austin: University of Texas Press, 1983.

Campbell, Lyle. "Préstamos lingüísticos en el Popol Vuh." In *Nuevas perspectivas sobre el Popol Vuh,* edited by Robert M. Carmack and Francisco Morales Santos, 81–86. Guatemala: Piedra Santa, 1983.

———. *Quichean Linguistic Prehistory.* University of California Publications in Linguistics 81. Berkeley: University of California Press, 1977.

Carlson, John B. "The Grolier Codex: A Preliminary Report on the Content and Authenticity of a 13th-Century Maya Venus Almanac." In *Calendars in Mesoamerica and Peru: Native American Computations of Time,* edited by Anthony F. Aveni and Gordon Brotherston, 27–57. BAR International Series 174. Oxford: British Archaeological Reports, 1983.

Carmack, Robert M. "Indians and the Guatemalan Revolution." *Cultural Survival Quarterly* 7, no. 2 (1983): 52–54.

———. *Quichean Civilization: The Ethnohistoric, Ethnographic, and Archaeological Sources.* Berkeley: University of California Press, 1973.

———. *The Quiché Mayas of Utatlán.* Norman: University of Oklahoma Press, 1981.

———. Review of Munro S. Edmonson, *The Book of Counsel. American Antiquity* 40 (1975): 506–7.

Carmack, Robert M., and Francisco Morales Santos. *Nuevas perspectivas sobre el Popol Vuh.* Guatemala: Piedra Santa, 1983.

Carrasco, Pedro. "Don Juan Cortés, cacique de Santa Cruz Quiché." *Estudios de Cultura Maya* 6 (1967): 251–66.

Casas, Bartolomé de las. *Apologética historia de las Indias.* Madrid: Serrano y Ganz, 1909.

Chávez, Adrián I. *Pop Wuj.* México: Ediciones de la Casa Chata, 1979.

Ciudad Real, Antonio de. *Diccionario de Motul, Maya-Español.* Edited by J. Martínez Hernández. Mérida, 1929.

Coe, Michael D. *The Maya*. Revised edition. New York: Thames and Hudson, 1980.

———. *The Maya Scribe and His World*. New York: The Grolier Club, 1973.

———. "Supernatural Patrons of Maya Scribes and Artists." In *Social Process in Maya Prehistory*, edited by Norman Hammond, 327–47. London: Academic Press, 1977.

Craine, Eugene R., and Reginald C. Reindorp. *The Codex Pérez and the Book of Chilam Balam of Maní*. Norman: University of Oklahoma Press, 1979.

Davies, Nigel. *The Toltecs*. Norman: University of Oklahoma Press, 1977.

Davis, L. Irby. *A Field Guide to the Birds of Mexico and Central America*. Austin: University of Texas Press, 1972.

Earle, Duncan MacLean. "La etnoecología quiché en el Popol Vuh." In *Nuevas perspectivas sobre el Popol Vuh*, edited by Robert M. Carmack and Francisco Morales Santos, 293–303. Guatemala: Piedra Santa, 1983.

Edmonson, Munro S. *The Ancient Future of the Itza: The Book of Chilam Balam of Tizimin*. Austin: University of Texas Press, 1982.

———. *The Book of Counsel: The Popol Vuh of the Quiche Maya of Guatemala*. Middle American Research Institute Publication 35. New Orleans: Tulane University, 1971.

———. *Quiche-English Dictionary*. Middle American Research Institute Publication 30. New Orleans: Tulane University, 1965.

Fox, David G. Review of *Quiche-English Dictionary*, by Munro S. Edmonson. *Language* 44 (1968): 191–97.

Fox, John W. *Quiche Conquest: Centralism and Regionalism in Highland Guatemalan State Development*. Albuquerque: University of New Mexico Press, 1978.

Guzmán, Pantaleón de. "Compendio de nombres en lengua cakchiquel." Manuscript (1704) in the collection of E. G. Squier. Photocopy in the Gates collection in the library at Brigham Young University, Provo, Utah.

Hammond, Norman. *Ancient Maya Civilization*. New Brunswick: Rutgers University Press, 1982.

Harrington, John P. "Popol wuh." Transcription of an oral rendition of the Quiché text by Cipriano Alvarado. Manuscript (1922) in the Harrington collection at the National Anthropological Archives, Smithsonian Institution, Washington, D.C.

———. "Quiche Grammar." Manuscript (1948) in the Harrington collection at the National Anthropological Archives, Smithsonian Institution, Washington, D.C.

Heyden, Doris. "An Interpretation of the Cave Underneath the Pyramid of the Sun in Teotihuacan, Mexico." *American Antiquity* 40 (1975): 131–47.

Hunt, Eva. *The Transformation of the Hummingbird: Cultural Roots of a Zinacanteco Mythical Poem.* Ithaca: Cornell University Press, 1977.

Hymes, Dell. *"In Vain I Tried to Tell You": Essays in Native American Ethnopoetics.* Philadelphia: University of Pennsylvania Press, 1981.

Ichon, Alain. "Arqueología y etnohistoria en Cawinal." In *Nuevas perspectivas sobre el Popol Vuh,* edited by Robert M. Carmack and Francisco Morales Santos, 237–46. Guatemala: Piedra Santa, 1983.

Kaufman, Terrence. "Common Cholan Lexical Items." Photo reproduction. Pittsburgh: University of Pittsburgh, 1979.

Kelley, David Humiston. *Deciphering the Maya Script.* Austin: University of Texas Press, 1976.

La Farge, Oliver. *Santa Eulalia.* Chicago: University of Chicago Press, 1947.

Laughlin, Robert M. *The Great Tzotzil Dictionary of San Lorenzo Zinacantán.* Smithsonian Contributions to Anthropology 19. Washington: Smithsonian Institution Press, 1975.

Lehmann-Nitsche, R. "La constelación de la Osa Mayor y su concepto como Huracán o dios de la tormenta en la esfera del Mar Caribe." *Revista del Museo de La Plata* 28 (1924–25): 101–45.

León-Portilla, Miguel. *Pre-Columbian Literatures of Mexico.* Norman: University of Oklahoma Press, 1969.

Lévi-Strauss, Claude. *From Honey to Ashes.* Translated by John and Doreen Weightman. New York: Harper & Row, 1973.

Lounsbury, Floyd G. "Astronomical Knowledge and Its Uses at Bonampak, Mexico." In *Archaeoastronomy in the New World,* edited by Anthony F. Aveni, 143–68. Cambridge: Cambridge University Press, 1982.

———. "The Base of the Venus Table of the Dresden Codex, and Its Significance for the Calendar-Correlation Problem." In *Calendars in Mesoamerica and Peru: Native American Computations of Time,* edited by Anthony F. Aveni and Gordon Brotherston, 1–26. BAR International Series 174. Oxford: British Archaeological Reports, 1983.

———. "The Identities of the Mythological Figures in the 'Cross Group' Inscriptions of Palenque." Undated mimeograph. New Haven: Yale University.

Lowy, Bernard. "*Amanita muscaria* and the Thunderbolt Legend in Guatemala and Mexico." *Mycologia* 66 (1974): 188–91.

Maynard, Gail, and Patricio Xec. "Diccionario preliminar del idioma quiché." Mimeograph, 1954.

Mendelson, E. Michael. "Maximon: An Iconographical Introduction." *Man* 59 (1959): 56–60.

Miles, S. W. "The Sixteenth-Century Pokom-Maya." Transactions of the American Philosophical Society 47: 735–81. Philadelphia: The American Philosophical Society, 1957.

Molina, Alonso de. *Vocabulario en lengua castellana y mexicana y mexicana y castellana.* Estudio preliminar de Miguel León-Portilla. México: Porrua, 1970.

Mondloch, James L. *Basic Quiche Grammar.* Institute for Mesoamerican Studies Publication, no. 2. Albany: State University of New York, 1978.

Morán, Pedro. "Bocabulario de solo los nombres de la lengua pokoman." Manuscript in the Bancroft Library, University of California, Berkeley. Copy in the Tozzer Library, Harvard University, Cambridge, Massachusetts.

Recinos, Adrián. *Crónicas indígenas de Guatemala.* Guatemala: Editorial Universitaria, 1957.

———. *Popol Vuh: Las antiguas historias del Quiché.* México: Fondo del Cultura Económica, 1947.

Recinos, Adrián, Dionisio José Chonay, and Delia Goetz. *The Annals of the Cakchiquels.* Norman: University of Oklahoma Press, 1953.

———. *Title of the Lords of Totonicapán.* Bound in the same volume with Recinos et al., *The Annals of the Cakchiquels.* Norman: University of Oklahoma Press, 1953.

Recinos, Adrián, Delia Goetz, and Sylvanus Griswold Morley. *Popol Vuh: The Sacred Book of the Ancient Quiché Maya.* Norman: University of Oklahoma Press, 1950.

Robicsek, Francis, and Donald Hales. "Maya Heart Sacrifice." In *Ritual Human Sacrifice in Mesoamerica,* edited by Elizabeth H. Boone, 49–90. Washington: Dumbarton Oaks Research Library, 1984.

Roys, Ralph L. *The Book of Chilam Balam of Chumayel.* Norman: University of Oklahoma Press, 1967.

Sahagún, Bernardino de. *Florentine Codex: A General History of the Things of New Spain.* Translated by Arthur J. O. Anderson and Charles E. Dibble. 12 vols. Santa Fe: School of American Research and University of Utah, 1950–69.

Schele, Linda. *Notebook for the Maya Hieroglyphic Writing Workshop at Texas.* Austin: Institute of Latin American Studies, 1984.

Scholes, France V., and Ralph L. Roys. *The Maya Chontal Indians of*

Acalan-Tixchel: A Contribution to the History and Ethnography of the Yucatan Peninsula. Norman: University of Oklahoma Press, 1968.

Schultze Jena, Leonhard S. *Popol Vuh: Das heilige Buch der Quiché-Indianer von Guatemala.* Stuttgart: W. Kohlhammer, 1944.

Shaw, Mary. *According to Our Ancestors: Folk Texts from Guatemala and Honduras.* Norman: Summer Institute of Linguistics, 1971.

Siegel, Morris. "The Creation Myth and Acculturation in Acatán, Guatemala." *Journal of American Folklore* 56 (1943): 120–26.

Smith, Mary Elizabeth. *Picture Writing from Ancient Southern Mexico: Mixtec Place Signs and Maps.* Norman: University of Oklahoma Press, 1973.

Stern, Theodore. *The Rubber-Ball Games of the Americas.* Memoir 17 of the American Ethnological Society. Seattle: University of Washington Press, 1966.

Stross, Brian. "The Language of Zuyua." *American Ethnologist* 10 (1983): 150–64.

Taylor, Dicey. "The Cauac Monster." In *Proceedings of the Tercera Mesa Redonda de Palenque,* edited by Merle Greene Robertson and Donnan Call Jeffers. Palenque: Pre-Columbian Art Research Center, 1978.

Tedlock, Barbara. "El C'oxol: un símbolo de la resistencia quiché a la conquista espiritual." In *Nuevas perspectivas sobre el Popol Vuh,* edited by Robert M. Carmack and Francisco Morales Santos, 343–57. Guatemala: Piedra Santa, 1983.

———. "Earth Rites and Moon Cycles: Mayan Synodic and Sidereal Moon Reckoning." In *Ethnoastronomy: Indigenous Astronomical and Cosmological Traditions of the World,* edited by John B. Carlson and Von Del Chamberlain. Washington, D.C.: Smithsonian Institution Press, forthcoming.

———. "Quichean Time Philosophy." In *Calendars in Mesoamerica and Peru: Native American Computations of Time,* edited by Anthony F. Aveni and Gordon Brotherston, 59–72. BAR International Series 174. Oxford: British Archaeological Reports, 1983.

———. "Sound Texture and Metaphor in Quiché Maya Ritual Language." *Current Anthropology* 23 (1982): 269–72.

———. *Time and the Highland Maya.* Albuquerque: University of New Mexico Press, 1982.

Tedlock, Dennis. *Finding the Center: Narrative Poetry of the Zuni Indians.* New York: Dial, 1972; Lincoln: University of Nebraska Press, 1978.

———. "Las formas del verso quiché." In *Nuevas perspectivas sobre el Popol Vuh,* edited by Robert M. Carmack and Francisco Morales Santos, 123–32. Guatemala: Piedra Santa, 1983.

———. "Hearing a Voice in an Ancient Text." In *Native American Discourse: Poetics and Rhetoric*, edited by Joel Sherzer and Anthony C. Woodbury. New York: Cambridge University Press, forthcoming.

———. "The Sowing and Dawning of All the Sky-Earth: Astronomy in the Popol Vuh." In *Ethnoastronomy: Indigenous Astronomical and Cosmological Traditions of the World*, edited by John B. Carlson and Von Del Chamberlain. Washington: Smithsonian Institution Press, forthcoming.

———. *The Spoken Word and the Work of Interpretation*. Philadelphia: University of Pennsylvania Press, 1983.

Thompson, J. Eric S. *A Commentary on the Dresden Codex*. Philadelphia: American Philosophical Society, 1972.

———. *Ethnology of the Mayas of Southern and Central British Honduras*. Field Museum of Natural History, Anthropological Series 17, no. 2. Chicago: Field Museum Press, 1930.

———. *Maya Hieroglyphic Writing*. Norman: University of Oklahoma Press, 1960.

———. *Maya History and Religion*. Norman: University of Oklahoma Press, 1970.

Tirado, Fermín Joseph. "Vocabulario de lengua kiche." Manuscript (1787) in the Tozzer Library, Harvard University, Cambridge, Mass.

Tozzer, Alfred M. *A Comparative Study of the Mayas and the Lacandones*. New York: Macmillan, 1907.

———. *Landa's Relación de las cosas de Yucatán*. Papers of the Peabody Museum of American Archaeology and Ethnology, v. 18. Cambridge, Mass.: The Peabody Museum, 1941.

Vare[l]a, Francisco de. "Calepino en lengua cakchiquel." Manuscript copy by Francisco Ceron (1699) in the library of the American Philosophical Society, Philadelphia, Pennsylvania. Typescript paleography by William Gates (1929), in the Gates collection in the library at Brigham Young University, Provo, Utah.

Villacorta Calderón, José Antonio. *Popol Vuh*. Guatemala: José de Pineda Ibarra, 1962.

Wasson, R. Gordon. *The Wondrous Mushroom: Mycolatry in Mesoamerica*. New York: McGraw-Hill, 1980.

Ximénez, Francisco. "Arte de las tres lenguas 3a3chiquel, Quiche y 4,utuhil." Manuscript (1701?), with the Popol Vuh as an appendix, in the Ayer collection at the Newberry Library, Chicago, Illinois.

———. *Escolios a las historias del origen de los indios*. Sociedad de Geografía e Historia de Guatemala, pub. 13. Guatemala, 1967.

———. *Historia de la provincia de San Vicente Chiapa y Guatemala*.

Biblioteca "Goathemala" de la Sociedad de Geografía e Historia, 3 vols. Guatemala: Tipografía Nacional, 1929–30.

———. *Las historias del origen de los indios de esta provincia de Guatemala*. Introduction, paleography, and notes by Carl Scherzer. Vienna: Academia Imperial de las Ciencias, 1857.

———. *Popol Vuh*. Facsimile edition with paleography and notes by Agustín Estrada Monroy. Guatemala: José de Pineda Ibarra, 1973.

———. "Primera parte de el tesoro de las lenguas cacchiquel, quiche y tzutuhil." 2 vols. Manuscript in the Bancroft Library, University of California, Berkeley, California.

Zúñiga, Dionysio de. "Diccionario pocomchí-castellano y castellano-pocomchí de San Cristobal Cahcoh." Manuscript in the Berendt collection at the University of Pennsylvania library, Philadelphia. Photocopy in the Tozzer Library, Harvard University, Cambridge, Massachusetts.

Outstanding Paperback Books from the Touchstone Library